Monastic Bodies

DIVINATIONS: REREADING LATE
ANCIENT RELIGION

Series Editors: Daniel Boyarin, Virginia Burrus, Derek Krueger

A complete list of books in the series
is available from the publisher.

Monastic Bodies

Discipline and Salvation
in Shenoute of Atripe

Caroline T. Schroeder

PENN

UNIVERSITY OF PENNSYLVANIA PRESS

Philadelphia

10 9 8 7 6 5 4 3 2 1

Published by
University of Pennsylvania Press
Philadelphia, Pennsylvania 19104-4112

Library of Congress Cataloging-in-Publication Data

Schroeder, Caroline T., 1971–
    Monastic bodies : discipline and salvation in Shenoute of Atripe / Caroline T. Schroeder.
        p.   cm. — (Divinations)
    Includes bibliographical references (p.   ) and index.
    ISBN-13: 978-0-8122-3990-4 (cloth : alk. paper)
    ISBN-10: 0-8122-3990-3 (cloth : alk. paper)
    1. Shenute, ca. 348–466.   2. Monasticism and religious orders—Egypt—History.
3. Monasticism and religious orders—History—Early church, ca. 30–600.   I. Title.
II. Series.

BR1720.S48S37   2007
271.0092—dc22
[B]   2006051414

For Pearl Meeske, Theresa Murphy, and Edna Taylor

Contents

Introduction

Shenoute in the Landscape of Early Christian Asceticism

IN THE EARLY 380S, in a monastery in Upper Egypt, a young monk named Shenoute stormed out of the monastic residence. Deciding to live as a hermit in the nearby desert, he accused his spiritual father of allowing acts of impiety and impurity to proceed unchallenged in the monastery. One might expect that this story would end with the monk's receiving a harsh punishment or a humiliating reprimand in order to serve as an example of the dangers of youthful pride to other potentially brash ascetics. Instead, he became the next spiritual leader of that community, succeeding the very person whom he had criticized openly before his colleagues. Indeed, he would become a central figure in late antique Egyptian Christianity, earning the lofty title of "archimandrite" in honor of his monastic leadership. He would also be revered as one of the Coptic Orthodox Church's most important saints.[1] How this monk came to lead that monastic community and how he developed a sophisticated ideology of the ascetic life constitute the subject of this book.

Over the course of a long career as a monastic father, Shenoute used his skills as an author and an orator to carve out a space for himself on the early Christian landscape, a landscape dominated during his lifetime by such theological heavyweights as Jerome and Augustine. Shenoute—the leader of a community of possibly thousands of male and female monks and author of at least seventeen volumes of texts—is best known in modern historiography for his attendance and influence at the Ecumenical Council of Ephesus in 431, his destruction of "pagan" religious sites in Egypt, and his significant contributions to the development of the Coptic language and literature.

Yet, as Stephen Emmel has so aptly noted, Shenoute himself identified as, "first and foremost, a monk."[2] He was born in the mid-fourth century, and in about 371, he joined a monastery located outside of the town of Atripe, which is now the modern city of Sohag. Atripe sat on the west bank of the Nile River, across from ancient Panopolis, now the mod-

Figure 1. The late antique basilica of Shenoute's monastery, known as Deir Anba Shenouda, or the White Monastery. Originally built during Shenouda's tenure as leader of the community, many of the church building's original architectural and sculptural features remain today. Viewed from the southwest, recent excavations of other late antique monastic buildings are visible in the foreground. Photograph February 2006, courtesy James Goehring.

ern city of Akhmim. The site of the ancient monastery is frequently called the White Monastery by some scholars and tourists in reference to the towering white walls of the church building that remain standing there. (See Figure 1.) The name "White Monastery" distinguishes it from the late antique monastery a few kilometers away, Deir Anba Bishoi, which is called the "Red Monastery" because of the reddish tint to the stones of its church building. Archaeologists and contemporary Coptic Orthodox Christians now call the White Monastery "Deir Anba Shenouda," or "Father Shenoute's Monastery," after its most famous spiritual leader. Shenoute became the third father of this community around 385, not long after his public dispute with the second father. During Shenoute's tenure, the monastery actually consisted of at least three monastic partners housing potentially thousands of monks, both male and female. The site known as the White Monastery functioned as the headquarters, but a smaller men's residence existed, as did a women's residence to the south. Shenoute writes of the entire monastic community at times in the singular, as the congregation (*tsunagōgē*), or in the plural, as the congregations (*nsunagōgē*).[3] He remained the leader of this large institution until his death in approximately 465.[4]

Recent scholarship has turned its attention to Shenoute's identity and activities as a monk, and thus also to the importance of his writings for understanding the many worlds constructed and inhabited by early Christian ascetics.[5] My work explores the contours of the ascetic space that Shenoute created for himself and his monks by outlining an ideology of the monastic life centered on the discipline of the body. I argue that this ideology lies at the heart of Shenoute's theology, his asceticism, and his style of monastic leadership. I ask how Shenoute's constantly evolving ideology of the communal ascetic life relates to the production of theologies, ascetic practices, and a Christian subjectivity distinctive to his monastery.

The Monasticism of Shenoute of Atripe

In his ideology of the communal ascetic life, Shenoute envisions the monastery as one corporate body in which the individual monks (both male and female) are its members. These two bodies—the individual monastic body and the corporate monastic body—have parallel natures, such that the salvation of each and every monk, whether male or female, depends on the salvation of the community as a whole. Likewise, the salvation of the community rests on the spiritual status of each of its members. Central to this relationship between the corporate and individual bodies are Shenoute's notion of sin as polluting and his related advocacy of bodily discipline as the means to combat the defilement of sin. Shenoute's ascetic discourse foregrounds purity of the body, and he categorizes as defiling not only traditionally polluting activities (such as sex) but disobedience and transgressions more generally. Sin pollutes the body of any monk who violates his or her ascetic vow or the monastic rule, and this sin will spread throughout the monastery, corrupting and defiling the corporate monastic body and thus threatening the salvation of other members of the community. Shenoute thus paints a portrait of two monastic bodies whose fates are irrevocably tied together either by the impurities of sin or by the virtues of discipline: the individual monastic body (namely, the monk), and the corporate monastic body. The purity of the corporate body depends upon the purity of the individual monastic body.

At the heart of the relationship between monk and community lie the important practices of discipline, or *askesis*. *Askesis* is "the training of the self by the self,"[6] usually through renunciatory practices. For the individual monk, this training constitutes the discipline of the body through chastity, fasting, prayer, and obedience to the monastic rule.[7] For the community, ascetic discipline comprises unified submission to the will of God, the community's leader, the monastic rule, and the "orthodox" Christian tradition. The practices of ascetic discipline are both redemptive and theologically productive in Shenoute's writings. Through the language and rituals of ascetic discipline, Shenoute constructs his vision of the relationship between the monastery and God.[8] As Rebecca Krawiec has observed, Shenoute's concern for bodily purity is embedded within the very monastic oath monks were required to take upon entering the community: "Thus, each person shall speak as follows: In the presence of God, in his holy place, I confirm what I have spoken and witness by my mouth. I will not defile my body in any way; I will not steal; I will not bear false witness; I will not lie; I will not do anything deceitful secretly. If I transgress what I have agreed to, I will see the kingdom of heaven, but I will not enter it since God, in whose presence I have established the oath, will destroy my soul and my body in fiery Gehenna because I transgressed the oath I established."[9] Protecting the body from pollution takes pride of place in this oath as the first in a litany of transgressions to avoid. Remarkably, Shenoute does not define what constitutes bodily defilement. Is this a subtle allusion to sexual behavior? Or to breaking a fast? Rather than attempting to circumscribe Shenoute's ambiguity, I propose instead that this ambiguity plays an important role in Shenoute's ideology of the monastic life. *All* sin is defiling—to both body and soul. Moreover, as the oath indicates, a monk's purity (or impurity) will determine the fate of his resurrected body and soul on judgment day. As I explain in Chapter 4, it is with respect to theological concerns such as the resurrection that Shenoute's ascetic sensibility (predicated on the discipline of the body) bleeds into his understanding of Christian identity more broadly. Despite the prevalence of pollution language in his discourse, Shenoute nonetheless fiercely defends the sanctity of the human body according to "orthodox" Christian theology. Because the body is holy and will some day be resurrected, monks, and even lay people, must protect its purity. Shenoute's faith in God's embodiment, as enacted in Jesus Christ's incarnation and bodily resurrection, is manifestly tied to his faith in the salvation of his monks through bodily discipline.

By no means is Shenoute unique in Egyptian monasticism for his attention to bodily purity. A monk named Theodore, who joined the network of Pachomian monasteries in Upper Egypt, is reported to have said upon his conversion, "If the Lord leads me on the way that I may become a Christian, then I will also become a monk, and I will keep my body without stain until the day when the Lord shall visit me."[10] Nor am I the first scholar to comment on Shenoute's particular attention to bodily purity. Krawiec, also pointing to the connection between the social body and the individual body in Shenoute's writings, has described bodily purity as "the main symbol for purity in the community."[11] Yet the role of bodily purity in Shenoute's discourse deserves continued attention.[12] As I argue in Chapter 2, purity and pollution language characterize his writings to a greater degree than they do the texts from the more famous monasteries founded by Pachomius. Moreover, as I maintain throughout, the discourse of purity is central to his formulation of the nature of salvation as well as to his own political aspirations.

For Shenoute, the body is the site of redemptive transformation. It is also the site for theological development, social control, and the construction of Christian identity. In *The Body and Society*, Peter Brown writes of the relationship between Clement of Alexandria's *askesis* and Clement's understanding of the self in society: "Sexual renunciation might lead the Christian to transform the body and, in transforming the body, to break with the discreet discipline of the ancient city."[13] For the archimandrite Shenoute, ascetic discipline transforms the body, and in transforming the body, situates the Christian monk into a social and theological position subordinate and obedient to God, to Christian orthodoxy (rather, orthodoxy as defined by the bishop of Alexandria), and to the monastery's leader. Like Clement, Shenoute constructs an understanding of the Christian subject in relation to his or her social world that is deeply ascetic. The notion of the person as a subject has a dual meaning: the individual who is "subject to someone else by control and dependence," but who also acts as an agent in developing a self-identity in relation to these mechanisms of power by means of "conscience or self-knowledge."[14] *Subjectivity* is both "the way in which the individual establishes his [or her] relationship to the rule [of conduct]" at work in one's society and "the basis of one's own identity through conscious self-knowledge" and consciousness.[15] In Shenoute's work, the particular sense of the self as subject consists of a negotiation between the individual and his or her position within society, which is expressed in the discipline of the body. The cultural paradigms that inform Shenoute's asceticism, that shape Shenoute's subjects, and by which these subjects shape themselves have changed from Clement's. The rhythms of institutionalized prayer, scriptural recitation, and monastic work replace the pulse of the cosmopolitan city. The centuries-old legacies of the ancient philosophical schools fade in prominence as the theological tradition of the Alexandrian bishops rise in importance. And whereas Clement's discipline may have constituted a "break" with that of the dominant culture, Shenoute's bodily discipline promoted a much more sustained engagement with many of the dominant, or soon-to-be dominant institutions of power in late antique Egypt.

Although Shenoute's asceticism has not been neglected by Western scholarship, it has been relegated to the background while his other activities have caught the eyes of historians. When Shenoute's name is recognized by Western historians, it usually is for his vigilant campaigns against heretics and pagans. Shenoute is known as the monk who attended the Council of Ephesus in 431 and, representing the politically influential Egyptian monastic movement, threw his weight behind the bishop of Alexandria.[16] His violent encounter there with Nestorius must count as one of the most memorable episodes attributed to Shenoute's career. The event is narrated in the *vita* attributed to Besa, his successor as monastic father. The literary account suggests that Shenoute's appearance was one of the more dramatic moments of the council. Shenoute accompanied Cyril of Alexandria to Ephesus to denounce Nestorius, bishop of Constantinople and Cyril's political and theological opponent. At a meeting of these figures, Nestorius removed a copy of the gospels from the only "unoccupied" chair in the middle of the room and placed it on the floor. He then seated himself on the chair instead. His actions offended Shenoute, who immediately arose and hit Nestorius in the chest. When Nestorius questioned Shenoute's audacity as a mere monk to attack physically a bishop, Shenoute responded, "I am he whom God wished to come here in order to rebuke you for your iniquities and reveal the errors of your impiety. . . . And it is he who will now pronounce upon you a swift judgment!" Nestorius immediately fell to the ground possessed by the devil. Shenoute's actions earned him the cloak and staff held by Cyril as well as the title of archimandrite.[17] Although this account certainly possesses more than a few narrative and hagiographical flourishes, it is one of the most well-known anecdotes in Shenoute's legend.[18] On another heresiological front, historians point to Shenoute's denunciation of Origenist texts as evidence of the penetration of Origenism into Middle and Upper Egypt.[19]

Scholars of religion in antiquity also remember Shenoute as a leader of frequent attacks on "pagan" religious sites neighboring his monastery. One of the most vivid images of Shenoute is one he himself crafted, that of the destroyer of pagan idols and temples. Shenoute describes a campaign against a nearby elite man in which Shenoute and his monks broke into the man's home, stole his pagan religious objects, posted a writ renouncing the pagan onto his door, and dashed pots of urine against his doorway.[20] The *vita* recounts other incidents in the campaign with pride.[21]

Scholars have often used Shenoute's writings as evidence for dramatic Christian and pagan interactions in Egypt. In this context, Shenoute is also offered as an example of the late antique holy man whose increasing power and influence accompanied the Christianization of the once polytheistic Roman Empire.[22]

Another historiographic narration of Shenoute renders him a symbol of an early Egyptian nationalism. In this paradigm, Shenoute the Egyptian Christian who wrote in Coptic, routed the Eastern Greek-speaking Nestorius, and destroyed the temples of pagans (*hellenes*) becomes Shenoute the defender of Egyptian faith in the face of a dominant Greek culture. He becomes the harbinger of a primitive ethnic Egyptian nationalism which would later resist the dominant Muslim culture. This particular portrait of Shenoute is crystalized in Johannes Leipoldt's 1903 monograph, *Schenute von Atripe und die Entstehung des national ägyptischen Christentums*, and was occasionally reinscribed by later scholars.[23] This portrayal of Shenoute clearly represents a projection of prewar nationalism in Europe and its colonial endeavors; it and the whole notion of early Egyptian "nationalism" quite appropriately have been critically questioned over the past decade.[24]

Shenoute's ascetic endeavors have received significant scholarly attention only recently. Most notably, Krawiec's book, *Shenoute and the Women of the White Monastery*, uses letters Shenoute wrote to the female monks of the community in order to reconstruct a series of conflicts between the women and the male leader. Krawiec situates her analysis of the asceticism practiced by the monks on the one hand and that advocated by Shenoute on the other within the context of late antique monasticism more broadly. Susanna Elm undertakes a more limited analysis of some of the same sources in her wider examination of women's asceticism, *Virgins of God*. Krawiec's 2002 book is the first monograph devoted to Shenoute since the publication of Leipoldt's biography almost a hundred years earlier.[25]

While my work necessarily builds upon the important insights of other scholars, this book's contribution to the history of monasticism is substantive as well as methodological. I examine the development of Shenoute's ideology of the monastic life over a wide array of his sources—texts written primarily for the monastic community and texts written for a wider audience; texts written as a young monk (before he assumed leadership of the community) and texts written as an old man; texts published and texts as yet unpublished (or with unpublished fragments). Also, this book is a study of Shenoute's monastic *ideology*—a study which draws on the methodologies of a variety of disciplines, including theology, literature, anthropology, art history, and history but which also consistently maintains as its

object of inquiry the systems of theological, political, and historical meaning generated by Shenoute during his production of these texts over a
lifetime spent mostly as the leader of a large monastery. One could describe the content of Shenoute's rules, letters, and sermons to the community as ascetic theory or a theology of monasticism. Such understandings
of these sources' potential, however, conjure up images of scholarship
framed by traditional intellectual history or historical theology. It raises up
one side of the age-old divide between theology and praxis, ideology and
realité, or even the history of theology and social history, or literary methods and historical methods. On the other hand, to describe Shenoute's
writings as an archive for a documentary study of ascetic practices privileges the other side of that intellectual divide. Such divisions between theology and practice represent a fundamental misunderstanding of the
nature of the monastic life, particularly as lived by Shenoute and the
monks of his monastery.

     As a monk and an author, Shenoute inhabits a world in which ideolo-
gies and material practices not only coexist but hold equally significant
positions of authority. Shenoute the monk was not and cannot now be
understood apart from his activities as a theologian writing on the nature
of God and the relationship between humanity and God, as a prolific author of antiheretical treatises, or as an orator lecturing against pagan religiosity. Nor can Shenoute the thinker be separated from the man who
took a vow of chastity, fasted extensively, prayed several times daily, and
provided detailed instructions on the physical positions and manners in
which one should pray. The theology produced by Shenoute as a member,
and as a *leader*, of his monastery was inseparable from, and in fact produced by, the language and material existence of the ascetic life, and it in
turn shaped the concrete experiences in the daily lives of all the monks.
Shenoute and his community *live* this theology and ideology in the ways
that they structured the rituals of daily life. Moreover, Shenoute's theological and literary endeavors played a part in his attempts to establish and
then maintain a specific authority structure for the monastery and perhaps,
one could argue, for the church at large.

Shenoute's Ideology of the Communal Ascetic Life

The principal element at issue in this study of Shenoute is his conception
of the relationship between the salvation of the individual monk and that
of the monastic community with respect to the role of the body in ascetic
discipline. I refer to the systems of meaning that Shenoute constructs

about the body as his *ideology* of the monastic life. By ideology, I do not mean a "purely" cognitive, and perhaps illusory, theorizing removed from the material conditions of "real life." Rather, I follow John B. Thompson's understanding of ideology as "meaning in the service of power," meaning that is produced by and that in turn impacts those very material conditions in which it is generated: "Ideology, broadly speaking, is *meaning in the service of power*. Hence, the study of ideology requires us to investigate the ways in which meaning is constructed and conveyed by symbolic forms of various kinds, from everyday linguistic utterances to complex images and texts; it requires us to investigate the social contexts within which symbolic forms are employed and deployed; and it calls upon us to ask whether, and if so how, the meaning mobilized by symbolic forms serves, in specific contexts, to establish and sustain relations of domination."[26] Shenoute's ideology of the "body" is the central focus of this study for several specific reasons. The ascetic discipline of the body (along with Shenoute's position of authority as monastic father to define, supervise, and control this discipline) provides *both* the "specific context" of Shenoute's literary activities as an author *and* the symbolic language through which he writes his texts. For example, in Chapter 1, I discuss Shenoute's references to sexual sins in his earliest letters to the monastery. One of the foremost obligations of ascetic men and women in late antiquity was, of course, celibacy, and Shenoute's explicit enumeration and castigation of behaviors that would be considered illicit sex acts surely were understood by his audience as a denunciation of any violation of the vow of celibacy. It might even have been interpreted as an allusion to specific sexual transgressions that had recently been committed in his monastery. Additionally, however, there are significant philosophical implications to Shenoute's sexual language. Shenoute uses the specific monastic discourses of sexual renunciation—and their complementary discourses about the dangers of sex—to write about sin and disobedience more generally. For Shenoute, to disobey the monastic father or rules, or to transgress the boundaries of the communal ascetic life in any way, is a form of fornication and a complete lapse of bodily discipline. He takes a page from the prophetic books of the Bible by using sexual terms to portray sin and disobedience as faithlessness to God. The language of bodily discipline is the language with which Shenoute constructs his understanding of sin.

Two other important terms from ideological and cultural criticism which I utilize quite freely are "discourse" and "power." I follow Michel Foucault's usages of both terms, and although his employment of them in poststructuralist theory is now widely known, it would be prudent to explain the ways in which they operate in my work. Power, argues Foucault, is not a static phenomenon but a system of "force relations" that are always in "ceaseless struggles and confrontations."[27] Consequently, these force relations are always unstable, and no one person or constituency in a social system "holds the power." Rather, positions of authority are constantly being challenged, defended, and negotiated by the various constituencies. In the case of Shenoute, the contesting constituencies include Shenoute, his former leader, different individual monks or groups of monks in the monastery (especially, as Krawiec has shown, the female monks and the highest-ranking female elder), the bishops of Alexandria and other ecclesiastical authorities, Christian groups Shenoute regards as heretical, and non-Christians in and around Atripe. Throughout, the book also refers to various "discourses" of the body, which again are meant in a Foucaultian sense, in which discourses are specifically linguistic expressions of systems of meaning. Discourse is also implicated in systems of power; linguistic utterances, including Shenoute's texts, are never "innocent" of the power relations in which they are formulated and upon which they have an impact. As discourse, systems of meaning—or, more bluntly, *knowledge*—are never separate from the negotiations of power in which the discursive authors and audiences are embedded.[28]

At this point, my use of "discourse" must sound quite similar to what I mean by "ideology," since both concepts seem to refer to the development of systems of meaning within complex systems of power. And indeed, I discuss the "discourses" of the body in Shenoute's writings as well as Shenoute's "ideology" of the body. But I refer to my primary thesis as an analysis of Shenoute's *ideology* of the body for three important reasons. First, I understand discourse as a component of ideology, or that ideology is a matter of "certain concrete discursive effects."[29] Second, I prefer to focus on Shenoute's ideology because the term "ideology" itself does convey a pressing sense of the material and political effects of ideas and discourse.[30] As Thompson has phrased it, the study of ideology "requires us to investigate the social contexts within which symbolic forms are employed and deployed." Or as Terry Eagleton has written, "[T]he concept of ideology claims to disclose something of the relation between an utterance and its material conditions of possibility, when those conditions of possibility are viewed in the light of certain power-struggles central to the reproduction (or also, for some theories, contestation) of a whole form of social life."[31] Eagleton's framing of ideology, and subsequently ideological criticism, are particularly apt for any study of Shenoute. Nearly all the historian has left of Shenoute are precisely his linguistic utterances—his texts—but these utterances are quite explicitly formed and deployed within a particular social and historical context—a context with a tradition that he in fact is attempting to reshape through his own discourse. More-over, his discursive strategies are indeed formulated under the conditions of "power struggles" over a whole "form of a social life"—namely, Christian asceticism.

This leads me to the third reason I choose to describe Shenoute's work as "ideology": the term also conveys a stronger sense of an attention to issues of power, and particularly to how ideology perpetuates or challenges systems of domination and subordination. Shenoute writes these texts to produce at least two effects: to contest the authority of certain other members of the monastery (or the larger Christian community) or to consolidate his own authority over the community, and to refashion both the theological meaning and the very material conditions of his particular form of "social life"—the late antique monastery. The texts are embedded within localized power struggles for leadership within his community and empire-wide power struggles to define the nature of orthodox Christianity and the leadership of the church. Thus, I employ the term "ideology" because I wish to hold onto the political edge that its usage conveys.[32] Shenoute attempts to achieve these two effects through the production of his ideology of the body.

In arguing that the body and various "technologies of the body"[33] (such as ascetic discipline) are the sites of political transformation and theological expression, I follow in now well-established lines of scholarship in literary theory, history of Christianity, and anthropology. The human body, as Mary Douglas has argued, is a "symbol of society," and "the powers and dangers credited to social structure" are "reproduced in small on the human body."[34] Thus an analysis of the regulations of the individual human body will reflect larger cultural concerns about a group's identity and social systems. Similarly, regulations or technologies of the body are also in themselves epistemologically productive. Restrictions and constraints upon the body, such as the classic ascetic disciplines such as fasting, sexual abstinence, night vigils, and corporal punishment, are not simply repressive. Instead, they fashion the body "with a much 'higher' aim"[35] and in order to produce (not merely inhibit) a particular kind of social subject and participant in society. I am also deeply indebted to a tradition of feminist theory which argues that sex, gender, and sexuality are not biologically and universally determined categories. Rather, the conceptions of male and female as well as the definition of normative sexual desire are social constructions with different manifestations in different cultures and different historical periods.[36] Moreover, I loosely follow Judith Butler's contention that the very human body is itself a social construction; that there exists no universal, essential norm of the human body. Even the "materiality" of the body, and particularly the sexual identity of the body, is socially constructed through the ritualized, repetitive performance of social norms regulating sexual expression.[37] The construction of the body occurs not as a result of a passive acceptance of cultural inscriptions from some "external" authority or "cultural source." Rather, the body is defined and reified through its active (and often shifting) performances within a particular society. For example, one prominent particularity in the social construction of Shenoute's monastic body was the ability for sin to travel with ease from one body to another; the social "performance" (to use Butler's term) of sexual abstinence in the particular social world of Shenoute's monastery participated in the cultivation of a normative and virtuous monastic body because it prevented sin from polluting the body of the individual monk as well as his or her monastic colleagues.

In late antiquity, the cultivation of the body was part of a larger "care of the self," in which the discipline of the body was intimately connected to the cultivation of virtue in the soul.[38] Medical literature and philosophical writing conform in such a way that the body was construed as a reflection of the soul. Physiognomists and philosophers alike argued that the condition of the body revealed the condition of the soul, and that the literal physical reshaping or manipulation of the body could affect the soul.[39] Where medical discourses of the body overlap with philosophical discourses of body and soul is also where understandings of the social body and the individual body overlapped.[40] The standards by which the body was created and cultivated in order to produce a virtuous subject were, of course, determined in part by broader social concerns about what constituted a virtuous society. The shared philosophical and medical discourses about the body were an instance of the way in which the individual human body was, to quote Dale Martin, "but an instance of the social body."[41]

This was particularly true with respect to ancient understandings of pollution. A polluting disease carried with it implications about an individual's moral state; in the words of Ruth Padel, there existed an "intermingling of moral and physical corruption."[42] Disease often was associated closely with moral corruption, and purification addressed both.[43] Martin has identified two conceptions or etiologies of pollution and disease in the first centuries of the Common Era. In the "imbalance" etiology, disease was conceived of as an imbalance in the humors inside of the human body (e.g., hot and cold, wet and dry), and pollution was not viewed as an invasion by an "alien infectious agent" but as an internal "putrefaction or corruption of the normal elements of the body."[44] According to the "invasion" etiology of disease, illness was considered to be caused by exterior elements that acted as "invading pollutants."[45] The first model was originally more dominant in classical Greek literature and medical theory and, according to Martin, reflected a more secure sense of one's place in society; the healthy body symbolized a more "secure microcosm of a balanced universe."[46] The invasion model, however, reflected a much more anxious view of society, in which the body, like society, is "a site of cosmic battles between good and evil."[47]

Shenoute's ideology of the body reflects the same concerns about the relationship between the individual body and the social body and about the close association between pollution and sin. His theology of salvation rests in large part on his understanding of the parallel nature of the individual monastic body—that of the monk—and the communal monastic body—that of the monastery, and the tendency of pollution to spread from one to the other. The spiritual statuses of the individual body and the corporate body are evaluated in terms of purity or pollution. Permeating Shenoute's writings is a conviction that for the individual monk to maintain a holy state, the entire community must be free from sin and corruption. The purity and integrity of the community depend on the purity and integrity of its members, and vice versa, because for Shenoute, sin is a polluting principle. The defilement of sin runs through the individual and corporate monastic bodies as disease.[48] Although much of early Christian literature (beginning with the first Christian author, Paul) reflected the invasion etiology of disease, Shenoute's writings rely upon *both* models. Sin can be an invasive agent, penetrating the monastic body from the outside, but it also can be a slow corruption of the monastic body, originating from the inside, infecting and eating away at the other members and expressing within the human body the strife existing in the social body. Thus, in Shenoute's ideology of the body, pollution language does not always reflect a concern with strict communal boundaries. In the classical anthropological analysis of Mary Douglas, a heightened concern with bodily pollution often indicates anxiety about the dangers posed by the porous nature of the boundaries of the physical body *and* the social body. For Shenoute, however, the source of sinful corruption was often not an agent or principle outside of the monastic body but a *member* of that body. The sources of pollution that proved *most* threatening to the monastery were not nonascetic outsiders—lay Christians and non-Christians beyond the monastery's walls—but the very people who were living within the community, monks who might, in a variety of ways, violate the monastic rule and provide a refuge for defiling sin inside the corporate monastic body. In Douglas's analytical framework, purity and pollution language is often understood as an identity marker as well; it sets those who must maintain ritual purity apart from those who need not. As I argue in Chapter 4, however, Shenoute's purity language does not mark the ascetic as particularly different from the lay Christian, either, since his discourse of purity and discipline informs his theological defense of Christian orthodoxy, which applies to all Christians.[49] Thus, Shenoute's ascetic subjectivity, striking in its attention to bodily purity, ultimately becomes a Christian subjectivity.

With respect to the origins of pollution in the individual monk, Shenoute for the most part lays the blame for sin's defilement of the body not on external temptation but on something interior to the monk, that is, the corrupt state of that monk's soul. In this way, Shenoute also adheres to the ancient ideologies of the body that posited that influences of the soul on the body were at least as strong as the influences of the body on the soul. Like the neo-Platonic philosophers of late antiquity, Shenoute believed, to paraphrase Teresa Shaw, that the body physically reacted to the diseases of the soul, diseases otherwise known as the soul's passions.[50] Disciplines of the body, such as fasting and sexual abstinence, were widely believed to temper the passions of the soul. For Shenoute, inasmuch as the discipline of the individual monastic body directly impacted the state of the monk's soul and thus the monk's salvation, that discipline also affected the salvation of every other monk, since the sins of any one monk spread throughout the corporate monastic body to threaten the spiritual status of every monk's soul.

This ideology of the monastic body has important political implications for the social structure of the monastery. In Shenoute's system, each monk has a vested interest in the degree to which every other monk practices proper ascetic discipline; each monk is thus implicitly and explicitly encouraged to monitor the ascetic progress of his or her colleagues and report back to the appropriate monastic authority. Nothing can exist beyond the limits of public scrutiny. This understanding of sin as polluting disease also provides the leader of the community (and potentially other authority figures on the lower levels of the monastic hierarchy) with justification for a fairly rigorous implementation of disciplinary practices in the monastery and a strict enforcement of the ascetic rule. If *all* monks are endangered by the sins of any one monk, this ideological system requires the swift and stern curtailment of even seemingly trivial sins.

Because Shenoute's ascetic ideology was configured as deeply entrenched in what were rapidly becoming institutions in late antique Egyptian Christianity—for example, the emerging office of the monastic leader and developing orthodox theology (orthodox in the Alexandrian sense, that is)—Shenoute presents an ascetic subjectivity that is surprisingly nontransgressive. Many aspects of the burgeoning Christian ascetic movement could be characterized as resisting or challenging dominant cultural and political paradigms.[51] Although Shenoute's ascetic ideology produces, or at least strives to produce, a distinctive Christian subjectivity, it is an identity that for the most part defines and understands itself as decidedly not marginal or alternative.[52] Although Shenoute's valorization of celibacy, poverty, and the life of prayer partakes of the world-renouncing discourse that has led many to characterize early Christian asceticism as actively resisting cultural norms (such as marriage, family ties, inheritance laws, political allegiances, etc.), Shenoute's ascetic subjectivity presents a subject whose bodily discipline simultaneously produces a subject that is submissive to other dominant (or ascending) cultural paradigms and that is aligned with some of the institutions seeking to maintain or strengthen those paradigms. Shenoute often depicts himself as embattled, one of a small group of righteous combating seemingly overwhelming forces of evil in the world—be it the pollution of sin, lingering paganism, threatening heresies, or Satan himself. And as an author, Shenoute often partakes of the writerly enactment of ascetic virtues, including humility and obedience.[53] But despite this authorial persona, Shenoute usually writes from a position of power and authority in his social world, not one of marginalization. His texts outline a vision of the monastery as *institution*, an institution that seeks to "normalize" its members by "turning them into meaningful subjects *and* docile objects."[54] It is possible that Shenoute's ascetic subjectivity, marked by its strident purity language, was perceived by people outside of his sphere of influence as an "alternative symbolic universe" that legitimated *alternative* authorities and ways of life.[55] Yet, for those within Shenoute's sphere of influence, especially the monks, Shenoute's definition of the virtuous self was the dominant worldview, and one with clear ties to authorities and authoritative institutions outside the monastery and the region. Shenoute's writings exemplify the ways in which power's "material force operating on the body" produces forms of knowledge about the self and society.[56]

Shenoute the Author

The act of writing held an almost sacred place in early Christianity. In putting word to parchment or papyrus, the Christian author ritually and mimetically recalled the incarnation of the divine Word (*logos*) in material form. As Derek Krueger has written, "From the perspective of late antiquity, the connection between logos and body always already underlies the craft of composition: the practice of writing is the embodiment of the logos."[57] For his ancient readers and listeners, Shenoute's writings about the body constituted a writing of the body as a sacred and powerful site for the renunciation of evil.

For the historian of Christianity, Shenoute's writings hold a certain power as well. The nature and scope of Shenoute's written sources are vast. His texts provide an exceptional resource for the study of early monasticism in general and the social construction of the body in particular because his corpus currently represents the largest library of texts written by such a prominent figure in early Egyptian monasticism. Over the course of his long life, he produced volume upon volume of letters, sermons, monastic rules, and treatises, all in the Sahidic dialect of the Coptic language. Much of the remaining Shenoutean research to date has come in the form of linguistic studies and textual translations. As one of the largest single collections of Coptic literature, Shenoute's writings have provided an important resource to linguists of Coptic and other Egyptian languages.[58] The publications of Leipoldt, Amélineau, Elanskaya, and Young, in particular, have made Shenoute's writings more accessible to scholars of late antiquity.[59] Some have claimed that Shenoute's monastery housed one of the primary libraries responsible for translating the Christian scriptures and other Greek Christian writings into Coptic.[60] But his texts also provide a rare literary source for life in a fourth- and fifth-century ascetic community as it was portrayed by a contemporary participant. Shenoute supplies provocative descriptions of significant disputes in the monastery's community, a lengthy reproduction of their monastic rule, extensive biblical interpretations in support of his decisions and rulings, elaborate parables and prophecies regarding the spiritual state of the community, detailed accounts of his own and his monks' activities, and considerable theological sermons and tractates.

When the extant texts of Shenoute's corpus are measured against the remaining documents from better-known figures, such as Pachomius or Antony, the textual legacies of the more famous monks seem sparse by comparison. Moreover, some of the most frequently used sources on Egyptian monasticism either are one or two generations removed from the circumstances that they describe or were written by authors who were not Egyptian ascetics. For example, James E. Goehring has established that many of the texts purporting to document the history of Pachomius's founding and leadership of his monasteries present that history filtered through a thick hagiographical lens; only the few authentic letters of Pachomius and his successors Theodore and Horsiesius "do not participate in the anachronistic developments discernable in other Pachomian sources."[61] Samuel Rubenson and David Brakke have lucidly documented the difficulties in relying on the *Apophthegmata Patrum* and *Life of Antony* for accurate information on the "founding fathers" of Egyptian monasticism.[62]

Unfortunately, such a prolific author is still relatively unexamined by historians of Christianity for several reasons. First, Shenoute remains unmentioned in Greek and Latin writings about Egyptian monasticism.[63] Second, Shenoute has been depicted in historiography as a man more violent and less intellectually sophisticated than his other monastic contemporaries. One historian of monasticism has contended that Shenoute is "a man whom all agree in calling authoritarian, harsh, and violent," and "without theological formation." His theology and spirituality are described as "lacking any mystical dimension."[64] Another prominent scholar, writing about the Council of Ephesus, describes Cyril's entourage of Upper Egyptian monks (including "the famous archimandrite" Shenoute) as "fanatic and untutored."[65] Although Shenoute did not write traditional, systematic treatises on Trinitarian or Christological topics, he did write extensively on the nature of God and on the relationship of his community with God. His theorizing about the nature of coenobitic monasticism and its role in Christian salvation is as sophisticated as the list of his violent actions against pagans, heretics, and fellow monks is long. An analysis of his asceticism does not lead Shenoute to shed his image as a strict and sometimes violent man. He does, however, emerge as much more than a simple monk, strong of faith; Shenoute's violence was neither untheological nor unique in Egyptian monasticism. Although Shenoute's use of corporal punishment may be more widespread and more severe when compared to other monasteries, such punishment was no novelty in Upper Egypt.[66] The penalties meted out in any early Egyptian monastery must surely be considered reprehensible by modern standards, and likely even more so in the case of Shenoute's monastery. I do not argue against either point. What concerns me is not so much the degree of the severity of the punishment, but the particular social function of the punishment in the authoritative system established by Shenoute and the theological meaning Shenoute urges the other monks to derive from their experience of punishment.

Third, Shenoute's monasticism has been viewed as derivative of an "original" (and hence more historically relevant) Pachomian monasticism. Beginning at least as early as Paulin Ladeuze's 1898 dissertation on Pachomius and Shenoute, scholarship has narrated a fairly linear evolution of coenobitic monasticism and the Egyptian monastic "rule" in which Shenoute's monastery is characterized as a later stage of a Pachomian monastery. According to this tradition, Pcol (the first leader of what would later be called Deir Anba Shenouda) adapted Pachomius's rules for his new community by making them significantly stricter. Upon becoming the monastic father, Shenoute then adapted and edited Pcol's rules.[67] Some subsequent scholars have followed Ladeuze in constructing this chain of textual transmission from Pachomius to Shenoute, and thus describe Shenoute as "Pachomian."[68] These conclusions, unfortunately, are not based on a thorough comparison of the texts from the two communities, but rather on a long-standing tradition that honors Pachomius as the "father" of coenobitic monasticism. Ironically, we have more evidence for studying the asceticism of Shenoute than we do for the asceticism of Pachomius, and I would argue that the unique nature of the Shenoutean sources requires scholars to rethink this trajectory of coenobitic monasticism. It may indeed prove to be true that the rules and daily practices at Deir Anba Shenouda were adapted from the Pachomian traditions; but only a detailed examination of the monasticism depicted in Shenoute's writings can begin to provide us with an answer to this question. Krawiec's monograph and a recent article by Bentley Layton on the regulation of food consumption in Shenoute's monastery mark an important beginning to this scholarly endeavor.[69] This book offers just one contribution to a much larger and long-term investigation of this community which must be pursued by a number of scholars.

By far, the primary reason behind the lack of research on Shenoute remains the sorry state of the manuscript tradition. Almost all of the manuscripts containing Shenoute's works were preserved only in the library of Deir Anba Shenouda.[70] Most of the extant manuscripts date from the ninth to the twelfth centuries.[71] As time passed, knowledge of the Coptic language was lost, and these texts were eventually considered refuse by the monastery.[72] Western Europeans "discovered" Shenoute's monastery in the seventeenth century and began plundering the remains of the library in the eighteenth century. Throughout the eighteenth through twentieth centuries, the manuscripts were dispersed to libraries and private collections in Europe and the United States. Frequently a codex was removed piece by piece to different locations, and as a result, parts of the same codex—and even the same text—currently reside in collections in different countries, or even continents.[73] Lamentably, none of the original codices has survived in its entirety, even scattered among various collections.[74] Although most of the extant Shenoutean documents likely have been identified, scholars nonetheless hope to continue to locate new fragments that currently reside undiscovered or unidentified in museums, libraries, or possibly even private collections.[75]

The turn of the twenty-first century has witnessed somewhat of a renaissance of Shenoutean scholarship, due in large part to Stephen Emmel's codicological reconstruction of the remaining manuscripts of Shenoute's writings, completed in 1993.[76] For the first time, scholars may reconstruct individual texts written by Shenoute and examine them in their entirety. Nonetheless, serious obstructions persist, since much of the literature remains unpublished and located in a variety of different libraries. The historian must piece together the remaining fragments—published and unpublished—to reconstruct individual texts. No critical editions exist, and for American and British scholars, few English translations have been published.[77]

In his codicological reconstruction of these disparate fragments, Emmel has discovered that the surviving texts were divided into two major categories: the *Canons* and the *Discourses*. The *Canons* of Shenoute (*nkanōn*) contain texts written primarily to the women and men of the monastery and seem to have been organized and compiled into nine volumes by Shenoute himself. The *Discourses* consist of public sermons, letters, and other texts that seem to be written for a more public audience and are referred to in the codices as *epistolē* or *logos*. The eight volumes of the *Discourses* were probably organized for liturgical or lectionary purposes and likely were not compiled by Shenoute himself. They also contain miscellaneous letters to and from Shenoute that have been used to fill up extra space in the back of the codices.[78] Deir Anba Shenouda's library contained additional lectionary codices that were not designated as volumes of the *Discourses*. Emmel is currently coordinating a team of senior scholars who plan to publish critical editions of the *Canons* over the next decade.

I follow Emmel's system of citing Shenoute's texts and manuscript copies. I refer to each of Shenoute's writings by its incipit (the opening line of the text). This may cause confusion for readers familiar with the titles given to texts by Leipoldt or other scholars who have published selections of Shenoute's corpus. For example, the text Leipoldt published under the heading "Adversus Saturnum II" is really one fragment of a longer text. Since Emmel's codicological reconstruction, it has been designated *Not Because a Fox Barks*. Occasionally, a text's incipit has been lost, and I follow Emmel's numbering of these "acephalous" works as *Acephalous Work 2* (or *A2*), *Acephalous Work 14* (or *A14*), and so on. I also provide the volume of the *Canons* or the *Discourses* containing each text as well as the codex sigla and page numbers of the codices in which the texts I utilize are found. These two-letter codes (e.g., XL, YW, YY) have been assigned to every codex originating from Deir Anba Shenouda's library. In the absence of a critical edition correlating each extant copy of the *Canons* or *Discourses*, these codex sigla are crucial in identifying the sections of any

given Shenoutean text and their relationships to each other in the manuscript tradition. Finally, I have provided publication information for the
text and English translation of the texts whenever such publications exist.
If the text remains unpublished, the location, catalog number, and relevant folio numbers of the unpublished manuscript have been provided.[79]
For scholars who wish to investigate any of these texts further, I have
provided descriptions of each text at the beginning of each relevant chapter, and I direct the reader to the pages in Emmel's codicological reconstruction that pertain to the reconstruction of the particular texts under
consideration. Unless otherwise indicated, all English translations are
my own.

The Scope of This Study

This book engages texts from both the *Canons* and the *Discourses*. The
Canons contain important sources for understanding the asceticism practiced at Shenoute's monastery. Letters from Shenoute to the community
and monastic rules form a large part of the *Canons*. Although the *Discourses* are directed toward an audience of lay people, clerics, church officials, and non-Christians as well as monks, some of the sermons, treatises,
and letters pertain to Shenoute's monastic ideology of the body. His more
explicitly theological texts address such important issues of embodiment
as the incarnation of Jesus Christ, the resurrection of the body, and the
relationship of the soul to the body. The current fragmentary and scattered nature of the manuscripts prevent a completely thorough examination of Shenoute's writings on any one topic; consequently, this study will
be confined to a select number of texts in the *Canons* and even fewer in
the *Discourses*.

I also limit the book to one aspect of Shenoute's thought: the problems and potentials of embodiment. Given the paucity of scholarship on
Shenoute, it is tempting to try to address every facet of his work. But for
the same reason, it is impossible to do so. Other important aspects of
Shenoute's writings and asceticism have necessarily been left for future
scholars. For example, Shenoute's exegesis of the Christian Old Testament
and the New Testament is central to his argument in every one of his
writings. At times, Shenoute's writing style even resembles a series of biblical quotations. Shenoute is representative of a style of Coptic theological
writing that is also characteristic of one of Pachomius's successors, Horsiesius. James Goehring's description of Horsiesius's writings as "replete with
quotations" from the Christian scriptures applies to Shenoute as well: "He

has integrated the scriptural language so completely into his thinking that he simply expresses his ideas through it."[80] This book examines several aspects of Shenoute's hermeneutical strategies, but a thorough analysis of Shenoute's exegetical system or the versions of the Coptic Bible from which he quotes lies well beyond the scope of this study.

I begin in Chapter 1 with the first formulations of Shenoute's ideology of the monastic life in letters the monk wrote to the community before he became its leader. These two letters make up the first volume of the *Canons* and document Shenoute's public argument with the second father about some incident(s) of sin in the monastery. During this period, Shenoute decided to remove himself from the living quarters of the monastery and retreat to the desert. In these open letters to the entire monastery, Shenoute berates the current leader for his poor management of the situation, arguing that the presence of undisciplined sinners threatens to destroy the entire community. This chapter reconstructs some of the events surrounding the conflict. It also examines Shenoute's depiction of sin as polluting and his use of sexual language to describe sin. Shenoute's sexual references, concern for pollution, and warnings about the demise of the community are parts of a larger ideology of monasticism in which sexual relations are a metaphor for the pollution of the corporate monastic body. Shenoute draws on imagery in the prophetic books of the Bible in which the religious community is seen as a feminine entity in relation to God; sexual transgressions are a metaphor for faithlessness to God and the ascetic life.

The second chapter examines the ritualization of Shenoute's discourses of the body in the monastic rules. I read Shenoute's rules alongside regulations from the Pachomian regulations in order to highlight unique elements of Shenoute's *Canons*. Regulations cited by Shenoute in *Canons 3, 5,* and *9* are examined with respect to three themes. First, as in *Canon 1,* the rules demonstrate an increasing concern for sexual purity when compared to other monastic rules, and they also exhibit a greater degree of pollution language in their discussions of sin. Second, Shenoute explicitly articulates a "one-body" ideology by claiming that all monks are "fellow members" of each other and are obedient to only one authority or head. He also argues that removing a sinful member from the corporate body is often required in order to protect the "virtue and purity" of the community.[81] Expulsion, thus, is required for protecting the remaining members. Third, I examine Shenoute's explicit use of the language of disease to depict the spread of sin throughout the community.

I devote Chapter 3 solely to *Canon 7,* which contains two sets of texts: sermons preached on the event of the construction of a new church building at the monastery, and sermons and treatises describing the efforts of the monastery to house the large numbers of refugees displaced by invasions from the south. In the first portion of *Canon 7*, Shenoute praises the construction of the church and uses it as a symbol of the monastic life. The beauty of the building is merely a reflection of the members who constructed it and worship in it. Shenoute interprets 1 Cor. 6:15 and 12:12–27 to declare the monastic body the body of Christ and its members the members of Christ. Any sin committed against a member of the monastery constitutes a sin against the body of Christ. The sins of the community, which Shenoute often calls "unnatural acts," will drive God out of the church, and will be reflected in the physical deterioration or possible destruction of the building. In the second set of texts, written a few years after the construction of the new church, Shenoute describes the presence of what presumably would be nonmonastic and therefore disruptive refugees who have brought their families, animals, and earthly possessions inside the monastic grounds to seek shelter from a series of raids on their towns. He does not, however, decry this as an invasion of sacred space, but seems to welcome them into the monastery's body of Christ. *Canon 7* thus illuminates what sorts of behaviors and actions constitute the defilement of the corporate monastic body and the body of Christ. The presence of nonascetics, their animals, and their earthly belongings do not pose a threat to the purity of the monastic body, for they are not a corruption or degeneration from the ascetic life. It is not outsiders who must be feared but rather insiders. Finally, I compare Shenoute's theology of architecture to other late antique texts written about church buildings in ascetic contexts.

Chapter 4 examines Shenoute's ideology of the body in the context of his more explicitly theological writings. Up until this point, the book will have concentrated on the ways in which Shenoute understands the body to be susceptible to corruption. This chapter will place Shenoute's views on the corruptibility of the body and the spiritual dangers inherent in the human embodied existence in the context of Christological and antiheretical writings from the *Discourses* that champion the sacrality of the body. The texts under consideration are *I Am Amazed* from *Discourses 7*, *The Lord Thundered* from *Discourses 4*, *Who Speaks Through the Prophet*, and *Acephalous Work 5*. Shenoute's Christology and his theology of the resurrection both contain a passionate insistence on the inherent goodness of the human body. The human body was created by God; it was the site of the incarnation of the second person of the trinity (Jesus Christ); Jesus Christ was resurrected in the body; and all human bodies will too be resurrected at judgment day. For Shenoute, the sacrality of the human body and its potential eventual to return to God at the resurrection are the reasons behind the need for ascetic discipline. One must discipline the body and keep it pure because it is the body that will be resurrected.

This examination of Shenoute's views on "the body" demonstrates that Shenoute engaged many of the same questions as his other monastic counterparts. Shenoute thus participated fully in the widespread ascetic movement that shaped late antique Christianity. Shenoute's answers to these questions, however, demonstrate the diversity of monastic experience in Egypt. Shenoute's development and enforcement of his ideology of the monastic life requires us to rethink the issues of authority in Egyptian monasticism. The conflicts in the monastery, and Shenoute's handling of them, challenge the somewhat romantic view that monks became authorities or community leaders because other ascetics adhered to them due to their sage advice and established ascetic discipline. This analysis of his ideology also requires us to rethink the roles of all Egyptian monks in the controversies and developments of Christian theology during this period. As this book demonstrates, although Shenoute certainly pledged his allegiance to his bishops in Alexandria, he did not merely rehearse for his monks the theological principles handed down from his ecclesiastical superiors. Shenoute's deep and critical engagement with the theological issues prevalent in his era surely was not unique.

Shenoute's representation of life in the monastery is a one-sided portrait. We glean the perspectives of the other male and female monks only through Shenoute's eyes. Nonetheless, this detailed vision of coenobitic monasticism in its formative period by one of its own remains one of our most significant and underanalyzed depictions of the ascetic life. This book investigates the means by which this arrogant youth transformed himself into the leader of a large community of female and male monks, and how Shenoute's own ascetic theory and monastic discipline helped to propel him to a position of authority that stretched beyond the bounds of his community.

Bodily Discipline and Monastic Authority: Shenoute's Earliest Letters to the Monastery

IN THE YEAR 381, a weary and embattled Gregory of Nazianzus, the former archbishop of Constantinople, lamented the politicking required of an urban bishop and cosmopolitan theologian. His words dripping with sarcasm, he proclaimed himself unsuited for the prestigious and powerful office he had recently vacated, because he had failed to "hunger for the enjoyment of the goods of the poor" and to compete with more overtly political animals such as "the consuls, the governors, the most illustrious generals."[1] Gregory contrasted the bitter infighting of the debates at the Ecumenical Council of Constantinople that year to the quiet serenity of his country retreat. A philosopher and ascetic, he resigned his episcopal post with a mournful plea, "Give me my desert, my country life, and my God, whom alone I may have to please, and shall please by my simple life."[2] Gregory's yearning for the "desert," where he could devote himself to God rather than to the tumult of human rivalries, was a nostalgiac longing for something that perhaps never existed. Although the "myth of the desert" as a space removed, set apart from the mundane and the urban, "captivated the late antique mind,"[3] politics did not end at the desert's edge or the monastery's gate. The death of Pachomius, founder of the most famous federation of Egyptian coenobitic monasteries, provides a case in point; strife over who would succeed him took years to resolve. Nor were competition and rivalry easily disentangled from deeply held theological convictions in dispute in the late fourth century. Gregory's separation of the pristine devotion of the desert from the corrupt politics of urban councils is a political critique of the "ecclesiastical establishment" as much as it is a statement about the nature of "true" asceticism or theological reflection.[4] Theological reflection was never fully extricated from politics, and neither, it could be argued, was asceticism.

Meanwhile, in another corner of the Mediterranean, at almost pre-

cisely the same time, a young Egyptian monk was composing similarly
critical invectives to his colleagues. Like Gregory, this ascetic claimed to
be leaving behind the corruption of his environment for the isolation and
tranquility of desert withdrawal. This monk, of course, was Shenoute,
who, despite his relative obscurity in the Greek and Latin worlds, would
become as important a figure to Coptic Orthodox Christianity as Gregory
is to Eastern Orthodoxy. Unlike the Nazienzen, however, Shenoute was
just beginning his career in the early 380s, when he issued his critical salvo
against his peers. His retreat was not a country estate but likely a desert
cave, and his audience was not bishops, but fellow monks—men and
women with whom he had lived, prayed, and worked since joining the
monastery as a youth. In his thirties—but still merely a monk rather than
a famous theologian, bishop, or even ascetic master—he announced his
intention to leave the residence of his monastery, leaving in his wake these
grim words as justification:

> But know this: A voice came three times around our congregation saying, "The
> destroyer came among you; the destroyer ruled over a portion of you, and he took
> it prisoner to a distant land; the destroyer overturned the enclosing wall of your
> congregation, and he destroyed the choice bunches of fruit of the grapevine, and
> he stripped its twigs; he crushed the fig trees; he destroyed the pomegranate trees
> and the apple trees and the olive trees; he gathered or he collected their fruit; he
> caused them to fall down to the earth; he chopped down the choicest of the tall
> trees in your midst (cf. Joel 1:7, 12); he destroyed the lambs of the fold; he de-
> stroyed the mature rams. For apart from the fact that among us a remainder exists
> from the Lord, we would become like Sodom and those of Gomorrah (Isa 1:9)."[5]

Shenoute's stark vision of his monastery's fate constituted a harsh and
public criticism of his community and its current leadership. This dramatic
passage provides a glimpse into his bold and uncompromising character,
revealing a person (like Gregory) unafraid to use his sharp yet eloquent
tongue to make his views known, regardless of their popularity. The passage appears in the first recorded letter of Shenoute, one of two letters he
wrote before becoming the next leader of this ascetic community. This
correspondence marks Shenoute's literary, theological, and political debut
and formed the first volume of his *Canons* in the library at Deir Anba
Shenouda. The texts were written as open letters to the entire community.
They contain his account of a dispute with the head of the monastery
(Shenoute's predecessor) over the discipline of a group of sinful monks.
They also outline Shenoute's prophetic vision of the destruction threaten-
ing to befall the monastery because of its sins. In the wake of these events,
Shenoute vowed never again to eat in community with his brothers, sis-

ters, and monastic father. While he indeed remained affiliated with the community, he no longer lived among the other monks. Instead he chose to dwell alone in the nearby desert as a hermit associated with the monastery. Embedded within Shenoute's criticism lies a call-to-action directed to his ascetic brothers and sisters, urging them to change their way of life, and perhaps even their monastic leader, or face destruction. In these early letters, Shenoute crafts the beginnings of an ideology of the monastic life with deep theological and political implications that would resonate throughout Shenoute's ascetic career, well into his own tenure as leader of the very same monastery.

Although a careful reading of almost any late antique ascetic literature belies Gregory's dichotomies, *Canon 1* opens a new and illuminating window on the complicated relationship between politics, theology, and ideology inside ascetic communities. It provides two important insights into Egyptian monasticism. For social historians, the letters present a rare first-person account of a dispute over monastic discipline between a monastic leader and the monk who would become his successor. But equally important are the theological and ideological apparatuses with which Shenoute frames both the events and his response to them. Out of *Canon 1*, an ideology of the communal ascetic life and a theology of salvation emerge. Shenoute begins to articulate an ideological and theological position, which holds that the salvation of the community as a whole depends on the righteousness of its individual monks, whether male or female. The sins of one monk have profound effects on the rest of the community, because sin is perceived to be a polluting agent. Events that precipitated the letters threaten the monastery's stability and the spiritual health of its members. Shenoute uses the language of ascetic discipline, or rather, of transgressions against that discipline, to formulate a vision of the monastic life that explicitly criticizes the monastic vision of his current leader. This chapter reconstructs the narrative of some of the events leading up to the crisis Shenoute describes in *Canon 1*, analyzes the rhetorical, theological, and ideological elements of Shenoute's response to the crisis, and theorizes about the social function of the correspondence—its rhetorical and practical effects upon the monastery.

Interpreting the scriptural quotations and allusions in Shenoute's writings is central to any reading of *Canon 1*. In both of these early letters, Shenoute frequently cites or refers to specific passages in both the New Testament and the Christian Old Testament. He also writes in a prophetic style throughout much of the volume, lending his own words a biblical feel even when he does not cite the Bible directly. The letters are so steeped in scriptural quotes or a scriptural writing style that the reader is

faced with the question of how to relate these biblical passages to Shenoute's particular context. Are the passages metaphors for the situation in
the monastery? Do references to biblical events and characters provide
examples of the kinds of activities that are actually going on in the community? Or are they unspecified admonitions to pursue virtue and avoid vice?
For example, how does one interpret the reference to Sodom and Gomor-
rah in the passage quoted above? As a reference to sins of sexual indiscre-
tion or inhospitality that have occurred in the community? As an example
of the destruction facing the monastery? As a generalized warning of the
potential of God's retribution against sinners? Or as all of these options?
This hermeneutical challenge poses a particularly acute problem with respect to the sexual language Shenoute frequently employs in *Canon 1*,
language that occurs both within and outside of his scripturally stylized
passages. Are Shenoute's references to both specific sex acts and general
fornication concrete accusations of illicit activity against particular monks?
Or do they signify something else? As I argue in this chapter, the answer
is both.

One of the interpretive keys to unlocking Shenoute's often complicated or elliptical language is his self-representation as a prophet for his
community. In *Canon 1*, Shenoute conforms to the literary and anthropological model of the biblical "peripheral prophet," a figure who stands
outside of the community's primary religious and political authority system and speaks to the community from a marginal, but not wholly outside, position.[6] Shenoute also exhibits the other primary characteristics of
a peripheral prophet: acting as an intermediary between the community
and God by claiming to receive direct revelations from God; taking the
role of a Mosaic figure who reveals and interprets God's law for his community; calling on the community's leadership to enact reforms, especially
concerning their adherence to God's law; experiencing opposition, persecution, and/or isolation from the community's centers of religious and
political power.

The theological level of Shenoute's discourse has important implications for what Shenoute understands the monastery's self-identity and its
relationship to God to be. Throughout *Canon 1*, he expresses concern for
the purity of the community and argues that the sins of the wayward
monks are polluting and threaten the remainder of the community, even
its most devout members. His ideology thus emphasizes the vulnerability
of the holy to corruption by evil and consequent estrangement from God.

Shenoute's rhetoric serves at least two purposes. The first and most
transparent is to encourage a more vigorous enforcement of the current
monastic rule. The second and more subtle is to demand a change in lead-

ership for the monastery. Shenoute draws on the very foundation of the monastic life—communal living and interdependence—to convince his fellow monks that their own salvation is at stake because of the weak leadership of their current monastic father. The sin polluting some monks threatens to bring about the destruction of the monastery. Shenoute thus implicitly calls upon the community to choose a new leader. The very public nature of Shenoute's censure suggests that he is presenting himself as an alternative to the current leadership. His strategy ultimately succeeds in that he becomes the monastery's third father several years later. These texts, which so illuminate the history, theology, and politics of early Egyptian monasticism, have lingered in the scholarly shadows, albeit for legitimate reasons. Since *Canon 1* remains unfamiliar even to most scholars of late antique asceticism, an introduction to its nature and content is in order.

Canon 1: A Review of the Sources

The physical state of *Canon 1* itself poses some of the greatest hurdles to its interpretation.[7] In his codicological reconstruction of Shenoute's writings, Stephen Emmel has argued that the manuscripts under discussion may constitute the earliest extant letters by Shenoute. In a later text, Shenoute referred to the first of these as his first letter, hereafter *Letter One*.[8] Shenoute also addresses his "father," presumably the monastery's leader, in at least one passage, indicating that the letters were written prior to Shenoute's own tenure as leader, likely around the year 380.[9] Some years after Shenoute assumed leadership of the community, the letters were bound together into one volume that would be called the first volume of Shenoute's *Canons*.[10] According to the postscript of *Canon 1*, the leader of the monastery was supposed to read the volume to the community four times a year. In addition, *Canon 1* was to be available to the community's leader for consultation as well as to other monks who might wish to have them read aloud in the houses of the monastery.[11] Unfortunately, the remaining manuscript copies of *Canon 1* are fragmented, and large portions of the two letters have been lost, including the opening and closing of *Letter One* and the opening of the second letter (hereafter, *Letter Two*).

The original audience for whom Shenoute composed the letters seems to be the monastery as a whole, not just the leader. Much of *Canon 1* is addressed in the second-person feminine singular, to "the congregation" (*tsunagōgē*).[12] Shenoute occasionally writes to the leader specifically or to the leaders of the individual houses of the monastery, but often he addresses everyone, suggesting that these were open letters, intended to be read and distributed throughout the monastery. How these letters circulated remains unknown.[13] (Since the extant format of *Canon 1* dates from a time *after* Shenoute became leader of the monastery and compiled the *Canons*, it is difficult to determine if either textual content or rhetorical style was altered *after* the letters were copied and bound into *Canon 1*.) Shenoute expressly includes both male and female monks in his audience, which may indicate that he expected the letters to be circulated in the women's residence as well as the men's residences. Prior to Emmel's research, Shenoute was believed to be the second leader of the monastery. Emmel has discovered references to *two* monastic fathers prior to Shenoute: Pcol (whom Shenoute's *vita* chronicles as the monastery's founder), and Pcol's successor, who may have been named Ebonh. Very little is known about Ebonh, in part because Shenoute's *vita* makes no mention of him. *Canon 1* provides historians with most of what meager information remains about his tenure as leader.[14]

The first extant section of *Letter One* begins with a recitation of some monastic rules.[15] Eight rules pertain specifically to sex and three others to interpersonal contact that has sexual overtones. Two rules deal with theft—from one's fellow monks as well as from the altar (*pethustērion*)—and one forbids the sale of objects made in secret.

After a break, the text picks up again with a homiletic and prophetic section building on several biblical passages, including Isa. 1:9, Jer. 6:11, and Ezek. 7:9.[16] The overall theme is a condemnation of hypocritical monks who commit defiling sins but who nonetheless claim to be good monks fulfilling the proper ascetic discipline. This section also contains a passage about a group of monks who overpower their leader and disobey him. The subsequent fragments describe Shenoute's confrontation with the father of the monastery about some sins that have been committed, which the leader has chosen to ignore.[17] The letter breaks off after several allegories about the spiritual state of the community and the fate that will befall it if the monks do not repent of their sins.[18]

Letter Two is also fragmentary. In the first extant section, Shenoute scolds the community for their continued failure to address adequately the problems facing the monastery.[19] Most of the remaining fragments consist of allegories modeled on biblical parables, judgment oracles, and other biblical motifs that in Shenoute's perspective describe the state of the community.[20]

Shenoute's account of this crisis is one-sided. We have no letters from the monastic leader responding to his charges. We do not even possess

accounts of life in the community before Shenoute's presence.[21] Our
chronicle of the monastery begins with Shenoute, and his voice alone
dominates the annals of this conflict. Although it is possible to deconstruct
Shenoute's accounts of the events in order to reconstruct some opposing
perspectives, Shenoute's highly stylized rhetoric and tendency to favor
parables, metaphors, and biblical allusions over straightforward narratives
make any historical effort to filter through Shenoute's domineering gaze
difficult. Despite these textual and rhetorical difficulties, much of *Canon 1*
remains, from which we can draw a number of conclusions regarding the
dispute between Shenoute and his leader and the theology of the ascetic
life that informs Shenoute's perspective.

The Events Surrounding the Writing of *Canon 1*

The catalyst propelling Shenoute to write the letters of *Canon 1* is the
commission of sin in the monastery and Shenoute's perception that the
head of the monastery and other monks have not appropriately dealt with
the transgression(s). Although Shenoute does describe specific events and
conversations that had recently taken place in the community, unfortunately for social historians, *Canon 1* in its current form does not contain a
passage that explains in a transparent, unambiguous way the specific episodes in the monastery's history that concern Shenoute and his reasons for
writing the letters. Given the fragmentary nature of the remaining textual
witnesses to *Canon 1*, it is difficult to construct a coherent narrative of
events that might lie behind the letters. Moreover, much of *Canon 1* is
written in a prophetic style with frequent biblical citations, raising the
question of how to interpret the relationship between the scriptural allusions and the historical circumstances of the letters. In his work on Horsiesius, a leader of the Pachomian monasteries, James Goehring has
commented on the difficulties of determining a "precise historical setting"
for monastic texts completely permeated with biblical texts. "[Horsiesius]
has integrated the scriptural language so completely into his thinking that
he simply expresses his ideas through it." Goehring has proposed that one
can reconstruct a social-historical context for such texts because the author
has adopted the language of scripture for his own particular situation.
Scriptural citations "have become direct references to the monastic community and Horsiesius's own situation in it."[22] Following Goehring, Shenoute's scriptural style can be read with an eye to its monastic context as
well as to its biblical context. Shenoute's stylized or prophetic passages
about the state of the monastic community can be used alongside the few

narrative sections of *Canon 1* to provide some preliminary reconstructions of the historical circumstances of the letters. (As always in the case of Shenoute, it is hoped that additional witnesses to *Canon 1*, which could shed more light on these events, will be discovered or identified.) Based on the extant sources, however, several factors suggest that two types of incidents may lie at the heart of the dispute: theft of food and sexual misconduct.

Few passages in *Canon 1* can be read confidently as narrative accounts of incidents that occurred in the monastery. In one, Shenoute addresses the entire congregation (*tsunagōgē*) in the second-person feminine singular. He describes a group of monks within the monastery who disputed with the leader of the community and then illicitly consumed food and beverages at the refectory:

> But there is another thing that you did, which you did not consider to be a sin. There is a great evil upon you, which is to say that not only did you—in your envy and your hatred and your disobedience and your pollution and your defilement which you committed—not fear God, but a group of evil people formed another gathering with each other among you. They rose up against the father of your whole multitude so that they might afflict him very grievously, as they disputed with him, using violence against him. They fled like dogs into the refectory in order to eat and drink on that day, even though it did not please him (the father), since he wished you to avoid the evils into which you fell.[23]

This passage is striking because it depicts what seems to be a fairly significant uprising in the community. Shenoute's accusations point to three important elements of monastic discipline that have been lost. First, the monks disobeyed a direct order of their spiritual father and may even have gone so far as to commit acts of violence against him. Next, the monks violated their ascetic dietary regimen by stealing food from the refectory. They have compounded their sin of disobedience by breaking their commitment to fasting. Finally, Shenoute depicts the father as impotent in the face of this crisis. He has lost control of his community and can no longer discipline the monastery.

Shenoute rhetorically links the lapse in bodily discipline committed by the individual rebellious monks to the lack of discipline in the community as a whole. He refers to the rebellious monks in the third person: the "they" who disputed with the head of the monastery. Yet the passage is addressed to the entire monastery: the second-person feminine "you" that stands for the community, the "congregation" or *sunagōgē*. "They" (the individual monks) are an expression of the loose morals that characterize the entire monastery. A "great evil" hovers over *all* monks, and the community ("you") has committed pollution, defilement, and disobedience.

Shenoute's condemnations reach beyond the boundaries of the specific "group of evil people" to all of "you," who wallow in hatred, disobedience, pollution, and defilement.

In a later, brief narrative passage, Shenoute recounts a cover-up of a scandal in the monastery. The nature of the original deeds remains a mystery—perhaps it is the act of rebellion described above; perhaps it is something else. In the two folios that remain from this part of the letter, Shenoute spends most of his energy decrying monks who refuse to confess and repent of their sins. He accuses a monk or monks who are confronted with their deeds, most likely by the head of the monastery, of perpetually lying. Although Shenoute narrates the passage in a way that suggests an encounter involving a small number of individuals, he addresses the entire community by using the second-person feminine "you," again blurring the distinction between the culpability of the individual sinner(s) and the guilt of the wider monastery. "[Y]ou are wont to stand before him in hypocrisy. When he asks you about your sin, you tell a lie in his presence, saying, 'I am holy.' "[24] The monastery's leader, however, sides with the accused over Shenoute, causing friction between the two men.[25]

Shenoute later describes the resulting argument he had with the head of the monastery over this course of events. This dispute presages his vow to remove himself from the monastery's residence and live in the desert as an anchorite. Unlike the majority of *Canon 1*, which is addressed to a singular feminine entity, the monastery, this section is addressed to a masculine singular audience, the head of the monastery.[26] Shenoute expresses his disapproval of the leader's reaction to the sinful monks and raises the issue of monastic discipline. He indicts his superior for lacking the discipline required of the monastery's authority figure, and Shenoute accuses him of not punishing the monks properly. Satan, Shenoute charges, is inside the walls of the monastery wreaking havoc on the community.[27] Shenoute has asked to visit some of the monks in order to encourage them to repent from their sins, but the head of the monastery has forbidden it.[28] The head of the monastery instead has found Shenoute's unsolicited advice to be insolent and has become angry with the younger monk. Shenoute recounts, "But you even became an enemy to me because I counseled you as a son." Shenoute also reports that their argument almost deteriorated into a physical fight.[29]

Even if the head of the monastery refuses to listen to his warnings, Shenoute implores him not to trust a monk who is cajoling him into believing that the spiritual state of the community is healthy. This monk, charges Shenoute, lies through his teeth. "If you will not believe the thing I say to you from God, that the deceit is upon us, you still should not be inclined to trust this one who lies before God saying, 'Nothing deceitful is among us, nor any defiling or besmirching act.'"[30] Shenoute here depicts a monastery at odds with itself, divided into factions. Another group of monks—probably the accused monks or their allies—have countered Shenoute's accusations and have appealed to the head of the monastery.

Despite a few efforts to remain superficially polite to his superior, Shenoute's contempt nonetheless bubbles through his prose. In one sentence he reassures his monastic father that he does not seek to cause trouble, but in the next he declares his intention to leave the community residence, levying an implicit critique of his brothers and sisters in an act that undoubtedly fomented discord, despite his protestations otherwise: "Let your heart not grieve you, my father. I will not trip you up, nor anyone else in a matter of this sort. Behold, I say that if the Lord provides the means for me, I determine that I shall not eat bread in fellowship (with the community) until I die (lit., until I go before God)."[31] Shenoute also carefully presents himself in a manner that seems respectful on the surface. He claims to be a spiritual child in the presence of a more mature spiritual father, and at times he defers to the head of the monastery. "For you are worthy because you are a righteous man. But woe to me because I have sinned. For this reason, my heart has become afflicted."[32] But then Shenoute uses his lower position in the monastic hierarchy to shame the head of the monastery. Although Shenoute is a mere monk and not a "righteous man" and leader, *he* recognizes the sin in the community for what it is; he therefore makes the monastic father seem weak and ineffective by comparison. Shenoute berates the leader for ignoring his warnings and publicly ridicules his father's ignorance of the events that have occurred in the community. "Since you asked me not in a manner of speaking in which a father talks to his son lovingly but in a manner of speaking in which a person talks to his companion hatefully, you said to me, 'Do we know with assurance who it is who sinned?'"[33] Shenoute then remarks that if God has revealed something to so lowly a monk as himself, then surely God has revealed the sins to such a distinguished monk as the monastery's leader. He insinuates that the head of the monastery has participated in a cover-up of a scandal. "And this is the way I answered you, hard as hell: 'Doesn't God speak with ash or reveal a matter to dust?' (Gen. 18:27) If God will speak with me or if he will reveal a matter to me, then he will certainly have spoken with you. And he will have revealed to you our every deed since you are a man who is worthy. For it is I who acts foolishly."[34] Shenoute thus implies that either the head of the monastery has lost favor with God (and thus does not know what has occurred), or he has willfully chosen to ignore a revelation from the Lord. Either accusation undermines the father's authority to lead the community.

Shenoute ends this section of the letter with a stark and prophetic vision of the future of the monastery. The community resembles a prosperous grove of trees in which a fire now blazes, consuming it and dominating it.[35] The fiery judgment that will befall the monks serves as Shenoute's reason for leaving the residence. Shenoute indicates that he would not quit the monastic residence if the situation were not so dire.[36] His departure should serve as a sign of the seriousness of the transgressions that have occurred within the monastery's walls.

The events that precipitated *Letter Two* remain shrouded in some mystery, as well, for in the extant fragments, Shenoute describes the circumstances prompting his second missive primarily in the form of allegories. The amount of time that has passed between the two letters is also unclear.[37] What is evident is that Shenoute believes that the community has failed to heed his earlier warnings, presumably those he enumerated in *Letter One*.[38] One person, in particular, has captured Shenoute's attention, and the letter reveals that he is a house leader.[39] Because of the allegories, it is difficult to determine what this person has done, but Shenoute warns that this figure threatens the spiritual welfare of the rest of the monks.

Although some of the narratives in *Canon 1* contain rich descriptions of traumatic events at the monastery, none of them provides the full context of those events. Shenoute details the dispute between the rebellious monks and the head of the monastery, but he also indicates that it is but one among many problematic events that have occurred in the community; it is an "other" deed they have committed. Shenoute does not provide narrative explanations (or, at least, explanations that would satisfy the modern historian) for the events that sparked his dispute with the monastery's leader. We still know neither the nature of the sins committed by the monks nor the course of action Shenoute wished his leader had taken. What is apparent, however, is that some monk or monks have violated the monastic rules, and Shenoute feels that their leader has overlooked the infraction, professing ignorance of the culprits. More significantly, the narratives depict the monastery as undisciplined and beyond the control of the head of the monastery. A group of unnamed monks has challenged the father's authority and disregarded the regulations regarding fasting, and Shenoute himself has publicly shamed the father and removed himself from the community's residence.

Although none of these narrative sections addresses sexual sins and only one addresses theft, these two types of sins are featured prominently in the rest of *Canon 1*. Fornicators and thieves receive the brunt of Shenoute's condemnations. The dominant discourses in *Canon I* are of deception or thievery and sexuality or promiscuity. In reconstructing the historical context of the letters, it is possible that acts of theft and sexual misconduct lie at the heart of the dispute.

Shenoute first mentions the sin of theft in the monastic rules he quotes at the very beginning of *Letter One*. Two of the fourteen rules cited concern stealing: "Cursed is he who will steal from the share of his brother. Cursed is she who will steal from the share of her neighbor. Cursed is the person who will steal from the things of the altar, whether it is bread or wine or any other item."[40] A rule about deceit and greed follows: "Cursed is the person who will create an object in secret and will sell it to people outside the monastery against the judgment of our father who exists for us."[41] The connection between theft and deception is understandable in the context of monastic social practices. Monks generally do not own private property, and material possessions, including food, are closely monitored. To steal, whether from an ascetic companion or the altar, entails dishonesty. Creating and selling a "secret object" likewise involves theft and deception: the theft of materials with which the monk must create the item, the money dishonestly earned, and the deception of the monk engaging in the activity.

In an exegetical section later in *Letter One*, Shenoute condemns theft, deception, and unauthorized commerce. He interprets Jer. 6:11, in which the Lord tires of holding in his wrath and releases it on the people, who have sinned. His anger will pour over children, young men, husbands and wives, the elderly, and the extremely old. Shenoute next places the monastic prohibitions against theft and deception into the voice of the prophet Jeremiah. "I will not spare the one who sells and who buys deceitfully outside and inside (the monastery). Woe to the one who sells and who buys deceitfully with a junior monk together with the one who will steal in any manner and the one who will remove items from the storeroom (*diakonia*) of God and who sells them outside secretly."[42]

One can read Shenoute's references to this type of larceny with an eye to reconstructing the social history and daily life of early Egyptian monks. Shenoute seems be responding to one or more incidents of pilfering supplies from the monastery's storeroom or dispensary, which he calls the *diakonia*.[43] Recent excavations at Deir Anba Shenouda have identified the remains of a structure believed to have been a granary or storeroom near the monastery's basilica. According to later texts by Shenoute, the storeroom stocked bread and other food (including food reserved solely for sick monks).[44] The accounts of theft in *Canon I* resonate with two of the most basic impulses male and female ascetics sought to control: appetite and greed. Plundering the storeroom surely would have been considered an egregious surrender to the desires of the appetite. Shenoute's denunciations of the theft and resale of other items for personal gain also speak to the struggle against greed and the monks' vow to relinquish all earthly possessions. Stealing from the monastery's storeroom is mentioned amid other general references to theft and citations of rules prohibiting stealing, suggesting that Shenoute is targeting a particular act or event that has occurred recently in the community. Add to this evidence the rule Shenoute quotes at the beginning of the letter condemning the theft of liturgical items (objects from the altar), including bread and wine. Provisions of bread and wine would have been held in the storeroom before being moved to the sanctuary to replenish the supplies in the altar. Together, this evidence indicates that one of the events that prompted Shenoute to compose *Canon 1* involved a monk or group of monks stealing supplies (possibly even future liturgical supplies) from the monastery's stores.

Such an act breaks the monastery's rules on theft, lying, owning personal property (if they sell the objects for profit), and fasting (if the items include food). Shenoute also interprets the act as a betrayal of God's gifts to the faithful. The hypocrisy and treachery of monks to whom God has remained faithful is a resounding theme of *Canon 1*. According to Shenoute, God has saved them from every kind of crisis and has bestowed upon them the honor of their ordination as monks. Yet the monks betray these acts of mercy with their sins.[45]

In addition to theft and deception, sex comes under Shenoute's scrutinizing gaze in *Canon 1*. The numerous references to fornication in general and homoerotic encounters, pederasty, and masturbation in particular suggest that the misconduct under dispute between Shenoute and the head of the monastery involved sex as well as theft. In one typical passage, Shenoute chastises his brothers and sisters with explicit references to sexual activities: "[S]ome of those among you are devils: the ones who defiled your sons and your daughters, those who became effeminate [*malakos*] among you, and those who sleep with men; those who commit many kinds of defilements and pollutions, those who are thieves and liars and who swear false oaths, and who conduct themselves very deceitfully among you, from male to female and from male junior monk to female junior monk."[46]

Repeated and detailed references to specific acts of sexual misconduct open *Canon 1* and continue throughout the two letters. The portion of the monastic rule that begins *Letter One* contains graphic descriptions of the sexual behavior it purports to prohibit. One rule reads, "Cursed is anyone who will kiss or who will embrace each other in a desirous passion, whether small or great, whether father or son, whether male or female."[47] The same fate awaits monks who kiss or touch junior monks, who touch each other or themselves erotically, or who engage in other possibly erotic activity (such as shaving each other).[48]

Since this document dates to the time before Shenoute became leader, the rules he cites probably originated during the tenure of his predecessor, Ebonh, or that of the monastery's first father, Pcol.[49] It is difficult to determine whether Shenoute modified the established monastic rules as he cited them, or whether Shenoute (or subsequent scribes) during or after the compilation of *Canon 1* edited the rules quoted in the original letter in order to make them conform with the rules that governed the monastery in later periods. As of this writing, we know of no rules from the earliest periods of the monastery's history which have survived apart from the writings of Shenoute or his successors.

Shenoute, nonetheless, indisputably contextualizes and interprets these rules in his own particular voice in *Canon 1*. This becomes apparent early in *Letter One*, when he reinforces the rules through an extended exegesis of Jer. 6:11, a passage in which the Lord announces that he is "weary" of holding back his anger, and that he will pour it out over children as well as the elderly. Shenoute first explains the passage by noting that the Lord can restrain his anger if people repent, but he will not hold it back forever if people continue to sin; he will choose to release it at the proper moment, on people who commit evil deeds.[50] As Shenoute elaborates on the scriptural text, however, he continues speaking from the perspective of the Lord, as if he is quoting the Bible, even though he is embellishing it. " 'I will hold back my anger and I will spare the children who conduct themselves purely from this day [on],' says the Lord. 'I will pour out my anger and my wrath upon the children who are in defilement and pollution.' "[51] Then Shenoute links the purity and pollution of Jeremiah's children directly to sexual misconduct. Again speaking with the voice of the Lord: "I will pour out my anger and my wrath upon everyone who burns in their desire for their companions or also for a junior monk (or child) in their polluted desire, whether male or female."[52] Several additional and more explicit sexual references follow, along with another brief mention of theft. Shenoute explains that the Lord holds back his anger only for those who remain pure. The monks believe that God's restraint applies to them, but Shenoute corrects them, informing them that due to their polluting sins, they will receive the fullness of God's anger instead. The language of Shenoute's Jeremiah mirrors the language of the monastery's rules quoted at the beginning of the letter. The Lord's wrath falls on those who have broken the monastic rules. Later in the letter, Shenoute again reminds his audience of the rules by weaving together the words of scripture with the words of the rules: "God is not the God of the effeminate [*malakos*], those who lie down with males, thieves, and defilers of boys and girls."[53] Shenoute's speech is indistinguishable from the speech of the Lord. By combining the language and genres of monastic rules and scriptural prophecy, Shenoute has transformed the monastic rules from a text of human authorship into the direct commands of the Lord through Shenoute, who acts as a prophet in the role of a new Jeremiah. In this act of intertextual interpretation, Shenoute simultaneously enhances his own authority as an enforcer of the monastic rules and traces the genealogy of those rules back to the mouth of God rather than a human hand.

Shenoute's efforts to remind the monks of the rules against sex and to enumerate the consequences of breaking them suggests that an incident of sexual activity that Shenoute believes the monastic father has inadequately punished may be one of the catalysts prompting his composition of *Letter One*. Emmel has surmised that "the offender was in a position of authority in the community, probably a monk in charge of one of the houses within the monastery," and likely a "confidant" of the head of the monastery.[54] For this reason, Emmel proposes, the leader of the community is reluctant to believe Shenoute's accusations. Emmel points to this incident of "carnal sin" between two male monks—and one in a position of authority over the other—as a primary impetus for *Letter One* and the incident that forms the backdrop for Shenoute's arguments with the monastery's father. In this reconstruction, Shenoute's discovery of this sin set in motion the chain of events described in *Canon 1*.[55] Much of the evidence for this theory consists of the letters' prominent rhetoric of sexuality and Shenoute's use of pollution language, a discourse often associated with sexuality or other bodily concerns and in *Canon 1* used almost (although not entirely) exclusively in tandem with sexual language.

Although an incident of sexual sin probably comprises one of the episodes that lies behind *Canon 1*, there is equally compelling evidence for other events that troubled Shenoute. As we have seen, he frequently mentions theft, and he describes a small rebellion among a group of monks. Additionally, he uses pollution language during his treatment of theft and lying; pollution is not the result of sex alone. Thieves and liars appear alongside monks who have sex with each other in a list of defiled sinners.[56] Shenoute's pollution language does not single out sex as the sole problem in the monastery. Rather, it exposes Shenoute's understanding of sin as a polluting agent. Through a discourse of purity and pollution, Shenoute articulates what he believes are the consequences for breaking the monastic rules—consequences for the individual monk and the community as a whole. Sin, not solely sexual sin, infects the body of the monk who has committed the transgression and threatens to infect the social body of his or her community.

Historians of early Christianity also must problematize any literal interpretation of the sexual slurs Shenoute hurls at his opponents, especially when we have little to no concrete evidence for sexual misconduct in the monastery aside from Shenoute's charges. In the centuries leading up to Shenoute, "orthodox" Christians accused their opponents of degenerate sexual morals. Shenoute's frequent and explicit references to sexual improprieties must be read in the context of a long literary tradition based more on the rhetorical and political impact of such accusations than on their historical veracity.[57] Additionally, sexual language in religious literature often functions as a carrier of multivalent messages.[58] The meaning of a text is always contextual and never unified; as Mikhail Bakhtin has argued, meaning only "exists among other meanings as a link in the chain of meaning."[59] In the case of Shenoute's monastery, the discourses of sexuality are derived from multiple textual traditions: the ascetic discourses of bodily discipline (expressed in the monastic rules he recites), the biblical discourses of sexuality (expressed in his prophetically stylized passages), and possibly the early orthodox and proto-orthodox heresiological discourses that accused other Christian groups of sexual licentiousness. In Shenoute's writings, these discourses have fused.

The events that propelled Shenoute to compose the letters of *Canon I* may have included sexual activity on the part of two or more monks, and they also probably included one or more acts of theft (likely from the monastery's storeroom), a moment of rebellion by a group of monks against the monastery's leadership, and a heated argument between Shenoute and the monastic father over the appropriate punishment for the monks accused of misconduct. Shenoute's sexual language in *Canon I* does not point to a social context of rampant sexual licentiousness in the monastery, but it does hold deep ideological and theological implications, and it serves an important rhetorical function. Shenoute uses sexual rhetoric and pollution language to shame the entire monastery and to compel the community to enact the political changes he advocates.

Theological Implications of Shenoute's Accusations

Shenoute's concern does not end with the behavior and punishment of errant members of the community. The main focus of *Canon I* is not the wayward monks and their sins (sexual or otherwise), but the consequences their unpunished sins hold for the community as a whole. As I reviewed in the Introduction to this book, the human body, its gender identification, and its sexuality often offer a roadmap for a society's social values. For Shenoute, sexual purity codes regulate monastic life beyond the prohibited behaviors—they protect the spiritual integrity of the monastery. In his role as a prophet, he marshals the language of pollution, sexuality, and biblical judgment oracles to warn of the destruction of the entire community on account of the errant monks. In many ways, Shenoute's world is a monastic extension of the biblical world. In the world of ancient Israel, pollution language governing food, sex, and the treatment of disease expressed a community's concern with self-identity and self-cohesion. Purity codes protected the identity and integrity of the community as much as they did the health of the individual.[60] In the prophetic books of the Bible upon which Shenoute relies for much of his rhetoric, sexuality signifies more than carnality; it functions as a metaphor for the relationship between God and the community. The language of sexual misconduct signifies Israel's unfaithfulness to her God by philandering with other nations and other gods.[61]

Shenoute uses sexual language to represent his monastery as an uncontrolled entity, like unfaithful Jerusalem or Israel in the Hebrew Bible, in order to shame and discipline the community. The sexual discourse with which Shenoute expresses his understanding of the relationship between God and the community contains allegations of sexual immorality (discussed above), the polluting effects those and other sins have on the rest of the community, and Shenoute's construction of the community as a feminine entity highly susceptible to pollution, whose whose faith mirrors Israel's fidelity to or betrayal of her bridegroom, the Lord.

Shenoute frequently uses the language of pollution and defilement to paint the moral state of the monastery as corrupt. Moreover, Shenoute links discourses of pollution and sexuality to his prophetic discourse about the grim spiritual fate of community. For example, in this passage addressing the monastery as a whole, he describes the evil works that condemn the community to hell in terms of sexual defilement:

Whether from a hardening of the heart, or folly, or ignorance, or fornication, or quarrelling, or great impiety, God bore you out from them when you committed them in your worldly, bestial nature. Whether wisdom, or knowledge, or disposition, or holy commands, or virginity, or all of the other wondrous works that you knew when the Lord made you worthy of *this* ordination into which he has now brought you. And yet, as it is written, you have returned to your ways again. . . . You are forcefully closing to yourself the door to heaven after it had been open to you at another time, but now it is closed to you because of the sins of your worldliness. And you are forcefully opening to yourself the door to hell (*amnte*) after having closed it to yourself at another time, because a few of the good things that you did as a monk are now brought to naught by your evil works, in the way that your male virgins and your female virgins defiled themselves unsparingly.[62]

The sexual innuendo in this passage is indisputable. Shenoute's references to fornication, virginity, and defilement are all couched in a writing style that both implicitly and explicitly invokes the language of the biblical prophets, mimicking in particular Jer. 2. Nonetheless, evidence for a history of specific behaviors or events in the monastery eludes the reader. Rather, Shenoute uses the language of sexual defilement to describe the moral and spiritual state of the monastery, rather than actual sins that its members have committed. Shenoute depicts the entire monastery (again using the feminine singular "you") as sinful because they have allowed sin to remain in their community. This passage brings together two of the most important aspects of Shenoute's ideology of the monastic life in *Canon 1*: the interdependent nature of salvation in the communal ascetic life (as expressed by his pollution language), and the use of sexuality as a symbol for the monastery's disobedience.

Shenoute's pollution language presents an understanding of sin on a continuum of defilement, in which sin in general is polluting, but sexual sin is particularly corrupting. In this passage and throughout the letters in *Canon 1*, Shenoute associates sexual misconduct (albeit not exclusively) with impurity and pollution. Ascetics who sleep with other monks, who kiss or touch each other or themselves sexually, and who experience sexual desire for each other are characterized as polluted or defiled, or their desires are described as polluted.[63] In the rules at the beginning of *Letter One*, half of the forbidden sexual activities are described as polluted, unclean, or defiled.[64] However, sex and sexual desire are not the only sins associated with pollution. For example, in Shenoute's account of the rebellion of a few monks, "pollution" and "defilement" plague a community in which theft and disobedience are committed. In one of his allegories, Shenoute counts thieves and liars as well as people who have committed general "defilements and pollutions" or sexual transgressions among the people who are trapped in a pit of impiety and lawlessness.[65]

Shenoute's sexual language is nonetheless pronounced and persistent in *Canon 1*, and his sexual allegations crescendo as his first letter progresses. Ironically, as they become more explicit, his rhetoric becomes even more stylized. At precisely those moments when he describes sexual misdeeds in their greatest detail, he also uses direct quotations from prophetic scriptures to characterize and condemn those acts. In doing so, Shenoute adapts the biblical trope of harlotry and fornication and applies it to the monastery, in fact accusing his own monastery of acting like a whore. Just as feminist biblical scholars have called into question the historical accuracy of charges of fornication and harlotry in books of Ezekiel, Hosea, and Jeremiah, so too should historians of Christianity question the relationship between Shenoute's rhetoric and the social reality in his monastery. Shenoute's use of these charged biblical passages in his condemnation of sex acts means that we must question whether or not the acts he describes have been or are being committed in the monastery, or if they operate as a device for Shenoute to shame and disgrace the entire monastery for the actions of a few monks, and possibly acts that are not sexual but nonetheless egregious in Shenoute's eyes.

For example, let us assess the following charges enumerated by Shenoute, which I examined earlier: people who "defiled" the monastery's "sons" and "daughters," who "became effeminate," or who "laid down with men."[66] Shenoute concludes his list of allegations by asking how the Lord will "spare" the monastery, and by citing the "the word that is written" (from Hos. 6:10): "They committed lawlessness in the house of Israel. I saw in your dwelling place fornication (*pornia*) that was bold, and the ones who defiled themselves among you, they defiled themselves unbeknownst to the Lord."[67] Does Shenoute cite Hosea here because it suits a social context in which monks are in fact fornicating? Or does he cite it because it suits a social context in which monks have sinned, and Shenoute wishes to condemn their sin by modeling his judgment on a severe form of scriptural denunciation?

Shenoute even compares the monastery to three different biblical fornicators or whores. Starting with the idolatrous Judah of Jer. 17, Shenoute asks his own community if she (Shenoute's *sunagōgē*) is "better than" her (Judah), "this one whose treasures the Lord gave for spoil as the price because of all of her sins which she committed in all her territory?" Shenoute then turns to Ezek. 16 and 23, asking his monastery if they are at all different from the biblical whore "whom the Lord handed over into the hands of the ones who hated her," who "stripped her naked," and who "made her shameless." For Shenoute, the answer need not be stated aloud, for it is unequivocally "no"—the monastery is no different than Ezekiel's whore, whose "disgrace" stemmed from her "fornication (*porneia*)." The third fornicating biblical figure who stands as a model for Shenoute's community is the wife in Hos. 2. Again, Shenoute proclaims that the monastery is no better than this whore: "You are not more beautiful than this woman who sinned before God, are you? . . . God took from her her grain, her oil, her wine, and her things, and her clothing (Hos. 2:9). He kept her according to the days of her giving birth, and according to the days when she came out of the land of Egypt (Hos. 2:15), as he [punished] her in the days of the Baals when she sacrificed (Hos. 2:13)."[68] Never the most subtle rhetoritician, Shenoute leaves no room for (mis)interpretation here: his Christian monastery has become a whore like the faithless harlots of scripture.

Harlotry is a literary trope and metaphor for another kind of faithlessness in the scriptures, and Shenoute, following the scriptures, uses this potent symbol in the same manner. He may not be accusing the monastery of physical fornication, but of a spiritual whoring, an adulterous affair with the wrong morals, the wrong interpretation of the monastic rules, the wrong kind of leadership. In their sins, they have stooped as low as a whore. In their fidelity to the alleged sinners (through their aversion to punishing the accused as strictly as Shenoute advocates), they have turned their back on the Lord and have committed harlotry.

The same fate that befell the faithless communities in scripture will be visited upon his monastery, charges Shenoute. The punishment for cheating on God will be estrangement from God, just as it was Yahweh's punishment on his people for entertaining other lovers.[69] The monks' disobedience to their rule constitutes a violation of their sacred commitment and devotion to God. In Shenoute's appropriation of the Bible, sexual regulations express the community's understanding of itself and its relationship to God. Violating those regulations violates that relationship. But in Shenoute's discursive system, in contrast to the biblical texts, illicit sex is not a metaphor for intermingling with an outsider or an outsider's gods. Illicit sex signifies a betrayal of God through intimacy with the devil. Sin, and especially sexual sin, defiles the monk, so that the devil may use the monk as an opening for penetrating the rest of the community.

Shenoute is not the first Egyptian Christian to equate his monastic community with the biblical Israel. Pachomius, who directed a string of male and female monasteries, also likened his community to Israel.[70] Pachomius's reference, however, is quite brief. Shenoute's explicit adoption of feminine and sexual imagery to describe the monastic faith clearly distinguishes his congregation from Pachomius's *koinōnia*.

Although Shenoute directs his criticism to all of the monks, regardless of their gender, his construction of the larger community is specifically gendered. Shenoute's term for the monastery, *tsunagōgē*, is feminine, and he often addresses his audience with the second-person feminine singular pronoun, the feminine "you." But Shenoute's feminization of the monastery runs even deeper, for he also implicitly draws upon two prominent, gendered discourses from the literature of his age: the biblical conception of the community as the faithful bride or fornicating whore, and the late antique medical discourse that characterizes the female body as more susceptible to desire and pollution than the male body. Women's very physiology was construed as softer and weaker than men's, and subsequently more vulnerable to impurities and particularly to sexual corruption.[71] Shenoute's monastery, likewise, is a highly sexualized entity, extremely susceptible to pollution, easily penetrated by corrupting elements, and readily swayed by seductive deceivers. The corporate monastic body is gendered, and that gender is female.

Returning to the issue of the most appropriate reading strategies for understanding the sexual language in *Canon 1*, I propose that reading for both the historical context and the theological meaning will provide important insights into the community at Shenoute's monastery. The modern reader should not have to choose between the literal and figurative interpretations of Shenoute's discourses, particularly regarding sexuality. The fourth-century audience that first received these letters would not have heard one meaning instead of the other. His audience consisted of monks who were probably familiar with some of the events that precipitated Shenoute's letters, or else they soon learned of them after his first letter appeared. Given the citation of rules prohibiting sex, these events may have included sexual misbehavior, and the monks likely understood the practical implications of his scripturally encoded references as well as their more symbolic implications. The thick, sexual rhetoric in Shenoute's letters, however, does not provide evidence of rampant sexual misconduct in the monastery, and in fact, it could be argued that the evidence does not prove that any sexual misconduct ever occurred. Even under those circumstances, Shenoute's accusations likening the monks' nonsexual misdeeds to the violation of such a prominent marker of ascetic identity—celibacy—would have had deep resonance for his audience. Understanding that Shenoute's condemnations of fornication and deception draw upon deeper, historical narratives of Israel's relationship with God does not diminish their more carnal resonance within an ascetic community. Nor does it preclude a more literal reading of *Canon 1*'s letters as denunciations of sinful acts committed by monks whose very identity is determined by their vows to chastity, poverty, obedience, and faith. Shenoute's accusations strike at the heart of monastic practice at the same time that they connect the monks' actions to God's historical relationship with humanity.

Shenoute describes the way in which the sins of individual monks render the rest of the monastic community vulnerable in a series of vivid omens modeled on the judgment oracles in the prophetic books of the Bible. Evil spreads through the community as a result of the monks' behavior and the monastic father's failure to punish them sufficiently. In these prophetic judgments, Shenoute sketches an ideology of the communal ascetic life based on the requisite discipline of the individual monks' bodies and the corporate monastic body, an ideology that he will continue to promote throughout his career. In *Canon 1*, he asserts that the failings of some monks threaten the spiritual integrity of the monastery's social body.

In the first letter, one image Shenoute uses to depict the threat to the community is that of fire. He describes himself observing a grove of fruit-bearing trees while in the classical throes of mourning: weeping, groaning, and throwing dust on himself. He mourns because an evil flame has filled the grove, burning its fig trees, apple trees, date palms, and most of the others.[72] Later in *Canon 1*, he returns to this image, comparing the sinful monks to a cluster of dried-up trees situated near an orchard.[73] The blaze engulfs the dry trees, threatening the neighboring orchard. Shenoute's judgment oracle evokes the imagery of scriptural prophecy, such as in the book of Joel, where locusts destroy apple trees and palm trees (among other crops), and a fire accompanying the Lord's host devours a land that once resembled Eden.

Shenoute revisits the imagery of trees and fire in *Letter Two*. Here he channels Jeremiah, employing a character called the "destroyer," the title of a figure in several judgment oracles from that biblical book.[74] Shenoute's version of the "destroyer" is evil personified. He approaches a tree in the midst of a forest, whereupon he attacks the tree with an ax, chopping off its chosen shoots and branches and leaving them to wither and die at the base of the tree. He later returns and sets the debris ablaze, engulfing the tree in flame and burning any lingering shoots on the tree. The only portion of the tree remaining in the end is a root which has been lying in a bit of moisture and some green shoots above it.[75] Shenoute's vision also evokes chapters 10–11 of Isaiah, in which the Lord burns and chops down forests,[76] and which then predicts that a "shoot" will emerge from the "stump of Jesse," with a "branch" growing from "his roots" (11:1).[77] If we interpret the tree in Shenoute's judgment oracle as the monastery, the dead branches become those monks who have succumbed to the devil, the "enemy" represented by the destroyer. The devil uses them to achieve his ultimate goal, the destruction of not just a few monks, but of the entire monastery. The surviving root and its few remaining shoots represent the very small number of monks who can survive such an attack—presumably, monks such as Shenoute.

Shenoute continues with his prophetic visions for the monastery in an allegory based on 2 Cor. 11:14–15 that is in turn an allegory of Shenoute's relationship with the community. A "man of light" (possibly meant to represent the monastic father?) encounters a "man of darkness" who has disguised his identity by kindling a false light, thus masquerading as another "man of light." The man of darkness deceives the man of light into trusting him and throws him into a deep, dark pit. A passing kinsman of the man of light (perhaps Shenoute?) is unable to convince friends and family to help him rescue the man of light; his companions instead mock him and accuse him of lying. In the end, the man of light remains in the pit. His kinsman remains tormented by distress over the situation even though God visits him.[78] Shenoute offers no solace for any of the characters involved.[79] His tale warns his brothers and sisters that the devil masquerades among them in the guise of a fellow monk, deceiving even the most respected of the brothers and sisters. This allegory is even bleaker than the previous one, in which at least a few green shoots survived the fiery destruction. In this story, even a devout monk such as the "man of light," may be deceived and drawn into the pit of damnation by a hypocritical colleague. Furthermore, he cannot lift himself out of the pit of damnation alone—redemption and salvation are community efforts.

This allegory also continues a motif that originally appears in an oracle in Shenoute's first letter, where "lawlessness" is represented by a group of people who have been pushed into a pit. They pull down on the hand offered by a passerby seeking to extricate them from the pit. To save himself from being heaved into the pit, the passerby must "shake them off of his hand and leave them in their current state." Thus, concludes Shenoute, shall be the fate "of everyone among you" who has "sunk" into deceit and evil and has refused Shenoute's aid.[80] Shenoute's allegories are both symbolic stories—thinly disguised narratives of what has happened from Shenoute's perspective—and prophetic alarms—warnings of the dangers still facing the monks, who remain condemned either by their fall into the pit of damnation or by their mocking denial on the sidelines.

Although Shenoute rarely uses the vocabulary of purity and pollution in these parables, they illuminate the core problem regarding the presence of particularly sinful monks. Their defilement renders the monastery as a whole vulnerable to the devil's work. Shenoute redirects the force of his disapproval away from specific individuals and toward the entire community. These allegories do not contain the same pollution language that Shenoute uses to characterize the monks' lack of discipline elsewhere in the letters, namely in sections discussing specific instances of disobedience or violations of the monastic rule. Nonetheless, these allegories convey a sense of the polluting nature of sin. Once sin enters the monastery, it threatens to destroy the other members. A lack of discipline on the part of one individual results in an undisciplined, and subsequently condemned, social body. Although destruction of the community is never absolute, because a few people endure, the threat of complete annihilation hovers over the community (as it did Israel, Judah, or Jerusalem in the biblical texts) for as long as they do not repent and reform. Shenoute maintains that only the vigilance of a few monks has protected them thus far, and that only those few may survive God's judgment over the community.

Throughout *Canon 1*, Shenoute defines and evaluates the discipline of the monastic community by the discipline of the body. Ascetic discipline is a communal concern in which salvation is perceived as interdependent. Sin defiles the body, acting as a corrupting agent, threatening to spread to other parts of the social body. The entire monastery is shamed by the actions of the sinful community, and as one social body, they face punishment from God. A well-disciplined monastery is composed of well-disciplined bodies: monks who do not succumb to the appetites of lust, greed, and hunger. Surrendering to these desires constitutes a betrayal of God. Not only is the monastery comprised of these well-disciplined bodies, but the community itself functions as a single unit—a unified and disciplined corporate monastic body. Through its ascetic discipline, it will be saved. Because of its lapses, the whole community is in peril.

The implications of Shenoute's theology in *Canon 1* are not limited to eschatological concerns. Precisely because Shenoute roots his theological discourse in the language of common ascetic practice, the texts function as powerful ideological tools. Shenoute's theology of the monastic life is deeply implicated in the social and political agendas he has for the monastery, not the least of which may have been a direct challenge to the current father for leadership of the monastery.

Shenoute's Political Challenge to His Predecessor

The writing of *Canon 1* represents a serious challenge to the authority of the second leader of the monastery. Shenoute charges that under this man's tenure, the monastery has abandoned God, and that those under his influence now face the specter of eternal damnation. The chance for salvation remains, but only if the community repents and changes course. Shenoute questions his superior's ability to lead the them under these circumstances. Because Shenoute mentions the second father's death in the postcript to *Canon 1*, it appears that he was not deposed. Unfortunately, no other direct literary testimony about his death or the selection of his replacement remains. We know that ultimately Shenoute would succeed him, and Emmel has speculated that *Canon 1* must have placed Shenoute "directly in the line of succession," in part by raising Shenoute's profile within the monastery.[81] Given the level of derision Shenoute claims the monks directed toward him after his accusations, the opposite might very well have been true. I contend, however, that with the writing of the two letters comprising *Canon 1*, Shenoute indeed threw his own hat into the ring for the position. He indirectly advocates for the removal of the current leader and presents himself as the best candidate to lead the community next.

Some monks clearly read *Letter One* in this way. In *Letter Two*, Shenoute mentions speculation about his intentions, and he insists that he has no aspirations to lead the community. In dismissing these rumors, Shenoute seizes the opportunity to levy yet one more reproach against the community by declaring that "not even the Lord's ministering angels want to get near" them.[82] Additionally, the remainder of *Canon 1* speaks against his denial in this passage. For despite his silence about political ambitions elsewhere in the letters, throughout *Canon 1* Shenoute implicitly mounts a multipronged attack upon the current leadership. His very theology of salvation functions to rally against the the monastery's leadership those monks who believe themselves to be pious, faithful, and obedient. He tells his colleagues that the behavior of others threatens their own salvation, thus giving them a distinct self-interest in changing the direction of the monastery. According to Shenoute, the interdependent nature of the monastic life necessitates a strict policy of ascetic discipline to which all members adhere. Even monks obedient to the monastic rule risk their own salvation when sinful monks are allowed to reside unpunished in the community. Witness the people in the pit or the "man of light" in Shenoute's allegories. The obvious disciplinarian, and the individual to whom Shenoute directs much of his displeasure, is the head of the monastery. Shenoute insists upon the necessity of identifying the sinful monks and taking some sort of action to bring about their repentance. It is the monastic father whom Shenoute holds responsible for enforcing the discipline. Shenoute places at the head of his monastic ideology a figure with significant centralized authority and responsibility and simultaneously accuses the current leader of failing to live up to that responsibility. In constructing the community as feminine, as a philandering woman, he rhetorically positions the monastery as a figure in need of discipline and punishment by a strong, masculine authority figure. The current father, whom Shenoute has shamed and demeaned, has lost his potency as a leader.

As he undermines the current leader's credibility, Shenoute casts himself as a person worthy of authority and responsibility. His every move, be it rhetorical through his exegesis of Jeremiah, or physical through his semianchoritic withdrawal to the desert outside the monastery, puts Shenoute in a position of greater perceived authority as both an ascetic and a prophet in the biblical mold. His condemnations of the community are crafted as prophetic visions from God in order to call the other monks to repentance. By taking on the persona of a biblical prophet, Shenoute solidifies his reputation as a spiritual leader. His rhetoric in *Canon 1* functions to present him as a compelling alternative to the current monastic leadership, despite his own silence on this very issue. As prophet, his role in the community is to peel away the monks' false sense of security in their salvation and reveal what he believes to be the true spiritual state of the monastery. He frames his censure of the monks' disobedience to the rule and of the leader's failure to exercise authority over the monks in the context of prophetic duty. He presents himself as the messenger of truth who must uncover and extinguish the falsehood and hypocrisy concealed in the monastery. As the one who speaks "the word of God," Shenoute must expose the iniquity that lies beneath a veneer of ascetic purity. He locates his challenge to the superior's authority within a tradition of prophetic expression. In the ascetic tradition, the young monk who challenges his elder could be severely chastised for exhibiting excessive pride. The harsh words of Shenoute, in contrast, are not merely sanctioned by God—they are mandated. "I saw visions and revelations of the Lord," he claims.[83] In adopting the trappings of prophetic wisdom, Shenoute simultaneously places himself in the tradition of authoritative ascetics whose charisma, ascetic practice, and purity of heart rendered them ascetic "masters" worthy of disciples.[84]

Shenoute uses the authority he has established as a prophet to justify his concerns about bodily discipline and purity. He exhibits apprehension that misguided monks use some of their ascetic practices as a shield to protect them while they secretly commit other sins. Shenoute decries their so-called monasticism, charging that they do not understand the true meaning of ascetic discipline. Despite their prayer, fasting, night vigils, and other *askesis*, the monks "suffer loss" of their ascetic endeavors because of "shameful" and "bitter" deeds.[85] They fail in their struggle against the devil because they commit other sins. Their ascetic practices do not inoculate them against sin incurred by other means: "On the one hand, you measure bread on scales, and you eat (it) in a fixed measure. You eat sin, however, until you are excessively sated. You know how to measure your prayer and your discipline and every good deed according to the rules that are established for you. You commit sin, however, without measure, with a lack of restraint, and without fearing the Lord."[86] Although the monks appear to follow many of the community's rules, they nonetheless have sinned in other ways, charges Shenoute. Their obedience to *some* of the rules does not protect them from God's judgment for their other misdeeds. He immediately follows this section on monastic hypocrisy by asking the monks whom they think the Lord will forgive—those who "defile your sons and your daughters?" those who "defile themselves with their companions?" those who "defile themselves?" those who "blasphemed" and "lied?"[87] His questions are filled with sexual suggestion, and he again combines the discourses of pollution, sexuality, and deception to characterize the sins that plague the community. Despite some overt acts of ascetic discipline, the monks nonetheless remain undisciplined—they are loose, wanton, and defiled. Their fasting, night vigils, and prayers cannot make up for their other lapses. Although the monks fast, they partake of other pollutions.

He portrays the monastery as under the grip of widespread deception and hypocrisy. The defilements of some render the whole community vulnerable to sin. And by failing to bring their colleagues to repentence, the others are culpable for their fellow ascetics' sins. In its efforts to hide its "abominations" and "bitter deeds,"[88] the community, Shenoute charges, has crafted a web of lies so intricate that they have even fooled themselves into believing that they have done no wrong. God, however, is not fooled, and Shenoute warns that their self-deception will not save them at the final judgment.[89] He asks, "Where will you conceal yourself on that day? . . . Where are our lies and our falsehoods and our hypocrisy? Let them come and let them save us from the hands of God on the appointed day."[90] Shenoute accuses some monks of even abandoning their monastic rules for "lawlessness" justified by a "false covenant."[91] According to Shenoute, they have become obedient to falsehoods, rather than the truth of their monastic heritage. The sinners have "trampled over the truth" and have become ruled by a lie, to the point that monks "who are taught the teaching of our fathers" no longer know or understand it.[92] The monks' deceptions may save them from self-castigation, but they do not protect them from the penetrating and judgmental gaze of the Lord. Under the current leadership, the community has "defiled" the "grace of monasticism" to which they were called, and the monks have abandoned their true rule and have instead pledged their obedience to a fraud.[93] Shenoute thus uses his prophetic role to challenge the legitimacy of the current leader's authority and to question the wisdom of the community's continued deference to that authority.

Shenoute seems acutely aware of the possibility of being charged a false prophet himself. After one of the many accusations hurled against him, he testifies somewhat defensively, "I call upon God as witness upon my soul that I do not lie."[94] Moreover, he takes care to frame his lengthy (and somewhat creative) exegetical passages and judgment oracles as revelation rather than heretical speech. The allegories at the end of *Letter One* and the beginning of *Letter Two*, such as the stories of the man of light and the destroyer, could be called parables. However, Shenoute's tendency toward hyperbole apparently has been questioned by other members of the community, for he insists rather forcefully that his edifying stories are not parables but revelation: "They are not parables, lest you say, 'This one opened his mouth against me in some parables and a speech that I do not recognize.'"[95]

Such accounts of Shenoute's rejection by the community only serve to enhance his prophetic identity and his authority. Shenoute resembles his biblical predecessors who are shunned and maligned by the very people they sought to save. Just as Israel refused the words of its prophets, so too does the monastic community plunge itself further into damnation by its refusal to listen to Shenoute. Given that Shenoute eventually succeeded the second father as head of the monastery, it would be erroneous to assume that Shenoute had no supporters in the community. Instead, in the biblically charged environment of Egyptian asceticism, Shenoute's claim to the position of outcast increased his authenticity as God's prophetic witness.

Shenoute's overt eschewal of any pretensions to a leadership role likely made him a more appealing candidate in the eyes of the men and women in his community as well. The ascetic's reluctance to accept a position of power, even when invited, was legendary. As Conrad Leyser has observed in his study of asceticism and authority in late antique Europe, the ascetic ideal of modesty when facing an accession to power dated back "to the Platonic tradition of the philosopher king, the man who could be trusted with power precisely because it was distasteful to him."[96] Hagiography from the Pachomian monasteries also promoted this ideal; the monk Theodore, widely expected to succeed Pachomius as abbot, reportedly fell from favor after he verbalized his willingness to accept the post.[97] It seems that "the two principal gestures of good faith" performed by ascetics in public office in sixth-century Europe apply equally well to the politics of Egyptian monasticism: "the disclaimer of all interest in power," and "a demonstration of constant purity of heart and hence spiritual expertise."[98] Shenoute, too, disavows any claim to political authority—and especially any claim to power—for himself as an individual. In these first letters, he offers his readers a rather humble self-portrait of a monk who understands and accepts his subordinate position in the community, even appropriating the label of sinner for himself.[99] In retelling his disputes with the monastic father, Shenoute represents himself as a son who speaks with some reticence to a father, and he avers respect for his superior, whom he declares "worthy" and "righteous."

This admiration, however, veils a stinging rebuke. He wears the mantle of humility not as a man content at a lower rank, but as a monk engaged in the common ascetic practice of status negotiation through the rhetoric of humility. As Maud Gleason has argued, in monastic literature, "The tension between the ideal of impassivity and the reality of competitiveness was perpetual."[100] Gossip about fellow ascetics played an important role in community formation among loosely organized desert anchorites. "[E]ven if being one of the 'old men' was only an informally achieved status, how was its attainment to be ratified and recognized, save by word getting round through informal channels? Status recognition *required* gossip."[101] Although a monastic "ideology of humility" held competition between monks in check, tales about desert ascetics suggest that monks frequently revealed "damaging" information about their peers in order to "one-up" each other and thereby prove their own ascetic mettle. In the *Apophthegmata Patrum* and other such literature, revered monks model the preferred responses to gossip: they disagree with "disparaging" remarks about others and respond with humility themselves, often admitting to committing the very error their colleague scorns. Such a move of "one-downmanship," often made by a more advanced abba or amma, is "socially stabilizing" in that it reaffirms an ideology of humility in order to prevent competition between monks from reaching ugly proportions. At times, the ascetic grapevine also served as a means to shame monks in leadership positions for perceived inappropriate disciplinary action they took toward disciples or junior monks.[102] *Canon 1*'s revealing and indeed disparaging letters certainly constitute "gossip" and "news" dispensed in order to shame and regulate the behavior of other monks, including a superior. In the *Apophthegmata*, however, the "behavioral regulation" of senior ascetics was usually undertaken by ascetics with comparable "star status." Additionally, in our coenobitic drama, Shenoute does not play the role of the gossiping monk who is implicitly rebuked by his audience's "socially stabilizing" response of humble "one-downmanship." Shenoute rather anticipates his audience's discomfort with status negotiation through gossip. He tempers his bold and public criticism with an embrace of the ascetic virtue of humility. Like the authors of literature about eremitic and anchoritic monks, Shenoute balances his monastic competition

for authority—which, as the letters reveal, unsettled many of his colleagues—with rhetorical humility. In doing so, he girds his own reputation
as a skilled ascetic and underscores his claim that his censure stems from
authentic spiritual concern rather than a bald grab for power.

Shenoute's ideology of the monastic life as it develops in *Canon 1*
carries theological commitments as well as political implications. Theologically, Shenoute appeals to the monks' concerns for their own salvation by
arguing that undisciplined, sinful behavior threatens the efficacy of their
own ascetic discipline, since the sins of individual monks have threatened
the moral integrity of the monastery's social body. Shenoute then presents
himself as the alternative leader of the community by portraying himself
as a worthy ascetic and prophetic bearer of God's truth, in contrast to a
regime of lies and deception. Some members of the community must have
found his argument persuasive, because our next glimpse of Shenoute
comes after he has been installed as their third leader. As an examination
of his later writings reveals, *Canon 1* lays the foundation for an ideology
of the monastic life that he will implement once he takes office.

2

The Ritualization of the Monastic Body: Shenoute's Rules

THE RULES AT DEIR ANBA SHENOUDA were a crucial way of shaping a communal identity. As Shenoute himself explains, they defined the very boundaries of the ascetic community: "Everyone who will dwell in our domain shall be bound by the canons that are established for all the brothers (and sisters) who gather together."[1] Through the rules, all the members of the monastery were joined by a common set of ritual practices that forged new ascetic subjects out of those who performed them. The rules set forth the activities of daily life in the community, such as work, cooking, meals, prayer, rest. They also lay out prohibitions on forbidden behavior, including theft, overeating, unauthorized visits from outsiders, and sex. But the regulations to which the men and women in Shenoute's monastery pledged their obedience functioned as more than a list of "do's" and "don't's" by which the monks structured their routine. As Patricia Cox Miller has observed, in the world of late antique Christianity, "ascetic practices are viewed as performative ritual acts that induce the perceptual construction of ascetic bodies as bodies of plenitude."[2] The rituals outlined in Shenoute's rules—be they the daily program of eating and work, the extraordinary asceticism of affiliated hermits in the outlying desert, or the punishments imposed for breaking the precepts—produced bodies filled with meaning, whose purity and discipline was meant to be mirrored in the purity and discipline of the monastery as a whole. In this way, the rules in subsequent *Canons* continue the ascetic project Shenoute began in *Canon 1*, when he charged that the actions of sinful monks threatened the salvation of the other monks as part of his challenge to the authority of the monastery's leadership.

The regulations contained within the *Canons* composed once Shenoute became the third leader of the monastery bind the monks together through a set of ritual practices that express both their identity as members of that monastery and their submission to Shenoute's ideology of the communal ascetic life. The rituals cultivate a monastic subjectivity particular to Deir Anba Shenouda, in which the acts of joining the community and gathering together as one unit four times a year affirmed their participation in the monastic social body:

Everyone who will dwell in our domain shall be bound by the canons that are established for all the brothers (and sisters) who gather together. Four Sundays each year, these ones that our father established for us, every one who is in the desert around us shall gather themselves also with the brothers (and sisters) so that they come together, unless they are sick. But as for every one who dwells in the desert who will not want to conduct themselves according to the ordinances that our fathers established for us, if he (or she) is in our congregations, we will cast him (or her) out from them, whether that person is a man or a woman. And if he (or she) is in the desert around us, we will gather so that we will go out to the place where he (or she) is and we will cast him (or her) out from our domain. But if in an argument, he (or she) disputes with us, we will destroy the place where he (or she) lives so that we cast him (or her) out from there out of necessity. . . . And we shall cast down the place where he (or she) dwells so that we destroy it down to its foundations, so that no person shall reside in it ever again, because it might cause difficulty for its neighbor.[3]

As this passage illustrates, the monastic subjectivity Shenoute envisions and articulates builds on the ascetic theory outlined in *Canon 1*. Fidelity to the group, to the communal monastic body, is paramount, and that allegiance is expressed as submission to the canons that "bind" the community together as one. Disturbance and disputation by some members threaten the integrity of the community, and in the name of preserving the harmony of the social body, those members merit expulsion.

As he describes the practices outlined in the rules, Shenoute articulates his vision of the path to salvation as relational, even interdependent. The monk at Deir Anba Shenouda—even the seemingly loosely affiliated desert hermit—shares in a communal identity that is continuously reified by the rules. This particularly Shenoutean ascetic subjectivity is marked by a contention that monks must maintain a strict ascetic discipline in order to avoid personal pollution or impurity that might negatively impact the spiritual status of others in the community. Shenoute also allows for the possibility that the virtues of some honorable monks might redeem their delinquent brothers and sisters. Shenoute's regulations generate a literary and material space for the ritual performance of asceticism, where ideology and practice are indistinguishable from each other. The very execution of the rules by the monks through their asceticism produces disciplined individual monks and a disciplined corporate monastic body obedient and subject to the rules, to Shenoute's leadership, and to God. These monastic bodies, which constantly enact, evoke, and inspire the rules, inform and are informed by the ideology of the communal monastic life crafted in *Canon 1.*

This chapter will explore how the rules explicitly fashion the monastery as one corporate monastic body in which the spiritual status of each member affects the other monks in the community. The rules are infused with the same language of purity and pollution that permeated *Canon 1.* The sexual discourse used to control and shame monks in *Canon 1* also reappears in the rules—and with a vengeance. Shenoute's frequent admonitions against sexual desire seek to purge sexual expression from the community, yet ironically they also serve to position sexuality as one of the foremost markers of monastic identity. Additionally, expulsion appears again and again in the *Canons* as an appropriate punishment for disobeying specific rules or participating in forbidden activities; through expulsion, the monastery removes sinful and disobedient members of the community, at times in order to protect the salvation of the other members. Shenoute cites passages from the Pauline letters about the Christian congregation as one body comprised of many members in order to justify, explain, or elaborate upon the rules he is providing for the community. Together, these aspects of Shenoute's rules construct a monastic subjectivity based on bodily purity and communal interdependence, in which the individual ascetic subject signifies a disciplined ascetic community.

What was presented in Shenoute's first letters as an alternative monastic model offered during a time of tumult and conflict becomes reality in these later texts. In editing and codifying the rules, he constitutes and reconstitutes the monastic bodies we first encounter in *Canon 1.* Shenoute's rules participate in a process of cultural production and identity formation that Teresa Shaw has termed "the 'making' of the early Christian ascetic ideal."[4] In making the corporate monastic body, Shenoute organizes, regulates, and orchestrates its members, the monks, in such a way as to produce a well-ordered and pure social body. Through the implementation of the monastic rules, Shenoute also produces that social body's members. Through the ritual performance of enacting the monastic rules, the monks not only conform themselves to the established boundaries of good behavior, they also position, perform, and transform themselves into the well-disciplined, pure bodies Shenoute longs for them to be. They are performing the self-same ideology Shenoute inscribes in the texts.

The combined work of four cultural theorists—Michel Foucault, Judith Butler, Pierre Bourdieu, and Catherine Bell—provides the framework for my analysis. I am indebted to Foucault for the insight that discipline of the human body results not only in a "subjected body," one that is

disciplined by, constrained by, and subject to at times physical (even violent) and at times ideological expressions of power, but also in a "productive body," one that through the acts of domination committed upon it
in turn produces knowledge about the body, the self, and the power relations in which it is implicated.[5] The end of discipline is not repression; it
is the production of knowledge.

From Butler (who, like Bell and Bourdieu, follows Foucault), I take
the notion that gender, and specifically the gendered and sexualized body,
is not an essential, universal *thing*. As I discussed in the introduction, I
treat the body as a socially constructed entity whose identity, sexuality, and
gender are constituted not through any biological essence but through its
performance within a particular cultural context.[6] Though Butler theorizes
only about sex and gender in contemporary society, the work of Shaw,
Peter Brown, and others has suggested the malleability of the late antique
body as well.[7]

To understand the ways in which the cultural norms that produce
gendered and sexualized bodies and are then in turn re-produced by them
within the context of a highly regulated religious community, I draw upon
the theorizing of Bourdieu and Bell. Bourdieu and Bell conceive of social
systems as informed by both cognitive or discursive theories and the material conditions and activities of everyday life. Bell urges scholars of religion
to think beyond the binaries of ideology/materiality and thought/ac-
tion—or *theology/praxis*—by thinking about religious or ritual practice as
something that is not removed from ideological or theological systems.[8]
Ritual practices produce, and are intended to produce, ideological and
theological meaning. The practitioner, however, is unable to recognize
fully their implications for the society, its values, and its structure. Aside
from the intended, strategic systems of meaning and social relations people
understand themselves to be producing through their ritual practice, rituals produce, reproduce, or reconfigure a particular vision of how the
world, society, or community *should be*. Bell calls this final aspect of ritual
practice "redemptive hegemony": the reproduction or reconfiguration of
"a vision of the order of power in the world."[9] Ritual practice creates a
reality through its performance, but it is a reality that is already constrained
and determined to a certain extent by the social reality in which it is being
performed. In the context of Shenoute's ascetic community, the monastic
"rule" as a social institution provides a ritualization of daily life, not in
the sense of making practices routine, but in the sense of making them
redemptive, such that "everyday" practices become transformative. Ritual
is a social performance that "constructs an argument" about the way in
which the world is or should be; it does not symbolize an idea, concept,

or thing outside of itself—it is power and the performance of power and social relationships.[10] Ritualization is the process by which ritual subjects are formed; it is a process "rooted in the body."[11] Bell envisions a dialectic between the social and individual bodies that ritual executes, during which the body itself is molded and restructured.[12] The ritual act of kneeling serves as an example: kneeling does not symbolize the subjection or submission of one class of subjects to another; it *produces* a subordinate subject.

The ritual practices in Shenoute's monastic rules reflect and reify a particular monastic subjectivity, which is bound to Shenoute's ideology of the communal ascetic life. This monastic subjectivity is informed in part by what Pierre Bourdieu has termed "habitus," that is, "systems of durable, transposable *dispositions*" or "principles of the generation and structuring of practices and representations which can be objectively 'regulated' and 'regular' "[13]—in other words, a historically conditioned, collective, and material ethos that is inscribed and inculcated within each person through the activities of daily life. The monastic subjectivity formed through this process at Deir Anba Shenouda is reflected within and further instilled in the monks through the monastic rules.[14] It is characterized by two key elements of Shenoute's ideology of the communal ascetic life: an interdependence of the monks' material and spiritual existence and an intense concern for purity. It is cultivated and given meaning through the process of ritualization.

Shenoute's rules also produce the ritualized subjects who, through enacting the ritual practices in the rules, form a unified, harmonious, disciplined, and pure social body that mirrors the disciplined and pure ascetic bodies of the monks themselves. Both the ritual reading of the rules and the everyday performance of the rules produce these ascetic subjects. In late antique liturgical rituals featuring the recitation of a text about a particular saint, that saint, through the "process of ritual representation," became the "one whose body . . . imaged the body of the worshipping community in that form it gained through the salvific process of the liturgy."[15] In similar ways, the regular reading of the rules, the recurring gatherings of the monks to affirm their allegiance to the rules, and the daily performance of the rules result in a monk whose body images the ascetic community.

In this chapter, I trace the ritual production of an ascetic subjectivity in Shenoute's community and highlight its particularities by reading Shenoute's rules alongside the rules of another late antique Egyptian monastic system, the Pachomian monasteries. To introduce the material, I will first account for the sources and genres that comprise both sets of rules and address issues of authorship in the texts. Shenoute's rules do not conform to what we typically consider the genre of monastic *regulae*. Interspersed between lists of approved and proscribed behaviors are interpretations of the rules, hortatory or instructional passages, biblical exegeses, or descriptions of events that have occurred in the monastery. Consequently, the regulations delineated in several volumes of Shenoute's *Canons* are a far cry from more familiar monastic *regulae*: the moderately sized, clearly defined lists presented in Jerome's translation of the Pachomian rules, the rule of Benedict, or even Basil's shorter and longer rules.[16] The longer descriptive or narrative sections in the Shenoutean rules explicate the social and soteriological consequences of following the rules. Then I will turn to three aspects of ritualization in Shenoute's rules. First, I will address the contents of the rules as they pertain to bodily *askesis*, and the particular practices (e.g., fasting, sexual renunciation) that relate to the discourses of the body seen in *Canon 1*. I also will place his rules side by side with the Pachomian rules to foreground the nature and prominence of the discourses of the body in Shenoute's texts. Next, I will examine the ways in which the punishment of expulsion participates in the ritual production of this monastic social body. Finally, I will turn to narrative passages interspersed among the rules in which Shenoute explicitly draws upon bodily metaphors such as Pauline biblical discourses of the body and etiologies of disease. The monastic rules in these texts illustrate a ritualization process whereby the vision of the monastic community presented in *Canon 1* is materially and theologically constituted.

Shenoute's Monastic "Rule": Sources, Genre, and Authorship

Shenoute's "rule" differs in genre, style, and contents from other monastic rules of late antiquity. In fact, it would be a mistake to call it a "rule" or *regula* as such, for that term conjures an image of a list of required and proscribed behaviors that is contained within the defined limits of a particular text. When compared to the early medieval *regulae* of Europe, whose genre "was an opportunity to imagine a community not beholden to the generosity of a donor," the rules in Shenoute's *Canons* seem generically unstable. His "*regulae*" vascillate between, on the one hand, registers of anonymous and concise precepts that represent an external authority to which *both* monk and abbot must pledge submission, and on the other hand, exhortations or justifications from a personalized and personally invested author and individual.[17] However, even Shenoute's very language requires the reader to rethink any attempt to judge Deir Anba Shenouda's rules by the standards of other late antique *regulae*. As Shenoute writes, the monks are bound by the "canons" established for them; *kanōn* is the word Shenoute uses to name his ascetic writings as a whole—the nine volumes of *Canons* that contain Shenoute's letters, rules, and sermons to the monks. Shenoute's "rules" are canons within *Canons*; they are at times lists of precepts, and at times explanations of those precepts. Shenoute's rules do not consist of one identifiable, free standing, or self-contained text or set of texts. Instead, they appear dispersed throughout several volumes of the *Canons*.[18] Rule texts alternate between lists of rules, descriptions or interpretations of those rules, and admonitions or praise for those who disobey or obey the rules. Shenoute's letters, which at times quote from the rules, are collected in the same codices as the rules. The rules also contain lengthy narrative descriptions of the ways in which the monks should follow and enforce the rules as well as substantial interpretive, homiletic, and hortatory passages similar in style to Shenoute's letters and sermons. Many rules are inserted within or appended to other prose or epistolary pieces.[19]

Shenoute's rules are distinct even when read alongside regulations attributed to his fellow Egyptians from the Pachomian monasteries. Pachomius, who lived from approximately 292 to 346 C.E., is credited with founding one of the earliest monasteries in Egypt, which later grew to a large federation of perhaps eleven male and female communities. Several sets of rules attributed to him and to one of his successors, Horsiesius, survive primarily due to a Latin translation by Jerome. I refer to them throughout as the "Pachomian rules" because of their provenance. The rules attributed to Pachomius were likely revised, adapted, and expanded under his successors, and the texts extant today do not necessarily represent the original rules established by Pachomius, himself. Moreover, these and the regulations attributed to Horsiesius come to us in their final, and their only extant full form, in the Latin translation. Although both figures died before Shenoute took control of his monastery, Jerome's translation in 404 C.E. is precisely contemporaneous with Shenoute's *Canons*.[20] In contrast to the Shenoutean rules, the "Pachomian" rules are specific, self-contained lists of regulations: the *Precepts, Precepts and Institutes, Precepts and Judgements*, and *Precepts and Laws* attributed to Pachomius, and the *Regulations* attributed to Horsiesius. When placed alongside the collection of Pachomian rules, the sheer volume of Shenoute's rules is also remarkable. Those published in Leipoldt's edition alone run over one hundred pages. Add to these the rules in other publications as well as the unpublished texts, and one can sense the enormity of their scope.

The diversity of styles of Shenoutean rules is apparent upon reading the *Canons*. One segment of *Canon 3*, for example, begins with a description of prohibited methods of personal hygiene and continues with a condemnation of people who perform evil works, who command others to do them, and who see sins committed but do not report them. Here are excerpts of the rules in the passage:

> Cursed is the person who slanderously appoints to his (or her) neighbor a matter that is sinful . . . whether it is a man or a woman. . . .
> Cursed is everyone who commits deceitful acts in all the congregations of the Lord. . . .
> As for everyone among us who will see a deceitful act in a pollution or in a theft or in any other sin that leads to death, and as for them, if they do not tell me who it is or what those wicked works are, all these curses shall come upon them from God, whether that person is a man or a woman.[21]

This list of regulations leads into an extended discussion of the merits of the rules, the character of monks who disobey them, and the relationship between God and the rules.[22] The ordinances cataloged in this passage resemble one of the preferred rhetorical styles for listing the rules in the *Canons:* listing prohibited activities in a formulation beginning with "Cursed is. . . ."[23] But the rules also appear in more descriptive styles, as in this passage regarding eating and food preparation:

> Now, if some need a little vinegar that has not been diluted with water or so that it may be mixed outside (the refectory) with any other thing like all the brothers eat, the elder shall first be told, and he for his part shall not turn them away. But whether he wants them to eat in the refectory or he wants them to eat in the infirmary on this occasion, he is held accountable only when they do not eat at the table with all the brothers. None among us, whether male or female, shall finish eating and go to the infirmary and eat there again, or shall finish eating in the infirmary and go to the refectory and eat there again. If ever a need arises such that some go to the refectory, but they cannot eat in the refectory as they assert, "It is in our innards or in our body that we are ill," while they (in fact) want to go to the infirmary and eat there again, their claim shall be brought to the male elder, and he shall decide the matter first before they go there—that is to say, (he shall decide) whether they have truly fallen ill and whether they cannot eat in the refectory. And also the female elder for her part, and the woman who is appointed with her: any matter of this sort shall be brought to them, and they shall deliberate until they know the certainty in any matter.[24]

The Pachomian rules also contain both short lists of regulations and longer descriptive rules.[25] Yet, the Pachomian texts much more closely resemble self-contained lists of regulations, and they do not contain the lengthy hortatory, prophetic, or exegetical passages that the Shenoutean rules do.

Finally, the problems of the authorship of the rules in the Pachomian and Shenoutean communities vary. Most of what are labeled the rules of "Pachomius" have survived only in the Latin translation. Some fragments attributed to Pachomius remain in Sahidic Coptic (presumably their original language), and the *Regulations of Horsiesius* survive in their original language, Coptic (though little work has been done on Horsiesius's corpus and particularly on the authenticity of the rules).[26] Yet the bulk of the rules, and the format in which they are published, come from Jerome's translation of an earlier Greek translation of the Coptic rules—a translation dating sixty years after the death of Pachomius. Although Jerome's translation corresponds fairly closely to the extant Coptic fragments, Jerome seems to have occasionally made changes or additions to the text. As Philip Rousseau warns, it is unlikely that Jerome's translation, no matter how faithful to the text he had in hand, accurately corresponds to regulations issued directly by Pachomius during his lifetime. Rather, they can only be considered authoritative and authentic for the monasteries as they existed some decades *after* Pachomius's death—late in the fourth century or early fifth century.[27] Thus, the issue of authorship for these rules is murky, yet taken together, these four sets of Pachomian regulations do provide a rough sketch of the organization of the community during the same period Shenoute was consolidating the rules in the *Canons*.[28] Consequently, the are an ideal corpus for reading alongside the Shenoutean rules, as they represent an Egyptian monastic *regula* from the same time period.

The rules in Shenoute's *Canons* cannot be taken as original documents of pure Shenoutean authorship either. The "Shenoutean rules" likely consist of Shenoute's edits, additions, and explications of a previously existing set of rules.[29] How faithful Shenoute remained to the prior rules is difficult, if not impossible, to determine. The precepts in Shenoute's *Canons* are a document of Shenoutean authorship in the sense that they contain the unmistakable stamp of Shenoute's voice and convictions, but they nonetheless possess roots in an earlier tradition of community regulations. Shenoute quotes from a set of rules in *Canon 1*, before he ever became the monastery's leader. Even these early, possibly pre-Shenoutean regulations, however, are not transparent representations of monastic daily life under Pcol or the second monastic father; the rules in *Canon 1* address both the men's and women's monastic congregations, even though the women's community was not formally under the White Monastery's authority until after Shenoute became the monastery's leader.[30] The *Canons* contain rules developed over an extended period of the community's history, a period in which the authority structure and demographics of the monastery were still evolving.

There is also some evidence to suggest that the Shenoutean rules borrowed from the Pachomian rules. Although a full and detailed textual comparison of the sources from both monastic systems is beyond the scope of this study, both Leipoldt and Hans Quecke have found borrowings from the Pachomian rules in Shenoute's writings, and copies of the *vita* of Pachomius were found in the library of Deir Anba Shenouda.[31] At the turn of the twentieth century, scholars postulated that Shenoute's rules were entirely derived from the Pachomian rules. According to this theory, Pcol (the first leader of Shenoute's monastery) adapted Pachomius's rules for his new community by making them significantly stricter. Upon becoming leader, Shenoute then adapted and edited Pcol's rules. This historical narrative, however, has not been based upon a thorough comparison of the rules from both communities. Moreover, as Emmel's research has demonstrated, because of the inaccessibility of Shenoute's own writings and the tendency of the *vita* to dominate historical reconstructions of Pcol and Shenoute, traditional accounts of the early history of the monastery must now be reconsidered. For example, Emmel's discovery that Shenoute did not directly succeed Pcol as the second leader (but was rather the third leader) has problematized the traditional accounts of the monastery's origins. For similar reasons, I would argue that the traditional account of the textual evolution of the rules in Shenoute's monastery must be reexamined as well.[32]

Another important issue of authorship remains, however, beyond the question of the "true" author of the actual words of the text. That is the question of authorial *attribution*: to whom do the texts in the *Canons* attribute their authorship? Though Shenoute wrote the texts found in the *Canons*, he also insisted that the regulations for the community came not from his hand but from God, scriptures, and the traditions of the "fathers." In *Canon 3*, Shenoute labels the monastery's rules "the ordinances that our fathers established for us" rather than commands that he himself issues.[33] The "curse" rules from *Canon 3* cited above provide another example of this rhetorical strategy. To justify the rules, he pushes their authorship even further back in time. Both the rules Shenoute cites in the *Canons* and the unwritten conventions that govern the monastery originate with traditions that date back to before Shenoute's time. He claims that some were derived directly from the teachings of Jesus in the gospels: "All the other things that it is fitting to write in this letter and which we have not written, behold! They are all written in the pages written since the beginning.[34] As for the holy words of our Lord Jesus that are written in the scriptures and in *this* letter, I will tell you what they are like."[35] Time and again, Shenoute distances himself from claims to authorship of the monastery's rules. Usually, as in this passage, he insists that the regulations are the words of God. Thus the rules that Shenoute outlines in this section of *Canon 3* come not, he insists, from his hand, but from Jesus and the Bible. He continues:

[These words] are like lamps that are kindled in dark places. And they are like the light of the day. And the senseless people who are extremely foolish are like bats. And just like bats[36] that are struck down or that flee into darkness or into caves[37] if ever they see the light of the flame of lamps and the light of the day, so also the senseless people and the extremely foolish people will be struck down in their passions and their desires and the darkness of their false knowledge before all the words of our Lord, whether they are not only from the scriptures or from this very letter, but also before all the other things that are written in these pages that were written since the beginning. So also, the holy words of our Lord Jesus are like the light of lamps that are in the hands of a wise man. They shine for him in dark places when he does his work as it is written, "Your word is the lamp at my feet." And they are like the light of the day, and the one who trusts them will not stumble, according to the scriptures, "The person who walks during the day does not stumble." For this reason, blessed are the children of light, who are the ones who conduct themselves in the openness of every subordination or every obedience or every good deed. But woe to the children of darkness, who are the ones who conduct themselves in every disobedience or every ignorance. Into or toward the darkness of every evil deed they have fled, like bats that have fled into or toward deep, dark caves.[38]

He follows this passage with an extended interpretation of the biblical command to love one's enemies. He first instructs monks to love their enemies and strangers but to cut themselves off from any "brother" who sins against God. He then concludes with a call to the unity of the monastic community.[39] Certainly, this small homily on the light of Jesus' words would have been read and heard by Shenoute's monks as a reference to the monastic rules—certainly to the rules quoted just prior to this passage, but to the rules more generally as well. For Shenoute, the rules "in these pages" in "this very letter" are not simply approved or sanctioned by Jesus; they are authored by Jesus. They have become a natural extension of the biblical word. They are monastic canons inseparable from the scriptural canon.

Shenoute appeals to the authority of tradition to enforce his rules, as well. In *Canon 5*, in the midst of a series of rules about the burial of dead monks (both male and female), Shenoute berates those who question the authority of his letters and instruction. It rapidly becomes apparent that some monks have raised doubts about the divine provenance of his instructions. Shenoute reminds the monks of the longevity of their tradition when he bemoans those who have "transgressed" or "renounced" the "law of the Lord" and have "departed from the teachings that their fathers commanded to them in their letters."[40] In this way, Shenoute anticipates the tradition of some early medieval monastic *regulae* in Europe, in which an unnamed "master" or *magister* presents the rules to subsequent generations of monks. The anonymity of the master means that the monastic authority, in the words of Conrad Leyser, "is not a particular individual, but a personification of the *magisterium* of tradition." As a result, the audience learning or relearning the rules are meant to think that they are not "idiosyncratic" but "rather the accumulated wisdom of an unbroken tradition of spiritual expertise."[41] Shenoute's deference to tradition of "their fathers" gestures precisely to this point: the rules speak from an unimpeachable source. Behind tradition stands the monks' God, who watches it with intensity; God will bless, protect, and save everyone, "whether male or female," who keeps "all the words that our fathers commanded to us." Shenoute's articulation of the authorship and authority of his letters and rules for the monks presages the later traditions in the early medieval *regulae*, which dictate, "When the disciples ask a question, it is the Lord who speaks through the *magister*."[42] The monks' spiritual ancestors are the vehicles for relaying God's commands to the monastery. The Lord, Shenoute claims, acts through a long-standing tradition which has produced the rules; Shenoute's contribution is merely to set them to paper: "As it is written, it is not according to glory or according to speech that they command to us teachings of human commandments, according to the scriptures, but (it is) in all their power that they speak to us the word of the Lord with their entire soul while they wish that we would receive eternal life."[43] God speaks virtually unmediated to the community through the rules.

Shenoute presses this point even more forcefully in *Canon 9*. In another defensive moment, Shenoute at first appears to claim authority and authorship for the commands laid out in his writings. But then, he quickly shifts gears and admits only to playing the role of God's agent and conduit. His authority is derived solely from a higher authority—the ultimate "author" of all of the community's regulations:

Who knows that these and other numerous counsels are not my words with him, because if God did nothing without God—that is to say, if the Father did nothing without the Son Christ Jesus, and neither did the Son do anything without the Father, since God is from God and light from light, as he said, "I do nothing for myself alone, but in the way that my father taught me I speak," and, "According to the way that he commanded to me, this is the way that I do it,"—then how will

I do a thing without you? You yourself do not do anything without me, nor by yourself. It is not because of me that you will submit to me, nor (is it) because of you that I will allow you to do everything, but (it is) because of Jesus, who was presented to us as a model.[44]

Just as Jesus does not act apart from God the Father, neither does the monastery act apart from Shenoute. Likewise, Shenoute does not act on his own behalf for his own benefit but rather on behalf of Jesus, carrying out God's wishes for the benefit of the community. Notably, Shenoute also quotes from the Nicene Creed ("God from God, light from light") in this passage and in doing so explicitly roots his genealogy of monastic authority within the boundaries of an orthodox church community.[45]

Shenoute thus constructs for the rules a chain of monastic authority that originates with God. He does not avoid stating that he himself issues commands. For example, in *Canon 9*, he orders that no one act without first obtaining permission from the person Shenoute has placed in charge of the men's community: "For before today, I said, 'No person shall work without (the permission of) the male elder.'"[46] Yet he justifies his own commands as coming not *from* him, but *through* him from God. The chain of authority begins on earth with Shenoute's deputies, such as the "male elder" who represents Shenoute's interests. It stretches back first to Shenoute himself and then to the aforementioned "fathers," who might be previous monks or figures from scripture. The "fathers," however, do not speak for themselves either; they speak the "word of the Lord." God not only authors but also defends the scripts that regulate the monastery. Using language from the prophetic books of the Bible, Shenoute graphically describes how God will curse and then cast into a "fiery furnace" anyone who dares to evade the rules or who keeps others from learning the rules.[47] Not only the rules have a divine origin; punishments for disobeying the rules also emanate but from God.

Shenoute's displacement of both authorship and authority away from himself onto God forms an essential aspect of the ritualization process inscribed in the rules. As Bell has argued, "Ritualization interprets its own schemes as impressed upon the actors from a more authoritative source," usually a source beyond the community or even human agency.[48] Shenoute's rules promote a redemptive hegemony by establishing a common set of practices that bind the entire community, including Shenoute, in an act of common submission to God. Submission to Shenoute's authority is masked by or reframed in terms of submission to a higher authority that Shenoute claims he must also obey. Following Bell, I argue that there are two levels of cultural production in the ritual practices contextualized in the monastic rules: the overtly stated goal of the rituals—"the evocation of a consensus on values, symbols, and behavior that is the end of ritualization"—and the social repercussions of the ritualization—"the way in which the hegemonic social order is appropriated as a redemptive process and reproduced individually through communal participation in the physical orchestration of a variety of taxonomic schemes."[49] That is to say, in the case of Shenoute's monastery during his tenure as leader, the ritual practices produced two effects. First, "the consensus or values" is Shenoute's stated goal of salvation and redemption. As the opening words to *Canon 5* read, "Some canons from the word of the Lord so that every one who loves God truly, whether male or female, might stand in a true measure according to the scriptures, 'For I stood in a true measure.'"[50] They submit to the rules in order to receive God's promise of "eternal life."[51] The ascetic discipline that is required to attain "eternal life" also generates *social* consequences for the individuals and the community that practice the *askesis* of the rule. The enactment of the bodily disciplines of fasting, celibacy, work, and prayer may produce subjects capable of obtaining salvation, but they also produce ritualized subjects that participate in Shenoute's vision of the communal ascetic life: disciplined bodies that comprise members of one, harmonious, unified body obedient to one head (Shenoute). This vision of the obedient monastic subject is the "redemptive hegemony" that Catherine Bell describes. The social organization of the monastery—the social body—produced by the practice of the rules is inextricably connected to the "consensus" that is the stated end of the rituals. Salvation can only be achieved when this particular social body is produced, for when one member removes him or herself from the communal ritual by ceasing to follow the rules, the redemption of the entire community is threatened.

Ritualizing the Monastic Body

Although the rules in Shenoute's *Canons* share common elements with other late antique monastic rules, they articulate a monastic subjectivity particular to the Shenoutean community. When comparing the discursive and ideological framing of some ascetic practices common to both the Pachomian and Shenoutean communities, three distinctive elements of the Shenoutean monastic subjectivity emerge. First, Shenoute's rules place a much stronger emphasis on bodily disciplines in order to curb fleshly desires. Second, in the rules Shenoute invokes the ideology of the communal ascetic life as interdependent to justify the expulsion of monks for dis-

obeying specific rules or participating in forbidden activities; the
monastery cuts off offending impure and disobedient members in order to
protect its purity and salvation. Third, in his narrative passages explaining,
clarifying, or enforcing the more formulaic rules, Shenoute articulates a
one-body ideology of the communal monastic life in order to justify, illustrate, or elaborate upon the rules.

THE PRACTICES OF BODILY ASKESIS IN SHENOUTE'S RULES

Reading Shenoute's rules alongside the Pachomian rules highlights the
distinctive aspects of the asceticism practiced at Deir Anba Shenouda.
Both Shenoute and the Pachomian authors demonstrate a preoccupation
with what Evagrius might have considered the practical aspects of the monastic life, as opposed to the contemplative life that Evagrius thought all
monks should strive to achieve.[52] But when reading the rules attributed to
two of the earliest leaders of the Pachomian community—Pachomius and
Horsiesius—alongside the rules in Shenoute's *Canons*, one notices the
very different aspects of the practical life that concern the authors. Although they share many of the same regulations, the regulations gesture
toward different goals for monastic discipline. Shared ascetic practices can
"have different and even contradictory meanings" in different ascetic
communities.[53] The Pachomian rules evoke a sensibility oriented toward
work and industrious harmony, in which the community's regulations
function to produce a smoothly and efficiently run monastery. As Goehring has noted, the Pachomian monasteries engaged in a great deal of commerce with the "outside" world, and their economic industriousness is
well documented in the rules as well as other Pachomian texts.[54] Concerns
for communal purity in the rules, however, are rare. The *Canons*, on the
other hand, present intense concerns for individual and communal purity
predicated on bodily discipline (and particularly the control of sexual desire).

Philip Rousseau concludes that the Pachomian monasteries' greatest
values were for "peace and concord" among the monks.[55] For Rousseau,
"peace and concord" effected by obedience to the rules "provided a
framework within which each monk could thrive," or in other words,
where each monk could individually achieve spiritual growth and possibly
"perfection."[56] Rousseau also insists that efficiency and productivity
should not be considered the most fundamental aspects of Pachomian monasticism: "Spiritual success, as it were, did not depend for Pachomius on
the creation of some smooth-running, uniform community." The accent

on obedience, efficiency, and industry is subordinate to the greater goal of the illumination of individual monks' souls.[57] Yet, one might also contend that no division existed between the goals for the community and the goals for the individual monk. I would argue that communal concord, efficiency, and production are construed as being in service to the goal of personal salvation. They are essential to the spiritual needs of the community and constitute defining elements of the community. Individual salvation cannot be achieved without them. For example, regulations about the assembly of the monks for prayer in the opening to the *Precepts and Institutes of Pachomius* make the connection between the salvation of the individual's soul and respectful behavior in this social setting.[58] The *Precepts and Institutes* continue by describing the manner in which monks should work and pray, the public penance required of monks who break the rules, and the manner in which the housemasters should manage their units of monks.[59] It then lists a variety of inappropriate manners and behaviors (e.g., "He shall not be of divided faith," and "He shall not be led by the lusts of his thoughts").[60] The community and individual needs are united, since the monastery's regulations enhance the spiritual life of the monks as individuals *and* as a community. This "smooth-running, uniform community" creates a space in which monks can pray, fast, avoid lust, and therefore spiritually thrive.

This image of the efficient monastic machine comes from the Pachomian community's emphasis on procedures. Rules outline when and how to pray, receive instruction, eat, work, manage smaller groups of monks, farm, and harvest. On kneading and baking bread, the *Regulations of Horsiesius* provide detail on the general procedures as well as guidelines on preparing extra crusts or loaves for the sick and warnings about the delicacy sweetbread.[61] The monks' work is an integral part of their devotion to God, for work done "in the fear of God and without any relaxation" will prove to be "a relief" to them "on the day of the great judgement."[62] Even many of the rules that do not pertain explicitly to the manual labor of the monks nonetheless contribute to the image of a "smooth-running" machine: "At work no one shall sit without the superior's order"; "No one shall light a fire in his house before the brothers have been so commanded"; "Reflecting on the instruction, they shall not plait or draw water until the housemaster says so."[63] A large number of the rules pertain to this kind of emphasis on work or procedure.

While many precepts suggest concern for the importance of bodily disciplines such as fasting and celibacy, few precepts express their commands for the stated purpose of curbing fleshly desires. Rules justified by a reference to desire are overwhelmed by rules regulating monks' work,

monks' private cells and prayers, the community assembly for prayer, procedures for admitting new monks, and the general discipline of wayward
monks. For example, the Pachomian rules instruct monks to "sit with all
modesty," to avoid lifting garments too high when doing laundry, not to
bathe another or shave another's head, not to pull a thorn out of another's
foot, and not to be intimate with a young monk.[64] These instructions are
cursory, however, when compared to the pages devoted to the manner in
which monks should knead dough, bake bread, plait mats, work in groups,
harvest plants, read and memorize scripture and prayers, govern their
houses, irrigate crops, and care for animals. Moreover, the precepts about
bodily disciplines are, for the most part, not couched explicitly in terms of
a concern for purity or preventing fleshly desire, even when those rules are
presumably enacted precisely to prevent sexual contact between monks.

   Of course, a few exceptions to this generalization exist. The conclud-
ing passages of the *Precepts and Institutes* sum up the judgment dealt to
those who do not follow the preceding regulations and characterize their
disobedience as "adultery" by means of a reference to Jer. 3:9 and the
common biblical motif of idolatry as adultery: "If he neglects any of these,
it shall be measured out to him with the measure he has used, and he shall
be paid as his works deserve. For he has committed adultery with the trees
and the stones; for the glitter of gold and the sheen of silver he has set
aside judgment, and for desire of temporal gain he has enmeshed himself
in the nets of the wicked."[65] The passage somewhat resembles Shenoute's
language about sin in that although it does not draw on discourses of
purity and pollution, it does describe disobedience and sin in a term with
strong sexual overtones. Additionally, the *Precepts and Judgements* describe one punishment as "cleansing" and even, "cleansing" the monks
from "filth."[66] The *Regulations of Horsiesius* also instruct monks to quote
the Psalms as they pray for purity at the *synaxis*, or general assembly.[67] Yet
references to pollution and the "desires of the flesh" remain surprisingly
infrequent.[68] When the admonitions to avoid interpersonal contact and
overeating are read within this context, they become part of the rules'
larger emphasis on producing disciplined bodies that constitute an efficient, orderly, and productive community.

   In reading Shenoute's *Canons*, there is a comparatively greater emphasis on the importance of the bodily disciplines of fasting and chastity
as such and much more detail within these very rules. Like the Pachomian
sources, Shenoute does provide meticulous instructions on work activities,
including mat weaving, but what distinguishes his rules from the others is
his unabashed attention to bodily desire.[69] The rules on disciplining desires of the flesh are more prominent and more detailed. Compare the

following admonitions to modesty in the two sets of texts. First, the Pachomian *Precepts*, which instruct the monk to arrange his tunic prudently: "He shall sit with all modesty and meekness, tucking under his buttocks the lower edge of the goat skin which hangs over his shoulder down his side, and carefully girding up his garment—that is, the linen tunic without sleeves called *lebitonarium*—in such a way that it covers his knees."[70] Shenoute's *Canons 9* and *5* contain similar regulations on the manner in which monks should wear their clothing to ensure modesty. Yet Shenoute's instructions go into more detail about the areas of the body that should not be exposed. Monks must not roll up or tuck in their clothing in such a way that it exposes themselves more than if they were to let it hang loosely. They may roll up their sleeves and hems only if it is necessary for completing their work: "I said concerning the edges of your garments, 'Do not tuck them in and do not become anxious,' because you did not know that it is not fitting to expose your arms up to your shoulders. For this reason, no person among us shall tuck in or pull in the edges of his garments, so that they are bound up to their neck for obvious reasons, except out of necessity, when they are working in mud or even some other task. Their edges shall cover them from their arms to their elbows."[71]

Differences between the regulations in each community are not limited to their level of detail. Unlike the Pachomian sources, Shenoute's writings frequently refer to sexual desire as the reason for the rules. In a passage on modesty, he cautions monks not to cross their legs when they sit because it encourages sinful "passions."[72] When compared to Shenoute's *Canons*, the language of the Pachomian rules are almost as modest as the monks, in that the rules rarely openly betray the concern for sexual desire that surely underlies them. Shenoute, however, places the specter of sexual desire in high relief.

An excerpt of *Canon 3* exemplifies both the emphasis on physical desire (especially lust) and the greater detail in Shenoute's rules. In a passage unparalleled in the Pachomian rules, Shenoute lists all of the situations in which a monk might risk immodest exposure and instructs the other monks to avert their gaze:

Cursed are men or women who will peer or look with lust upon the nakedness of their neighbors in their bedrooms, or stare at them in any other place, either when they are on a wall or up a tree, or when they urinate or walk in mud or bathe, or while they are sitting down and uncover (themselves) inadvertently, or when they are dragging a log up to a high spot, or when they are working with one another or washing their clothing . . . or when the brothers who make the bread reach into the ovens or (are busy) at any other task which some would be doing in our domain or in your domain too and unwittingly bare (themselves).

And those who will gaze at them in lust with a shameless eye shall be cursed. And also those who will look passionately upon their own nakedness shall be cursed.[73]

In attempting to suppress sexual desire, Shenoute implicitly reifies his monks' identities as sexual beings. Even inadvertent nakedness or seeing one's own naked body can inspire a lustful gaze. Inherent in the monasticism practiced at Deir Anba Shenouda is the understanding of the self and the body as a sexual self and body, one that must always be controlled and constrained through the discipline of that body, but whose very self-expression is nonetheless defined in terms of the sexual. Thus, a brief reading of passages on modesty in the two sets of rules demonstrates distinct differences between the two, differences that result in a distinctive monastic subjectivity produced at Shenoute's community.

The sexual tension in Shenoute's texts also reverberates throughout his treatment of visits between male monks and female monks. Not surprisingly both the Pachomian and Shenoutean rules place strict limits on the conditions under which men and women could see each other. In the Pachomian monasteries, the women lived in a separate residence across the river. The Pachomian *Precepts* allow a man to visit the women only if he has relatives in the women's community, if a visit is necessary for "some obvious reason," and if an older monk accompanies him.[74] At Shenoute's monastery, the women also lived in a separate residence or "congregation."[75] Shenoute's *Canons* have similar restrictions on visits, but add that male and female monks should not kiss each other on the mouth "openly" when they greet each other.[76] He also justifies his detailed regulations about the ways in which men and women will communicate or work together by a concern for "purity."[77]

In instructions regarding food and eating, as well, the two sets of rules construct the practice of fasting using different frameworks. The *Regulations of Horsiesius* forbid monks from eating before the common signal, eating between noon and the midday *synaxis*, and baking bread that is different from the bread baked for everyone else. The sick, however, may receive extra food.[78] Similarly, Shenoute provides rules for how to eat and allows extra food and wine for ill monks.[79] Shenoute also provides considerable additional details. For example, he allows monks to add vinegar to food if they receive prior permission from their superior, but he also forbids monks from being fastidious with their food—"testing it as to what is tasty and what we like and eating that."[80]

The rules in the *Canons* differ in tenor as well as detail. Most significantly, the Pachomian rules mention the difficulties of fasting only obliquely. Consider the following regulations:

Let no one put away in his cell anything to eat, except what he has received from the steward.

As regards the small loaves given to the housemasters to be distributed to those who dedicate themselves to greater abstinence and do not want to eat in common with the others, they must see to it that they give them to no one as a favor. . . .

No one shall eat anything in his cell. . . .[81]

. . . Hence, even if we are laboring at perishable things in order to sustain the body—which is necessary—let us be watchful not to render our soul, which is worth more than our nourishment, a stranger to eternal life under the pretext of a necessity which will disappear.[82]

These rules allude to the difficulties of following the restrictive monastic diet. They intimate occasions in which monks broke their fasts or ate more than their allotted share. Yet the texts rarely explicitly place these rules in the context of the relationship between the bodily discipline of fasting and the salvation of the soul; the last passage above is the only such reference I could find within the rules from the Pachomian community.

The *Canons* contain rules similar to those in the Pachomian texts about eating and fasting. Yet Shenoute's regulations openly address the social and theological difficulties associated with fasting in more detail and in a broader context. Where the Pachomian rules hint at monastic lapses, the Shenoutean rules wag a very accusing finger. Shenoute instructs monks to eat "truthfully," and he writes that those who pretend to be sick in order to receive more food will be "despised before Jesus."[83] He also warns of monks who seem to be quite resourceful in supplementing their diets. In *Canon 5*, Shenoute lists rules against going to the infirmary for an extra meal.[84] He also cites regulations prohibiting cooking extra food, since the monks in the kitchen are required to eat any leftovers that remain after feeding the monks:

They shall not cook at any time in the day in which they cook so that it (the food) might satisfy them for two days, but rather (they shall cook only) the amount to eat for one day for them and the strangers who sojourn at the gate and everyone who comes to us on that day. But if a little is left over for the next day, they shall not take (it) to the gate, but they shall eat it for themselves alone, only without being dishonestly hasty, such that they might cook enough for themselves for two days at a time, and so that God would be angry at them and would cast them out with the ones who commit lawless deeds, according to the scriptures, because even though they think that they are doing a good thing, they are really doing a more evil thing, and they do not know it.[85]

Here, Shenoute warns against deliberately cooking more food than is required for one day of meals, suggesting that monks in charge of meal preparation might do so in order to have more for themselves to eat. Finally, Shenoute cites regulations condemning monks who pretend to fast, only to hoard food that they eat later, out of sight of their companions. "They shall not be [allo]wed at all to do this among us, because deeds of this sort in his (God's) congregations are abominations of God."[86] In *Canon 9*, Shenoute addresses this problem again, portraying those who "eat their bread freely" as "fleshly people," and charges that those who hypocritically claim to be "spiritual people" will be reproached.[87]

When compared to the Pachomian texts, the rules in Shenoute's *Canons* place the agonizing details attendant to the discipline of fasting at the forefront, providing a different tone to the rules about food and eating. The personal struggle to curb the desires of the appetite is a much more urgent and explicit concern. What the Pachomian texts term a hindrance to the soul Shenoute depicts as "lawless," "an abomination," and "despised" by Jesus. Disciplining the desires of the flesh holds significant import in configuring the monks' relationship to God. We can also sense worries over the effects of overeating on the larger community that extend beyond concerns for administration or individual weakness. Shenoute places the breaking of rules about food within the context of communal life: people who eat inappropriately do not belong in the monastery; God, acting through Shenoute, will "cast them out."

Although Shenoute's rules and the Pachomian rules provide instructions about the ways in which monks should or should not implement bodily renunciations such as fasting and celibacy, and both sets of rules share a commitment to fasting and celibacy, the rules nonetheless illustrate different subjectivities produced by the same practices. For both, the practices of ascetic renunciation are ritualized throughout the course of the monk's day. Each monastery views its *askesis* as central to salvation, and it values the same activities—work, prayer, fasting, celibacy, and so on. Yet, the rituals in which monks perform these activities are constructed differently in the two sets of rules. Any potential desire for sex or food in the hearts of his monks lies naked and exposed in the *Canons*. The "redemptive hegemony" implicit in these rules lies in individual and communal purity and the discipline of the flesh. In the Pachomian rules, purity and its nemesis, desire, are mentioned far less frequently. That Shenoute's rules embody a unique "redemptive hegemony" which then produces uniquely ritualized monastic bodies becomes even more apparent upon examination of the punishments imposed upon monks who break the rules.

DISCIPLINE AND PUNISH

Punishment for unacceptable behavior played a significant role in the rules governing these two early Egyptian monastic federations. Punishment, however, was not simply about repressing unwanted behaviors. It was about creating a desirable ascetic subjectivity, as well. As Foucault remarked in his landmark book *Discipline and Punish*, systems of discipline and punishment purport primarily to mold the soul or character of criminals and (more importantly) potential criminals through "constraints," "privations," "obligations," and "prohibitions" imposed on the body.[88] Foucault insists that "it is always the body at issue—the body and its forces, their utility and their docility, their distribution and their submission."[89] Juridical and punitive systems have a "hold" on the soul that is effected by technologies of the body implemented in order to make useful members of society. Consequently, systems of punishment reflect a community's larger understandings about the relationships between mechanisms of power and the production of knowledge. The body becomes both "productive" and "subjected." Just so at Shenoute's monastery, where punishment was one piece of the redemptive hegemony that guided the community. Even though Shenoute's rules and the Pachomian rules do list some of the same penalties for transgressive monks, the juridical codification of punishment exposes another aspect of the particularity of the Shenoutean monastic subjectivity.

Each monastery used corporal punishment for some of the most severe violations of the rules. Moreover, in both communities the beatings are justified as actions that purify the offending monk from sin. In the case of a monk who entreats other monks to sin, the Pachomian *Precepts and Judgements* order that he first be "admonished three times." Then if he does not reform, he should be beaten outside of the gates and fed only bread and water "until he is cleansed from his filth."[90] Shenoute instituted corporal punishment in the women's community as well as the men's.[91] Yet, despite a number of shared punishments, the Shenoutean rules contain a punitive ritual lacking in the Pachomian ones: expulsion. At Deir Anba Shenouda, expulsion furthered the monastery's larger goal of ritually producing pure monks and a pure community by removing from the community irredeemably polluted members. In the implementation of expulsion, the soteriological and social goals of the monastery's redemptive hegemony collide most visibly. Ridding the community of its most unruly members ensures the sanctity of the monastery *and* the stability of the monastery's social hierarchy.

The Pachomian sources rarely require or even condone the exile of a sinful monk from the *koinonia*. Instead, they frequently prescribe public rebuke and penance, or even the withdrawal of food.[92] They also often demand the demotion of monks to a lower rank in the community, as in this precept:

If someone is irascible and violent, and frequently gets angry without reason or for some light and unimportant reason, he shall be admonished six times. The seventh time, he shall be removed from his seating rank and placed among the last ones, and he shall be given instruction, that he may be cleansed from this agitation of mind. And when he can bring three trustworthy witnesses to promise for him that he will never again do anything of the kind, he shall be given back his seating rank. Otherwise, if he remains in his vice, he shall lose his former rank and remain among the last ones.[93]

Disobedience requires a demotion in rank, and monks may not resume their original status without proving their worthiness to their companions. This passage also contains one of the few references to purity in the Pachomian rules, in that it characterizes the process of restoring a monk to obedience as a cleansing; the erratic behavior that constitutes disobedience also indicates impurity, which must be "cleansed."[94] The purification that accompanies the monk's demotion, however, is limited to the individual monk. The Pachomian rules do not require the permanent exile of a monk in order to cleanse the community.

Expulsion appears only in other literary sources, such as various versions of the *vita* of Pachomius. Even there, the sources expose ambivalence about this penalty. In one episode, Pachomius decides to expel a monk, only to find that the rest of the community follows the monk out. Given the paucity of references, this form of punishment likely was, as Rousseau concludes, a "rare sanction."[95] Rousseau even goes so far as to argue that the expulsion of a monk would contradict the goal and purpose of the communal ascetic life and would undermine the monks' responsibility to assist each other in their monastic discipline. "Simply to reject the sinner, therefore, was to repudiate that responsibility: only within the *koinonia* could the requisite healing, enlightenment, and growth take place."[96] The underlying principle of the Pachomian *koinonia* was a sense that ascetic perfection could come only in community, only with the assistance and support of other monks. Expulsion, he concludes, "robs" the monks of the opportunity to repent. This explains Pachomius's reconsideration of the aforementioned monk's expulsion: "Henceforward, the integrity of a monastery will be measured by effort and growth and by renewed endeavor after weakness and failure, not by the achievement of some exclusive purity."[97] This interpretation of the story highlights what I have been arguing is a central distinction between the ascetic ideologies inscribed in the ritual practices of the Pachomian and Shenoutean communities. The "effort," "growth," and "endeavor" of the individual monk is supported by actions of the larger social body.

Although Rousseau's use of this anecdote to explain a broader ascetic theory at play in the Pachomian monasteries may hold true for some strains of Egyptian monasticism, this interpretation cannot be generalized to coenobiticism throughout Egypt.[98] For in contrast to the Pachomian regulations, expulsion from the monastery appears frequently in Shenoute's rules. Monks are ordered to be "made strangers," "cast out," or "cut off" from the community as punishment for a range of unacceptable behaviors. Shenoute, too, extols the value of repentance and enacts other methods of punishment besides expulsion. So, it would be disingenuous to claim that monks at Deir Anba Shenouda were "robbed" of the opportunity to repent.[99] Rather, both repentance and expulsion appear as legitimate responses to transgressions. The frequency of the latter punishment points to Shenoute's comparatively greater emphasis on communal purity. The act of expelling monks contributes to the ritual enactment and production of the pure social body that is the goal of Shenoute's monasticism, since expelling sinful monks excises impure members from the corporate monastic body. Moreover, at Deir Anba Shenouda, the penalty was no mere threat; Shenoute himself refers to specific moments in the monastery's history when such a punishment was meted out.[100]

A variety of sins trigger its execution, accentuating expulsion's ritual and ideological importance. Monks who cook two days' worth of food for only one day of eating may be cast out. As for people who take items belonging to the monastery without permission from their superiors, the monastery's leaders will make them "strangers" to the community.[101] Members who are preoccupied with the amount of resources they donated to the monastery when they arrived also risk expulsion: "If men or a woman are found among us who murmur and who throw words from their wicked heart so that they do not wish to comply with our canons, saying so impiously, 'I brought how much when I arrived!' and 'I gave such-and-such to this place!' . . . If they are taught but do not heal their language from more wickedness, they shall be cast out."[102] Ironically, castration—the physical excision of anatomy that may have been viewed as offending or polluting—merited immediate expulsion, even if the man were still bleeding. Castrated monks are themselves regarded as contaminants, people "polluted by the blood of their wound" who must not be allowed to remain members of the monastery, even if removing them from the community requires manually placing them on a bed and dumping them in a nearby "populated area."[103]

Monks who contribute to the sinful behavior of others are particularly prone to expulsion. Contributing to the delinquency of junior monks[104] and defending the actions of sinners are two examples.[105] High-ranking members of the monastery are allowed a certain amount of discretion in

determining whether to expel such monks, monks whom Shenoute brands
"enemies to their companions." If the monastic superiors examine the
monks' behavior, they may deem it acceptable to allow these monks to
stay. Otherwise, the monks will be "cast out."[106] These precepts illuminate the social function of expulsion: expulsion removes the threat to the
integrity of the community. Monks who encourage sin, defend sin, or are
generally "enemies" to their fellow ascetics must be removed, presumably
to preserve the spiritual progress of their companions and the community
as a whole. The punishment applies to anchoritic monks associated with
the community as well as monks in the residence. The passage examined
at the beginning of this chapter orders that affiliated monks who live in
the desert and do not visit the monastery at the required four times a
year, or who otherwise ignore the community's rules, be cast out. It even
authorizes Shenoute or his designated representative to enforce the rule
by leading a group of monks out to the dwelling place of an identified
troublemaker in order to remove the monk and vandalize the residence.
The expulsion of the monk and destruction of his or her residence are
justified by an appeal to community stability: "And we shall cast down the
place where he (or she) dwells so that we destroy it down to its foundations, so that no person shall reside in it ever again, because it might cause
difficulty for its neighbor."[107] The last sentence in this passage is difficult
to translate because of the many pronouns. Both "place" and "person"
are masculine nouns. Hence, the last phrase could also read, "so that no
one can reside in it ever again because he (or she) might cause difficulty
for his (or her) neighbor." In either translation, the monk or the residence
carries the potential to disturb the other ascetics, and thus the residence
must be destroyed. The goal of the punishment is to preserve the harmony
and unity of the corporate monastic body.

Shenoute also recounts more general rules demanding expulsion of
sinful monks. General obstinacy justifies expulsion in *Canon 9*: "Whenever
people are found in these congregations who say, 'We will not comply
with the ordinances that are established for us,' whether he is a man or
she a woman, they shall be cast out from us."[108] Later in *Canon 9*, Shenoute cites another general rule for expulsion, ordering the censure of
monks who do not subject themselves sufficiently to the bodily disciplines
of the monastic life. The appropriate punishment is an increase in the severity of the discipline they resist; their food is restricted until they are
essentially forced to leave. Any male or female monk who is not "ashamed
before the truly self-disciplined and suffering brothers" and who does not
"subjugate" his or her body after instruction "shall be prohibited from
going to eat by the fathers of these congregations, and under compulsion

they shall depart."[109] Conversely, monks who follow the rule must not be removed from the community: "But as for everyone who conducts himself (or herself) according to the canons that are established for us, no one shall be able to be jealous of him (or her) to cast him (or her) out, whether he (or she) is in the desert around us or in the congregation with us in our domain or in your domain."[110] Shenoute seems cognizant that expulsion might be perceived as unreasonable, and he takes pains to justify the punishment. He defends it by attributing the expulsions to God, claiming that monastic officials who remove monks from the community are merely God's agents; God—not Shenoute, his successors, or the other "elders" in the monastic hierarchy—exact the penalty.[111]

Moreover, the monks who remain in the monastery should not feel sorry for those who have been expelled, because the latter do not belong in a community of the faithful: "Do not let a merciful person who fears God among us, whether male or female, be pained over people who flee from these congregations (*eupēt ebol hn neisunagōgē*) or who are cast out, as long as I live. Nor let anyone regret concerning them or pity them, even if they are male senior monks or female senior monks or they are male junior monks or female junior monks. For it is Jesus who is pursuing them (*IC gar petpēt nsōou*)."[112] While it is possible to interpret this passage to mean that Shenoute is consoling the remaining monks by assuring them that Jesus will pursue and look after their lapsed colleagues, it seems unlikely. Shenoute's use of the verb *pēt* (from the infinitive *pōt*) to describe the activity of both Jesus and the fleeing monks suggests that Shenoute instead is justifying his expulsion of the wayward brothers and sisters by implying that Jesus is the one who has encouraged, and perhaps compelled, their departure from the monastery.[113]

In *Canon 3*, Shenoute defends the expulsion of sinful monks by returning to his vision of the monastery as a corporate, almost corporeal, social body. He first explains that the community must "cut off" a monk who refuses to repent for his or her sins because the person has sinned against God. He then traces the monastic practice of expulsion back to Jesus' command in the gospels to love God more than one's family. In a novel way, Shenoute asceticizes Jesus' claim that he has come to separate a son from his father and daughter from her mother.

But when he (the Lord) says, "If your brother does not listen to you, let him be for you an enemy, like one whom you have never seen," because the Lord first wishes that we cut him off from us after we reproach him in order that he perhaps indeed might regret after he has become a stranger with respect to God, since he is our brother, and so that he might return and repent, and we might forgive him up to seventy seven times, such that he does not sin again, since we know to cut him off from us because of it (his sin). But if it does not please him to turn from sin—because of which we know to cut him off from us—then we will cut him off from us, and he shall not return to us, and we shall not love him. But he shall be for us an enemy with respect to God, even though he is our brother. And in this way, the person who loves God reveals all of his desire for the Lord, since he loved him (the Lord) more than his brother and more than his father and his mother. For it is a great perfection for the person to cut himself off from his brother or his son or his daughter or his father or his mother or any other person because of God, whenever they sin against God who created them.[114]

Shenoute does *not* make the expected exegetical move of citing the gospel passages about leaving behind one's father, mother, and other biological kin in order to support the monastic requirement to abandon family in the pursuit of the ascetic life. Instead he suggests that the monastery itself is one family which at times, in order to please and love God fully, must forsake one of its own members. Thus the monastery forms a family according to the spirit, rather than a family according to the flesh. He returns, however, to discourses of the flesh and the body and describes this spiritual family in corporeal terms, arguing that they are indeed united by ties of blood. The monks are sons and daughters begotten and birthed by the same parents, and they are borne from and bound by the blood of Jesus Christ. They are "in community (*koinōnos*) with each other" because they are "children of a single man, who is God" and "children of a single woman, who is heavenly Jerusalem." The spiritual parents trump the biological parents. "Are our father and our mother who begot us and who nourished us according to the flesh truly more chosen than our Lord Jesus, our father and mother? This one who begot us in his holy blood . . ."[115] Unfortunately, the manuscript breaks off here. In this tantalizingly brief passage, Shenoute draws on the discourses of reproduction and family relations to depict the monastery as a single social unit, from which problematic members must be excised. In this passage, although the monastic corporate "body" is not described as a human body, it is envisioned as a family unit, a social body whose members are joined together by blood— the sacrificial blood of Jesus Christ. The relations of the spirit in the monastic congregation are transformed into new blood ties that are no less unifying and binding than traditional biological ties. Expulsion is thereby warranted as a means to maintain the sanctity of the community.

The social and soteriological roles of expulsion are further illuminated by an examination of other biblical discourses of the flesh and the body that Shenoute uses to justify the rules. In the narrative sections of the rules, he provides an ideological and theological context for the way that the juridical implementation of expulsion, and the monks' subjection of themselves to it, produces a particular kind of social body among those who remain in the monastery. The inclusion of expulsion in the rules was not a message directed solely toward those monks who had already sinned. Rather, as Foucault has aptly noted, the juridical codification of punishment is geared as much, if not more, toward those members of a community who have not broken the law—yet. At Deir Anba Shenouda, the rules defined what a community was and should strive to be: "Everyone who will dwell in our domain shall be bound in the canons that are established for all the brothers (and sisters) that gather together."[116] By obeying the rules, the monks forged a community and a communal identity.

THE MONASTERY AS ONE BODY

At several places in *Canons 3* and *9*, Shenoute uses corporeal language about the monastic social body to underscore the social and soteriological effects of the ritualization process embodied in the rules. In narrative passages interspersed throughout the rules in *Canons 3* and *9*, he explains the ideology embedded in his monasticism by depicting the community as one body with many members.[117] The monastery possesses three corporeal characteristics. First, the monks are all "fellow members" of each other. Second, the monks form one body obedient to a single head (the authority figure who enforces the rule). Third, sin functions as a disease spreading through the body. In these three ways of explaining and justifying the rules, Shenoute explicitly connects the bodily discipline performed by monks obedient to the rules with his vision of the monastery itself as one unified, disciplined body. The integration of theology and practice, or ideology and materiality, is most obvious in these sections of the rules, because Shenoute himself openly theorizes on the nature of the monastic life and the monks' relationship to God in the specific context of articulating and enforcing rules for proper ascetic practices. In the following examples, Shenoute candidly outlines the "redemptive hegemony" intrinsic to the ritualization process. To be saved, monks must obey and enact his regulatory system.

In *Canon 3*, Shenoute defines the monks' relationships with each other as being each other's "fellow members." As a result of the connection between them, the disobedience of some monks afflicts the other monks. In this passage, Shenoute describes the web of relationships that make up the monastery, with the consequence that salvation is inherently interdependent. Shenoute's fate hangs on the prayers of the other monks, and all the monks are spiritually "afflicted" if any one of them breaks the vow of monastic obedience. This passage occurs between two sets of rules in *Canon 3* prohibiting indulging in fleshly desires. Shenoute seems to be discussing the trials and tribulations of directing a monastery for so many years. Possibly facing the end of his life, he writes that he has spent "more than one hundred years in the desert" and ponders the effectiveness of his efforts as a leader.[118] He begins by insisting that his own salvation depends upon the prayers of the other faithful monks. During his prayers, he claims, he weeps over his own prospects at the final judgment, and acknowledges that God may "treat [him] mercifully" thanks to the prayers of his own brethren on his behalf. But he also bemoans the disobedient actions of "God-hating" monks who are "polluted" and "defiled" in their "conscience."[119] These monks stand in stark contrast to those who have remained loyal to Shenoute, for he then thanks high-ranking monks (the "male elder and elders") for their unwavering obedience. Because they obey him "in every submission, working for their salvation in fear and trembling," God will grant them "every rest in heaven."[120] For those monks who are disobedient, however, he has harsher words. Their disobedience disrupts the rest of the monastery: "But as for the ones who are disobedient in every work, who make the word of the Lord angry in their disobedience and their confidence in themselves, we know who they are. For this reason, the Lord shall forgive them because they are our brothers and they are our fellow members, and because they labor themselves in their stupidity, and because we ourselves are afflicted on account of them."[121] Shenoute's complaints illuminate his core beliefs about the nature of the communal ascetic life. The hegemonic hierarchy at Deir Anba Shenouda truly is redemptive. Obedience to Shenoute and his rule promises salvation not only for the individual monk, but for the monks' errant colleagues and even Shenoute himself. Conversely, the disobedience of a few can disrupt the community. His use of the curious phrase "our fellow members" (*nenšbēr-melos*) to describe the monks' relationship to each other indicates that the monks are all integrally, almost organically connected. Shenoute here evokes the rhetoric of Paul in Rom. 12:5 ("so we, who are many, are one body in Christ, and individually we are members one of another"). Because of this close bond between monks, the disobedience of some members "afflict" the other obedient members. Ironically, Shenoute does not here, as he does in other passages examined above, use this close bond between monks to justify the expulsion of the disobedient monks who incur God's wrath.[122] Instead, in a moment of mercy, Shenoute uses this notion of the corporate monastic body to explain the way in which the obedient monks' virtue will cause God to look with compassion upon their wayward brothers and sisters.

Further on in this same section of *Canon 3*, Shenoute employs another element of Paul's rhetoric of the body: circumcision. Drawing on Romans, Shenoute likens monastic purity and discipline to the circumcision of the heart. Fleshly desire and disobedience equal an uncircumcised heart:

> We shall not put you to shame as we speak these things to you, but we teach you as a beloved brother, so that we shall not be condemned with the world, and so that we shall escape the word of the prophet, "Behold, I will bring evil things upon these people and upon the fruit of their disobedience, because they did not observe my word, and they renounced my law." For this reason, I pray for you, brothers, that you remove yourselves from every struggle or every dispute, and every evil thing, and every fleshly desire. These who fight against your souls so that we circumcise our uncircumcision of our hard heart, so that the Lord will raise you up in every good deed, so that you do his will for him. . . . For this is the will of God—your purity—so that we might be pure for him, and so that we might love our companions, just as he commanded us according to the scriptures. What is the circumcision of the heart, or the uncircumcision? The ones who exist in every time in hard-heartedness and stiff-neckedness and stubbornness and ignorance and disobedience and cruelty and struggles and disputes and jealousies and hatreds and pollutions and very wicked thing, it is they who are uncircumcised in their heart and also their ears, according to the scriptures. But as for the ones who are always humbly and gently and patiently and lovingly and wisely in every submission or every obedience or every propriety, it is they who are circumcised.[123]

In adapting yet another discourse of the body—that of circumcision—to his ideology of monastic discipline, Shenoute aligns ascetic discipline with a familiar biblical purity system and with obedience to the "law."[124] In the social context of a monastery, "the law" surely designates the monastic rules. Whereas Paul attempted to transform a fleshly marker of faith (circumcision) into a spiritual marker, Shenoute turns Paul on his head by returning circumcision back to the realm of the flesh by using circumcision as a code for ascetic discipline. Shenoute's circumcision of the heart is still simultaneously spiritualized; it requires cutting away one's "stubbornness," "ignorance," and "disobedience." Yet, Shenoute's use of purity and pollution language and his overt mention of "fleshly desire" bring the metaphor back to the realm of the physical body. Circumcision of the heart *is* the discipline of the flesh. It is the purity that is attained through obedience to Shenoute and the monastic rules.

Shenoute also models the social system of the monastery on Paul's vision of the Christian community as one body. In one set of rules in *Canon 9*, he applies the Pauline discourses of the body in 1 Cor. 11–12, in which the church forms one body in Christ, to his monastery. In Shenoute's construction of the Christian social body, the monks who follow the rules form a single body and thus must work together as one unit obedient to its head. Shenoute describes this hierarchical system in an explanatory passage that appears in a collection of rules on social order in the community. These rules govern visits to the other residences in the monastery, the punishment of disruptive monks, and the admission of novices.[125] Shenoute appeals to the anatomy of the human body to explain the rationale for his hierarchical system. Here he confirms the authority of his deputy ("the male elder") to carry out his wishes:

> This is what I will say now, "It is a single head which is upon the person which the whole body and members follow." For it is a disgrace and a derisive act for the head and the body to follow after the foot or the feet, because it is unnatural for us to drag upon the earth, dragging our body behind. Just as it is possible for us to walk forward according to our nature now, indeed as long as the body is free from paralysis and the head is not stupefied, this is the way. For before today, I said, "No person shall work without (the authority of) the male elder." That one knows what I say.[126]

Just as the body must follow the head, the monks must obey Shenoute's second in command, the elder. Using the example of the body following the head, Shenoute naturalizes the authority structure of the monastic system. To obey anyone other than the "male elder" would be unnatural, indeed almost impossible, just like the act of the feet dragging the body and the head on the ground behind them. The "male elder" here functions as a kind of proxy in Shenoute's absence, and he derives his authority entirely from submitting his will to his own head—Shenoute. This person has earned his privileged position in the monastic hierarchy through his own unflinching obedience to Shenoute. Shenoute goes on to describe him as a person who never acts without Shenoute's permission and concedes to Shenoute's authority in everything.[127] Thus, the real head of the corporate monastic body is Shenoute. The "male elder" and other "elders" and "senior monks" below him as well as those who lead the individual houses of the monastery are Shenoute's agents.[128] Whatever independence they might possess in supervising the monastery is severely restricted: "The ones whom we judged and selected to assign over these places, they shall not be able to work without me," insists Shenoute.[129]

One authority and one set of rules bind the community together. Just as it is harmful for the corporate monastic body to follow the feet, rather than the head, it is harmful for the corporate body to attempt to follow more than one head: "As for the congregations that have many heads that teach them—each one with his word and his rule and the thing that he

will think to speak—there is not a single head over them, and no one
teaches them, and there is no one who thinks about the right thing."[130]
Monasteries that consider more than one person authoritative—
monasteries with more than one head—in fact possess no head at all. And
without a head, they lack wisdom, righteousness, and salvation. Shenoute
charges that the instability at these sorts of monasteries threatens to destroy their souls. The rules are not the creation of humanity but commands of God. "What is the inappropriate matter or ordinance that those
who are in these places do not do or change? . . . As for the one who
destroys a wall, it appears that he destroys a wall and not a soul, neither
his own nor that of another one. But the one who destroys the things that
are built by Jesus destroys his soul and the souls of others with him, and
he sends them down with him."[131] To change the rules or abandon the
rules in favor of different rules is a serious form of monastic disobedience.
Shenoute finds fault with such monks on two levels. First, they are forsak-
ing a command of God. Second, the disobedience of one monk affects the
spiritual health of other monks in the community, for this monk destroys
the souls "of others with him."

As in *Canon 1*, Shenoute's concern for the effect of sin on the entire
monastery permeates the texts. We have already seen this in his explanation
of the rule that dictates the destruction of the home of an anchorite in
Canon 3; the monk or residence causes difficulties for neighboring ascetics.
Here in *Canon 9*, Shenoute explains the communal effects and consequences of sin by constructing the monastery as one corporate body. It is
one body with one head, and the failure of any members to obey the head
endangers the body's other members.

Shenoute further develops this understanding of the monastery as one
corporate body by characterizing sin as disease, especially in *Canon 9*.[132]
Here, a lengthy passage about illness precedes rules about sick monks,
deception, and junior monks. Writing in a prophetic style, Shenoute devotes several manuscript folios to a condemnation of some monks, whom
he calls the "sons and daughters of the devil." To describe the effects of
these monks' actions, Shenoute turns to the language of disease. Once a
disease infects one part of the body, it will devour the rest. Shenoute writes
of an illness wracking his own body, and a close examination of the passage
suggests that the diseased body to which Shenoute refers actually consists
of multiple bodies. His own sick, human body manifests a disease spreading through the corporate monastic body, and that disease is sin. Krawiec
has demonstrated that in other texts in the *Canons* Shenoute interprets his
own sickness as an expression of the sins of the women in the community.[133] Disease is not a literary metaphor for Shenoute—it is the physical

manifestation of sin. This section of *Canon 9* begins soon after the narrative segment containing the exegesis of Paul that constructs the monastery
as one corporate body with only one head. Shenoute's exegesis of Paul
provides the hermeneutical key to understanding his later complaints
about his sickness. When he speaks of an illness ravaging a body and all of
its members, that body is the monastery.

In the first extant fragment of this section, Shenoute mentions an
"illness in my bones and flesh" and its effects upon him. He makes this
self-reflective observation as he explains his command that the monks tell
him about any wicked behavior they see in the monastery. Although they
need not inform him of absolutely every activity, all sins must be reported.
He complains that his illness prevents him from sleeping and resting, but
he does not allow it to inhibit his communication with the monks.[134] In
the next extant fragment, he again mentions his disease and the difficulties
he faces in enduring it.[135] He then describes the way in which disease
spreads from one part of the body to another, affecting the entire body.
Again, the context is discussion among the monks about what inappropriate behaviors are (or are not) transpiring in the monastery. According to
Shenoute, words of love, or "deceptive enticements," are being spoken
privately between monks who are related to each other.[136] He urges his
monks not to listen to such "demonic" utterances. As he continues, he
suggests that his disease is an expression of the illicit talk running through
the monastery. His illness, like the sinful speech, is also communicable:

Because of a professed love,[137] do not become subject to sufferings or afflictions
and unable to escape them, when you forsake the words of the one who prays that
this disease will disappear from his body, at least that it ceases or does not attack
the small members (of the body) and weaken them and (thus) afflict the entire
body. If there is a person who inquires what are the harmful effects of this disease,
let him approach this (afflicted man), who is fearful lest those who visit him will
dislike coming to him, and he will tell you, "If the lips of the foolish will sink him,
the ears of the foolish will also sink him."

As for the serpent, it was on account of its tongue that God cursed it. As for
Eve, it was because of her ears that she succumbed to all these things. As for those
who do not believe this (afflicted man), who has not liked to stop talking about
this disease, they do not know whether they will recognize even its symptoms, nor
have they understood its crushing effect; also, they have not been amazed at it,
but verily it waxes in them and they have grown accustomed to enduring it and
hiding it and instructing others not to tell anyone that they have it.[138]

Though Shenoute writes of an illness spreading from one part of his own
body to another, the context of this passage within *Canon 9* suggests that
his individual body is an exemplar for the monastery.[139] Just as the disease

attacks and afflicts Shenoute's "entire body," it "waxes" within the other members of the community, particularly among those monks who refuse to acknowledge its existence. Professions of love will "sink" and "curse" those who listen, but some kinds of confidences are appropriate. Listening to speech that exposes sins for what they are—sin—is rehabilitating. The cure for the disease is to listen to Shenoute, who prays for an end to the illness. Those who do not listen to Shenoute and do not understand the disease will succumb to it. Shenoute, as the head of the body, desperately attempts to prevent the spread of disease from one member/monk to another.

Shenoute's illness afflicts more than his and his monks' physical health. His disease *is* the manifestation of the spiritual corruption in the community.[140] This is evident in Shenoute's response to the rhetorical question about the effects of the disease. He writes not about pain or fever but the earliest portions of the book of Genesis, alluding to Eve sinning in the Garden of Eden. "All these things" to which Eve succumbed are likely the disease and its symptoms, which also have befallen the monks. For this disease to be cured, it must be exposed, not "endured" and "hidden." The sickness is a consequence of listening to "demonic" words, just as Eve listened to Satan; sin, thus, *is* the sickness. Eve succumbed to the ailings of sin because she listened to the evil words of the serpent. Listening to Shenoute, however, inoculates a monk against sin: his words will teach the monks to recognize the symptoms of sin and prevent the illness from flourishing in them. Ignoring or hiding sin provides no cure.

Shenoute later equates sin with disease even more explicitly. Condemning monks who hide transgressions that occur in the monastery, he uses the language of disease to explain the effect of this behavior on the community. The sin affects the "whole body," even monks who have not participated directly in the sinful acts: "What members will I condemn so that I forgive what (others)? Or what members will I make miserable so that I bless what (others)? It is this single body from which these diseases eat. Thus, wretchedness exists for the whole body, even if there is a member in it that does not cause pain or is not a part of the pain."[141] In this passage, the double entendres of the previous fragments become transparent. Sin is an illness that literally consumes an entire body, eventually afflicting even its undiseased members.

Shenoute returns to his depiction of sin as disease later in *Canon 9*, in the middle of a series of rules about integrating novices into the community. New monks should not insist upon receiving work and residential assignments that reflect the trades they practiced before joining the monastery. People do not become monks in order to continue in their trade but to repent from their past sins and to endeavor never to sin in the future, he says.[142] Shenoute then declares that monks who nonetheless demand specific work assignments are "abominations" to God's "holy place." Such obscenities manifest themselves as a sickness that plagues them as well as Shenoute. He continues, "[T]his one there (Shenoute?) brought his hands up to heaven . . . saying, 'God is my witness as to what way this disease is in the members of my body.' Who is it who will be able to recognize it in themselves, or know its function in his members, so that he might be told, and so that he might believe? *God*, however, knows it."[143] Sin is a disease that must be diagnosed before it may be treated. Monks who persist in holding on to their worldly possessions and desires may be hiding their maladies from themselves, but they fool neither Shenoute nor God. The symptoms of their sinful behaviors present themselves for all who have the eyes to see.

The potent anxiety about pollution is one of the primary characteristics of the monastic subjectivity particular to Shenoute's community and writings. The goal of the rituals outlined in the rules is the production of physically and spiritually pure bodies which then form one pure corporate monastic body. This process marks Deir Anba Shenouda during Shenoute's tenure as a monastic space different from even its closest neighbors, the Pachomian communities. In Shenoute's system, physical and spiritual pollution deny a monk salvation, and then spread like a disease throughout the community, threatening the salvation of the other monks, male or female. Obedient adherence to the rules and performance of the rituals prescribed therein maintain the physical and spiritual purity of each monk. They also bind the monks together into one pure, corporate social body, in the hope that they all will stand righteous before God at the final judgment. In this way, the rules reflect and reinforce Shenoute's ideology of the communal ascetic life.

The deep regard for purity is manifest in texts outside of the monastic rules as well. This aspect of the monastic subjectivity produced at Deir Anba Shenouda pervades another element of Shenoute's management of the monastery: maintaining the sanctity of the places in which the rituals of ascetic life occur. As Shenoute explains, God, too, resides in the monastery with the monks. Allowing the disease that is sin to remain in God's holy places offends God. The ritualization process entailed in the rules sanctifies both the monks and their ascetic space. Breaking with the community ritual incurs sin in the form of disease, and just as that disease can spread to the other members of the communal monastic body, it can spread to the ritual space, as well. The purity so central to the monastic life extends to places the monks inhabit. The next chapter explores how Shenoute develops this concept further in *Canon 7*, where he argues that the evil deeds of monks contaminate more than their own bodies and souls; they defile the very dwelling place of God—the monastery's church.

3

The Church Building as Symbol of Ascetic Renunciation

MANUSCRIPTS OF SHENOUTE'S WRITINGS are not the only material legacy of Deir Anba Shenouda. On the edge of the cultivated land outside of the modern city of Sohag lie the remains of its church building. According to a twelfth- or thirteenth-century inscription in the sanctuary, the basilica was originally built c. 450–55 C.E. on the instructions of Shenoute himself.[1] It sits at the foot of desert cliffs dotted with caves that have been home to ascetic hermits from Shenoute's time to the modern era[2] (Figure 1, p. 2). Although the original building was partially destroyed by fire (likely in the seventh century) and then reconstructed and modified during succeeding years, some of the early reconstruction utilized the same materials as the original building, and it was rebuilt along almost the same site plan.[3] Volume seven of Shenoute's *Canons* opens with several sermons preached by Shenoute on the occasions of the construction, inauguration, and use of the original church. The archaeological remains of this site, when read in tandem with the ancient texts, provide an important interpretive lens for understanding the asceticism practiced at Deir Anba Shenouda specifically and early Christian asceticism more broadly.

In reading many early Christian texts from and about Egypt, one is struck by the importance of space for the ascetic life. Whether it be Antony locked in his desert fortress, the tightly arranged cells of Kellia in the *Apophthegmata Patrum*, or the landscape of the desert in so much hagiographical literature, the space in which the early Christians practiced ascetic renunciation was as infused with as much meaning as the ascetic practices themselves. Since few texts with descriptions of early ascetic space survive, studies have been left largely to archaeologists and art historians, not historians of Christianity.[4] Only a handful of ascetic authors from the fourth through sixth centuries wrote about the theological significance they found in the building of churches. These include Shenoute, two anonymous members of the Pachomian monasteries in Egypt, and the wealthy Latin patron Paulinus of Nola, Italy. The sanctuaries built for each of these late antique communities held deep theological significance. They symbolized the ascetic endeavors undertaken at those communities. Since for each writer, the ascetic struggle was constituted in slightly different terms, with different goals, practices, and interpretations of those practices, so were the church buildings imbued with different meanings. Yet, in each case, the church held meaning beyond its mere walls. Each was constructed as much by a theology and a discourse of ascetic discipline as it was by wood, brick, and stone.

Although each building performs an important ideological function in its community, Shenoute's texts articulate the most complex relationship between monk and church. This chapter examines through archaeological and textual sources the role of physical space and architecture in ascetic practice at Shenoute's monastery and in Shenoute's ideology of the monastic life. A comparison of the ascetic significance of the churches described in the comparatively sparse sources from Paulinus and the Pachomian texts forms the conclusion to the chapter. Both the literary and archaeological evidence from Deir Anba Shenouda are difficult to date, and each presents its own interpretive difficulties. Nonetheless, they are an invaluable resources for understanding concepts of ascetic purity and discipline, the significance of the eucharist, the function of communal worship, and the role of architecture in the ascetic life. For when compared to the scant evidence from the Pachomian monasteries or the early ascetic communities of Europe about their understandings of ascetic architecture, this site at Deir Anba Shenouda, in both its literary and material manifestations, is an unparalleled resource for the scholar of late antiquity. The church at Deir Anba Shenouda signified to its monks the creation of a new and richly layered symbol of the monastic life.

For Shenoute the church is first and foremost a house of God, and its primary meaning lies in its status as a monument to the community's relationship with God. Shenoute incorporated the building into his theology of communal asceticism, and in doing so he expanded the contours of the symbolic landscape in which he believed the monks dwelled. The building embodies a theology of the ascetic life in which the monument is the material testimony to the purity of the monks' bodies and souls. Yet, it is the very materiality of the church that also poses its greatest hermeneutical difficulties. Although the church's beauty stands as a testament to the greatness of the God who resides in it, the monks must take heed not to admire its physical attributes too much, for fear that they might be drawn too deeply into the desires and concerns of the flesh, and away from the desires and concerns of God. As this chapter will show, the church, like the body of the monk, becomes the space in which the ascetic struggle between the spirit and the flesh is undertaken.

As Chapter 1 demonstrated, even before he became the leader of the monastery, Shenoute began constructing his ideology of the monastic life based on the parallel natures of the individual monastic body and the communal monastic body. He used this model of monasticism to structure his leadership in the community, his relationship with the monks, and his revisions of the monastic rule (Chapter 2). It pervaded another aspect of life in the community, as well—its communal worship and the building in which the rituals of communal prayer and the eucharist occurred. Shenoute rhetorically constructs the new church on a template similar to that of the individual ascetic's body. In the kind of asceticism that Shenoute practiced, the human body was seen to house both the flesh (*sarx*) and the spirit (*pneuma*).[5] Through ascetic discipline, one turns oneself and one's soul away from matters of the flesh and toward matters of the spirit. The flesh was considered a "burden" pulling on the spirit and the soul, keeping them apart from God. Bodily discipline trained the body and soul and directed their attentions away from the flesh to the refinement of the spirit.[6] In Shenoute's writings, the building itself becomes a body that houses both the spirit (God) and the flesh (its material construction).[7] Like the human body, the church is the space in which the monks struggle to extricate themselves from the desires of the flesh. It forms a third body, linked to the individual monk's body and the corporate monastic body (the monastery), that the ascetic inhabits. Additionally, the building serves as an expression of this second body, the social body. According to Shenoute, the sins and faults of the monastic congregation are echoed in the structure of the church. Finally, this building—the site where the monks partook of the eucharist—also links the monastery to another body constituted by the community: the body of Christ. In this intricate paradigm, the monk of Shenoute's monastery existed in a four-part relationship in which ascetic discipline affected not only his or her own body and soul, but also the community, the church building, and even Jesus Christ. As Shenoute exhorts the monks to turn their attentions to matters of the spirit rather than of the flesh, he uses the building as both metaphor and exemplar in his instruction on the spiritual life. Before beginning an examination of the way in which Shenoute used the new church as a model for the monastic life, it may be useful to introduce the sources on which this chapter is based.

Canon 7: The Textual and Architectural Remains

Most of this chapter assesses heretofore relatively unscrutinized literary sources in *Canon 7* about the construction of Deir Anba Shenouda's church. *Canon 7* is difficult to date, since in the extant fragments, Shenoute makes no reference to specific, independently dateable events, such as the current length of his own tenure as abbot, the episcopacies of major bishops, or church councils that may have occurred.[8] The only external event mentioned is a series of "barbarian" invasions, which have proven difficult to date precisely. Stephen Emmel has proposed a period in the later years of Shenoute's life—perhaps the middle of the fifth century—for *Canon 7*.

Although this *Canon* survives only in fragmentary copies, fortunately a handful of its texts have endured almost completely intact.[9] *Canon 7* contains at least eight texts, all of which appear to be sermons. They span several years in which two major events occurred. First, a substantial construction project involved multiple buildings. Second, the monastery sheltered numerous refugees from nearby villages who were displaced by the aforementioned invaders from the south. Although some of the first texts in *Canon 7* seem to have the monastic community as their intended primary audience, it is possible that people who were not monks also attended the original preaching of the sermons. The texts that conclude *Canon 7* are directed to a mixed audience, for they were written and delivered during the refugee crisis. Shenoute describes the first event as the construction of "this great house" and sometimes "these great houses."[10] The former, also called the "house of God," likely refers to the monastery's main church, whose archaeological remains still stand.[11] *Canon 7* also contains one of Shenoute's most well-known works: his colorful descriptions of the effects of the invasions on this region of Egypt. The texts treating these two seemingly disparate events seem to have been collected together in one codex due to their chronology. In one sermon about the refugees, Shenoute claims to be preaching two years after the construction of the new church.[12]

This chapter will concentrate on the first five texts in *Canon 7*, each of which relates to the new church. The sermon *God Is Holy* opens the volume and may date to the beginning of the construction.[13] The colophon concisely summarizes its contents: "A discourse about the temple of God the almighty and the house of Christ, concerning his houses and all his holy and honored places, and about the unnatural things into which we have descended, instead of what belongs to our nature."[14] A small fragment of a second sermon follows, and since the incipit has been lost, it is known as *Acephalous Work Twenty-three* or *A23*.[15] The third sermon, *This Great House*, is the longest concerning the building program.[16] In it, too, Shenoute capitalizes on an opportunity for moral exhortation: "This is the way that they are blessed—those who walk according to the values of the Gospel and according to the values of the house of God, or the

houses, and all of his places." The opening pages also list the time and
effort required to construct the buildings, as well as their purpose ("that
we might become holy in them.").[17] *I Myself Have Seen* and *If Everyone
Errs* conclude this section of *Canon 7*.[18] (The final texts of *Canon 7—The
Rest of the Words, Continuing to Glorify the Lord,* and *It Is Obvious*—date
to the refugee crisis.)[19]

The site of Shenoute's monastery is singular in the history of early
Christian asceticism. Not only did *Canon 7* survive, with its extensive theorizing on the significance of the community's church for ascetic purity,
but the remains of the building itself have survived, as well. Deir Anba
Shenouda lies on the western outskirts of Sohag, a modern city 465 kilometers south of Cairo. The Coptic Orthodox Church has reactivated the
monastery, and it serves as the home for approximately ten male monks.[20]
Its most prominent structure is still the ancient basilica originally constructed during Shenoute's tenure as monastic leader. (See Figure 1.) This
church is currently used by the monks of Deir Anba Shenouda, local Coptic Orthodox Christians, and the thousands of pilgrims who visit the monastery each July for the month-long festival honoring Shenoute's feast day
on the Coptic liturgical calendar (July 14). These contemporary demon-
strations of piety occur on the grounds of one of Egypt's most important
Christian archaeological sites. Excavations have uncovered the remains of
a number of other buildings in addition to the visible basilica: monks'
living quarters, latrines, a kitchen, a refectory, a well, and storage rooms.[21]
(Some recent excavations are visible in the foreground of Figure 1.) At
least as far back as the famous Egyptologist Flinders Petrie in 1908, archaeologists and art historians have been drawn to the site because of its historical value and the church's aesthetic features.[22] Peter Grossmann, who has
excavated Deir Anba Shenouda for the past several decades, has declared
the church to be "beyond doubt the most important monument of early
Christian architecture in Upper Egypt," and one of the most architecturally influential churches in all of Egypt.[23] Its architectural sculpture, some
of which dates to the original construction, also constitutes some of the
most significant Christian art in Egypt.[24] The archaeological site is currently threatened by a variety of sources and was listed along with the
nearby monastery Deir Anba Bishoi (also known as the Red Monastery)
as one of World Monument Watch's most imperiled cultural heritage sites
for 2002–2003.[25]

Despite renovations over the intervening centuries, the church at Deir
Anba Shenouda in many ways resembles the original basilica built by Shenoute and discussed in *Canon 7*. Grossmann concurs with the tradition
recorded in the aforementioned inscription, which dates the original

building to Shenoute's era, circa 450–55 C.E. Although fire partially destroyed the fifth-century construction, most likely during the Persian invasion around 619 C.E., the church was rebuilt soon afterward, and on a scale almost exactly contiguous with the configuration of the original structure.[26] Figure 2 provides a detailed plan of the building.[27] It was quite rare in this era to rebuild a structure so closely to the original design, suggesting that those who reconstructed the church less than two centuries after Shenoute's death were attempting to remain faithful to a monument they knew to have been built by their famous archimandrite.[28] A prominent medieval wall painting of Shenoute in the sanctuary provides further testimony to the powerful association of the memory of Shenoute with the building.

A visit to the current archaeological site still provides a sense of the space in which the monks from Shenoute's era worshipped. Stone from an Egyptian temple, possibly the abandoned Ptolemaic temple to the goddess of Triphis (from whose name Atripe comes), comprised much of the building material for the church.[29] Hieroglyphs are still visible in several places in the church today, including one stone on the floor of the nave.[30] From the exterior, the building's style, with its straight and striking white walls, is even reminiscent of a pharaonic temple, thus distinguishing it from Roman basilicas elsewhere in the Mediterranean.[31] Much of the limestone for the building's walls (see Figure 1) and interior survived the fire, but where original materials collapsed, brick was used as replacement. Some original limestone was reused in reconstruction after the fire.[32] The building's architecture also incorporates elements from North Africa and Italy. The triconch sanctuary (see the plan in Figure 2) has been compared to the apse of Paulinus's New Basilica in Nola.[33] The large nave (see Figure 3) would have accommodated thousands of monks, as there were upper galleries in addition to the ground floor. Benches in the nave provided seating.[34] The remains of a colonnade are still visible as well. (Compare Figures 2 and 3.) Some of the original, fifth-century columns were destroyed and replaced, but others that were merely damaged were "encased with fire brick masonry" and reerected.[35]

Additions and renovations continued into the medieval and modern eras, changing some of the worship space. A ninth-century *khurus* with a medieval domed ceiling now separates the nave from the sanctuary. The domes over the sanctuary and *khurus* have been replaced over time, but some date to the thirteenth century.[36]

Shenoute himself writes of the building's ornamentation in *Canon 7*, and despite the building's later reconstructions, the artistic and architectural remains can provide a glimpse into the style of ornamentation in the

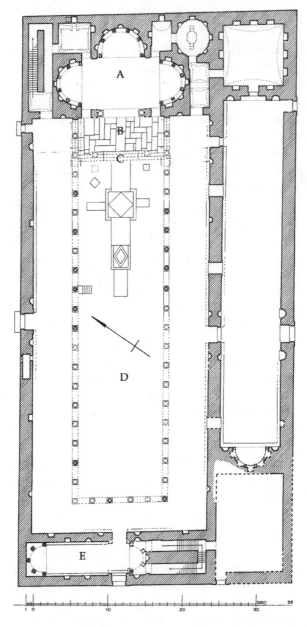

Figure 2. Site plan of the late antique church of Deir Anba Shenouda. Courtesy Peter Grossmann.

A. Triconch sanctuary
B. *Khurus*
C. Current entry to *khurus* and sanctuary
D. Nave
E. Narthex

Figure 3. Nave of the church at Deir Anba Shenouda, viewed from the roof of the sanctuary. (Item D in Figure 2.) February 2002.

basilica during his lifetime. Despite Shenoute's own ambivalence about the theological meaning of the beauty of this building, its original artistic program is considered ornate by ancient standards. The sculptural décor still extant in the west narthex (see Figure 4) was designed for the original building. The capitals also visible in Figure 4 are also late antique—specifically "spolia," or pieces of earlier (likely Diocletian-era) buildings reused for the construction of Shenoute's church. Many of the wall niches lining the nave (visible in Figure 3) are original, fifth-century construction, and some niches contain intricate sculptural decorations, as in Figure 5. The sculpture in the baptistry (the octagonal room in Figure 2) is entirely orginal.[37]

Although the sanctuary has sustained several stages of rebuilding, some of the sculptural and wall ornamentation may date to late antiquity, even the fifth century, including some of the elaborately sculptured wall niches underneath the three semidomes of the triconch.[38] Two of the three semidomes in the sanctuary display medieval paintings. The eastern, or central, semidome contains a portrait of Christ enthroned, and the southern semidome shows a large draped cross flanked by Mary, John, and two angels.[39] Icons of Shenoute, Mark, and Mary (whose skin tone is dark in

Figure 4. Narthex of the church at Deir Anba Shenouda in July 1999. (Item E in Figure 2.) The architectural sculpture is original construction for the building in Shenoute's era. The capitals also date to late antiquity. Sometime before February 2002, structural supports were added to prevent collapse. These supports now obscure most of the decorative details.

Figure 5. Decorative wall niche in the church building at Deir Anba Shenouda. Many of the niches in the nave date to the original, fifth-century construction of the building. February 2002.

her portrait) are painted directly onto the lower walls. And even though the only paintings currently visible in the sanctuary are certainly medieval, there is reason to believe that the original sanctuary was painted in late antiquity. The interior of the sanctuary at the nearby Deir Anba Bishoi is painted extensively. Deir Anba Bishoi's church is also built in the form of a basilica with a triconch sanctuary, with an architectural plan similar to Deir Anba Shenouda's church. As of this writing, study and conservation of Deir Anba Bishoi's wall paintings are underway, and new redatings attribute them to late antiquity. They adorn all three of the semidomes in the sanctuary. As at Deir Anba Shenouda's sanctuary, decorative niches articulate the wall below the monumental semidomes. But at Deir Anba Bishoi, both figural and nonfigural paintings adorn virtually the entire sanctuary interior. We should imagine the interior of the sanctuary at its architectural and ascetic counterpart, Deir Anba Shenouda, being painted in late antiquity as well.[40] Thus, the material remains at both monasteries provide the historian reading Shenoute's writings about the beauty and ornamentation of the church with a sense of the building as an adorned and decorated space in that period.

Shenoute himself marveled at the architectural magnitude of this monument. In *This Great House*, he celebrates the building by detailing what was required to construct it: four or five months of labor and sacrifices, plus expenses that according to Shenoute amounted to "everything we had."[41] The size of the monument belies this modest construction time.[42] Perhaps Shenoute refers to one stage of the project[43] or deliberately minimizes the earthly efforts expended upon it. Whatever the time required, the church seems to be somehow bound to the monks through the labor they invested in building it.[44]

Yet, the physical attributes and adornments of the church that entailed such labor held ironic significance for the monks who gathered there. According to Shenoute, the physical beauty of the building should not be revered for itself alone, but only as a manifestation of the community's ascetic purity. The building functions as an extension of Shenoute's larger ideology of the monastic body in his theology of the ascetic life. He argues in the *Canons* that the nature of salvation is interdependent; the sins of any members of the monastery threaten the salvation of the entire community. In *Canon 7*, Shenoute discursively constructs the building as a symbol and exemplar of ascetic purity. Shenoute's interpretation of the apostle Paul's writings on the body, especially in 1 Corinthians, is central to his project.

From the Corinthian Body to the Shenoutean Body

Beginning in the first sermon of *Canon 7*, *God Is Holy*, Shenoute develops a theology of ascetic architecture through his interpretation of Paul's writings on the body. Following Paul's claim that the Christians have been "baptized into one body" in which their own bodies are the members of Christ's body and members of each other Shenoute conceives of the monastery as one body in Christ, with the male and female monks as the members of Christ. Moreover, again adapting Paul, Shenoute believes the human body to be susceptible to pollution caused by sin—pollution that can spread to the other members of the communal monastic body.[45] He maps this monastic interpretation of the Pauline ideology of the body in 1 Corinthians onto the church building in *God Is Holy*. The relationship between the construction of the church, the sacrality of the building, and ascetic holiness is made explicit early in the sermon. Shenoute visualizes the monastery as a physical space which the monks, their buildings, and their God all inhabit. "As for the holy and good places of God, it is hoped that some people who are holy and good also reside in them. For the

temple is not for gods of wood or stone and other remnants."[46] Much of
the sermon is devoted to denouncing sin, and Shenoute uses Pauline language of the body to connect his moral message to the church building:
"[If a] thunderbolt strikes those who do not know that a person is a temple of God and his Holy Spirit, then what will happen to those who despise
him, even though they hear and they know that humanity is a single body
in Christ (1 Cor. 12:12–27) and also that humanity is the members of his
body (Eph. 5:30)? What also is it that he says, that we are each members
of one another (Eph. 4:25)?"[47] Unfortunately, the pages immediately preceding and following the folio containing these Pauline references have
been lost. It is clear, nonetheless, that Shenoute is blending passages from
1 Corinthians and Ephesians to establish a relationship between four different entities: the individual person, people collectively, the body of Christ,
and a "temple of God." Although "temple of God" in this passage clearly
refers not to a building but to a Christian person, Shenoute's language
("temple") connects the person to the building to which he dedicates the
larger sermon. Throughout, he speaks repeatedly of physical houses and
buildings, including the church or "house of God."[48] Thus in this one
brief passage, Shenoute links the church building to the Pauline ideology
of the body. All the members of a community—in this context the monastery—are interconnected through the body of Christ. The church building
symbolizes that relationship.

The community's shared existence as the members of Christ's body
has both positive and negative repercussions. On the one hand, it is proof
of the goodness of creation. In *This Great House*, Shenoute argues that a
person, as the "member of Christ" and "dwelling-place of his spirit," is
the most glorified of God's creations. Indeed God created the rest of the
world for humanity. Shenoute develops this argument in conversation
with some opponents who submit that humanity is evil because it was
created by a "demiurge."[49] Interpreting Gen. 1:31, Shenoute contends that
humanity is inherently good because it was created by God. People become wicked only through their own disobedience to God. They are not
inherently evil:

Concerning the submission of creation, it suffices for the Lord to say, "It is good,"
as it is written, and, "God saw everything that he created, and behold, they were
very good." With respect to the fighting and the disobedience of humanity, it
suffices for God to say that a wicked thing is before him. All of creation is good
according to that which he spoke since the beginning. Creation exists on account
of humanity. . . . It is not fitting for them to say that humanity is evil because the
demiurge formed it—since it is very good. . . . And how is humanity not more

chosen, since it is the seed of God, and the member of Christ, and the dwelling-place of his spirit?[50]

Through an exegetical layering of the creation account and Pauline anthropology, Shenoute declares humanity essentially good and at the top of the hierarchy of creation because humanity was created directly by God, as a "seed" of God, and as a "member of Christ." The rest of the created world is subordinate to people, because it was created for them; people are subordinate only to God. They are considered "wicked" for subverting this hierarchy through their disobedience.

Shenoute then uses this exegesis to expound upon the relationship between the monastery and its church. As a building and a creation of God, the church is not more glorious than humanity. It is built for humanity's worship of God; it is built because of humanity. Shenoute explains the order of creation using the metaphor of light. People light lamps not to illuminate the lamps, but to illuminate other things. Similarly, the church, and even all of the created world, exists on behalf of humans: "Is it the case that the house is built because of itself alone? Or is the lamp kindled for the purpose of lighting itself? Also, what is more chosen—is it the house or humanity, because of whom it was built? Is it the light of the lamp or humanity? And how is humanity not a great thing that is glorified very much, since the Lord God created heaven and built the world because of humanity, and since he made luminators exist because of it?"[51] In contrast to his opponents, who attribute the evil in the created world to the creator, Shenoute attributes evil to humanity's actions alone. Sin separates people from God: "And humanity is the race (*genos*) of God. We use it badly, in unnatural things without fear. For sin made humanity ignorant that it was from God and that it was a child of God."[52] People, and more specifically the monks to whom Shenoute preaches, are the seed, race, and children of God as well as the members of Christ's body.

Participation in the body of Christ also brings the potential for great dangers. Although humanity and creation are both essentially good because they derive from God, human sins do corrupt. Sin destroys the soul, heart, and body of the sinner.[53] Because people are the members of Christ's body, sinful people also threaten to pollute Christ himself. Shenoute accuses his monastery of doing this very thing. Instead of becoming one body in Christ as Paul commanded, the community has become one body in sin. This renders the community unfit to partake of the eucharist: "We have become sin. Sin has become a single body with us. Our members have been united with unnatural things instead of making us holy. . . . We became unclean, and we were not ashamed before your goodness—

we, impious people, even though you will give your only-begotten Son on behalf of us. Truly, we are not worthy of eating from his flesh and drinking from his blood."[54]

Throughout *God Is Holy* and *This Great House* in particular, the terms Shenoute uses to describe the effects of sin are "pollution," "defilement," "uncleanness," and "corruption." Shenoute develops his concept of pollution using several overlapping discourses, one of which is a sexual discourse that relies once again on the Pauline ideology of the body. In both *God Is Holy* and *This Great House*, Shenoute turns to 1 Cor. 6 to describe the way in which humanity corrupts the members of Christ, and he transfers the Pauline understanding of sin as pollution onto the monastery. Sinners are like the man in Paul's church who made the members of Christ members of a prostitute. Employing the language of familial kinship to denote the ascetic relationships that monks have formed with each other (their monastic sisters and brothers) or monks of a lower rank (their sons and daughters), Shenoute describes in *God Is Holy* how the sins of one monk will affect the others, following the Pauline model:[55]

If your member is the one to whom you say, "My son," and "My brother," or as a woman speaks to the one next to her, "My sister," and a mother to the one whom she calls, "My daughter," why were you not ashamed to sin against yourselves? For if you did not fear nor feel shame before Christ not to make his members members of a prostitute, since his members are your members in turn, then how will you be ashamed to make the members of your sons and daughters and your brethren unnatural members?[56]

Prostitution proves a potent theme in *Canon 7*. In *This Great House*, also, he warns, "It is the first practice for each person to avoid making the members of Christ members of a prostitute, unnatural members."[57] Prostitution could be read figuratively as a sexual metaphor for the mingling of the holy with the impure. Alternatively, it could signify the broader sin of "fornication," a more general sense of sexual sin frequently rebuked in monastic texts, rather than prostitution per se. Finally, it could be read symbolically as an ascetic adaptation of a biblical trope for disobedience and unfaithfulness, one that Shenoute used in *Canon 1*.[58] Here, Shenoute adjusts Paul's sexual language and bodily imagery for a monastic context. Pollution travels from one member of the monastery to another and even to Christ because all form a single body in Christ.

Shenoute also links another Pauline discourse, albeit one from Romans rather than 1 Corinthians, to his purity and pollution discourse. As we have already seen, many passages in *Canon 7* that contain some condemnation of sin also refer to acts that Shenoute characterizes as "unnatu-

ral" (*paraphusis*, or *mparaphusis*—unnatural things or acts). "Unnatural"
acts are associated with and even produce defilement, uncleanness, and
impurities; they pollute the corporate monastic body. Unfortunately, in
typical Shenoutean fashion, he often remains ambiguous about the definition of these activities, and even as to whether he refers to specific events
in the monastery's history or to general concepts of sinfulness.[59] Shenoute
and his audience probably were familiar with Paul's condemnation of "unnatural" sexual acts in Rom. 1 and likely heard a Pauline subtext in this
monastic usage of "unnatural." The term may distinguish the truly pious
from the impious, the pure from the impure, but it also conjures up Paul's
discourses of the flesh in Romans, in which the Greek *para physin* carries
a decidedly sexual tone. Paul's usage, as contested as it is, is itself oblique,
such that it is not sufficient to determine what the precise meaning of the
term may have been for Shenoute.[60] Though the textual memory of Romans may imply that homosexual relations are under discussion in *Canon
7*, the context provided by other ascetic literature belies such a simplistic
interpretation. As Elizabeth Clark has demonstrated, "naturalizing discourses" proscribe and prescribe a variety of conduct. "Natural" activity
can refer to food, sex, social relations, physical appearance, adornment,
and more. Taking sexuality as an example, either virginity or certain forms
of sex are considered "natural," depending on the author.[61]

Although Shenoute does not always outline specific deeds or behaviors that may be characterized as "unnatural," he does construct a discourse of natural and unnatural built upon the ascetic practices of bodily
discipline, obedience, and devotion. In particular, he turns to the language
of the biblical prophets and adapts their discourses of idolatry and fornication for his monastic context. Unnatural deeds are associated with sexual
excess, violence, and other defiling acts.[62] But idolatry also qualifies as
"unnatural" activity: "Consider now our shame. Know now our scorn.
For when he sees the person who knew other gods beyond the Lord God
alone, and who did not obey this voice, 'There will be no new god among
you. Nor will you worship foreign gods,' when he saw humanity being
impious by means of unnatural things, abominable acts. . . ."[63] Here Shenoute highlights not only idolatry, but also the disobedience against God's
commandments that is inherent in that act. Disobedience and idolatry are
thus enfolded into Shenoute's ideology of the body through his use of the
term "unnatural." In the end, the term's meaning lies not in specific actions or behaviors to which it might allude, but to the larger concept of
the orientation of the ascetic to or from matters of the flesh. In the discourses of the body that Shenoute adapts from Paul, fulfilling the desires

of the flesh signifies spiritual disobedience more broadly. Humanity's "natural" state is one of devotion and submission to God.[64]

Shenoute maps his interpretation of the Pauline body and his vision of ascetic discipline onto the new church in three ways, each of which I will explore at length in the following three sections. First, he explicitly links the purity of the individual monks to the spiritual status of the building; the monks' ascetic discipline (or lack thereof) is reflected in the building. Second, he develops parallels between the exterior and interior of the church building, the external building (the church) and internal buildings (the worshippers within it), and the material and the spiritual. Third, through an elaborate series of exegetical passages and parables based on the scriptural parable of the wheat and the weeds (Matt. 13:24–30), he compares the interdependent nature of salvation to the interdependent nature of buildings, walls, and spaces in the created world.

Holy Bodies and Holy Buildings: Two Temples of God

Much of *Canon 7* concerns the church building as a metaphor for the person of the monk, and at times, specifically for the body of the monk. The human person and sacred places are created to become dwelling places for God. Yet, both spaces can also be defiled through sin, driving God out of those places and effecting their destruction. Shenoute's parallel construction of monk and church as dwelling places for God rests on his use of the Pauline ideology of the body as the operating frame for the community's relationship with God. Just as the community participates in the body of Christ as Christ's members and separates itself from God by means of the sinful corruption of its members, so also the community and the building participate in the body of Christ as residences for God and separate themselves from God by the defilement of sin.

Shenoute first establishes the relationship between body and building in *God Is Holy* in a passage I have already discussed: "A person is a temple of God and his Holy Spirit."[65] Throughout *God Is Holy*, Shenoute characterizes both people and places as residences of God, and the link between them is the purity and discipline required of both. Just as the purity of the individual monk affects the purity of the community, the purity of the monk also affects the purity of the building. The first line of the sermon reads, "God is holy: he dwells among those who are holy, and he rests himself among those who are holy."[66] In Coptic, the word usually translated as holy also may be translated as pure; in Shenoute's discursive system, holiness is virtually equivalent to purity.[67] The opening line may also be translated, "God is pure: he dwells among those who are pure, and he rests himself among those who are pure." Thus, Shenoute introduces the sermon's main argument: that the community must maintain the ascetic purity and holiness of its space (both spiritual and physical) if it wishes to continue to experience the presence of God.

Like a community, an individual person can be a dwelling place of God. Those who do not maintain their purity, however, will become homes for Satan.[68] This applies to spaces and places as well. "If there is freedom from every defilement where the spirit of the Lord exists, then there is also slavery of all pestilential things where the unclean spirit exists."[69] Community, monk, and place share a common nature. They can welcome God within them, or they can become defiled and unclean.

Although God blesses his places and fills them with his mercy, people often defile them.[70] The same holds true for human beings, whom Shenoute compares to buildings. Just as the measure, dimensions, and sides of the places of God are beautiful, so too is it fitting for "the measures of people's hearts, the dimensions of their souls, and the uprightness of their living within them" to be beautiful.[71] Similarly, Shenoute asks, if no one dares to claim that a "defiled" house is a house that belongs to a king, how could anyone say that an "unclean person" belongs to Christ?[72] Shenoute's house expresses the virtue or wickedness of its residents, but it is also a metaphor for its human inhabitants.

Shenoute builds on his architectural symbolism by arguing that the church and the monk's body possess the same purpose. Both are spaces in which a monk should worship and glorify the Lord. Each monk should follow Jesus' instructions to Peter to transform him or herself into a sanctuary; they should "edify" themselves " 'like a living stone' " of a " 'spiritual house for holy worshipping.' "[73] Later, he returns to the image of the person as a place of worship, citing the human body specifically as the space in which the glory of God should be celebrated. He reproaches his congregation for failing to use their bodies in this manner: "You did not establish your body as a holy sacrifice for God. You did not allow others to establish themselves for him. You did not glorify the [spirit] that mixes with your body. You did not allow others to glorify him in their body. Woe unto me! Because instead of our marveling upon the creation of God and all his members and our glorifying him, you caused many to marvel upon the destruction of their world."[74] The human body is the offering presented to God. But it is also the space in which the offering is made.[75]

The bodily discipline inherent in physical labor also connects the monks to the church. Work was an essential element of the discipline required in most early Christian monasteries, and this certainly held true for

Shenoute's community: "Some others, namely the respectful and righteous or the good and honest, are humble and perfected in all righteousness, are holy in the holy house of God, and are a model for other multitudes through labor and skills. And the house appears as a house that is perfected, that is bound to its companions through labor and skills. The ones who will be in it, but even more the ones who are in it, will thrive and show forth as righteous."[76] Labor and work on the part of monks produce an ascetic perfection that parallels the perfection of the "house." The church will reflect the holiness of the people who worship inside it. It is irrevocably tied to the community both materially and spiritually, through physical labor and moral righteousness.

Calamity occurs when God abandons the church and its community. Since both are dwelling places of God, both can drive God away with their sin. The salvation of the monastery depends upon God's presence among them: "Who will save you? Who will strengthen you, congregation, if the Lord will not dwell among you . . . ?"[77] Houses that God enters will be renewed by God and will shine with his light. Houses that God leaves, however, will be cast down to their foundations and will remain dark.[78] The spiritual state of these buildings and spaces depends upon the spiritual status of those who dwell and pray within them. The houses of God are places in which to forsake sin, not places to engage in disrespectful "laughing matters" or to commit sins, such as theft or slander.[79] The souls of those who defile the houses of God will be given up as dwelling places for demons, just as God abandoned Jerusalem of old.[80] Such people become "dwelling places of the devil."[81] Before God abandons the unclean houses, he will first destroy the souls of those who defiled them.[82]

In Shenoute's hermeneutics, the places made desert or wasteland by God in the Christian Old Testament are allegories for the bodies and souls of Christian sinners. In *I Myself Have Seen*, Shenoute interprets the destruction of Zion in Isa. 61:4 as the death of sinful Christian bodies and souls: "But as for the soul, and also the body or the whole person of those who became desert and who were laid waste, it will be said about them instead of places and cities, 'They will build up the deserted places. As for the ones who first laid waste the cities that are deserted, they will renew them forever, and for generations.'"[83] Despite the promise of redemption and renewal in this passage, Shenoute executes an exegetical bait and switch. He immediately tells his congregation that they, in fact, will *not* experience such redemption because of their sins. If God removed Adam and Eve from paradise because of a single transgression even though they did not know Jesus, he asks, then how could the monks, who know Jesus and yet have committed many wicked deeds, expect more?[84]

The relationship between the community and its space, its buildings, and its church is not one of equality. The purity and holiness of the church depend upon the people who gather inside it. Polluting activities sever the monastery from the body of Christ and drive God out of the church. A building is not in its essential nature sinful—it is only made sinful by the people who live in it. The church, which should be a house of God, faces material destruction if it has already been spiritually destroyed by people who have sinned inside it. "This house was laid waste or already cut down in its turn, but in this way I will say that he (God) does not make people foreign to him because of the house. What wicked thing did the house do? Or does the house sin? But he makes people foreign to him because they made the house foreign to him in defilement. God will not live in the house because of it."[85] God, notes Shenoute, resides in the heavens and does not actually *need* a building in which to live. Rather, "For our sake he lives in it—if we are holy."[86] The piety of the people saves their house, place, and community, not the reverse: "What person was ever righteous because of the beauty of the house and all of its construction . . . ? But if we guard the regulations and the laws of the Lord God which are in them, listening to them and reading them, we will be saved."[87] Likewise, the sins of the people draw God's wrath upon their houses, land, and communities: "For indeed from of old the Lord God was not angry at the place or city or land or field if they had not first sinned against him."[88] God is neither capricious nor arbitrary; eternal prayer and devotion can spare a place from God's punishment.[89]

Christianizing the judgment oracles of the prophetic books of the Hebrew Bible, Shenoute compares the sins of his day with the defilement of the temple condemned in Jer. 7. In Shenoute's exegesis, the temple signifies the house of God in which the monks now worship. He writes his own judgment oracle about the eucharist, a ritual performed inside the building of which he speaks:

> If God did not spare those who defiled the thing in which the calf or sheep or birds were offered up to him, then will he spare those who defile the thing in which the body and blood of his Son is offered up to him because he is patient with us now? . . . Those whom we are not worthy of calling "our fathers" wrote to us about their manner of work, and not only did they teach us to guard the house of God and his holy Christ, but also they did not cease wishing to tell us that the one who will wound him (Christ) will be destroyed.[90]

The monks' holiness determines whether God will be present in the building and the community. Their sins defile the very building in which they celebrate the sacrifice of Christ's own body.

This relationship between the church and the monks hinges on Shenoute's understanding of the created order of the universe, and particularly the subordination of the rest of the world to humanity. Although
Shenoute disagrees with those who argued for the inherently evil nature
of humanity and creation, he upholds a hierarchy between humanity and
the rest of creation. This hierarchy is based on humanity's participation in
the divine through its status as the members of the body of Christ. The
church *reflects* (but does not *affect*) the monks' spiritual status because it
stands below humanity on the hierarchy of creation.

This leads to the second way Shenoute maps his theology of ascetic
discipline onto the church: its structure and design epitomize a series of
relationships that are corollaries to his hierarchy of the divine and the created. Each hierarchical relationship consists of two elements: interior and
exterior, spiritual and material, and spirit and flesh. Although Shenoute
rhetorically opposes these elements to outline an ascetic conflict between
the material and the spiritual, he carefully avoids the dualisms that he has
rejected in his opponents' schema. His hierarchies become hermeneutical
extensions of the architecture of the church building. Interiority, including the interior of the church building, is associated with the spiritual, the
eternal, the heavenly, and the divine. Exteriority, including the exterior
of the church building, evokes materiality, temporality, worldliness, and
createdness. The conflict between the material and the spiritual, or the
exterior and the interior, becomes a metaphor for ascetic practice. In the
church as in monastic discipline, Shenoute privileges the spiritual and interior over the material and the exterior.

From Exteriority to Interiority, Material
to Spiritual, and Flesh to Spirit

Shenoute establishes these hierarchies most clearly in *God Is Holy* by making the interior and exterior of the church building symbols for the ascetic
struggle between spirit and flesh. He implicitly links the function of the
church to the function of the monastic body by describing the church
building as the place in which the temptation to adorn the earthly must be
resisted with an impulse to attend instead to the matters of God. Shenoute
minimizes the church's material importance by contrasting its external and
physical aspects with its interior and spiritual elements. "Just as adorning
the outside is good, adorning the inside is better."[91] That which pertains
to the "outside" consists of material goods, that is, "the church of bricks
or stones or beams, or the rest of the things in which they work." The

"inside" is associated with "the people who will be inside it or who live in it."[92] The monks should concern themselves less with material matters, such as the physical adornments of the church building, and more with their own salvation.

The distinction between external and internal symbolizes a distinction between the material and the spiritual. Shenoute develops this metaphor by contrasting the material concerns of people and the spiritual concerns of God. Although the "interior" of the building represents humanity, people themselves seem inevitably and adversely drawn to the exterior. They "pay heed to the adornment of the house on the outside." Jesus, however, "pays heed to the adornment of the houses that are built inside them"—the people.[93] Likewise, while both people and God concern themselves with the flawed structure of a faulty building, the meaning of those flaws differs for each viewer. People look at the "angles of houses or walls which have weakened or fallen," but Jesus watches over the complete destruction of such houses, down to their very foundations.[94]

The monks should turn their attentions away from the material elements of the building, because God will not receive the architectural elements at the final judgment. The monks' salvation will transpire as a result of their asceticism, not solely because of their successful completion of construction projects: "It is not the ornamentation of the house and the writings that are inscribed on its edifications and its beams that will reconcile us to Jesus if we destroy his members but the souls that become ornaments by purification and that are inscribed in this single commonwealth of the angels."[95] Monks should not focus on the edification of the church to the detriment of their other ascetic efforts. And yet, Shenoute uses those same edifications as symbols of the ascetic goal to which the monks aspire. The building thus operates as a *distraction* from the primary goals of ascetic discipline and as a *symbol* of that discipline.

The hierarchical relationships between the material and the spiritual, the church and the monk, should not be interpreted as dualistic. Although the material is subordinate to the spiritual, there remains an intimate relationship between the two. The house is saved only if the souls of the monks who worship in it are saved. Physical holiness is reflected in the cultivation of spiritual holiness. Shenoute (or rather Shenoute's God) does not reject the body or the building. One can tend to material adornments, or matters of the flesh, only if the perfection of the spirit remains the ultimate goal. Just as in the ascetic struggle between flesh and spirit, cultivating physical purity results in a certain level of spiritual purity. The flesh may even be made spirit, as exemplified in the church: "I said another time that every adornment that is in the house of God in wood, in stone, in walls, in every place in it, and everything that is of any sort or any color, they are good, and it is possible for us to bring them to the spiritual, since they are fleshly things, like water that became wine in Cana of Galilee."[96] "Fleshly things" can be made "spiritual" precisely because "fleshly things," although subordinate to the spiritual, are nonetheless part of creation and good. Monks who discipline their flesh likewise will receive divine assistance for their spirits.[97] Tending to the material aspects of the church building is a metaphor for the monastic discipline of the body.

Keeping one's body holy and pure in a community of all-too-fleshly humans proves difficult, however, as a series of allegories roughly drawn from the gospel parable of the wheat and the weeds illustrates. In these allegories, Shenoute serves up figurative readings of both building and text to map his ideology of the body onto the church in a third way: just as the fate of the entire monastery depends on the purity of each of its members, the impurities of buildings or places will render neighboring buildings or places impure, thus removing them from the congregations of God.

Sifting the Wheat from the Weeds and the Holy from the Defiled

In *This Great House,* Shenoute uses the construction of the new church to address a crisis he depicts as facing the monastery when sinful members are allowed to remain unpunished. The physical space in which the monks live and worship serves as a model for his theological and anthropological paradigm. He begins with the ways in which the good and the pure in a community or a house can save their companions through their holiness. The interdependent nature of the monastic life thus has positive benefits for the community; the pure and holy can assist in the salvation of the other weaker members. His first parable on this topic describes a person who sees a stone rolling down from a hill or high place threatening to crush those who sit below. This person shouts to the people in danger, warning them. Shenoute summarizes, "The ones who heard saved the ones who did not hear."[98] In this analogy to the monks' situation, the *actions* of the people who heard the message led to the salvation of the others. Good ascetics of course mentor their fellow monks in the classic tradition. Shenoute also concedes that the mere *presence* of holy people can contribute to the salvation of a community. Although God makes some communities and places strangers to Jesus because of their sins, God dwells in congregations that contain holy people "because of the righteousness of those who reside among them," even if "enemies" dwell there, too.[99] By extension, even the whole world may be spared "because of the holy places" in it.[100] He continues, "If there is a single grain on the bunch, the bunch will be spared because of the grain. That is to say, Jesus is patient with a congregation because of the ones within it who fear him. Woe to that bunch on the day that the grain is removed from it!"[101] God spreads his mercy over the earth on account of the presence of holy people in his places.[102] Nonetheless, Shenoute only reluctantly concedes that the presence of righteous people can save a community containing unrepentant sinners, for he easily slips from praising the righteous to condemning the sinful (and those who harbor them). As the sermon progresses, he almost abandons his concessions regarding the positive influence of the righteous on sinners. He concentrates instead on the corrosive influence of sinners on their companions. Allowing sinners to remain in the monastery is tantamount to rejecting Jesus Christ.[103]

The church building again provides fruitful material for allegorical interpretation. Decrying hypocrites and sinners, Shenoute begins an exegesis of Ezek. 13:10, about a wall that is "daubed" or "whitewashed." In Ezekiel, the wall is faulty (representing Israel's weaknesses or sins) and false prophets attempt to hide its weaknesses by whitewashing it. For Shenoute, Ezekiel's wall symbolizes the church building as well as the congregation of monks—two places of God that have been weakened by human evils: " 'This one built a wall, but it was daubed.' Know this building, but also know this daubing, that is to say, the ones who honor wicked things."[104] God will cast down the wall or the house to its foundations, bringing down with it the neighboring walls and houses.[105] The new church building is the tangible manifestation of the lesson they should glean from Shenoute's exegesis. As a successor to Ezekiel's wall, it serves as a reminder of the threat posed by sinners to the communities and houses of God. A church weakened by sin will fall, as will the rest of the monastery.

Shenoute's next parable has no direct references to the church itself, but it builds upon the same motifs of communal contamination and mutual destruction. To prevent soteriological catastrophes, the community must remove the impure people from its social body. Using the parable of the wheat and weeds of Matt. 13: 24–29, he chastises monks who leave an "unclean person" in the midst of holy people, like farmers who leave weeds "in the midst of wheat."[106] Some in his audience have excused monks who neglect to call their fellow monks to task by citing instructions of Jesus and Paul not to judge one another.[107] Shenoute parries such exegetical moves with the parable of the wheat and weeds. In the original passage, Jesus instructs farmers to leave the weeds among the wheat until the harvest time, suggesting that at the final judgment sinners will be routed from the faithful. Shenoute, however, argues that the parable applies to the present day. The division of wheat from the weeds must occur immediately. He ridicules the consequences of an incorrect reading of the text: "Leave the weed, so that it rises in the place of a grape vine or the place of green plants, and you will benefit from them greatly, senseless farmer. Or you will be honored greatly before the Lord of the earth, true fool among wise gardeners."[108] Another scriptural interpretation along the same theme is a morbid twist on the parable of the sheep and the good shepherd: "What shepherd ever left a sheep in the flock and the sheepfold while it died or while the beast destroyed it?"[109]

As a cautionary tale, Shenoute raises the specter of Achan in Josh. 7, who was stoned and burned with his family and possessions by the ancient Israelites. Achan illustrates both the potential fate awaiting a community that harbors a sinner and the preventative measures required to avoid such a fate. "As for Achan, it was not only he who was killed because of his sins. Did he alone suffice? But when he was killed, he also was obliterated with his whole household, including his beasts, so that God would not forsake them (Israel) and they would not fall beneath their enemies."[110] Achan's story exemplifies Shenoute's belief that sin affects more than the individual. Achan's entire household suffered the punishments meted out to him. The larger community protected itself by destroying the offending members.

According to Shenoute's logic, even Jesus called for the separation or destruction of impure members of the corporate monastic body. The Jesus of Matt. 10:34–35 separates "a father who is holy from an unclean son, or even a son who is holy from a pestilential father," and, "a mother who is holy from a daughter who is established in unnatural things, or even a daughter from a mother who was insane by means of them."[111]

Pestilence and disease are the final expressions of the ravages of sin on a community. Sins are "pestilential works"[112] that manifest themselves as disease in the corporate monastic body, spreading from limb to limb (or monk to monk) as a contagion. Shenoute compares the disease that "moves" among the "members of the body" to "snake poisons."[113] "Pestilential" people must be separated from the holy and pure.[114]

Finally, Shenoute sums up this section of *This Great House* by returning to the subject of the sermon itself: the necessity of keeping the monastery's church, or house of God, pure and holy. He again relies upon architectural motifs and revisits Ezekiel's wall. He equates the doomed structure to those who refuse to cast sinners out from the community: "The prophetic word is yesterday, it is today, and also it is every day until the consummation, since he (Ezekiel) says, 'Are not this wall and those who daub it the people who counsel and who guide and who urge us to leave unclean people in places of God, while they quarrel against those who say, "It is not fitting to leave them."'"[115] Like Ezekiel's wall, these monks are the weak point that will cause the collapse of the monastic congregation. With this, Shenoute ends the section of *This Great House* devoted to his various versions of the parable of the wheat and the weeds, and in doing so, he brings his monks back to the interplays of material and spiritual.

In exhorting his audience to keep themselves and their church holy and pure—to transform their "fleshly" selves and building into "spiritual" things, as he phrased it in *God Is Holy*—Shenoute turns to the virtues of ascetic renunciation. Staples of monastic life (celibacy, fasting, and obedience) will preserve their holiness. Here he clearly betrays the ascetic context of *Canon 7*. Celibacy and fasting trump marriage and the standard diet. Although the latter are "sweet," virginity and self-control (*enkrateia*) are sweeter.[116] The monks and monastery constitute the body of Christ, and it is this divine body to which they should turn their attentions, not the fleshly desires of this world.

In both *God Is Holy* and *This Great House*, Shenoute frequently condemns fornication. Citing the sanctity of the church as a reason for preserving their sexual purity, he writes, "Why have you become unclean when you live in the house of Christ with the one who has offered his body as a sacrifice . . . ?" He then bemoans the possibility that sexual transgressions and other sins might despoil this structure: "Woe to us. Because we have defiled ourselves and we have defiled all the earth including even the houses of God and his places. The earth was filled with adultery, fornication, rape, violence, every impiety, like these lands where every defilement that you can enumerate or that you can think of lives."[117] At times, Shenoute's rhetoric borrows heavily from the prophetic books of the Bible, making it difficult to determine whether Shenoute is exposing instances of monks breaking their vows of celibacy, or whether these denunciations function as rhetorical hyperbole in order to underscore sexual renunciation as a marker of monastic self-discipline. Nonetheless, sexual renunciation is clearly a fundamental imperative, according to Shenoute, and anyone who feels more concerned about other hardships should be ashamed. Shenoute berates those who fear violent barbarians more than God's retribution for fornication:

> If we speak the words to you God the almighty, "Do not give us into the hands of these nations who shed blood," then we act like someone who blasphemes. We

are people who gave ourselves to defilement for the commission of every unclean act. We filled the borders, we filled the cities and the villages and the roads crying out because of fear of barbarians, uttering, "Woe, woe"—some saying, "Because of my children," and some others saying, "Because of my parents and my siblings." Then where is the father, or where is the mother, or where is the sibling, or where is the person who weeps and who mourns because his daughter fornicated, and his son was impious, and his brother (was also)?[118]

Renunciation of the family accompanies sexual renunciation. Ties to biological family or sexual partners indicate a privileging of the things and the bonds of the world, the material, and the flesh over the things and the bonds of heaven, the divine, and the spirit. Leaving behind family and spouse is indeed a sacrifice, as Shenoute admits. Even Shenoute professes amazement at the many children, parents, husbands, and wives who have left behind those they love.[119] Yet, he insists, despite these difficulties, monks who pervert their calling, even those who have risen into the ranks of supervisors or house leaders in the monastery, will face condemnation by God. Their righteous peers will be "ashamed" of them for not loving God more than familial and sexual relationships.[120] Moreover, the more devoted monks will pray for everyone's steadfastness in renunciation, and they must condemn their fallen brethren. Otherwise, they will be judged alongside the sinners.[121]

Monks who turn their backs on their vows of celibacy will find all their other ascetic labors worthless at the final judgment. Their ascetic purity has been sullied, like an impure coin forged from precious metal.

For there are many people who do not know the quality of gold and silver—whether the metals are evil or polluted—and who are confident in them. . . . And if the necessity arrives at the time that they will all the more need them, then they will find that they are worthless. In this way, also, there are many people and many ones who will find their purity unclean when they are tested, and if their purity is unclean, their deeds also are unclean. Or if the silver that they gave deceitfully was reckoned as like a clay pot, why do those who commit these unnatural acts not know that their virginity is a clay jar and is not a virgin state? Rather, the jar is worth more than it because the jar is given for many uses many times in many works including the building of these great houses which are beautiful, of which we speak.[122]

Shenoute's comparison of a compromised virginity to a clay jar is telling. The jar, albeit irrefutably tied to the material, created world, nonetheless has greater redemptive value than does a flawed monk with an unvirginal virginity. The jar cultivates one of Shenoute's many "bodies" in these sermons—the house of God. The jar has at least turned its labors away from the things of the flesh and toward those of the divine in its attempt to perfect the body or building that houses the divine. Once again, the church building has become a metaphor for the monastic body: one can discipline and beautify the body in order to glorify God, or one can sully and defile it in order to please the flesh. Despite its base materiality, the clay jar has chosen between spirit and flesh, divine and material; the jar indeed holds the treasures of 2 Cor. 4:7, for it glorifies God.

Shenoute thus comes full circle, tying ascetic purity back to the church, arguing that monks should not look to the building for proof of God's favor. It is at this moment that he asks, "What person was ever righteous because of the beauty of the house and all of its construction . . . ? But if we guard the regulations and the laws of the Lord God which are in them, listening to them and reading them, we will be saved."[123] Obedience to God's laws equals obedience to the ascetic life. The physical structure of the church, while a symbol of spiritual redemption, provides in itself no proof such redemption. Only the ascetic renunciation outlined in the rules they vowed to obey can sanctify the building and the monks. "For every purity and every good exists in obedience. And every defilement and every wickedness exists in disobedience."[124]

In these sermons, Shenoute's advocacy of ascetic renunciation coupled with the ubiquitous purity and pollution language might suggest a strong sense of boundaries between the monks and nearby laity. The classical interpretation of purity codes in religious texts reads such language as a marker distinguishing high-status members within a particular group from that group's low-status members, or differentiating insider from outsider, fostering a strong group identity. In an example from late antique Europe, Peter Brown's reading of Ambrose of Milan's act to bar from his basilica emperors polluted by sin or tainted by "tolerance for pagans, heretics, and Jews" compares Ambrose's church to Mary's womb. For Ambrose, the building, like the womb of the virgin mother, forms a sanctuary "ringed by unbreakable frontiers," holding back the "intrusion" and "admixture" of the *saeculum*. Mary's purity, like the sacred walls of the basilica, marks the barrier between the sacred and the profane.[125] Although Shenoute contrasts those who commit defiling acts with those who successfully adhere to the ascetic lifestyle, Shenoute does not associate pollution with the laity, the *saeculum* outside the monastery or church, or the non-Christian world in *Canon 7*. Interpreting Shenoute's discourse of purity and pollution as establishing impenetrable boundaries between ascetics and nonascetics, or between the monastery and the world beyond its walls, is not the most compelling reading of the texts.

Rather, the reverse is the case, for perhaps only as few as two years after the church was constructed, the monastery served as a massive refu-

gee camp for nearby residents displaced by raiders from the south. Shenoute describes this experience in detail in several texts that were placed,
possibly by Shenoute himself, in *Canon 7*, alongside the sermons about
the construction of the church. Life in the monastery revolved around care
for the lay people—both Christians and non-Christians—who slept within
the monastery's walls, even alongside monks. *Canon 7* lists the amount of
food required to sustain the people and animals residing in the community, the number of doctors needed to care for the sick, and even the
money used as ransom for people captured by the invaders.[126] The reader
is overwhelmed by a sense of a space filled with very nonascetic and undisciplined bodies, vying for the attention of monks whom Shenoute presumably preferred be attending to God instead.

Today, Deir Anba Shenouda is annually transformed into a hostel for
visitors during the festival for Shenoute, which occurs during the entire
month of July. This modern influx of laity may provide a sensory aid for
imagining and understanding the tremendous impact the influx of refugees must have had on the experience of the space and the daily life in the
monastery over fifteen hundred years ago. Today, a tent city is erected on
the monastery's grounds and at least ten thousand Coptic Christians make
their pilgrimage at the height of the festival, bringing with them children
and animals, and even products for sale. Coptic pilgrims camp in the monastery's paths, orchard, and even inside the sanctuary of the ancient
church. Tents for shelter as well as commerce are erected in the nave.
Although the ancient and modern events cannot be equated, the tightly
packed tents, the amount of space and resources dedicated to feeding the
visitors, and the sight of people living in almost every corner of the monastery are evocative of Shenoute's textual descriptions of the monastery's
transformation into a place of refuge for the laity of his period.[127]

Yet, Shenoute did not consider the monastery polluted by this teeming mass of people who were most certainly *not* monks. As Emmel has so
aptly put it, the monks were "caring for the needs of the refugees' bodies
out of concern for the needs of their souls," and thus should be thankful
for all things, whether bodily or spiritual, that God has provided for this
task.[128] And here Emmel points to what must be the crux of the matter
for Shenoute—that everything the monks do for the refugees ultimately
is about preserving the community of God. In the ascetic context, that
community is envisioned primarily as the body of Christ represented by
the monastery and its church, but the community can be extended to
include those who are not monks.

Given that such a socially disruptive event as the refugee crisis is not
categorized as polluting or even dangerous for the monastery, the greater

threat to the monks' salvation and to the church building comes from the monks themselves, from those who break their vows by placing material concerns (such as the adornment of the church or sexual desire) before spiritual ones (such as prayer and obedience to God). Such monks drive God out of his house and sever the monastery from the body of Christ. The church building thus functions as a potent symbol of Shenoute's theology of the monastic life, emphasizing the interconnectedness and interdependence of asceticism at Deir Anba Shenouda.

In no other sources discovered thus far from late antiquity does a monastic leader use a church building to construct and enforce such an overarching principle of ascetic renunciation. Building projects receive attention in ascetic sources, but rarely do they serve as a moment for theological reflection on the nature of the *communal* ascetic life. Those few sources that juxtapose ascetic piety with building projects are exceedingly brief or produce different discourses of ascetic renunciation.

Ascetic Aesthetics in Late Antiquity: Shenoute, Paulinus, and the Pachomian Monasteries

Though the argumentation in *Canon 7* is unique, Shenoute was not alone in constructing a particular ascetic identity and ideology in constructing a church in late antiquity. Two other writers in Shenoute's lifetime interpreted the construction of a church in an ascetic context.[129] In Nola, Italy, the Latin author Paulinus renovated the town's old church and constructed a *Basilica Nova* to honor the local saint, Felix. In Egypt, a source from the Pachomian monasteries contains a brief passage about the small church at Pbow. Years later, a panegyric to the Pachomian abbot Victor (pseudonymously attributed to bishop Timothy of Alexandria) purports to celebrate the dedication of a church at Pbow. Paulinus provides an illuminating foil to Shenoute, for his construction projects endeavored to recast the aristocratic Roman tradition of patronage by means of monumental building projects into an ascetic obligation of almsgiving. Paulinus's architectural ventures and his writings about them constitute the sources closest to Shenoute's *Canon 7* and new church in late antiquity. Like Shenoute, Paulinus used the monuments to define and defend his ideology of the ascetic life. Yet, Paulinus and Shenoute diverged in their definitions of the act of ascetic renunciation and in their use of their buildings as symbols of that act.

It is difficult to imagine two fifth-century Christian authors located in more disparate social worlds than Paulinus and Shenoute. Born in Bordeaux in the 350s, a young Paulinus traveled in the elite circles of Roman senatorial families and served as the governor of Campania in Italy before returning to Bordeaux due to the political turmoil facing the western empire after the death of the emperor Gratian.[130] Baptized as an adult, Paulinus turned increasingly toward asceticism in the 380s and 390s. He ultimately was ordained as a priest and declared his devotion to the ascetic life.[131] In 395, Paulinus moved back to Italy, embarking on a series of building projects dedicated to Saint Felix of Nola. The obvious differences between Shenoute and Paulinus in wealth, social status, and geography are reflected in the cultural production of the two men, whose material monuments to ascetic piety functioned to produce radically different visions of the ascetic life.

One feature that distinguishes Paulinus's building projects from the church of Deir Anba Shenouda is that Paulinus funded the construction from his own personal wealth. The structures formed the axis of Paulinus's ascetic theology of "wealth turned redemptive," as coined by Dennis Trout.[132] Like the texts of *Canon 7*, Paulinus's *Epistle 32*, *Carmen 27*, and *Carmen 28* describe not only the material measures and adornments of his buildings, but also his own, his community's, and his God's relationship to them. Paulinus, however, devotes many more words than Shenoute to the monuments' architectural elements. He details their paintings, archways, columns, marble, inscriptions, mosaics, and relics.[133] The elaborate adornments testify to the magnitude of their donor's beneficence. They speak from a sensibility that the material testimony to God's splendor should always be embraced. The buildings' magnificence holds spiritual significance, for Paulinus's renovations represent the rebirth of the self through Christ.[134] In building or restoring these monuments, Paulinus evokes his own rebirth into asceticism.

Paulinus's discussion of sin is brief but vivid.[135] He shares with Shenoute a conviction that his buildings (despite their grandeur) represent a form of ascetic renunciation. The structures should inspire people to "abolish those things which are behind and to keep the mind tensely directed to what God will do, to cover bygone cares with suitable oblivion, and to bring care for the heavenly realms into our soul, . . . and to die to human troubles and to the morals of this world in the spirit." Body and soul must become "shining" and "clean" from the "muddy actions of our earthly form."[136] The new buildings stir Paulinus to ask how he can transform himself, as he has transformed the basilica, into "a suitable abode for Christ."[137] As in Shenoute's monastery, the church building should serve as a reminder of the true ascetic goal. Yet Paulinus rarely mentions the standard practices of renunciation, such as celibacy, fasting,

and poverty in these texts.[138] As Trout has demonstrated, the purpose of
Paulinus's literary and architectural constructions was not to promote obedience to a monastic rule, but to produce an ascetic reconfiguration of the
tradition of Roman patronage. It is an elite justification of Paulinus's own
refusal to renounce all of his wealth. While Shenoute's monks were required to relinquish their earthly assets upon entering the monastery, Paulinus received admonishments from Jerome and other colleagues for not
giving up his wealth as he embraced asceticism.[139] For Paulinus, wealth,
used properly, could be redemptive. Trout writes, "On the one hand,
riches bestowed on Christ through the medium of his saints, like those
used . . . to succor the poor, were cleansed of their debilitating taint.
Church building thus emerged as another mode of the appropriate use of
wealth motivated by a complex sense of *caritas*, but it was one that, like
Paulinus' conception of almsgiving, kept the benefactor very much at the
center of attention."[140] Paulinus decreed the sanctuaries of Felix, and even
the spirit of Felix himself, to be like his own house. Paulinus's basilica,
then, was not a representative of the social body that honored Felix in
Nola, but a monument to a "salvation economics" that was engineered
by Paulinus and that "confirmed and enhanced" his own social status as
community benefactor.[141]

Ironically, the ascetic and architectural aesthetics of Shenoute and
Paulinus do share an important ideological element. Ideologies often serve
to enhance or to mask social differences within a particular social body. In
Shenoute's monastery, *Canon 7* and its centerpiece function to eliminate
difference: despite Shenoute's use of the rhetoric of pollution to mark
sinful monks, he promotes a vision of monasticism in which all members
of the social body should operate smoothly and indistinguishably in their
collective obedience to the monastic rules. Together, the monks form a
homogenized, unified whole, represented by the church that they have
constructed. The elimination of distinctions between monks serves, however, to emphasize the particular role Shenoute plays in the monastic social
body: he is its head, its architect, and its prophet. The erasure of difference
is executed in the name of the benefit of the community, in that removal
of sin necessitates such an erasure. But the erasure of difference also ele-
vates the eraser into a position of extreme privilege. Similarly, Paulinus's
own architectural projects, performed as acts of *caritas* and benefaction
for Nola and as acts of piety to God, as Trout argues, maintain Paulinus's
status as a member of the privileged, Latin social elite and position him as
a new Christian patron for his community.

The two other literary examples of ascetic, architectural theologies
in late antiquity come from a social and cultural milieu much closer to

Shenoute's: the Pachomian monastery of Pbow. Unfortunately, due to the extremely brief nature of the first source and the extremely late date of the second, they are not as revealing as Paulinus's writings.

The first is a section of the Pachomian *Paralipomena*, a collection of traditions about Pachomius. The *Paralipomena* date to a period after Pachomius's death, the late fourth through fifth centuries—a time roughly parallel to Shenoute's lifespan. The relevant passage describes the renowned monk's supervision of the construction of an "oratory," which may be the small basilica whose remains have been found at the archaeological site of Pbow.[142] Due to the brevity of the passage, it is worth quoting in its entirety:

> The blessed Pachomius built an oratory and he made porticos for it and set up pillars of bricks, and he furnished it very well. He was pleased with the work, because he had built it well. Then he thought that it was through a diabolic activity that he was marveling at the beauty of the house. Therefore, he took ropes and tied them to the pillars; then he made a prayer in his heart, ordered the brothers to pull and bend all the pillars so they remained crooked. And he said to the brothers, "I pray you, brothers, do not make great efforts to adorn the work of your hands. But whatever may enter into the work of each one of you by the grace of Christ and from his gift, take great care that your mind may not stumble through the praise given to the art, and become a prey to the devil."[143]

Two features of this passage merit its consideration alongside the more substantive works of Paulinus and Shenoute. It has also been associated with a possibly authentic architectural monument. Moreover, it reveals a shared element in the ascetic ideologies of the Pachomian and Shenoutean traditions.

This passage has traditionally been read through the lens of archaeological history. James Goehring links this text to the site of the Pachomian monastery of Pbow in part due to the archaeological evidence: preliminary excavations have revealed the northern wall of the oldest basilica to be crooked.[144] The basilica likely dates to the mid-fourth century, possibly even during Pachomius's lifetime.[145] The dating of the church and its north wall has rendered this citation a potentially "authentic" piece of the Pachomian legends.[146] As Derwas Chitty proposed, and as Goehring has concurred, "This sounds like an attempt to explain the actual crookedness of a church the writer knew, due, in fact, to inadequate foundations, faulty material, or inexpert building."[147]

For the literary and social historian this strand of the Pachomian tradition is striking because it resonates with the themes in Shenoute's *Canon 7*. Generically, the two sources differ. One is comprised of sermons preached around the time of the construction of the structure under discussion; the other is one small legendary fragment in a collection of hagiographical traditions. Nonetheless, both sources were read and heard by their monastic audiences for their spiritual edification, and similarities in their ascetic ideologies should not be ignored. The Pachomian story promotes a form of ascetic contemplation that resembles Shenoute's: "the beauty of the house" cannot be regarded simply as a monument to the magnificence of God. It also serves as a potential trap for ascetics who believe themselves to be "marveling" at a holy thing but who really marvel at a work of their own hands. Instead of contemplating God—the reason for constructing an oratory or church—the monks praise a work of human creation. The monks engage in an egregious act of pride in admiring their own work. Pachomius resolves the paradox by mutilating the building so that monks will not be drawn into the devil's trap by the structure's beauty. The literary Pachomius expresses concerns similar to Shenoute's warnings about the dangers of attending to material adornments instead of spiritual edification. The anecdote reveals that the Pachomian communities wrestled with the same tensions between the material and the spiritual that Shenoute articulated. It also highlights a rift between Paulinus of Nola and his Egyptian peers: in Paulinus's eyes, his buildings housed neither theological paradoxes nor ascetic impediments.

The last literary source with parallels to *Canon 7* is a panegyric to Pachomius and to Victor, general abbot of the Pachomian monasteries in the early to mid-fifth century. It is pseudonymously attributed to bishop Timothy of Alexandria.[148] Though the text professes to have been delivered in the second half of the fifth century at the dedication of the large basilica at Pbow, it probably dates to the sixth century. It was neither written nor preached by Timothy.[149] Nonetheless, its professed genre and context situate it within this small pool of similar sources.

The panegyric narrates the construction of a church at Pbow, positioning Victor as the central character. The emperor instructs Victor and Shenoute to attend the Council of Ephesus (431) with Cyril of Alexandria. Victor learns from his mother, a fellow monk who had concealed her identity from Victor until his departure for Ephesus, that his father is none other than emperor Theodosius II.[150] On the way to the council, they stop in Constantinople where Victor reunites with his father and receives a promise of imperial support for his monasteries as well as imperial opposition to heretics such as Nestorius. Theodosius commits farmland and resources to Victor in order to build a new church as a fortress against the "barbarians."[151] Upon Victor's return, all the cities of Egypt assist him with the foundation of the church.[152] Construction, however, halts upon the death of Theodosius II and does not resume until after Victor's death, under the leadership of abbot Martyrius and the support of emperor Leo I.[153] The remainder of the text describes the consecration of the church, which occurred after Martyrius's death and was purportedly attended by no fewer than 880 bishops, 6000 monks from Pbow, 2300 monks from other monasteries, plus assorted laity.[154] The night before the ceremony, Timothy witnesses Jesus consecrating the church, and the next day Jesus distributes the eucharist to the gathering.[155]

Amidst the storytelling, "Timothy" inserts a few hortatory remarks entreating his audience to the "pure" ascetic life.[156] The model ascetic life for "Timothy," however, is devoted more to discerning heresy from orthodoxy than to encouraging obedience to the monastic rules. In this way, this text adheres to a trend seen in other later Pachomian literature to ally the monastery with the bishopric of Alexandria and its theological positions.[157] The author uses the building not as an opportunity to expound on the nature of the communal ascetic life but rather as a forum to praise individual and now "orthodox" exemplars—Pachomius and Victor. The building itself holds little symbolic relevance beyond an "earthly Jerusalem" parallel to the "heavenly Jerusalem."[158] The building symbolizes not the renunciation of the flesh but rather the renunciation of heresy.

The texts and buildings examined here highlight the intensely aesthetic nature of the experience of asceticism. All call attention to the interplay between ritual and the experience of physical space. The emphasis on the visual—be it in the details of the structures of the buildings, or in the numbers and kinds of people gathering in the buildings, or in the prophetic images of the buildings' destruction or salvation—speaks to an aesthetic sensibility described by Catherine Conybeare in her treatment of Paulinus. Church paintings, and one might add, the church itself, "should nourish the mind for reflection."[159] The visual aspects of the churches as well as the texts about them are designed to spark a specific "moral response" in the viewer and reader.[160] In the case of Paulinus, Shenoute, and the *Paralipomena*'s Pachomius, the architectural and artistic space should urge the mind to reflect upon the path to salvation by means of ascetic renunciation. In all four of these examples, the buildings acted in the same manner that Elizabeth Bolman has argued early monastic art functioned: they "point to something beyond them, to something beyond the words and . . . walls."[161]

For Paulinus, seeing these buildings, with their vibrant paintings and mosaics and their richly decorated ceilings and floors, inspired an act of ascetic mimesis. Paulinus sought to emulate the buildings themselves, to become as spiritually beautiful as the buildings were physically beautiful.

He articulated an ascetic aesthetic described by Bolman in her study of much simpler Egyptian cells: "Not only did these ascetics learn to see spiritual beings, they learned to become like them, and indeed to become them."[162] Paulinus hoped that those who entered his basilicas would become like the saints depicted on their walls and like the basilicas themselves—suitable abodes for Christ. The biggest obstacle Paulinus found was neither pride nor the glorification of material objects. Rather, he feared that people would not understand the pictures, and thus provided captions to guide the viewer in interpreting them.[163]

In the pseudo-Timothy panegyric, by contrast, the actual building fades into the background. It serves mainly as an opportunity to tout the orthodoxy of the Pachomian monastic tradition. The construction of the building is retroactively imbued with theological significance. The support it garners from emperors, the crowds of officials who attend its consecration, and even its mere existence, all prove the truth of a specific theological agenda, but one that could be seen as tangential to the project of ascetic renunciation per se. The church legitimates a particular brand of asceticism—Pachomian—but the structure provides little commentary on or symbolism for the acts of renunciation that the monks engage.

For both Shenoute and the *Paralipomena*'s Pachomius, however, the visual and physical experience of the church buildings is more complex. The buildings are indeed "material traces of spiritual work" that involved viewing an architectural exemplar.[164] Shenoute in particular directed the monks to construct more than a new building in which to pray; he ordered them to create for themselves a new, material symbol of the monastic life he wished his monks to enact. Yet, for both Shenoute and Pachomius, the impulse to imitate this exemplar was tempered by the monastic imperative to squelch both individual pride and the glorification of the created world. The churches exemplified ascetic renunciation in part because of their fragility. Pachomius's oratory stands flawed in perpetuity as a reminder of the fragility and vulnerability of human embodied existence.

Likewise, in the backdrop to Shenoute's church lie visions of the destruction of other houses and communities of God. Shenoute's church is also an object of mimesis, in that like Paulinus, Shenoute urged the monks to make themselves along with the building into suitable abodes for Christ. The structure becomes the nexus of a four-part relationship between the ascetic individual, the community, the building, and God. As a place of worship, it connects the monks to each other. As a house of God, it unites the monks with Christ. It is the earthly and material embodiment of the dwelling place of God. For Shenoute, only ascetic renunciation can make the monk worthy of entering the building. Shenoute's church, and perhaps Pachomius's oratory, provides no proof of righteousness. The building's physical beauty is insignificant in comparison to what should be the spiritual beauty of the monks that tend to it and worship in it. It serves as a model for the bodily discipline of the monk and becomes the site of ascetic transformation.

The church building thus proves to be a powerful symbol for late antique authors who sought to express their particular visions of asceticism both textually and architecturally. Just as these writers articulated different understandings of what renunciation entailed and signified, so too did they diverge in their interpretations of the buildings they constructed. For all, however, the embodied experience of living and worshipping in a consecrated physical space enriched their representations of the ascetic life. For Shenoute, in particular, this ascetic theology of sacred architecture is but one piece of his ideology of the monastic life. His writings in *Canon 7* promote the same monastic ideology as in many of his other writings: an understanding of the monastic community itself as an ascetic body, an ascetic subjectivity strongly informed by purity codes, a notion of salvation as interdependent and relational among the members of the corporate monastic body, the repression of differences in members of the social body, and the elevation of Shenoute as the prophetic leader and head of the monastic body.

Defending the Sanctity of the Body:
Shenoute on the Resurrection

SHENOUTE'S LETTERS, RULES, AND SERMONS to monks are suffused with the sense that the human body was a problematic site for the ascetic Christian. Throughout the *Canons*, he writes of the desires, impulses, and activities that monks experienced in the human body as sources of deeply polluting sin, sin that rendered both monk and monastery condemned before God. Just as the monastery was one body in Christ, the members of the community were members of Christ's body. In the same way, the church building was the home for the Holy Spirit, and Christ would abandon the building should it be polluted by the abominations of its members. Yet, the human body was also the site of religious transformation and potential holiness for Shenoute. Through the rituals of embodied monastic existence—such as prayer, work, fasting, and chastity—the monks demonstrated their devotion to God.

As David Brakke has recently demonstrated, Egyptian ascetic writers for generations after Shenoute continued to express a deep ambivalence about the human body.[1] Brakke describes an internal conflict on the part of monks who on the one hand found the body to be the primary source of sinful corruption, yet who on the other hand had to concede to the orthodox church's stance regarding the inherent goodness of the human body. Antiheretical campaigns in Egypt were waged against monks who were perceived to be denigrating the body through their ascetic interpretations of the writings of the third-century theologian Origen. These Origenists were indicted for disavowing God's creation of the human body, denying the reality of a bodily resurrection, and crafting an ascetic theology based on the unique divinity of the soul.[2] Monks who wished to avoid charges of heresy had to temper their notions about the inherent dangers of the body. Brakke writes, "While language that associates bodilessness with purity and corporeality with defilement comes easily to these preachers, the needs of their lay audience and the dangers of appearing Origenist demand a moderation of this privileging of the soul."[3] Some of this "typical" Egyptian ascetic "ambivalence about the body" exists in Shenoute's work as well.

Admittedly, Shenoute spends little if any time overtly praising the body in his sermons and letters to the members of his monastery. Despite his profound anxiety about the body's desires and susceptibility to sin, he nonetheless maintains in the *Canons* that the body does not sin without the aid of the soul.[4] In *Canon 7*, for example, Shenoute consistently asserts that inner purity—purity of the soul—is paramount for monks, and he insists that material and corporeal corruption is only an expression of a monk's bankrupt spiritual state. For Shenoute the ascetic goal is to purify both body and soul. Consequently, it should be no surprise that Shenoute passionately defends the sanctity of the body, and particularly the truth of the bodily resurrection, in texts directed to monks and laity. While for Shenoute the body is a site of tremendous potential hazards to the spirit, it is also the site of the glorious and ultimate spiritual transformation. The very bodies he urges his monks to purify through ascetic discipline will, after the final judgment, either live joyously with Christ or experience the physical torments of hell, depending on the success of their ascetic endeavors.

Shenoute indeed prevails as the most prominent Coptic author to defend the sanctity of the body. Two recent works have drawn attention to Shenoute's role in the anti-Origenist debates about the nature of the resurrected human body. Tito Orlandi's publication of a large portion of one of Shenoute's antiheretical treatises reveals Shenoute to have positioned himself squarely in the midst of broader fourth- and fifth-century debates about Origenism.[5] Of particular concern in the Egyptian context of the Origenist controversy were the contentions by some monks that God did not create the body simultaneously with the soul, and that the resurrection after death would be a spiritual one or a resurrection of the soul alone—not the body. Elizabeth Clark points to Shenoute's writings as proof of the extensive reach of both the Origenist ascetic practices modeled after the monasticism of Evagrius Ponticus and the anti-Origenist fervor of "orthodox" clergy.[6] Like many other Egyptian monks of his own and later periods, Shenoute found himself at the receiving end of a variety of missives from his ecclesiastical superiors regarding the dangers of heretical Christians who might seek refuge in nearby monastic cells. Most notably, bishop of Alexandria Dioscorus corresponded with Shenoute about the influence of an Origenist monk in upper Egypt, and Shenoute received the festal letter of 401 from bishop of Alexandria Theophilus regarding the heretical nature of Origenism.[7]

Origenism was only one of a number of theological controversies

concerning embodiment that were swirling around the Mediterranean
during Shenoute's lifetime. Disagreements over the relationship between
the human, embodied aspect of Jesus Christ and his status as the divine
son of God fractured the church. "Orthodox" and Melitian Christians
argued over the veneration of relics, the corporeal remains of martyrs. Debate raged in the Latin-speaking world over the proposition that sin had
been embedded within the very fabric of human, embodied existence since
the original sin of Adam and Eve. In each of these controversies, the meaning of embodied existence was deeply contested. Into this theological
maelstrom stepped Shenoute. His writings show a keen awareness of a
number of these disputes and a deep, personal investment in more than
one.

For the most part, Shenoute conforms to the theological doctrines
promoted by the bishop of Alexandria. His adherence to the Alexandrian
"orthodox" view of the body, however, stretched well beyond mere repe-
tition of episcopal talking points. The centrality of the body in the ascetic
theology Shenoute developed in the *Canons* finds expression in the more
public sermons and treatises in the *Discourses* in the form of a theology of
the resurrection that places belief in the resurrection of the body at the
center of Shenoute's definition of the Christian faith. In the *Canons*, Shenoute insists that monks who failed to discipline their bodies and souls
through proper *askesis* would suffer grievously in their afterlife. In the *Discourses*, Shenoute develops a more sophisticated theology of the resurrected body in the context of a far-reaching antiheretical and antipagan
polemic. He does not limit his condemnations to Origenists alone.

Shenoute defends the sanctity of the body and the resurrection of
the body against opponents he labels both pagans and heretics, including
Melitians, Arians, Manichaeans, Origenists, and Nestorians.[8] This chapter
begins by examining how Shenoute's theological writings on embodiment
rhetorically conflate pagans and heretics and what ideological purposes
that conflation serves. The chapter then presents three arguments that
form the framework of Shenoute's defense of the body in the *Discourses*.
First, Shenoute insists upon the truth of the full fleshly incarnation of Jesus
the son of God and his subsequent bodily resurrection from the dead.
Second, he contends that Jesus' resurrection provides the foundation for
Christians' faith in their own bodily resurrection. Finally, Christians who
rise above sin in their earthly lives prefigure their future bodily resurrection
from death. Before examining Shenoute's theological arguments in more
detail, however, it is necessary to review the sources in which his writings
on embodiment are found.

Shenoute's Writings on Embodiment in the *Discourses*

At least four of Shenoute's sermons or treatises address the topic of the resurrection body.[9] While the exact sociohistorical context for most of these texts remains uncertain, at least two are found in volumes of Shenoute's *Discourses*—that portion of Shenoute's corpus written for a mixed audience of monks, lay Christians, church officials, and possibly even non-Christians.[10] Unfortunately, the dating of the texts in the *Discourses* is problematic. Unlike much of the *Canons*, the texts of the *Discourses* have not been proven to follow a roughly chronological order. The sources for this chapter are presented in the order in which they appear in the *Discourses*.

The first sermon, known by its incipit, *The Lord Thundered*, chastises both pagans and heretics in large part because of their disbelief in both the resurrection of Jesus and the bodily resurrection of all from the dead. It appears in volume four of the *Discourses*.[11] It is one of only two of the four sources with a clearly established social context. The scribal preface reads, "These are the words that Shenoute spoke in an instruction during the days when he came to Antinoou (Antinoopolis) at the time that the priests who serve idols accused the Christians, whom they brought there to the squadron of soldiers of the current commander when they (the Christians) destroyed the temple in Pneueit."[12] Although the rest of *The Lord Thundered* contains no other information about either the destruction of the pagan temple or Shenoute's testimony in Antinoopolis, some have hypothesized that Shenoute himself was involved in the devastation of this temple.[13] The sermon is written in a prophetic style, framed by an account of God creating the world in a cataclysmic, thunderous moment at the beginning of the text and a description of God's judgment over unbelieving Jews and pagans at the end.[14] Interestingly, in a sermon delivered presumably in defense of Christian anti*pagan* activities, Shenoute takes aim at a variety of opponents of what he regards as the "orthodox" Christian faith. He launches a broad invective against Jews, philosophers, Manichaeans, and heretics in addition to pagans. He specifically targets those who deny Jesus Christ's birth from the virgin Mary,[15] who worship idols or multiple gods,[16] who deny the bodily resurrection of the dead,[17] or deny Jesus Christ's divinity.[18] All of these charges easily could apply to non-Christians, especially given the context of this sermon's delivery. Yet Shenoute's primary concern is people who claim to be Christians and nonetheless profess such beliefs. They share condemnation with pagans precisely because of the intolerable nature of these doctrines.

The second source is one of Shenoute's most famous texts, the so-

called anti-Origenist treatise now known as *I Am Amazed*.[19] Emmel has
suggested that it was written originally not as a sermon but as an antiheretical instruction or treatise. It is difficult to determine the precise mo-
tivation for the composition of the text. Since Shenoute quotes
Theophilus's sixteenth festal letter condemning Origenism, apparently in
its entirety, many scholars speculate that Shenoute wrote *I Am Amazed*
somehow in connection to the circulation of the letter against Origenism
written by bishop of Alexandria Dioscorus, between 444 and 451.[20] Shenoute also mentions the city of Ephesus and the person of Nestorius, who
was condemned as a heretic at the Council of Ephesus in 431.[21] Emmel
suggests a date somewhat late in Shenoute's life, probably circa 445.[22]
Building on Orlandi's characterization of *I Am Amazed* as an anti-Origenist
treatise, Clark has identified the primary object of Shenoute's wrath here
as Gnosticizing Origenists upholding beliefs similar to those of the Origenist monastic writer Evagrius.[23] As Clark has demonstrated, some of the
doctrines mentioned by Shenoute bear the hallmarks of a philosophical
and theological tradition that has often been labeled "Gnostic" in modern
scholarship: the existence of a plurality of worlds, the notion of Jesus as an
angel, the belief that Mary did not conceive Jesus.[24] It bears remembering,
however, that Shenoute himself brands his adversaries with a variety of
labels: generic heretics,[25] Melitians,[26] Origen and his supporters,[27] pagans
(*nhellēn*),[28] and Nestorius.[29] Shenoute also brandishes the words of Athanasius of Alexandria in addition to those of Theophilus to support his
positions.

   The third text under consideration appears only in two codices, codices which belong neither to the *Canons* nor the *Discourses*, though it is
likely that the work originally belonged in a volume of the *Discourses*.[30] In
Who Speaks Through the Prophet, Shenoute presents words of "light" to
counter "dark words of the pagans and every heretic."[31] Almost all of the
extant fragments are devoted to the resurrection of Jesus and the resurrection of the body. One brief section addresses people who insist that John
the Baptist did not recognize Jesus as the Christ.[32] The original sociohistorical context for this text remains elusive, as does the date of its composition.

   One extremely fragmentary text, which has yet to be placed within a
specific volume of the *Canons*, *Discourses*, or lectionaries from Deir Anba
Shenouda, also discusses the resurrection of the body at length. The incipit
has been lost, and I will refer to it by Emmel's designation, *Acephalous
Work Number Five* (hereafter, *A5*). The extant fragments all urge Christians to remain steadfast in the face of persecution or martyrdom.[33] In *A5*,
Shenoute reminds his audience of the inevitable sufferings and persecu-

tions of Christians in this world, and he reassures them that all martyrs, including those who have been decapitated, who have been torn limb from limb, or who have had their eyes plucked out, will rise again in a whole body.

One of the most intriguing features of those texts in which Shenoute actually names the people against whom he writes is precisely the list of names itself. *I Am Amazed* has been labeled an antiheretical treatise. Given its social context, one would expect Shenoute to address primarily pagans in *The Lord Thundered*. Yet, in *The Lord Thundered*, *I Am Amazed*, and *Who Speaks Through the Holy Prophet*, Shenoute condemns pagans and heretics alike. Shenoute's critique of both groups contains an impassioned defense of the goodness and divine origin of the human body. Indeed, Shenoute brands as pagans those heretics whom he deems to have forsaken this central premise.

Heretics as Pagans and Pagans as Heretics

In the three antiheretical texts under consideration in this book, Shenoute discusses at length the beliefs and practices of both heretics (*nhairetikos*) and pagans (*nhellēn*), often in reference to their views on theological issues concerning embodiment. For example, in *Who Speaks Through the Prophet*, which concerns "false" doctrines about Jesus and the resurrection, Shenoute explicitly addresses both *hellenes* and heretics.[34] Although the term *hellene* usually refers to pagans in late antique Christian writings, at times Shenoute seems to ascribe to his *hellenes* identifiably Christian beliefs and religious practices.[35] Additionally, he refers to heretics or to doctrines deemed heretical by the "orthodox" church in passages that also mention "pagans." Pagans are even called heretics, and heretics are sometimes identified with "pagans."

Considering the limited scope of Shenoutean scholarship thus far, a substantial amount of ink has been spilled attempting to determine precisely who Shenoute's *hellenes* are, in an effort to determine the audience and social context of the sermons. Scholarship usually has addressed these elusive "pagans" without tending to the "heretics" that inhabit some of the very same texts. One hypothesis posits that Shenoute's *hellenes* are upper-class hellenized Egyptians, regardless of their religion.[36] Another scholar concludes that they are people who might have been identified as Christians but "lived as those within the urban patronage system had lived since the Ptolemies" and "maintained behaviors appropriate to the pre-Christian empire," including participating in traditional Egyptian cultic activities.[37] Both positions concede that Shenoute's "pagans" might have considered themselves Christians.

David Frankfurter has interpreted Shenoute's references to *hellenes* as evidence for economic conflicts between two social groups in Upper Egypt—conflicts that Shenoute used to his own political advantage as he consolidated his authority and influence in Middle and Upper Egypt. Shenoute, Frankfurter argues, rhetorically positions wealthy landlords in his region as "pagan" and oppressive in opposition to Christians, whom he presents as poor and oppressed, and with whom he would like the Egyptian peasant class to identify.[38] Shenoute thus uses religion to play the two socially and economically distinct groups against each other and to build his own base of support as a political and religious leader. Frankfurter concludes that Shenoute's rhetoric against traditional Egyptian religion strives to convince local Egyptians to shift their allegiances away from their traditional patrons—the often pagan landlords—to Christian patrons, like Shenoute. Shenoute's sermons against *hellenes* and polytheistic Egyptian religion "functioned as a rhetorical means of convincing a peasant audience of the appropriateness, indeed the protective power, of Christianity through identifying traditional religion exclusively with the people who own the land and patronize the culture (and, to be sure, would occasionally oppress them)."[39] Central to his argument is a passage in *The Lord Thundered*, in which Shenoute describes and condemns the worship of stone, wood, clay, silver, or gold idols, or the heavenly bodies such as the sun and moon, or even animals such as crocodiles.[40] Frankfurter reads *The Lord Thundered* alongside Shenoute's most famous sermon against pagan religiosity, *Not Because a Fox Barks*, in which "Shenoute berates his nemesis Gesios, a local noble," whose home Shenoute raids because it contains a pagan temple or altar.[41]

Frankfurter's compelling reconstruction of the political conflicts and maneuverings in Shenoute's Panopolite nome does not address one important aspect of Shenoute's discourse: the antiheretical rhetoric in *The Lord Thundered*, which appears in and around the passages decrying traditional polytheistic religion. Just prior to the excerpts in which Shenoute describes people who worship a variety of "idols," he writes, "Woe to a pagan or a Jew or any other heresy." And in the midst of his anti-idolatry polemic, he writes, "And every heretic who serves and who worships many gods is unbelieving in him. They are godless ones who abandoned God who created them."[42] The socioeconomic interpretation of Shenoute's rhetoric with its accompanying model of local religious conflict sidesteps the role heresy plays in his rhetoric. Shenoute here casts pagans as heretics and heretics as polytheists. The content of Shenoute's heresiology will be addressed in greater detail later in this chapter, but for now it is sufficient to note that it is inextricably intertwined with an antipagan polemic. In these nonascetic texts, we see Shenoute's efforts to impose a rigorous theological and ideological discipline on the people of Middle and Upper Egypt, a discipline that excises heterodox Christianity and traditional polytheism alike. Like Shenoute's heresiological work, the controversy over "idol worshipping" engages theological questions of embodiment, namely how divinity takes material or corporeal form. Despite efforts to reconfigure the Roman Empire as a Christian empire, the worship of traditional Greco-Roman and Egyptian gods continued, and these deities often took corporeal forms, forms denounced as "idols" by Christians who argued that God becomes corporeal only in Jesus Christ.

The slippage between Shenoute's use of the labels "heretic" and "pagan" suggests that perhaps religious identity in late antique Egypt was much more fluid than these monikers imply. Although Shenoute uses highly charged labels to stigmatize people who challenge him or disagree with him, his rather flexible application of the labels exposes a disjuncture between the signifier (the term *hellenes*) and the signified (polytheists). In *The Lord Thundered*, Shenoute quotes a slogan he attributes to one of his opponents, a man who has been identified by some scholars as the aforementioned wealthy landowner, Gesios. Gesios is referenced in Shenoute's *vita* as well as several of Shenoute's own writings. The quotation from Shenoute's own writings in the *Discourses* reads, "But the one who says that Jesus the son of God is not divine in the way that this pestilential son spoke, might not his tongue be bound to the toes of his feet on the day of his need and he be cast into the depth of hell and Nun swallow him."[43] The slogan Shenoute attributes to this rival—that "Jesus the son of God is not divine"—evokes the language of the Trinitarian or Christological debates of the era as much as it references the continuing conflict between Christians and pagans.[44] Although Jesus's status as a divine figure/son of God/son of a god was contested by pagans well into the fifth century, the "orthodox" Christians also accused "heretics," such as the Arians and Nestorians, of contending that Jesus was not divine.[45] This slogan has traditionally been interpreted as a quote from an unambiguous pagan who was referencing polytheism, since the *vita* also reports that Shenoute uttered this very curse against the wealthy Gesios. According to the hagiographical account, after Gesios's death, Shenoute then had a vision of Gesios in hell with his tongue tied to his toe.[46] Moreover, because of Shenoute's own account of destroying Gesios's pagan ritual objects, Gesios and this slogan, until recently, have not been presumed to have been anything but unmistakeably polytheistic. As I have proposed, the slogan may evoke heretical (or intra-Christian) discourses as well as pagan anti-Christian ones. Additionally, Emmel's recent work on Gesios has confirmed the fluidity and complexity of "pagan" and "Christian" identities, for he has posited that Shenoute's Gesios is Flavius Aelius Gessius, a provincial governor in the Thebaid who might have been what Emmel has termed a "crypto-pagan"—someone who publicly "passes" as a Christian but privately keeps to traditional pagan cultic practices. Shenoute's raid on Gesios's altar may have served to expose Gesios's continuing worship of traditional deities, despite a professed allegiance to the monotheistic religion of Christianity.[47]

Although it is difficult to nail down Gesios's own understanding of his religious identity, the interweaving references to traditional polytheists and heretical Christians in *The Lord Thundered* and the ambiguity of the slogan Shenoute quotes suggest that Shenoute is attempting imposing a theological discipline on a social world in which religious identity is not so easily sorted or classified into mutually exclusive categories. In the texts examined in this chapter, Shenoute rhetorically groups "pagans" together with heretics. Some of these pagans seem to possess a Christian self-identity, hold recognizably Christian beliefs, or follow Christian ritual practices.

Shenoute's antipagan rhetoric overlaps so extensively with his antiheretical rhetoric that he verges on eliding the distinctions between pagans and heretics. The conflation of these two categories of the "unorthodox" is most apparent in *I Am Amazed*, where he accuses Christians who disagree with him on theological doctrines about embodiment of practically becoming *hellenes*; in their denial of the bodily resurrection, they are "like the pagans" in Shenoute's eyes.[48] Both pagans (*hellenes*) and self-avowed Christians ("the ones among you") are reported to deny that the bread and wine of the eucharist are the body and blood of Christ: "Truly, the one who says that it is not his body and blood—especially the ones among you and not only the pagans (*hellēn*)—they are more wicked than dogs and sows."[49] Shenoute also shames Christians who question his understanding of Jesus Christ as the embodiment of God by insinuating that these heretics are even worse than pagans: "So, is this not a new piety that was not manifest among the pagans (*nhellēn*)? For the work of those is always to slander the scriptures. But it was a new lawlessness that was revealed among you, which is this, 'Mary did not conceive the savior,' and again, 'It is not his body and blood that you receive.' You see how many are those among us who do not have God, like these very godless ones."[50] Shenoute charges that the godlessness of the pagans has entered into the Christian church ("you" and "us") in the form of new heresies that seem to dispute the full embodiment of Christ, whether with respect to Christ's bodily conception in Mary's human womb or to Christ's bodily presence in the bread and wine of the eucharist. Although he characterizes these "lawless" beliefs as "new," Shenoute nonetheless likens the heretics to the "godless" *hellenes*. Finally, Shenoute concludes a lengthy section on the sanctity of the human body, Christ's resurrection of Lazarus, and Christ's own bodily resurrection by asking how people who disagree with him and "speak this great lawlessness" can even be considered "Christians"?[51] As I will address in more detail below, what is at stake for Shenoute in these theological debates is the full humanity of Christ as the embodiment (or *incarnation*) of God.[52] In Shenoute's logic, if Mary did not conceive the Christ, then Christ was not simultaneously fully human and fully divine. The eucharist is redemptive precisely because it is Christ's (God's) body and blood. The incarnation's authenticity and power paradoxically lie in its corporeality. Shenoute here uses the language of "paganism" to besmirch contrasting views as something even worse than paganism.

Both heretics and pagans are also clear targets of Shenoute's wrath in *The Lord Thundered*, a text with an occasion for a more obvious antipagan platform than a heresiological one. Shenoute often berates the two in the same breath, and even his separate criticisms of each group have parallels. He associates pagans and heretics with the devil or demons.[53] Both, he claims, serve multiple gods.[54] He charges that the Holy Spirit has withdrawn from both pagans and heretics and will not be present for them during the resurrection.[55] Although the categories of "pagan" and "heretic" might appear almost interchangeable in his rhetoric, his coupling of these two groups goes beyond simply dumping them both in a common discard pile. Shenoute uses the labels "heretic" and "pagan" to challenge the identities that self-avowed Christians may have constructed for themselves.

People who identify themselves as "Christians" but still participate in polytheistic rituals are stigmatized by the label of pagan and then doubly stigmatized by the charge of heresy: "Would that also the word of truth not find some who share in the faith and who are mixed with the pagans or the heretics and fault them, saying, 'You are not able to take from the table of the Lord and the table of the demons. You are not able to drink from the cup of the Lord and the cup of the demons,' (1. Cor 10:21) as I say to the ones who state, 'We became Christians. . . .' Woe to the one who will worship the sun and the moon and the whole army of the sky, while turning to them as if to a god."[56] Not surprisingly, Shenoute here condemns people who worship traditional gods in some form or another even though they call themselves Christians. More shocking is that the

label of "heretic" appears among the epithets hurled at people who participate in traditional Egyptian polytheistic worship. The line between *hellenes* and heretics is so blurred that paganism actually becomes heresy:

> Who will not say: Woe to every heretic who does not believe in God and Christ
> Jesus, and who did not repent until now. Woe to a magician or a healer[57] or an
> enchanter who partakes of the body and blood of the Lord, even though they have
> not left behind their evil works. Woe to a pagan or a Jew or any other heresy, as
> they mock and they deride the mystery of God and all the righteous works among
> every work that the Christians do. Woe to every one who takes the holy baptism
> of the Lord while he is of two hearts. Woe to the one who puts his hands to his
> mouth, worshipping, saying, "Praise the sun," or, "Hail the moon," as he blesses
> the creatures and glorifies them more than the creator, even though every person
> must glorify God the almighty, the one who caused them to shine upon the
> earth.[58]

Here, Shenoute categorizes *hellenes* as a subset of heresy by characterizing
pagans and Jews as just another heresy (*celaau nhairesis*). Elsewhere in the
sermon, Shenoute again almost conflates the two groups, accusing heretics
of being the descendents of idol worshippers.[59]

This slippage also occurs in his portents of the ultimate punishment
awaiting pagans and heretics. Shenoute transitions easily from a portrait
of heretics—Satan's "friends" who keep him company in "the fiery furnace"—to a description of "faithless" and "impious" idol worshippers—
the *ethnos* or peoples of the biblical world. The heretics who reside with
Satan in hell are contrasted with the faithful who will dwell in heaven with
Jesus. Abraham, who offered to sacrifice his son to God, is Shenoute's
paradigm for the heavenly faithful. Shenoute then immediately turns his
attention to people he accuses of sacrificing their children to demons—
people like Gog, Og, and King Herod. He contrasts these historical figures
with the ancestors of true Christians, such as kings David and Solomon,
"who destroyed your temples and who cast down your idols."[60] Does
Shenoute here address accused heretics burning in hell or the allegedly
polytheistic descendents of Gog, Og, and Herod, or both? Is the idolatry
of Gog, Og, and Herod merely a metaphor for the "lawlessness" of the
heretics (*tanomia de hōōf nnhairetikos*) cited earlier in the passage?

Shenoute's rhetoric raises a number of broader questions as well:
What ideological or political traction does Shenoute gain by classifying
pagans as heretics, and by associating heretics with pagans? What aspects
of *hellenes'* religious identity do not fit so easily into the pagan stereotype?

In this ideologically fluid period in late antiquity, when the boundaries between orthodox and heresy were deeply disputed, labeling was a

strategy church leaders deployed in order to position their political and theological opponents as beyond the boundaries of true faith. In the city of Rome in the 440s, at almost precisely the same moment Shenoute was countering pagans and heretics in Upper Egypt, the orthodox bishop Leo of Rome ("Leo the Great") mounted a campaign against Manichees who had fled to Italy after the Vandal conquest of North Africa. The Manichees were worshipping within orthodox churches, alongside the laity. As Harry O. Maier has argued, in the sermons, Leo used the rhetoric of disease and defilement to move the Manichees from a position of "insider" and "dissenter" within the church to one of "outsider" and "heretic." When perceived by the laity as dissenters *inside* the church, the Manichees occupied a position that was more politically and ideologically threatening to the orthodox; as simply another expression of Christianity, Manicheanism might seem like a legitimate, even appealing, option to the Roman Christians. To counter this perceived threat, Leo urged Rome's congregations to expel or "extirpate" the Manichaean "plague," "contagion," and "pestilence" from their midst. Leo rhetorically constructed the Manichees as "heretics" who threatened the unity of the church, rather than as mere "dissenters" with "alternative" ritual practices that could be tolerated.[61]

As did Leo, Shenoute uses labels to condemn as "outsiders" individuals and groups who may nonetheless consider themselves Christian "insiders." Given the broad use of the term *hellene* as a generic referent to pagans, or any polytheists, Shenoute's labeling of certain people as *hellenes* or pagans often reveals more about his definition of Christianity than it does about the social reality of the people against whom he writes. Shenoute uses the common, recognizable, linguistic currency of "paganism" precisely in order to place people outside of the Christian fold, not because they *are* socially or physically located outside of Christian communities in Egypt. Granted, some of the people whom Shenoute calls "pagan" seem to be easily identifiable polytheists who have never professed an interest in the Christian faith. They worship human-made idols and multiple gods, including a Greek and Egyptian pantheon that contains the sun, the moon, Chronos, Petbe, Rhea, Zeus, Ares, Hephaestus, Ptah, and Apollo.[62] Yet, these pagans are not the only sources of Shenoute's concerns. As I have demonstrated, some of Shenoute's pagans bear a decidedly Christian cast, albeit a heretical one.

Shenoute's labels of "heretic" and "pagan" do not signify discrete social groups, but rather function as more flexible rhetorical categories with which he stigmatizes those who deviate from his definition of orthodoxy. In *I Am Amazed*, "heretics" are characterized as "pagans." In *The Lord Thundered*, "pagans" are but one category of "heresy." Heresy,

there, is the framework by which Shenoute organizes intolerable and unorthodox religious practices and beliefs, and he subsumes both pagans and
Jews under this classification. The power of this act of labeling lies in the
stigma attributed to the term "heresy." Polytheism becomes an act of
heresy, a stigma that would perhaps be more troubling to people who self-
identify as Christian and do not see their continutation of traditional ritual
practices as in conflict with their identities as orthodox Christians. Shenoute, however, shatters this understanding of identity by classifying it as
heresy.

His act of labeling also stigmatizes and marginalizes certain Christians
by claiming that to deny the orthodox position (or, more accurately, what
Shenoute claims to be the orthodox position) on Christ's embodiment is
to deny the core message of the Christian faith. It is to become a *hellene*.
"Pagan" (like "heretic") becomes a fairly fluid label by which he identifies
certain beliefs as incompatible with his vision of orthodox Christianity;
they are not merely heterodox Christians—they are non-Christian. People
who profess "heretical" beliefs are labeled non-Christian regardless of
their own religious self-identity or the religious identity that might have
been ascribed to them in late antique Egypt. Shenoute uses both labels to
marginalize people who considered themselves Christians and may have
been considered as such by others.

This does not *preclude* the more obvious use of the term "pagan" to
refer to people who engage in traditional, polytheistic religious practices.
Rather, it is an additional nuance to the term. What makes heretical Christians "pagans" is their heretical beliefs. In the social world Shenoute attempts to construct, to challenge Shenoute's understanding of the full
embodiment of the divine Jesus Christ is to place oneself outside the
boundaries of the Christian church. Divergence from Shenoute's "orthodox" faith on matters such as the eucharist and the nature of Christ so
distances them from "the church" that they no longer deserve to be called
"Christian," even if that label is accompanied by the important modifier,
"heretical." In calling them "pagans," Shenoute communicates that heterodox Christians stand alongside Greco-Roman and Egyptian polytheists
completely beyond the limits of the Christian faith.

That Shenoute elides distinctions between heretics and pagans on issues of embodiment suggests the centrality of embodiment in Shenoute's
theology. As a closer examination of Shenoute's antiheretical arguments in
I Am Amazed, The Lord Thundered, and *Who Speaks Through the Prophet*
confirms, Jesus Christ's embodiment from birth to resurrection underpins
Shenoute's understanding of the nature of the human body. Christ's
earthly life and resurrection proves the sanctity of human embodied exis-

tence. The human body is good and sacred and thus will be resurrected after death. The sanctification of the human body hinges on the fact that *this* body is not discarded after death; it is *this* body—not some other kind of body—that the Lord will raise. The proof of humanity's ultimate resurrection lies in Christ's own bodily resurrection according to Shenoute's logic. Thus, disavowing any aspect of Christ's embodied human existence denies that Christ himself was crucified on the cross and then resurrected again in the body and hence denies the resurrection of humanity. The truth of Christ's embodied existence is the cornerstone of Shenoute's defense of the resurrection of the human body as well as the overall sanctity of the body.

The Human Birth and Embodiment of Jesus Christ

One of the cornerstones of Shenoute's theology of the body is God's complete embodiment in human flesh in the form of Jesus Christ. For Shenoute, Jesus Christ is the incarnation in the flesh of God himself. Shenoute defends what he understands to be the full humanity of the second person of the trinity and hence the reality of Christ's embodiedness on multiple fronts against a panoply of foes. Countering Nestorius and his followers, Shenoute insists that the divinity was conceived within and born of a human woman, Mary, and experienced death on the cross. Against Origenists, Shenoute argues that Christ labored in the flesh on the cross. To unnamed heretics who claim the eucharist is only a "type" or symbol of Christ's blood and flesh, Shenoute defends Christ's embodied presence in the bread and wine. What links these heretics for Shenoute's is their shared contempt for a theology that proclaims the full embodiment of the divinity of Jesus Christ from conception to death to resurrection. In what follows, I examine what links these heretics in *Shenoute's* mind and writings. I do not provide an analysis of Nestorians, Origenists, and other heretical groups per se. Rather, I present an appraisal of the theology *Shenoute* develops in opposition to beliefs he identifies (or misidentifies) as belonging to specific groups of "heretics."

In both *The Lord Thundered* and *I Am Amazed*, Shenoute participates in the Christological controversies about the nature and redemptive value of Christ's corporeal existence. He refutes people who he claims deny that Mary did conceive Jesus Christ, and thus (from Shenoute's perspective) assert that Jesus Christ was not always *both* fully human and fully divine. In two extended passages in *I Am Amazed*, Shenoute writes against Christians who disagree with him about the status of the Virgin

Mary, and whether Mary, in giving birth to Jesus, actually conceived and
bore God. He does not name his opponents in the first passage, but instead attacks their views on Jesus Christ's incarnation. He first presents
their doctrine (that "Mary did not conceive Christ") and then ridicules it
("[they ask] did her belly not swell up or collapse?"). Shenoute uses the
infancy narratives from the gospels of Matthew and Luke as the prooftexts
for his own position—that Jesus Christ was in fact conceived as human
inside of Mary: "Others blaspheme that Mary did not conceive the Christ,
and that if she did conceive then (they ask) did her belly not swell up or
collapse? Let them hear about this from us. If she did not conceive him
then the prophet spoke a vain thing, saying, 'Behold, the virgin will conceive and bear a son and his name will be called Emmanuel.' (Matt. 1:23)
And also, 'The birth of Jesus Christ was like this.' And, 'Behold, you will
conceive and bear a son and will call his name Jesus.' (Luke 1:31).[63] Although this passage is ostensibly about Mary, Shenoute utilizes her to
emphasize the human conception, birth, and *embodiment* of Jesus Christ
as the divine son of God.

The end of the passage reveals the significance of this Christological
debate for the resurrection. According to Shenoute, his opponents' claims
about Mary and about Jesus Christ's birth represent more than a crude
misinterpretation of the gospels. What is at stake for Shenoute is not simply the full veneration of Mary as the mother of God, but the truth of
Christ's resurrection. He presses his case that Christ's *divinity* was present
in Mary's womb and then born out of Mary. If the divine Christ had not
been conceived in and born of a woman, then he did not possess genuine
humanity, and he could not have died on the cross. "If she did not conceive him, then he was not born. If he was not born, then he did not
become human. If he did not become human, then he was not crucified.
And if he was not crucified, he did not rise on the third day, having gone
to his holy dwelling in which he was before, when his Father had not yet
sent him, so that he might exist from a woman who, for her part, is Mary,
the holy virgin."[64] Jesus Christ, for Shenoute, is the embodied divinity
from conception through the resurrection. Although Shenoute does not
refer to Jesus Christ as the "Logos" here, it is obvious that he is discussing
the divine, second person of the trinity—the Word who existed "before"
God the father sent him. The very meaning of the crucifixion and the
resurrection depends, for Shenoute, on a genuine embodiment of the divinity in the form of Jesus Christ, an embodiment that is proven by his
conception within Mary's womb.

It seems likely that Shenoute has in mind as his opponents followers
of Nestorius, the bishop of Constantinople who was declared a heretic at

the Council of Ephesus in 431 because of his Christology. During this period, the most prominent debate about the status of Mary as the mother of God was the argument between Cyril of Alexandria, Shenoute's bishop, and Nestorius, the soon-to-be former bishop of Constantinople. Shenoute himself was involved in this dispute, and he may have accompanied Cyril to Ephesus. According to the *vita*, Shenoute hit Nestorius in the chest at the council.[65] Moreover, after the council, Nestorius was exiled first to Antioch and then to the Great Oasis in Egypt, just 170 kilometers southwest of Shenoute's monastery.[66] Nestorius argued against the title of Mary as the "Theotokos," or bearer of God, because it implied that the divine Logos, "has need of a second birth from a woman"; moreover in speaking of the divinity's conception and birth, one attributed to the divine nature of God "the characteristics of the flesh" such as suffering and death, which Nestorius considered debasing to God and bordering on the heresies of Arianism or Apollinarianism.[67] Cyril and others accused Nestorius of claiming that only the humanity of Jesus Christ, and not the divinity, was conceived by Mary.[68] This seems to be at issue for Shenoute, as well, since he takes pains to follow Cyril in asserting that it was in fact the *divine* son (who existed eternally, with God the father) who came into Mary's womb; through the conception of Jesus Christ, the divinity *became human*. When Shenoute jests that his opponents think Mary's womb did not swell, he mocks Nestorius's alleged statement that Christ "passed through" Mary—a statement Cyril quoted and refuted.[69] Shenoute also uses some of the same biblical citations that Cyril used against Nestorius.[70]

Nestorius also was charged with making too great a distinction between Christ's divinity and humanity by arguing for two distinct and unmixed natures in Christ.[71] It is this issue that Shenoute raises in the second passage about Mary in *I Am Amazed*, and again he follows Cyril to a certain extent. Cyril argued, countering Nestorius, that Jesus Christ did not possess *two* natures but *one*, in which the divinity had actually become flesh and thus become human.[72] Shenoute takes from Cyril this emphasis on the incarnation of the divinity. Nestorius, however, is accused of distinguishing between Christ's divinity and humanity when he asserts that Christ's divine nature was not present in Jesus at the moments of his conception, birth, and crucifixion.

At the heart of Shenoute's critique lies his perception that Nestorius's insistence on two completely distinct natures in Jesus Christ denies the full humanity of the Christ and the complete embodiment of the divinity. Shenoute maintains that Jesus Christ himself made no distinction between his humanity and his divinity. Although Nestorius might have disputed the archimandrite's characterization of his doctrines, Shenoute finds that

Nestorius neglects the son's embodiment by separating his divinity from his humanity.[73] In a rhetorical argument with Nestorius, Shenoute chips away at his theology piece by piece. First, he quotes two of the most famous Christological claims attributed to Nestorius: that Jesus "is a man in whom God dwells," and, "After being born from Mary, the Word went into him."[74] He then addresses Nestorius's supposed pronouncement that God (Christ) was not crucified—only the man, Jesus, was—because the Bible never calls "the crucified one" God, and because Jesus himself professed that his resurrected body was not a human body. Shenoute replies, "Why did he (Nestorius) [not k]now this [. . .] that he (Jesus Christ) did [not s]ay, 'See the [hands] and fe[e]t of a man,' but simply he said, 'My own feet and hands,' since he did not separate the body from the divinity."[75] In other words the Son himself never claimed to be anything other than simultaneously and inseparably human and divine; he was always the embodiment of the divinity.

In a similar manner, Shenoute dismisses any assertion that the divine Christ did not experience a human death on the cross. He accuses Nestorius of stating that the divine Christ left the human body of Jesus before Jesus died:

And he (Nestorius) said, "The divinity went to the heights; it left the flesh on the wood." For he said in his writings, "This one who cried out, 'My God, my God, why have you forsaken me?' (Matt. 27:46) I worship him, too, with the divinity because he joined with it." But the words of the apostle put his foolishness to shame, "It was the Lord of glory who was crucified." (1 Cor. 2:8) . . . Not that the nature of the divinity died, but it was in the flesh that he died, as it is written, "Christ suffered in the flesh." (1 Pet. 4:1) For surely the divinity is not separated from the body while it is on the wood.[76]

The issue for Shenoute is again the embodiment of the divinity as it existed in the person of Jesus Christ. The divinity did not simply join with human flesh temporarily; it became flesh. Once again, Shenoute begins his counterarguments with his own proof texts to denounce Nestorius's exegesis of Matthew's passion narrative. This time, Shenoute cites Paul and 1 Peter to emphasize his point that the divine Christ remained on the cross "in the flesh."

Shenoute, however, is careful not to claim that God actually died. He builds his argument on the profession that Christ's divinity was fully incarnated in Christ's human body and thus inseparable from that body. Although God did not die, nonetheless, the man who died on the cross was the divine, embodied Christ:

When a person is killed, is it said, "A body was killed?" Is it not said, "We killed a whole person," even though [the so]ul does not die, but it is the body alone that dies? So it is with the Lord. He died in the flesh, even though he was immortal in his divinity. For just as he said, "He shared blood and flesh," so he said many times, "[The Word became] flesh." Where did he become flesh except in the virgin? . . . the Son is not different from the Father, nor is the Father (different). The Son is also a spirit, and he is God from God. And he is the Son from the Father who begot him.[77]

What makes Nestorius a heretic in Shenoute's eyes is his perceived denunciation of God's consistent, full embodiment in Jesus Christ, from conception to resurrection. What is at stake is no less than the meaning of the crucifixion and resurrection for human salvation. God created the possibility for humanity's redemption while embodied. Jesus Christ "tasted death for us," Shenoute insists, by willingly dying in the flesh on the cross. Moreover, Christ arose and returned to heaven all while in "the body."[78]

For Shenoute, Christ's embodied existence extends even beyond the crucifixion and resurrection. On judgment day, Christ will return corporeally: "It is also in it (the body) that he comes to judge the living and the dead. As he said, 'When the Son of Man comes down in his glory,' and the words that followed."[79] Thus, Shenoute concludes, Mary is rightfully proclaimed "she who bore God"—*tentasjpe-pnoute*.[80] Within her womb, the divine Christ assumed human flesh.

Shenoute makes a much more abbreviated version of this argument in *The Lord Thundered*, where he focuses on Christ's conception and birth. He may have Nestorians in mind here as well. His brief defense of the Virgin Mary emphasizes his contention that Jesus Christ was the embodiment of God, and he directly addresses "you, oh heretics" two sentences later. He maintains that the incarnate divinity (the "father of the entirety") was indeed born of the woman Mary. He continues, "It is you who will blaspheme that he did not exist from the Virgin Mary. But what I say is that the Lord the Christ Jesus, God of the Christians, chose for himself a pure virgin who had not known a man, as it is written. He existed from her, and he who was father of the entirety called Joseph father."[81]

The Nestorians are not the only faction with which Shenoute finds fault on the grounds that its adherents deny the full embodiment of God in Christ. He also accuses the Origenists on this score by claiming that they professed that Christ did not suffer on the cross. Whether or not Origenists did, actually, hold these beliefs may be debatable. Nonetheless, the section of *I Am Amazed* in which Shenoute's allegations appear is clearly addressed to Origenists. Shenoute first bitterly condemns "the shame of the multitude of words of Origen" as the "sweetness of a word

on the outside which hides cunning thought" on the inside. He then proclaims, "For indeed Christ after the crucifixion which he endured for us
did not cease being the Lord of glory according to the word of the blessed
Paul (1 Cor. 2:8). . . . But he labored in the flesh, and he hung on the
cross, and he appeared to the multitudes."[82] Unfortunately, this portion
of *I Am Amazed* is fragmentary; the folios preceding and following the
folio containing this passage have been lost. Consequently, we have no
slogan or quotation (whether accurate or inaccurate) from Shenoute of
his opponents' beliefs about the crucifixion. He follows his condemnation
of Origenism with a description of Christ "laboring in the flesh," suggesting that it is this aspect of Origenism (or what he labels "Origenism")
with which he disagrees most strongly at this point. He chafes at their
alleged interpretation of the crucifixion, because he believes that the "Origenists" are somehow denying or at least mitigating God's embodiment
by refusing to accept that Jesus Christ suffered bodily.

Shenoute also defends Christ's embodiment through his interpretation of the Christian ritual of the eucharist. In *I Am Amazed*, Shenoute
decries those who deny Christ's literal presence in the bread and wine of
the eucharist. As with his repudiation of the Nestorians, Shenoute's debate
with this unnamed group of heretics focuses on the nature of Christ's
embodiment.[83] Just as God became "flesh and blood" in the life and death
of Jesus Christ, so too is God physically present in the sanctified bread and
wine. Again, Shenoute begins by quoting his opponents: "Certain ones
also say that the bread and the cup are not the body and the blood of
Christ, but only a type."[84] In opposition to these Christians, Shenoute
provides his own interpretation of the gospel passages about the Lord's
supper: "If the Lord himself says, 'The one who will eat of my flesh and
drink of my blood will live forever,' (John 6:54) and also, 'This is my body
and this is my blood,' (Matt. 26:26–28) and these people, however, say, 'It
is not his body and his blood,' then great woe to them and great woe to
those who receive their words."[85] According to Shenoute's hermeneutics,
Jesus Christ's own words reveal the fallacy of his adversaries' claims.

Shenoute's primary concern, though, is not the doctrine itself—the
nature of the eucharist—but the doctrine's implications for other elements
of Shenoute's theology: the crucifixion and resurrection. He relates the
distribution of the bread and wine at the Last Supper to Christ's crucifixion and resurrection, because the bread and wine are Christ's sacrificed
flesh and blood. He criticizes any priest who administers the eucharist but
does not believe that the eucharist is Christ's actual flesh and blood. "Let
him stop his mouth when he prays and prays to the most high as he says,
'This is my body that shall be given to you for the forgiveness of your

sins,' and also, 'This is my blood that shall be shed for many, for the forgiveness of their sins.' "[86] For Shenoute, the eucharist provides a reminder and even a continual reenactment of Christ's embodied sacrifice on the cross. To deny the flesh and blood of the eucharist is to deny the true meaning of the crucifixion and resurrection.

Shenoute's championing of Christ's embodiment lays the groundwork for a sweeping defense of the sacrality of the human body in general. His anti-Nestorian arguments closely resemble his critique of the Origenist doctrine of the preexistence of souls. Just as he accuses the Nestorians of separating the humanity from the divinity of Jesus Christ, he charges that the Origenists have erroneously separated the human body from the human soul. "For the soul and the body exist in the womb together. The body is not before the soul, nor does the soul exist before the body. Rather, it was at one time that God molded soul and body in the womb."[87] The logic behind the integration of Jesus Christ's human and divine aspects is parallel to the logic explaining the human condition. The human Jesus was always also the divine Christ, and the soul was always with the body. Perhaps what underlies Shenoute's argument is unease with the denigration of the body that he perceives in the doctrines of these otherwise diverse heretics. In his Christology, Shenoute is quick to defend the potential for the human body to be completely joined with God's divinity in the second person of the trinity.[88] By making the case for Jesus Christ's embodiedness, Shenoute implicitly vindicates the sacrality of the human body itself, a cause he takes up more explicitly when he writes about the resurrection of the body.

The Resurrection Body

Christ's embodiment figures prominently in Shenoute's theology of the resurrection. In the process of defending the bodily resurrection of Christ, he explicates his views on the nature of the human body. Jesus's bodily resurrection, argues Shenoute, confirms the promise of a bodily resurrection for all people. He adamantly defends the resurrection of the body against pagans, Manichaeans, Origenists, and others who deny it. He bases the full sanctity of the human body on the full humanity of Jesus. All people will be raised in the body thanks to Christ's embodied life on earth and his subsequent bodily resurrection. Jesus himself performed resurrections, was raised in the body, and thus guaranteed a future bodily resurrection for humanity.

In *I Am Amazed*, Shenoute maintains that proof of the resurrection

lies in Jesus' actions even before his own death. Shenoute takes issue with
certain Christians who deny that Christ raised Lazarus's body from the
dead.[89] They have interpreted his resurrection allegorically, holding that
the figure of Lazarus represents the intellect or *nous*.[90] Shenoute, however,
argues for a literal reading of the story. Christ's raising of the dead becomes for him the fundamental mystery that provides the foundation for
God's miracles. All of Jesus Christ's other miracles disappear if one rejects
resurrection: "In brief, if the Lord did not raise Lazarus and if he did not
rise—as they think—then the others did not rise, and he did not raise
them; nor did he cause the deaf to hear and the lame to walk; nor did he
make water into wine. And he did not bless the five loaves and the seven
that all those multitudes ate, and they were sated, and they took those
other baskets of fragments. Nor did he walk upon the sea; he did not
command the winds. He did not do the other great things, the other
miracles and all the other signs."[91] The bodily resurrection, as exemplified
by Lazarus, underpins Shenoute's belief system. When one takes away the
resurrection, the Christian faith disintegrates.

Most significant for Shenoute's theology and anthropology is Jesus
Christ's own resurrection. In *The Lord Thundered*, Shenoute claims that
Jesus died and rose again precisely so that mortal people might also rise
from the dead. "For it is our Lord Jesus who died for us so that we might
rise not only bodily from death at the final day, but also so that we might
rise now from the death of sin."[92] Humanity's redemption lies the bodily
resurrection. Shenoute defends the sanctity and integrity of the human
body against those who would deny its resurrection. Just as Christ's body
was raised after the crucifixion, Shenoute insists that the fleshly human
body will be raised after death and will not be destroyed by death. In *Who
Speaks Through the Prophet*, Shenoute scoffs at people who doubt the final
resurrection because they dispute the resurrection of Jesus. He quotes a
refrain of skeptics suspicious about the likelihood of a bodily ascent; they
suggest that Jesus' body in the tomb was replaced with the body of another, live person after the crucifixion but before the "resurrection": "For
some on the one hand say, '*This* body will not rise,' and, 'They put another person in his place.'"[93] These skeptics find the whole concept of a
corporeal resurrection ludicrous, in part because they doubt that Jesus
himself was ever resurrected. Shenoute, however, dismisses their assaults
against the foundation of his resurrection theology. Anyone who rejects
Jesus Christ's resurrection or the resurrection of humanity will be consumed by flames, and their blasphemous words will disintegrate, dispers-
ing like dust in the wind.[94]

Shenoute is quite confident in his grand vision of a physical resurrection—a vision he takes great pains to depict for his audiences. Both *The Lord Thundered* and *I Am Amazed* contain vivid descriptions of this moment, which he pieces together using a sequence of biblical passages. Shenoute calls upon his audiences' senses of sight, hearing, and touch to craft an impression of a very material resurrection. In *I Am Amazed*, he begins with the aural heralding of the day of judgment. The Lord's archangels will "sound the trumpet" to indicate the moment when the dead "will rise imperishable." These once dead bodies will have transformed into " 'the likeness of the body of his glory.' (Phil. 3:21)." Then the dead shall "hear the voice of the Son of God and come forth. (cf. John 5:25)."[95] Mountains and earth break open, stones roll from the mouths of tombs, dead bodies exit their tombs, and trees rejoice.[96] The day of the resurrection is a momentous occasion, and Shenoute bombards his audience with detailed and palpable imagery, as if the overwhelming sensory experience will prove the truth of his claims, and he will overcome opposition with a relentless barrage of descriptions.

Shenoute uses this rhetorical strategy to great effect in *The Lord Thundered*, as well, where he depicts the resurrection of the flesh in even more graphic terms. He cites Ezek. 37:1–14 to describe the way in which dried, dispersed bones and rotted, decaying bodies will nonetheless reconsolidate and rejuvenate: "The bones that are scattered, the bones that are burned in a flame, the bodies that the beasts and the birds eat, the bodies that are rotted in the earth—they will hear the voice of the son of God, and they will gather together to each other, each one to the one to which it belongs, and sinews come upon them, and flesh comes over them, and skin spreads over them and a spirit comes into them and they live and they rise and they stand before the one who had commanded them, as Ezekiel the prophet said."[97] Shenoute then quotes in its entirety the biblical passage in which Ezekiel prophesies in a valley of dried bones; the Lord causes the bones to come to life as people and thus renews the "house of Israel" and promises their return to the land of Israel. Shenoute concludes by deploying this scriptural text in defense of the future resurrection of the body, writing, "See the command of God who will cause the dead to rise hurriedly."[98] In Shenoute's hermeneutic, this passage promises a literal resurrection of the body on judgment day, when the bones of each person will reunite only with each other—"searching" so that they do not "mix" with any other person's bones.[99] They will live again inside human flesh, sinew, and skin.

Shenoute's certitude regarding the resurrection of the body underlies his theology of martyrdom in *As* as well. In this fragmentary work, he uses the martyrs, whose bodies were often disfigured and dismembered, to explain his own confidence in the bodily resurrection. The text urges Christians to persevere during persecution. He levies recriminations against people who do not stand and fight for their faith but instead surrender almost suicidally to martyrdom without defending themselves.[100] He assuages fears that prolonged combat could result in bodily injury and disfigurement. "You fear lest your hands or your feet or even another member of your body be wounded, and you will not fight so that you will accept the martyr's crown. A gladiator does not accept the martyr's crown unless he fights well."[101] The bodies of martyrs, like the bones in Ezekiel's valley, will reassemble in the kingdom of heaven. Though the sufferings and torment that result from standing and fighting might mar the body, it is the refusal to fight, not the disfigurement of the body, that prevents one from receiving the martyr's crown. He cites examples of the apostles who suffered torture and imprisonment, earlier martyrs, and prominent biblical figures (such as Stephen, Zacharias, and Abel).[102] Shenoute suggests his audience find solace in the salvation of martyrs. Despite the torture they experience, they are resurrected whole. Inherent in the promise of the resurrection lies a promise of bodily integrity. "Even if they pluck out your eyes, you will not rise in the resurrection without eyes. . . . Even if they remove your head, you will rise again with it upon you. Even if they cut you apart limb from limb, not only will you rise and not be separated from the little digit on your hand or your foot, but you will also rise with a spiritual body."[103] Before the text breaks off, Shenoute cites prominent biblical figures such as John the Baptist, Micah, and Jeremiah, who endured torture before their deaths or were disfigured in death.[104]

One of the many striking aspects of this text is the excruciating detail with which Shenoute describes the resurrection of the body. Although the resurrected body is a "spiritual body," it is nonetheless the same human body with which everyone is familiar. It will have a head, toes, eyes, and fingers just like the earthly human body. The promise of a complete bodily resurrection should fortify all Christians, and the resurrection should dispel all fears of suffering, mutilation, dismemberment, and death. The resurrection body is the reward for righteous martyrs who have made the ultimate sacrifice for their faith—the sacrifice of their earthly bodies. *As* thus demonstrates the importance of the resurrection of the body for Shenoute's soteriology.

To those who deny his claims to a corporeal resurrection Shenoute devotes his treatise *Who Speaks Through the Prophet*. He again links the resurrection of Jesus Christ to his defense of the resurrection of the body. He prefaces one section on the resurrection with a humble nod to the resurrected Jesus: "[N]ot by the power of the one who speaks (Shenoute), but by the grace of the one who says, 'Now I will rise,' says the Lord."[105] In other words, Shenoute claims that his doctrine of the resurrection comes not from him, but from Jesus himself. He then cites a litany of challenges to the doctrine of the bodily resurrection. Some unspecified heretics or pagans believe the soul will enter a criminal or beasts. Others hold that it will become dispersed into the atmosphere. Some pagans believe that souls will join the celestial bodies in heaven.[106] Shenoute articulates similar arguments in *I Am Amazed*, where he defends the resurrection of the body against those who argue that at the "resurrection" the body will dissipate into the four elements (earth, air, fire, and water).[107] Shenoute asserts, however, that a person's material body is resurrected at the end of time because it was the material body that God created at the beginning from the stuff of the earth. "Listen, 'From the earth,' and not from elements. He molded him. He breathed into his face. The person became a living soul, this one whom he will also raise up, according to the scriptures."[108] Here Shenoute gestures to an important tenet of his theology of the resurrection: the body is good because it is a product of God's creation. At the final judgment, human life will come full circle. The body that God once created will rise up and return to God.

Shenoute develops this principle most explicitly in *Who Speaks Through the Prophet*. In this text, he enters into a dialogue with the Manichaean doctrines of the soul and the body. In his eyes, Manichaeans face particular censure because they believe that matter does not have a divine origin: "But as for the Manichaeans, they say, 'If a soul is killed, if it dies, it is changed to a husk of a body.' But they also advance in their godlessness by saying, 'The air is the soul of the living things and the people and the birds and the fish and snakes and everything which is in the world.' Just as they also say, 'This body is not something from God but something from matter.' And, 'It is dark, and it is bound also to become dark.' But as for the sky as well as the earth, they say, 'They are not things from God.'[109] For Shenoute, the Manichaeans' rejection of the resurrection reveals another equally (if not more) heretical principle: that the earthly matter that comprises the body is "dark" and was not created by God. Shenoute buttresses his argument by noting that Athanasius of Alexandria has already revealed the "wickedness" and "impieties" inherent in the Manichaeans' beliefs.

In his own critique, Shenoute explains another aspect of his theology of the resurrection: the body will return to God because the body was created by God—it is something *from* God.[110] Shenoute holds fast to this basic principle, that the body's goodness and potential for resurrection derive from its divine origins. The human and seemingly frail or flawed body will indeed rise because it is the same body that God himself created. Despite acknowledging that the body might somehow "change" or transform in the resurrection, Shenoute insists unflinchingly that it is *this* body that will rise at the end of time. No other body will appear. Some people, he claims, have read 1 Cor. 15:35–49 and have asserted the opposite. They interpret Paul's comparison of the body to a seed that will be sown and raised anew as a reference to a new and different resurrection body: "Thusly you have said, 'Another body comes on the day of the resurrection, so that this one now which we are in becomes earth and no longer exists.'"[111] Shenoute responds that such people have misinterpreted Paul's metaphor of the seed. Shenoute persists in his argument that the earthly body and resurrection body are one and the same: "As for this body, it is this one that will rise in the resurrection just as the Lord Jesus said, 'Do not be amazed at this, since an hour will come when every one who is in the tombs will hear his voice and they will come forth.' (John 5:28) Or, if according to your word, it is another body that will be released from this, then you err because you [re]ad the scriptures that the dead will rise, even though there are no readings that it is another body that will be released from the bodies of the dead."[112] Ironically, Paul does write of a "heavenly" and "spiritual" resurrection body that is different from the "earthly" body. Shenoute, however, insists that "it is this one that will rise," even adding, in another allusion to Paul, "not weakly but strongly, not shamefully but gloriously, according to the scriptures."[113] He mocks his opponents' hermeneutics by offering an example of the kind of scriptural passage that would have to exist in order for them to extract their particular theology of the resurrection from the Bible: "Or perhaps, indeed, your foolishness has a fault. When the prophets and the apostles spoke, they did not say in your manner that it is another body that will be released from the body of the dead, nor did they say, 'This is the way that Adonai, the Lord, said, "Rise up from these scattered bones, since behold, I myself will bring another body to you."'"[114] Shenoute insists that any theology positing a new or different resurrection body cannot be grounded in the actual Bible, but can only be based on a perverted scripture of false citations. He also imagines an alternative, heretical version of Ezek. 37:1–14, which would state that "other bodies" will spring forth from the valley's dried bones.[115] The Bible, of course, does not contain these citations—proof, for Shenoute, of the fallacy of his opponents' claims. A litany of biblical revivifications underscore what he believes to be the indisputable scriptural support behind his resurrection theology: the daughter of the synagogue leader in Matt. 9, the son of the widow from Nain in Luke 7, Tabitha of Acts 9, the corpse thrown into Elisha's tomb in 2 Kings 13, and, of course, Lazarus of John 11. The very stench of the newly risen Lazarus proves that his dead corpse arose, not some "other body" apart from his original, dead body.[116] Shenoute strives to cast his opponents' views as outlandish and fantastical, and to portray his own readings of scripture as the simple and obvious interpretations.

In the end, however, no matter what the rhetorical strategy Shenoute uses, the backdrop to his conflicts over the resurrection is his commitment to bodily integrity. The human body is not an object of contempt but of transformation. The ultimate proof is the resurrection, which will be a resurrection of the actual human body. And because it is the same human body that will rise again, Christians must vigilantly guard their moral and physical purity so that they will experience the heavenly life in the body.

The Ascetic Significance of the Resurrection

According to Shenoute, the ways in which Christians live their lives on earth have profound implications for the nature of their bodily resurrection. The very body in which people both sin and prevail against sin is the same body that will rise at the final judgment. A direct relationship exists between corporeal existence on earth and embodied existence in the afterlife. This relationship between mortal life and the afterlife relies on two elements of Shenoute's ascetic thought that I have addressed in earlier chapters: his understanding of how sin operates in the world, and his notions about the relationship between the body and the soul. Shenoute's theology of the resurrection is closely linked to his anthropology of the human condition. In explaining the significance of his theology of the resurrection for the daily lives of all Christians, Shenoute uses the language of purity and pollution to describe salvation and sin, and to urge his audience to prepare for an embodied resurrection. The purity language Shenoute wielded so deftly in the *Canons* to enforce his regimen of ascetic discipline of the body appears again in these texts directed to a wider audience; his monastic-based theology has a broader relevance.

Shenoute mounts four arguments to support extending his understanding of purity and discipline beyond a solely ascetic context. First, he asserts that the bodily resurrection at the end of time is prefigured by a spiritual resurrection from the death of sin. Second, Shenoute describes sinners, including heretics who challenge his views on embodiment, as polluting and defiling, and thus dangerous to the rest of the Christian congregation. Moreover, despite their disavowal of the belief in a bodily resurrection, they will experience all too palpably the physical torments of

hell after their own resurrection. Third, he maintains that purity in this life
ensures a satisfactory embodied existence in the next. Finally, this requisite
purity consists of more than physical purity; purity begins with the soul,
because for Shenoute, the body cannot sin without the soul.

In addition to the resurrection from death at the final judgment,
good Christians arise during their lives from the death of sin due to their
virtuous conduct. The resurrection that Jesus guaranteed through his own
resurrection is prefigured by another spiritual "resurrection" during one's
mortal life. Jesus sacrificed himself so that people might live free from sin
during their bodily existence on earth *and* so that they might live forever
with God after their resurrection: "Who among those who are restful will
not want to live until their old age? So too, who among the faithful will
not want to live righteously and completely without sin until he goes before God . . . ? For it is our Lord Jesus who died for us so that we might
rise not only bodily from death at the final day, but also so that we might
rise now from the death of sin."[117] Jesus' resurrection thus promises two
resurrections—a resurrection of the righteous from the death of sin, and a
resurrection of the body at the end of the age.

Shenoute's living dead, who have not risen "now" from the death of
sin, include people who disagree with the notion of a bodily resurrection.
He characterizes these living dead as "ungrateful" for Jesus' sacrificial
death and subsequent bodily resurrection. They lack theological discipline,
and thus remain polluted by their sin during their earthly lives:

Some of them, on the one hand glorified him, but some others, on the other hand,
condemned him. What will he do for them, except forgive those who were worthy
and lived prudently for an eternal life? But as for the unclean people, he covers
them with shame and he gives them up to death at another time. Likewise, some
people who are dead from sin remained in evil and were destroyed by every uncleanness, and also when they are raised from the death of sin by the command of
the one who died for us and was raised, some of them might endure in repentance,
glorifying God as a salvation and a blessing, but some others are ungrateful, and
they do not know the one who did the good thing for them.[118]

Those who do not recognize "the good thing" that Jesus Christ did—
dying for them and then being raised—are "unclean," and even figuratively killed by sin. Though they live, breathe, walk, and eat like any other
living person, they constitute the living dead, because they have not ac-
cepted the orthodox theology of the resurrection. In contrast, Jesus "offers" the faithful "immortality" and a promise that they will not "die in
sin as of this hour." Rather they will "live in righteousness" now and "rise
bodily" at the final judgment.[119] Because of their rebirth from sin during

their mortal lives, at the final judgment, they will live corporeally with Jesus forever.

Although Shenoute includes all sinners in the eschatological vision in this section of *The Lord Thundered*, he often singles out heretics, in particular. Faithful orthodox Christians, he insists, mourn heretics' spiritual demise just as they would mourn a physical death. "Who among these God-fearers is it who will see some dead people in their tombs and not be grieved? In this way also, which prophet or which apostle is it who will see every dead heretic in their impiety and not be grieved over them?"[120] The faithful can look upon a heretic and discern his or her status as a member of the living dead. Similarly, when God gazes upon sinners, their abominations manifest themselves physically in their very bodies: "How beautiful is the person while he is living in the body (as he stands) before the one who sees him? But how ugly is he (as he stands) before the one who sees him when he is dead and placed in the tombs? In the same way, how beautiful is the person (who stands) before God who sees him when he is in a sinless state? However, how ugly is he (who stands) before him who sees him amidst his evils?"[121] These people are as dead to God as any mortal killed by more mundane methods. To divine eyes, sinners' bodies appear rotted and dismembered. Observing them is like viewing corpses. Shenoute continues, "For just like those who see dead bodies with their members destroyed and falling off of them one by one, so too God sees the members of the bodies of those who sin—members which are destroyed, and which fall off one by one on account of the evil in which each person died."[122] When scrutinized by God's divine eye, the body betrays the sins a person has committed; evil reveals itself corporeally.

Shenoute's theology of the resurrection posits that one's torments in the afterlife will be commensurate with the sins committed in one's mortal life. The body, inscribed with its misdeeds, will feel pain in proportion to those evils. After death, a sinner's body will rise, only to languish in the tortures of hell.[123] There, eternal suffering will consume their resurrected flesh: "You shall be satiated by the torments of the hungry and by the thirst that shall burn like a fire within your miserable flesh, this (flesh) which you say shall not rise. Howbeit, it shall rise again, and you shall receive from your body according to your impieties. Sin reigned in your body on earth, or it devoured you. The fire and the worm will be satiated by your destruction. Death will devour you in hell, as it is written."[124] This grim, eschatological vision is based upon another fundamental premise of his overall theology. Because the resurrection body is the self same body in which people live, die, and sin, it is imperative for all Christians to maintain their moral and physical discipline. Precisely because *this* body is resurrected, *this* body must remain pure.

Shenoute's resurrection theology holds particular irony for heretics who dispute orthodox theology. People who challenge Shenoute's position on either Jesus Christ's embodiment or the body's resurrection will experience a most brutal version of the of the doctrine they denounce. The sin of heresy will materialize dramatically in their own bodies. Transgressions of faith render heretics polluted in such a way that their defilement is visible to God during their lifetimes. Their bodies writhe in pain and decay, ironically because they reject the embodied resurrection offered by Jesus Christ.

Purity and pollution language distinguishes these heretics from the orthodox in Shenoute's heresiology; heterodox theologies render the believing subject defiled. He argues that although heretics pretend to be "righteous" and "pure," they are instead "unclean" because they "blaspheme against God and his messiah."[125] The theologically undisciplined present a danger to the purity and discipline of the orthodox faithful. Just as he portrayed sinful monks in his monastery as a threat to the salvation of its other residents, Shenoute attempts to persuade the wider church of the danger posed by heretics in their midst. Jesus Christ himself will chase the heterodox out of the church "like a shepherd who chases wolves from his flock."[126] Like the wolf, the heretic threatens to consume the tender and vulnerable orthodox Christians. Purity includes orthodoxy of faith as well as righteous behavior. It also acts as a prophylactic against the heretic in orthodox clothing, since the faith of the truly orthodox summons God as their protector.

Theological sin, pollution, and defilement eventually find expression in the resurrection body, but they begin on a person's "inside"—inside the soul. In *I Am Amazed*, Shenoute condemns heretics who "make a division between the Father and the Son" as impure and compares them to the Pharisees and scribes who crucified Jesus but would not go into the Praetorium, in order to avoid pollution (Matt. 23:25–26). In Shenoute's reading, the "purity" of these Jews was only superficial, or "exterior"; similarly, he charges, the "purity" of heretics is equally hypocritical: "They do not know that the beauty of the outside will not be able to remove their defilement on the inside. The purity of the cu[p] and the [pl]ate will not be able to cleanse their defilement on the inside. It was in this way that the Lord taught, 'Blind Pharisees, first purify the inside of the cup and the plate, so that their other side, the outside, might be pure.' (Matt. 23:25) But who are they about whom he speaks? It appears just as he said, 'Outside on the one hand you appear as righteous people. But inside, on the other hand, is filled with hypocrisy or lawlessness.' (Matt. 23:26)"[127] The biblical Jews stand in for trinitarian heretics who "make a division between the father and the son." Quoting the gospel, Shenoute compares them to the "Pharisees, scribes, and high priests" of John 18:28, who "did not enter the Praetorium, so that they might not pollute themselves so that they might eat the Passover." They serve as an allegory for others whose form of "worship"—their external purity—does not compensate for their internal defilement. Heretics face the same bloodcurse as the Jews of Matt. 27:25: "These ones, their blood is upon them, and it shall not be removed from the crown of their heads forever, they and every heretic who blasphemes against him."[128] In Shenoute's heresiology, the heterodox are just as unclean, defiled, and dangerous as the monks who transgressed rules in the *Canons*.

Discipline of faith transforms the Christian self into a pure sacrifice to God, as Shenoute argues in a prelude to his remarks on the resurrection in *The Lord Thundered*.[129] A brief homily on obedience within the sermon shames the audience by recalling the examples of Noah, Abraham, Lot, and Jesus' disciples as the most faithful of God's followers. They obeyed God after only a single command.[130] In contrast, Shenoute complains that members of his audience have not lived up to these biblical standards: "But as for us, we did not obey. It was us who committed evil deeds even after all of these words from God (that were spoken), so that we might do a righteous thing and be saved by it."[131] Shenoute's biblical paradigm of unswerving and immediate faith implicitly condemns heretics for questioning the orthodox definition of faith and for deviating from that faith. Abraham and Isaac in particular provide an important example of the kind of faith Shenoute champions within the specific context of his defense of the bodily resurrection in this text. Shenoute finds in them the prototypes for moral and physical purity. Christians, he argues, should emulate Abraham and Isaac for two reasons. First, they should adopt Abraham as a model for their faith because he loved God even more than he loved his own son. Second, they should imitate Isaac, the son, who represents the pure sacrifice made to God—a sacrifice that *all* Christians should offer in the form of their very own bodies. "But as for us, we did not obey him up to now in all of his words, namely that we present our bodies to him as a sacrifice in complete purity and complete love."[132] The faith and purity in which Isaac was offered as a sacrifice to God provides the model for all Christians. They should emulate Abraham and Isaac in the combined steadfastness of their faith and purity of their bodies.

Shenoute thus enfolds into his antiheretical and antipagan theological framework the essence of his ascetic theology: the discipline of the body.

In these texts from the *Discourses*, however, that discipline includes theological discipline. Rebuking his listeners and readers for failing to imitate
the disciples who followed Jesus after only one command, he writes: "But
also, it is a single word that God spoke to his disciples, 'Follow me. I will
make you fishermen of people.' (Matt. 4:19, Mark 1:17) They quickly left
behind their nets and their boats and their father and their hirelings; they
followed him. And this is the way that they took these great honors and
these great glories from him in miraculous works. But as for us, we did
not obey him in all of his words—that we leave behind our desires and all
our sins so that we might be worthy of his mercy and his blessing."[133] The
disciples provide an ascetic model relevant for *all* Christians, in that the
disciples, in Shenoute's reading, followed Jesus' command to abandon *desire* and sin for the sake of God. In this public sermon at Antinoopolis,
Shenoute betrays his monastic roots. All Christians must partake of the
ascetic project, even if only modestly. Orthodox faith requires the aban-
donment of desire and the maintenance of physical and theological purity.
Shenoute's insistence on purity relates directly to his theology of the resurrection. The earthly body must remain pure precisely because it will be
resurrected and will join God in heaven after the final judgment. Moreover, the purity of a person's body is affected by theological discipline;
sinners' bodies are polluted and dismembered in the eyes of God. A Christian's bodily integrity depends upon the integrity of his or her faith. Sins
of the soul find their expression in the body of tomorrow as well as the
body of today. Theological discipline is as important for the salvation of
the average Christian as ascetic discipline is for the monk.

Shenoute's insistence in the *Discourses* that the inside must be pure in
order for the outside truly to be pure echoes sentiments he also expressed
in sermons and treatises in volume seven of the *Canons*, in which the physical appearance of his monastery's church building was only an expression
of the purity and virtue of the monks. If the monks (the "interior" and
heart of the monastery's church) were defiled, the church (the "exterior")
could not be holy. The same holds true for heretics. They cannot present
their bodies as a pure sacrifice to the Lord, as Isaac did, because inside,
they have become corrupted by their abominable beliefs.

Shenoute repeats this argument later in *I Am Amazed*, only this time,
he uses it to refute an unnamed heretical group that disputes the orthodox
definition of the resurrection. These heretics resemble "the pagans" because they claim that "the body is from the elements."[134] Though Shenoute does not label his opponents as adhering to a particular school or
heresy, he recounts their doctrines as follows: when a person "departs
from this life to the underworld, the bodies disperse to the elements, as

they were before, and they return again and are born."[135] They also purportedly assert that matter is reborn multiple times in many bodies, and that "the body is the prison of the soul and its jail."[136] To these theories, Shenoute retorts, "I, however, say that the body of the truly righteous person is the gladness and rest of the soul. For if the soul of the impious person becomes dark, the whole body becomes dark and is bound for Gehenna with the body. If the soul of the righteous person becomes light, it makes the whole body light."[137] The body reflects the spiritual state of the soul. The body itself is not mere matter, nor is it inherently evil or dark. The body's purity or corruption depends upon the righteousness or wickedness of the soul that inhabits it.

Shenoute's frequent anguish over the perils of physical pollution in the *Canons* is thus easily reconciled with his anti-Origenist, orthodox theology of the resurrection as well as his general adherence to Alexandrian Christology. For Shenoute, the body is not inherently defiled or evil because the body originated with God in the creation. Moreover, God himself took on an embodied form in the person of Jesus Christ. Monks and lay people alike should strive to maintain the highest levels of Christian purity because their earthly bodies will rise again at the final judgment, just as Jesus Christ's own body rose three days after his crucifixion. The resurrected human bodies will bear the markers and afflictions of the sins they committed during their earthly lives. These sins include theological sins, for Shenoute's definition of bodily discipline extends beyond a simple catalogue of prohibited behaviors. Discipline of the body involves a discipline of faith, since the sins of faith in heretical theologies will manifest themselves as corporeal defilement on earth and affliction in the afterlife. Above all, Shenoute defends the integrity and sanctity of the human body and urges his audiences to guard this integrity and sanctity with all their power. His theological writings on Christology, soteriology, and the resurrection thus participate fully in his more explicitly ascetic project to preserve the purity of the Christian body, and they can be understood as an extension of his monastic ideology regarding the discipline of the body.

Conclusion

SHENOUTE BUILT UPON prevailing late antique discourses of the body and gender to produce a Christian subjectivity informed by his ideology of the body. In his earliest letters, he developed a theology of salvation that articulated the nature of the communal ascetic life as interdependent; the spiritual status of each monk in the monastery—male or female—was impacted by the actions, and especially the sins, of other monks. He constructed the monastery as a whole as a feminine entity highly susceptible to desire, sexual temptation, and pollution, a feminine figure who was prone to disobedience and thus in need of masculine discipline. In fashioning the rules of the monastery once he became its leader, Shenoute drew explicitly on the writings of Paul and the discourses of pollution and sexual sin to conceptualize the monastery as one corporate monastic body which was comprised of many individual monastic bodies (the monks) and through which sin could flow as a polluting agent, influencing the other members. The ascetic discipline of the monk, through practices such as fasting, chastity, and the expulsion of sinful monks, produced a disciplined and purified corporate body obedient to its head. The construction of a new church building afforded Shenoute another opportunity to reflect upon the ascetic struggle between flesh and spirit through the discipline of the body. The structure itself served as both a model and an expression of the ascetic purity he urged the monks maintain; the building functioned as a symbol of the ascetic life he envisioned for his community. Finally, as a theological author as well as a monk, Shenoute crafted a theology that urged all Christians to participate in the discipline of the body. Because all human bodies would be corporeally resurrected at the final judgment, all Christians needed to protect the purity of their bodies.

If asceticism, in its discipline of the body, "attempts to control the play of the body as signifier" and seeks to "reimagine how the body can be read and what it can say," Shenoute's idealized ascetic body spoke volumes.[1] It spoke to the nature of monastic authority, the formation of a communal and deeply ascetic understanding of Christian identity, and to the physical, ritual, and mental discipline of religious orthodoxy. Shenoute's imagined monastic bodies argued for a continuity between the biblical past and the monastic present in their performative ascetic exegesis of the Christian Old and New Testaments. The individual bodies of the monks joined together into a corporate monastic body that mirrored Israel in its devotion (or infidelity) to God, and that constituted the very body of Christ itself. These bodies strived to provide a place for the Christian divinity itself to dwell. They provided a model for Middle and Upper Egypt of the fortitude of Christian orthodoxy amid a teeming sea of paganism and heresy.

Although this book has presented Shenoute's ideology of the body as a coherent, dare I say, systematic, ideology, there are nonetheless quite a number of cracks and fissures in Shenoute's theological vision for his monastery and the church as a whole.

In his writings about the body, Shenoute balances what seem to be two deeply held yet conflicting beliefs. On the one hand, he remains allegiant to the "orthodox" Christianity represented by the archbishops of Alexandria and embraces the sacrality of embodied life. On the other hand, Shenoute also was undeniably formed by the Egyptian ascetic experience, which frequently associated bodies with pollution and impermanence. The tension between the dangers of embodied existence and the holiness of embodied existence was a creative one, however. Shenoute used the ascetic anxiety about the body's ambiguous status as the starting point for an ideology of the monastic life based upon the discipline of the body, an ideology that he extended to other arenas in an attempt to influence the evolution of "orthodox" theology, the structure of monastic authority, and the daily practices of asceticism.

A more problematic tension for Shenoute was perhaps a political one. The degree of success Shenoute realized in populating the monastery's residences and the nearby towns with these particularly engendered bodies remains a question. The subjects whose meaning he sought to shape and control often resisted fixed signification. His deep and repeated concerns about discipline, desire, and purity reveal the extent to which his ideology was challenged by monks within his own community and by other Christians in Egypt. The power of Shenoute's own voice does not drown out the voice of dissent, although one must listen carefully to hear those protests. On the page, he crafts a coherent and (at least for many readers or listeners in late antiquity) compelling philosophy of the communal ascetic life and the relationship between God and humanity in human embodied existence. Nonetheless, Shenoute's very ambitious quest to extend his theology of the communal ascetic life over the monastery, its monks, and their desires leads us to question the true extent of that control. Shenoute offers the model of unwavering obedience to one's monastic superiors as the true form of communal asceticism throughout the *Canons*, yet his own actions as a young man in *Canon 1* belie that model. His insistence on labeling anyone who falls outside of his circumscribed definition of true Christianity as something other—Jew, heretic, or pagan—suggests that among the Egyptians to whom he speaks, those identities were much more fluid than he would care to admit. And that Shenoute's vision of the ascetic life remained so constant from *Canon 1* through to his later years is remarkable—indicative, perhaps, of a lack of creativity (though Shenoute's creative exegeses and literary imagery undermine this suggestion), or (more likely) of a project that remained always unfinished, continuously resisted, forever in need of reinforcement and justification. From *Canon 1* through to the rules, the sermons on the church building, and even the sermons on heresy and paganism, theological principles as well as relationships of power were constantly being negotiated.

Constructing the ascetic community as one body in which the deeds, and especially the sins, of members threaten the integrity of the other members (even the whole body) also raises questions about free will and human agency. Does Shenoute's pollution language suggest a model of living in which outside agents—be they contaminating heretics, transgressive monks, or the polluting agent of sin itself—overdetermine the spiritual status of the individual Christian? This question is particularly poignant for the ascetic, whose way of life is predicated on the belief that acts of renunciation and prayer by the individual will result in a future life with God. Shenoute's answer is a resounding "No." The individual Christian subject will stand alone before God, to be judged not on the basis of the deeds of others but on his or her own choices. He writes of the final judgment, "Either the person does good openly and does not fear any of those who see him, and he is received openly into the kingdom of God; or he does evil, looking this way and that, fearing those who see him, and he is taken with a threat by the angels down to hell."[2] Shenoute's ideology of the body engenders a self whose individual will is paradoxically at the core of his or her identity. His ideology of the body produces an ascetic Christian subjectivity in which the self is determined *in relationship* to others but not *by* others. It is a subjectivity in which transgressive ritual acts or theologies within the corporate body pose a threat to other individual bodies, a threat which, in Shenoute's ascetic and theological system, reinforces the need for increased vigilance in discipline on the part of those individuals. As Foucault has argued, effective disciplinary regimes produce subjects who willingly make themselves into objects of that discipline, who subject themselves to the practices that simultaneously are informed by and then reproduce desired systems of knowledge. In Shenoute's theology of the communal ascetic life, the ascetically and theologically disciplined Christian can protect his or her salvation, but only by living a life of constant watchfulness for the dangers posed by the others in one's midst. In the monastery, the choices of one's colleagues—be it an ascetic father whose misguided leadership threatens to bring God's punitive and cleansing fire over the community, a desert hermit whose refusal to obey the rules threatens to destabilize the monastery, or a transgressive monk whose acts may pollute the very house of God in which one worships— shape the self by providing further opportunities for the Christian ascetic to renounce sin. Shenoute walks a fine line in his presentation of salvation as interdependent due to the interconnectedness of the individual ascetic bodies within one communal monastic body. As members of one body, monks are all the more vulnerable to sin, because sin has so many potential entry points into the community. Yet, as a member of the body of Christ, the individual ascetic subject is empowered—even compelled—to reject sin through ascetic discipline. In doing so, that person will be invited to participate in the bodily resurrection promised by the orthodox theology of the body. Expelling troublesome monks, maintaining sexual purity, renouncing heresy and traditional Egyptian religion are all actions that simultaneously reinforce what is for Shenoute a fundamental truth—that sin, in its myriad forms, corrupts the potentially pure creations of God— and what is also (for Shenoute) an optimal system of power relations—the monastic hierarchy and the orthodox ecclesiastical hierarchy in Egypt—for enacting that truth in the world. The knowledge about the self and its relationship to the divine that Shenoute's asceticism expresses also expresses a vision of power relations in the monastery in particular, as well as in his region of Egypt.

In constructing his ideology of the monastic life and presenting his vision of the ideal Christian subject, Shenoute engaged many of the same questions as his ascetic counterparts elsewhere in the Mediterranean. Shenoute participated fully in the widespread ascetic movement that shaped late antique Christianity. His answers to these questions, however, demonstrate the diversity of monastic and ascetic experiences in this period. While this book has focused primarily on Shenoute himself, the significance of his writings can only be comprehended when his monastery is examined in the context of the broader Mediterranean world in late antiquity and not simply the physical borders of his ascetic "congregation." He must be read alongside not only other Egyptian writers such as Pachomius, Horsiesius, and Antony, but also the Greek and Latin writers of his era, such as Paulinus of Nola, Athanasius, Cyril, or Augustine. The theology and events at his monastery cannot be understood outside of the theological and political conflicts and the growth of monasticism elsewhere in the Roman Empire. Although Shenoute likely remained unaware of the specific doctrines promoted especially by the Latin authors of his era, his writings, in their own Shenoutean particularity, are illustrative of the debates about Christian identity that characterized the late antique Mediterranean.

Notes

Introduction

1. The current patriarch of the Coptic Orthodox Church, Pope Shenouda III, takes his name from Shenoute of Atripe. Additionally, the July festival celebrating Shenoute's feast day is one of the most popular Christian festivals in Egypt today.

2. Stephen Emmel, *Shenoute's Literary Corpus*, 2 vols., CSCO 599–600, subsidia 111–12 (Louvain: Peeters, 2004), 1:7. The following chronology comes from Emmel's reconstruction of Shenoute's life based primarily on Shenoute's own writings rather than on the *vita* attributed to Shenoute's successor, Besa. Scholars have debated Shenoute's dates for a century. See ibid., 1:7–13; idem, "From the Other Side of the Nile: Shenute and Panopolis," in *Perspectives on Panopolis: An Egyptian Town from Alexander the Great to the Arab Conquest, Acts from an International Symposium Held in Leiden on 16, 17 and 18 December 1998*, ed. A. Egberts, B. P. Muhs, and J. van der Vliet, Papyrologica Lugduno-Batava 31 (Leiden: Brill, 2002), 95–99; Rebecca Krawiec, *Shenoute and the Women of the White Monastery: Egyptian Monasticism in Late Antiquity* (New York: Oxford University Press, 2002), 175 n. 2.

3. See also Bentley Layton's analysis of the organizational structure of what he calls Shenoute's monastic "federation." For the most part it corresponds with my own conclusions from the texts. (Layton, "Social Structure and Food Consumption in an Early Christian Monastery: The Evidence of Shenoute's *Canons* and the White Monastery Federation AD 385–465," *Muséon* 115 [2002]: 25–55.)

4. Shenoute's exceedingly long lifespan seems unbelievable, but his longevity is documented by his own references to events in his life or historical figures with whom he corresponded, as well as by a reference to Shenoute's death in a sermon of Besa, Shenoute's successor. Emmel's chronology of Shenoute's early life differs from the *vita* attributed to Besa in several respects. Cf. Besa, *Sinuthii Vita* 5, in Johannes Leipoldt, ed., with the assistance of W. E. Crum, *Sinuthii Archimandritae Vita et Opera Omnia*, 3 vols. (numbered 1, 3, and 4), CSCO 41, 42, 73, SCopt 1, 2, 5 (Paris: Imprimerie nationale, 1906–13), 1:9–10; Eng. trans. in David N. Bell, *Besa: The Life of Shenoute*, CSS 73 (Kalamazoo, Mich.: Cistercian Publications, 1983), 43; and Armand Veilleux's introduction to Bell, *Life of Shenoute*, 1–9.

5. In addition to Emmel's work, see especially Krawiec, *Shenoute and the Women*. See also Andrew Todd Crislip, *From Monastery to Hospital: Christian Monasticism and the Transformation of Health Care in Late Antiquity* (Ann Arbor: University of Michigan, 2005), and Layton, "Social Structure."

6. Michel Foucault, "Writing the Self," trans. Ann Hobart, in *Foucault and*

His Interlocutors, ed. and introduced by Arnold I. Davidson (Chicago: University of Chicago Press, 1997), 235.

7. Layton charts some of the lists of "ascetic 'labors'" in Shenoute's writings. The most frequently mentioned labors (*hise*) are fasting, prayer, meditation, and labors in general. Night vigils, reading, virginity, purity, faithfulness, and repentance are also included. "Social Structure," 48.

8. Here I draw loosely upon Pierre Bourdieu's concept of "habitus" and Catherine Bell's appropriation of this concept in her theorizing on the meaning of ritual. The practices enacted by the historical subject(s) (here, Shenoute) in themselves produce systems of meaning, in this case a theological system. Pierre Bourdieu, *Outline of a Theory of Practice*, trans. Richard Nice (Cambridge: Cambridge University Press, 1977), esp. 78–87, 159–97; Catherine Bell, *Ritual Theory, Ritual Practice* (New York: Oxford University Press, 1992), 78–88. I examine the epistemological significance of ascetic practices at Deir Anba Shenouda more closely in Chapter 2.

9. Shenoute, *Canon 9*, XL 392–93, in Leipoldt, *Opera Omnia*, 3:20; Eng. trans. in Krawiec, *Shenoute and the Women*, 20–21. See also Karl Kuhn, "A Fifth-Century Abbot," *JTS*, 2nd series, 5 (1954): 175; and Janet Timbie, "The State of the Research on the Career of Shenoute of Atripe," in *The Roots of Egyptian Christianity*, ed. Birger A. Pearson and James E. Goehring, SAC (Philadelphia: Fortress Press, 1986), 264.

10. *Vita Pachomii* (Bohairic) 89 in Th. Lefort, *S. Pachomii vita bohairice scripta*, CSCO 89, SCopt 7 (Paris: E typographeo reipublicae, 1925; repr., Louvain: Imprimerie orientaliste L. Durbecq, 1953); Eng. trans. in Armand Veilleux, trans., *Pachomian Koinonia*, 3 vols., CSS 45–47 (Kalamazoo, Mich.: Cistercian Publications, 1980–82), 1:117.

11. Krawiec, *Shenoute and the Women*, 21.

12. Krawiec's central object of inquiry is not purity language but the relationship between the female monks and Shenoute, as it can be reconstructed through various letters from Shenoute to the women's community.

13. Peter Brown, *The Body and Society: Men, Women, and Sexual Renunciation in Early Christianity* (New York: Columbia University Press, 1988), 31.

14. Michel Foucault, "Afterword," in *Michel Foucault: Beyond Structuralism and Hermeneutics*, by Hubert L. Dreyfus and Paul Rabinow, 2nd ed. (Chicago: University of Chicago Press, 1982), 212.

15. Foucault, *The Use of Pleasure*, vol. 2 of *The History of Sexuality*, trans. Robert Hurley (New York: Vintage Books, 1990), 27; Richard Valantasis, "Constructions of Power in Asceticism," *JAAR* 63 (1995): 783.

16. C. Wilfred Griggs, *Early Egyptian Christianity from Its Origins to 451 CE*, CoptSt 2 (Leiden: Brill, 1990), 198–99. See also W. H. C. Frend, *The Early Church*, Knowing Christianity (Philadelphia: J. B. Lippincott, 1966), 228. Frend describes Shenoute's attendance in Cyril's colorful entourage as follows: "The Egyptian fleet included fifty bishops, to which were added a motley concourse of lesser clergy, fanatic and untutored monks, including the famous archimandrite Schnoudi of the White Monastery, strong-arm men called *parabolani*, who acted as Cyril's bodyguard, and Egyptian sailors."

17. Besa, *Vita Sinuthii* 128–30, in Leipoldt, *Opera Omnia*, 1:57–59; Eng. trans. in Bell, *Life of Shenoute*, 78–79. See also Michael Gaddis, *There Is No Crime*

for Those Who Have Christ: Religious Violence in the Christian Roman Empire, ClassHer 39 (Berkeley and Los Angeles: University of California Press, 2005), chapters 5 and 6.

18. Some might doubt Shenoute's presence at Ephesus, despite the account in the *vita*, especially considering that Shenoute would have been quite advanced in age. In addition, no evidence for Shenoute's presence remains in the council's records. Shenoute himself, however, mentions traveling to Ephesus. The dominant scholarly consensus is to trust the *vita*'s veracity on this issue, albeit perhaps not on the details of the excursion. (Emmel, *Corpus*, 1:8–9.)

19. Tito Orlandi, ed. and trans., *Shenute Contra Origenistas: Testo con introduzione e traduzione* (Rome: C.I.M., 1985); idem, "A Catechesis against Apocryphal Texts by Shenute and the Gnostic Texts of Nag Hammadi," *HTR* 75 (1982): 85–95; Elizabeth A. Clark, *The Origenist Controversy: The Cultural Construction of an Early Christian Debate* (Princeton, N.J.: Princeton University Press, 1992), 151–58.

20. Shenoute, *Not Because a Fox Barks, Discourses 4*. A fragment of this text can be found in Leipoldt, *Opera Omnia*, 3:79–84; Eng. trans. in John Barns, "Shenute as a Historical Source," in *Actes du Xe congrès international de papyrologues: Varsovie-Cracovie 3–9 septembre 1961*, ed. Jòzef Wolski, 156–59 (Wroclaw: Zaklad Narodowy Imienia Ossolinskich Wydawnictwo Polskiej Akademii Nauk, 1964). On Shenoute's antipagan activities, see also Frankfurter, *Religion in Roman Egypt: Assimilation and Resistance* (Princeton, N.J.: Princeton University Press, 1998), 77–78; Emmel, *Corpus*, 2:615–16, 621–22, 812; and idem, "From the Other Side of the Nile," 95–113.

21. Besa, *Vita Sinuthii* 125–27, in Leipoldt, *Opera Omnia*, 1:57; Eng. trans. in Bell, *Life of Shenoute*, 77–78. On the relationship between the *vita*'s description of Shenoute's rivalry with this man and Shenoute's own accounts, see Emmel, "From the Other Side of the Nile," and Chapter 4.

22. Peter Brown, *Authority and the Sacred: Aspects of the Christianisation of the Roman World* (Cambridge: Cambridge University Press, 1995), 77; Frankfurter, *Religion in Roman Egypt*, 80; idem, "Syncretism and the Holy Man in Late Antique Egypt," *JECS* 11 (2003): 339–85.

23. Leipoldt, *Schenute von Atripe und die Entstehung des national ägyptischen Christentums*. TU 25.1. (Leipzig: J. C. Hinrichs, 1903), 188. An example of Leipoldt's influence can be found in Frend's history of early Christianity. He credits Shenoute for what he sees as the enduring strength and independence of the Egyptian church after 451: "In the first half of the fifth century, there was no more formidable a figure in Christendom than Schnoudi . . . abbot of the White Monastery. . . . His was the leadership that ensured that the Coptic Church was to go its own way after the condemnation of the Patriarch Dioscoros at Chalcedon in 451." (*The Early Church*, 205.) He also describes Shenoute as representing a "self-conscious Coptic spirit" and new Egyptian identity that distinguished itself from the "previously dominant" Greek language, culture, and religion. (*The Rise of the Monophysite Movement: Chapters in the History of the Church in the Fifth and Sixth Centuries* [Cambridge: Cambridge University Press, 1972], 72–73.) On Shenoute—specifically his antipagan activities and his polemics against wealthy elites and governmental authorities—as an important turning point in the separation of the Egyptian church (represented by the bishop of Alexandria) from the

other early medieval and Byzantine churches, see E. Revillout, "Les origines du schisme égyptien. Premier récit: Le précurseur et inspirateur, Sénuti le prophète," *Revue de l'histoire des religions* 8 (1883): 401–67, 545–81.

24. The most thorough treatment of the subject is Ewa Wipszycka's "Le nationalisme a-t-il existé dans L'Egypte byzantine?" *JJP* 22 (1992): 83–128. See also Susanna Elm, *"Virgins of God": The Making of Asceticism in Late Antiquity*, Oxford Classical Monographs (Oxford: Oxford University Press, 1994), 299 n. 44; and Frankfurter, *Religion in Roman Egypt*, 79. Similarly, Tito Orlandi has also critiqued the notion that Shenoute rejected the Greek language and culture and argues that Shenoute quite artfully integrated Greek rhetoric into his writing. Tito Orlandi, "Coptic Literature," in *Roots of Egyptian Christianity*, ed. Pearson and Goehring, 69.

25. Krawiec, *Shenoute and the Women*; Elm, *"Virgins of God."* An earlier treatment of Shenoute in the context of Egyptian monasticism can be found in Janet Timbie, "Dualism and the Concept of Orthodoxy in the Thought of the Monks of Upper Egypt" (Ph.D. diss., University of Pennsylvania, 1979). On Shenoute's texts as evidence for homoeroticism in early Christian asceticism, see Bernadette J. Brooten, *Love Between Women: Early Christian Responses to Female Homoeroticism* (Chicago: University of Chicago Press, 1996). For an unusual instance of reading Shenoute (albeit a small bit of Shenoute) side by side with Augustine, see Peter Brown, *Authority and the Sacred*, 10, 21.

26. John B. Thompson, *Ideology and Modern Culture: Critical Social Theory in the Era of Mass Communication* (Stanford, Calif.: Stanford University Press, 1990), 7. Ideology, insists Thompson, is not a generic "social cement" or a set of "shared values" or an illusion (as opposed to material reality). It involves the "social uses of symbolic forms" (7–9). Terry Eagleton also finds the notion of ideology as something apart from reality—a "false consciousness"—problematic. Eagleton, *Ideology: An Introduction* (New York: Verso, 1991), 2, 11. For another ideological analysis of early Christianity, see Elizabeth A. Clark, "Ideology, History, and the Construction of 'Woman' in Late Ancient Christianity," *JECS* 2 (1994): 155–84 and esp. 156–60, where she reviews a wide variety of critical theory on the study of ideology.

27. Michel Foucault, *The History of Sexuality: An Introduction*, vol. 1 of *The History of Sexuality*, trans. Robert Hurley (New York: Vintage Books, 1978), 92–93.

28. In discourse, asserts Foucault, "power and knowledge are joined together." (Foucault, *History of Sexuality: An Introduction*, 100.) "These 'power-knowledge relations' are to be analysed, therefore, not on the basis of a subject of knowledge who is or is not free in relation to the power system, but, on the contrary, the subject who knows the objects to be known and the modalities of knowledge must be regarded as so many effects of these fundamental implications of power-knowledge and their historical transformations." (Michel Foucault, *Discipline and Punish: The Birth of the Prison*, trans. Alan Sheridan, 2nd ed. [New York: Vintage Books, 1995], 27–28). Moreover, argues Foucault, "power *produces* knowledge." (Ibid., 27, emphasis mine.)

29. Eagleton, *Ideology*, 223.

30. Foucault and other post structural theorists have come under fire for inattention to the material conditions of oppression (such as poverty, gender discrimination, racism) in discursive analyses. Nancy Fraser and Linda J. Nicholson

review some of the anxieties about poststructuralism among some feminist theorists in "Social Criticism without Philosophy: An Encounter between Feminism and Postmodernism," in *Feminism/Postmodernism*, ed. Nicholson (New York: Routledge, 1990), 19–38. See also Nicholson's introduction to the same volume.

31. Thompson, *Ideology and Modern Culture*, 7; Eagleton, *Ideology*, 223.

32. On ideology, discourse, and language, see also Eagleton, *Ideology*, 202.

33. I borrow this phrase from Foucault's "technology of the body." (*Discipline and Punish*, 24.)

34. Mary Douglas, *Purity and Danger: An Analysis of Concepts of Pollution and Taboo* (London: Routledge & K. Paul, 1966), 115.

35. Foucault, *Discipline and Punish*, 11.

36. I provide only a few examples of the most significant contributions to this field: Denise Riley, "Does Sex Have a History?" in *Feminism and History*, ed. Joan Scott (New York: Oxford University Press, 1996), 17–33; Joan Scott, "Gender: A Useful Category of Analysis," in ibid., 152–80; Judith Butler, *Gender Trouble: Feminism and the Subversion of Identity* (New York: Routledge, 1990); Sherry B. Ortner, *Making Gender: The Politics and Erotics of Culture* (Boston: Beacon Press, 1996).

37. This is an admittedly dramatic watering-down of Butler's theories. (*Bodies That Matter: On the Discursive Limits of "Sex"* [New York: Routledge, 1993], esp. 1–55.) Butler herself has shifted from these positions, but her early work nonetheless remains useful for the study of asceticism.

38. Foucault, *The Care of the Self*, vol. 3 of *The History of Sexuality*, trans. Robert Hurley (New York: Vintage Books, 1988), 133–44.

39. As Teresa M. Shaw states, "[A] practical recognition that the soul's condition and character are subject to bodily influence, and therefore also to bodily management, . . . runs throughout pagan and Christian ascetic literature of late antiquity," even while the same literature also simultaneously reveals an opposition or hierarchy of body and soul. (*The Burden of the Flesh: Fasting and Sexuality in Early Christianity* [Minneapolis, Minn.: Fortress Press, 1998], 33.) Physiognomists were practitioners of the science of physiognomy, "the art of interpreting a person's character and inner state on the basis of visible, physiological characteristics." (Dale Martin, *The Corinthian Body* [New Haven, Conn.: Yale University Press, 1995], 18; on physiognomy see 19, 33–34.) Also on the connections between medical and philosophical literature, see Foucault, *Care of the Self*, 54. Dominic Montserrat has shown that principles of physiognomy are evident in the descriptions of bodies found in Egyptian papyri from Roman Egypt. (*Sex and Society in Græco-Roman Egypt* [New York: Kegan Paul International, 1996], 60.)

40. As Ruth Padel notes, the "two-way traffic in medical and moral discourse" stretched from ancient Greece through late antiquity, even into Shakespeare. (Padel, *In and Out of the Mind: Greek Images of the Tragic Self* [Princeton, N.J.: Princeton University Press, 1992], 53).

41. Martin, *The Corinthian Body*, 37.

42. Padel, *In and Out of the Mind*, 54.

43. Ibid., 53–54.

44. Martin, *The Corinthian Body*, 146, 150.

45. Ibid., 153–59.

46. Ibid., 160–61. Champions of the imbalance model regarded "invasion" adherents as "superstitious." (153–57).

47. Ibid., 160–61.

48. In addition to the texts studied in this book, see *A Beloved Asked Me Years Ago, Discourses 4*, text and Eng. trans. in D. Bell, "Shenoute the Great: The Struggle with Satan," *CS* 21 (1986): 177–85. Shenoute draws on the biblical example of Job to depict the virtues of fighting sin wholeheartedly and to describe "bodily strength" as freedom from sin.

49. Here I diverge a bit from Krawiec, who states that the pollution language in the rules "reinforced the boundary . . . between the monastery and the surrounding society, between insiders who were living for their salvation, and outsiders, who were in a less certain position." According to Krawiec, Shenoute protected the monastery's boundaries in order to "keep the group pure from polluting activities that violated the integrity of the community." (Krawiec, *Shenoute and the Women*, 25.)

50. Shaw, *Burden of the Flesh*, 44–45.

51. Valantasis, "Constructions of Power in Asceticism," 797, 800, 813. See also Geoffrey Galt Harpham on Foucault's reading of Flaubert's *The Temptation of Saint Anthony*, in which the Egyptian monk Antony's ascetic body is read as "transgressive." (*The Ascetic Imperative in Culture and Criticism* [Chicago: University of Chicago Press, 1987], 224–25.)

52. In that sense, Shenoute's ideology of the body holds remarkable parallels to some of the disciplinary regimes examined in Foucault's writings on modern technologies of the body. Foucault's early writings argued that disciplinary systems sought to bring the subjected individual "to an awareness of his status as subject, responsible for his own actions," whereby through a process of internalization, the person *objectifies* himself or herself to the external authority or "other." (Dreyfus and Rabinow, *Michel Foucault*, 8.)

53. Derek Krueger, *Writing and Holiness: The Practice of Authorship in the Early Christian East*, Divinations (Philadelphia: University of Pennsylvania Press, 2004), 94.

54. Dreyfus and Rabinow, *Michel Foucault*, xxvii; emphasis mine.

55. Valantasis, "Constructions of Power in Asceticism," 813. Cf. David Brakke, "Ethiopian Demons: Male Sexuality, the Black-Skinned Other, and the Monastic Self," *Journal of the History of Sexuality* 10 (2001): 534–35. Although power always produces resistance, "this resistance is never in a position of exteriority in relation to power." (Foucault, *History of Sexuality: An Introduction*, 95.)

56. Harpham (writing about Foucault) in *The Ascetic Imperative*, 226.

57. Krueger, *Writing and Holiness*, 134.

58. Layton's exhaustive reference grammar on Sahidic Coptic provides an excellent example; Layton culls from Shenoute's writings illustrations for most of his grammatical categories. (Layton, *A Coptic Grammar with Chrestomathy and Glossary: Sahidic Dialect*, Porta Linguarum Orientalium Neue Serie 20 [Wiesbaden: Harrassowitz, 2000]). See also Ariel Shisha-Halevy, *Coptic Grammatical Categories: Structural Studies in the Syntax of Shenoutean Sahidic*, Analecta Orientalia 53 (Rome: Pontificium Institutum Biblicum, 1986).

59. Leipoldt, *Opera Omnia*; Émile Amélineau, *Oeuvres de Schenoudi: Texte copte et traduction française*, 2 vols. (Paris: Ernest Leroux, 1907–14); Alla I. Elanskaya, *The Literary Coptic Manuscripts in the A. S. Pushkin State Fine Arts Museum in Moscow*, Supplements to Vigiliae Christianae 18 (Leiden: Brill, 1994); Dwight

W. Young, *Coptic Manuscripts from the White Monastery: Works of Shenute*, 2 vols., Mitteilungen aus der Papyrussammlung der Österreichischen Nationalbibliothek (Papyrus Erzherzog Rainer), Neue Series 22 (Vienna: Österreichische National-bibliothek in Kommission bei Verlag Brüder Hollinek, 1993). On Amélineau's re-liability, see Emmel, *Corpus*, 1:25; Frederik Wisse, "The Naples Fragments of Shenoute's 'De certamine contra diabolum,'" *OC* 75 (1991): 127.

60. Orlandi follows a hypothesis proposed by Leipoldt in "Coptic Litera-ture," 70. He reevaluates the evidence for the library in "The Library of the Mon-astery of Saint Shenute at Atripe," in *Perspectives on Panopolis*, ed. Egberts *et al.*, 211–31.

61. Goehring, "The Fourth Letter of Horsiesius and the Situation in the Pachomian Community following the Death of Theodore," in *Ascetics, Society, and the Desert: Studies in Early Egyptian Monasticism*, SAC (Harrisburg, Pa.: Trin-ity Press International, 1999), 222. Philip Rousseau has also commented on these difficulties in *Pachomius: The Making of a Community in Fourth-Century Egypt*, rev. ed., ClassHer 6 (Berkeley and Los Angeles: University of California Press, 1999), xvii.

62. David Brakke, *Athanasius and the Politics of Asceticism*, OECS (Oxford: Clarendon Press, 1995); repr. as *Athanasius and Asceticism* (Baltimore: Johns Hop-kins University Press, 1998), 201–65 (page citations are to the reprint edition). Samuel Rubenson, *The Letters of St. Antony: Monasticism and the Making of a Saint*, SAC (Minneapolis, Minn.: Fortress Press, 1995), 126–62.

63. Emmel, *Corpus*, 1:14.

64. Armand Veilleux, preface to Bell, *Life of Shenoute*, v, xi.

65. Frend, *The Early Church*, 228.

66. Regarding the severity of corporal punishment in Shenoute's monastery, Krawiec discusses an important "innovation" of Shenoute's to the discipline of female monks: the beating of women on the soles of their feet as penance for transgressions of the rule. Prior to Shenoute's tenure as leader, women in the monastery were not beaten (although men were). Krawiec also discusses a point in the monastery's history during which a male monk was beaten so severely that he died. Both of these issues were points of incredible contention and strife between Shenoute and the female monks. (*Shenoute and the Women*, 40–46.)

67. Paulin Ladeuze, *Étude sur le cénobitisme Pakhômien pendant le IVe siècle et la première moitié du Ve*. (Ph.D. diss., University of Louvain, 1898; repr., Frank-furt: Minerva, 1961), 306–9.

68. E.g., Leipoldt, *Schenute*, 99–100; Frend, *The Early Church*, 205; Rous-seau, *Pachomius*, xix. Even Orlandi once described Shenoute as a "disciple" of Pachomius. ("The Future of Studies in Coptic Biblical and Ecclesiastical Litera-ture," in *The Future of Coptic Studies*, ed. R. McI. Wilson, CoptSt 1 [Leiden: Brill, 1978], 153 n. 47.)

69. Chapter 1 of Krawiec's *Shenoute and the Women* is the fullest recent de-scription of daily life in Shenoute's monastery available; although it is dependent upon Leipoldt's biography, it provides important updates to Leipoldt's work. Chapter 2 outlines women's daily life more specifically. In addition to document-ing the types and amount of food produced and consumed at Shenoute's monas-tery, Layton's "Social Structure" provides a preliminary description of the hierarchy of the authority structure in the community.

70. Emmel, *Corpus*, 1:29.

71. Orlandi, "Library," 211–31.

72. Emmel, *Corpus*, 1:13–14.

73. Ibid., 15–24.

74. Ibid., 29.

75. Ibid., 23.

76. Emmel's codicological reconstruction, *Shenoute's Literary Corpus*, was completed as a dissertation at Yale in 1993. Subsequent studies of Shenoute have relied upon his work. In addition to Krawiec's *Shenoute and the Women*, see Michael Foat, "I Myself Have Seen: The Representation of Humanity in the Writings of Apa Shenoute of Atripe" (Ph.D. diss., Brown University, 1996); Mark Moussa's forthcoming dissertation at Catholic University of America, which will provide a critical edition, translation, and introduction to Shenoute's work, "I Have Been Reading the Holy Gospels"; Layton, "Social Structure"; Crislip, *From Monastery to Hospital*.

77. Leipoldt's collection of texts, published nearly a century ago, continues to be the closest thing we have to a critical edition. Where available, Leipoldt compared different manuscripts of the same textual fragments and published a "critical edition" of a large number of these fragments. Unfortunately, other fragments of the same texts either remain unpublished or have been published (usually without the advantage of a comparison with parallel manuscripts) in a variety of different venues, including periodicals. Amélineau's collection is the other most substantial collection of Shenoute's writings published. See Emmel, *Corpus*, 1:25–27.

78. I follow Emmel in his description and reconstruction of the organizing schema of Shenoute's texts in his *Corpus*.

79. See pp. 218–19 below for abbreviations of designations of unpublished manuscripts.

80. Goehring, "The Fourth Letter of Horsiesius," in *Ascetics*, 226.

81. Shenoute, *Many Times I Have Said, Canon 8*, XX 196, in Young, *Coptic Manuscripts*, 1:35; Eng. trans. in ibid., 1:37.

Chapter 1

1. Gregory Nazianzen, *Oration* 42.24, in *Grégoire de Nazianze discours 42–43: Introduction, texte critique, traduction et notes*, ed. and trans. Jean Bernardi, SC 384 (Paris: Éditions du Cerf, 1992), 104; Eng. trans in *S. Cyril of Jerusalem, S. Gregory Nazianzen*, vol. 7 of *Nicene and Post-Nicene Fathers of the Christian Church, Second Series*, ed. and trans. Philip Schaff and Henry Wace (New York: Christian Literature Company, 1894; repr., Grand Rapids, Mich.: W. B. Eerdmans, 1952), 393.

2. Gregory Nazianzen, *Or.* 42.24, in Bernardi, *Grégoire*, 104; Eng. trans. in Schaff and Wace, *Cyril*, 393. On *Or.* 42, see Susanna Elm, "A Programmatic Life: Gregory of Nazianzus' *Orations* 42 and 43 and the Constantinopolitan Elites," *Arethusa* 33 (2000): 411–27.

3. James E. Goehring, "The Dark Side of the Landscape: Ideology and Power in the Christian Myth of the Desert," in *The Cultural Turn in Late Ancient*

Studies: Gender, Asceticism, and Historiography, ed. Dale B. Martin and Patricia Cox Miller (Durham, N.C.: Duke University Press, 2005), 138.

4. Neil McLynn, "Gregory of Nazianzus," in *Late Antiquity: A Guide to the Postclassical World*, ed. G. W. Bowersock, Peter Brown, and Oleg Grabar (Cambridge, Mass.: Harvard University Press, 1999), 476.

5. Shenoute, *Canon 1*, XC 13–14, in Leipoldt, *Opera Omnia*, 3:195–96. See also Stephen Emmel's translation and discussion of this passage in "Shenoute the Monk: The Early Monastic Career of Shenoute the Archimandrite," in *Il Monachesimo tra eredità e aperture: Atti del simposio "Testi e temi nella tradizione del monachesimo cristiano" per il 50° anniversario dell'Istituto monastico di Sant'Anselmo, Roma, 28 maggio–1° giugno 2002*, ed. Maciej Bielawski and Daniël Hombergen, Studia Anselmiana 140 (Rome: Pontificio Ateneo di S. Anselmo, 2004), 165–66. In addition to Joel 1:7, 12 and Isa. 1:9, Shenoute draws on language and imagery in Jeremiah (the "destroyer," see n. 74 below), possibly Hag. 2:19 (the destruction of the vine, fig tree, pomegranate tree, and olive tree), and Ezek. 34:8 (sheep as prey). "The enclosing wall of your congregation" (lit. "the wall of enclosure in your congregation" *tjo mpōrb ehoun ntetnsunagōgē*) may be a technical term for a wall that surrounds the monastery, marking off its boundaries.

6. The material in this chapter pertaining to Shenoute's self-representation as a prophet and his writings on sex receive much more extensive treatment in my article, "Prophecy and *Porneia* in Shenoute's Letters: The Rhetoric of Sexuality in a Late Antique Egyptian Monastery," *JNES* 65 (2006): 81–97. On the figure of the biblical peripheral prophet, see Robert R. Wilson's seminal study, *Prophecy and Society in Ancient Israel* (Philadelphia: Fortress Press, 1980). On Shenoute, see also Krawiec, *Shenoute and the Women*, 55–56; Emmel, "Shenoute the Monk," 166; Behlmer, "The City as Metaphor in the Works of Two Panopolitans: Shenoute and Besa," in Egberts et al., *Perspectives on Panopolis*, 13–29. On the biblical tradition of prophecy in Christian Egypt, see also David Frankfurter, *Elijah in Upper Egypt: The Apocalypse of Elijah and Early Egyptian Christianity*, SAC (Minneapolis, Minn.: Fortress Press, 1993).

7. I follow Emmel's codicological reconstruction of *Canon 1*. For a description of *Canon 1* and Emmel's reconstruction of its manuscript witnesses in codices XB, XC, YG, YW, YY, ZI and XL, see Emmel, *Corpus*, 1:125–45; 2:558–65, and 700–706. I have examined all the witnesses to *Canon 1* (apart from cases of textual parallels) known to Emmel except for unpublished folio AT-NB K 932.

8. Shenoute, *Canon 6*, XM 546–47, as cited in Emmel, *Corpus*, 2:561.

9. Emmel, "The Other Side of the Nile," 96; idem, *Corpus*, 2:564.

10. So indicates the postscript to *Canon 1* in YW 209 in Henri Munier, *Manuscrits coptes: CGC Nos. 9201–9304* (Cairo: Imprimerie de l'Institut français d'archéologie orientale, 1916), 115 and XC frg. 2, unpublished (FR-BN 130² f. 117); see also the translation and discussion in Emmel, *Corpus*, 2:562–63.

11. Shenoute, *Canon 1*, YW 210–211, in Munier, *Manuscrits coptes*, 116; Eng. trans. in Emmel, *Corpus*, 2:562–63.

12. See also Emmel, "Shenoute the Monk," 158 n. 16; idem, *Corpus*, 2:561.

13. Emmel, "Shenoute the Monk," 173.

14. On the second father (probably named Ebonh), see Emmel, *Corpus*, 2:558–60; idem, "Shenoute the Monk," 156–57.

15. Shenoute, *Canon 1*, XC 7–8, unpublished (AT-NB 9101R/V). On the contents of *Canon 1*, see also Emmel, "Shenoute the Monk."

16. Shenoute, *Canon 1*, XC 13–30, in Leipoldt, *Opera Omnia*, 3:195–208.

17. Shenoute, *Canon 1*, XB 43–46, 83–86, unpublished (FR-BN 130² ff. 89–92); XC 59–60, in Munier, *Manuscrits coptes*, 103–4, 189; YW 77–92, unpublished (FR-BN 130² ff. 1–8).

18. Shenoute, *Canon 1*, YY 86, unpublished (IT-NB IB17 f. 82V); YG 124–25, unpublished (FR-BN 130² f. 130); YG 128–29 with Eng. trans. in Elanskaya, *Coptic Manuscripts*, 234–38; XB 147–52, unpublished (FR-BN 130² ff. 94–96).

19. Shenoute, *Canon 1*, XC 111–12, unpublished (FR-BN 130⁵ f. 43).

20. Shenoute, *Canon 1*, YG 172–85 and XC frg. 1a–c, in Amélineau, *Oeuvres*, 1:445–60; YG 223–25, unpublished (FR-BN 130² ff. 47V–48V).

21. Although Shenoute's *vita* discusses the monastery's founder, Pcol, it is in the context of narrating his recruitment of Shenoute into the monastery. Besa, *Sinuthii Vita* 5–9, in Leipoldt, *Opera Omnia*, 1:9–12; Eng. trans. in D. Bell, *Life of Shenoute*, 43–44.

22. Goehring, "The Fourth Letter of Horsiesius," in *Ascetics*, 226.

23. Shenoute, *Canon 1*, XC 21–22, in Leipoldt, *Opera Omnia*, 3:201–2.

24. Shenoute, *Canon 1*, XB 44, unpublished (FR-BN 130² f. 89V): ⲛ̄ⲑⲉ ⲉⲭⲟⲟⲥ ⲭⲉ ⲉⲃⲟⲗ ⲧⲱⲛ ⲛ̄ⲅⲱⲃ ⲛ̄ⲧⲓϩⲉ ⲉϩⲟⲩⲛ ⲉⲣⲟ ⲉⲃⲟⲗ ⲭⲉ ϣⲁⲣⲉⲁϩⲉⲣⲁⲧⲉ ⲉⲣⲟⲩ ϩⲛ̄ ϩⲩⲡⲟⲕⲣⲩⲥⲓⲥ ⲉⲩⲭⲛⲟⲩ ⲙ̄ⲙⲟ ⲉⲡⲟⲩⲛⲟⲃⲉ ⲉⲣⲉⲭⲓϭⲟⲗ ⲙ̄ⲡⲉⲩϩⲏⲧ ⲉⲃⲟⲗ ⲭⲉ ⲧⲟⲩⲁⲁⲃ.

25. Cf. Emmel's interpretation of this event in "Shenoute the Monk," 161–62.

26. Toward the end of the passage, Shenoute speaks directly to "my father." (*Canon 1*, YW 78 unpublished [FR-BN 130² f. 1V]: ⲡⲁⲉⲓⲱⲧ.) Cf. Emmel's description of this incident in "Shenoute the Monk," 161–63 (including n. 27), 169.

27. "[I]t is Satan who is inside the wall, with his hands full of weapons, with which they (monks) are committing acts of violence against themselves." (Shenoute, *Canon 1*, YW 77, unpublished [FR-BN 130² f. 1R]: ⲉⲁⲓⲟⲩⲱϣⲃ̄ ϩⲱⲱⲧ ⲛⲁⲕ ϩⲛ̄ ⲟⲩⲛ̄ϣⲟⲧ ⲛ̄ϩⲏⲧ ⲭⲉ ⲙⲏ ⲛ̄ⲧⲁⲓ̈ϫⲟⲟⲥ ⲛⲁⲕ ⲭⲉ ⲉⲛⲧⲁⲟⲩⲱⲧⲃ̄ ⲉϩⲟⲩⲛ ⲉⲣⲟⲟⲩ ϩⲓⲃⲟⲗ· ⲭⲛ̄ ⲙ̄ⲙⲟⲛ ⲡⲥⲁⲧⲁⲛⲁⲥ ⲡⲉⲧⲏ̄ⲡϩⲟⲩⲛ ⲙ̄ⲡⲥⲟⲃⲧ̄ ⲉⲣⲉⲛⲉϥϭⲓⲭ ⲙⲉϩ ⲛ̄ⲥⲟⲃⲧⲉϥ ⲙ̄ⲙⲓϣⲉ ⲉⲩⲭⲓ ⲙ̄ⲙⲟⲟⲩ ⲛ̄ϭⲟⲛⲥ̄ ⲙ̄ⲙⲓⲛ ⲙ̄ⲙⲟⲟⲩ ⲉⲃⲟⲗ ϩⲓⲧⲟⲟⲧⲟⲩ ⲟⲩⲁⲁⲧⲟⲩ. Eng. trans. in Emmel, "Shenoute the Monk," 169.)

28. "If your heart was at ease with the fact that you did not want us to visit our fellow members for a repentance, and if your heart was agreeable with this—not wanting us to see if we might be able to pluck our companions from the fire—then God also would have added to your agreement." (Shenoute, *Canon 1*, YW 78, unpublished [FR-BN 130² f. 1V]: ⲉϣⲭⲉ ⲁⲛⲉⲕϩⲏⲧ ⲙ̄ⲧⲟⲛ ⲭⲉ ⲙ̄ⲡⲕ̄ⲟⲩⲱϣ ⲉⲧⲣⲉⲛϭⲙ̄-ⲡϣⲓⲛⲉ ⲛ̄ⲛⲉⲛϣⲃⲣ̄-ⲙⲉⲗⲟⲥ ⲉⲩⲙⲉⲧⲁⲛⲟⲓⲁ ⲁⲩⲱ ⲉϣⲭⲉ ⲁⲡⲉⲕϩⲏⲧ ⲧⲱⲧ ϩⲛ̄ ⲡⲁⲓ ⲉⲧⲛ̄ⲟⲩⲱϣ ⲉⲧⲣⲉⲛⲛⲁⲩ ⲭⲉ ⲧⲛ̄ⲛⲁϣⲧⲱⲕⲙ̄ ⲛ̄ⲛⲉⲛⲉⲣⲏⲩ ⲉⲃⲟⲗ ϩⲛ̄ ⲡⲕⲱϩⲧ ⲉⲓⲉⲡⲛⲟⲩⲧⲉ ⲟⲛ ⲉϥⲉⲟⲩⲱϩ ⲉⲭⲛ̄ⲡⲉⲕⲧⲱⲧ ⲛ̄ϩⲏⲧ.)

29. Shenoute, *Canon 1*, YW 77, unpublished (FR-BN 130² f. 1R): ⲙ̄ⲡⲕ̄ⲟⲩⲱϣ ⲁⲗⲗⲁ ⲁⲕⲣ̄-ⲡⲕⲉ-ⲣ̄-ⲭⲁⲭⲉ ⲉⲣⲟⲓ̈ ⲭⲉ ⲁⲓ̈ϫⲱ ⲛⲁⲕ ⲙ̄ⲡϣⲟⲭⲛⲉ ϩⲱⲥ ϣⲏⲣⲉ ⲁⲩⲱ ⲛⲉⲡⲁⲣⲁⲕⲉⲕⲟⲩⲓ̈ ⲡⲉ ⲛ̄ⲧⲉⲟⲩⲙⲓϣⲉ ϣⲱⲡⲉ ⲙⲛ̄ ⲛⲉⲛⲉⲣⲏⲩ ϩⲓⲟⲩⲥⲟⲡ. See also Emmel, "Shenoute the Monk," 169.

30. Shenoute, *Canon 1*, YW 80, unpublished (FR-BN 130² f. 2V): ⲉϣⲭⲉ ⲛⲅ̄-ⲛⲁⲧⲁⲛϩⲟⲩⲧ ⲁⲛ ϩⲛ̄ ⲡⲉⲧⲭⲱ ⲙ̄ⲙⲟⲩ ⲛⲁⲕ ⲉⲃⲟⲗ ϩⲓⲧⲙ̄ⲡⲛⲟⲩⲧⲉ ⲭⲉ ⲡⲉⲕⲣⲟϥ ϣⲟⲟⲡ ⲛ̄ϩⲏⲧⲛ̄ ⲛⲉⲕⲏⲡ ⲁⲛ ⲟⲛ ⲡⲉ ⲉⲛϩⲉⲧ ⲡⲁⲓ ⲉⲧϫⲓϭⲟⲗ ⲙ̄ⲡⲉⲛⲧⲟ ⲉⲃⲟⲗ ⲙ̄ⲡⲛⲟⲩⲧⲉ ⲭⲉ ⲙ̄ⲗⲁⲁⲩ ⲛ̄ⲕⲣⲟϥ ϩⲣⲁⲓ̈ ⲛ̄ϩⲏⲧⲛ̄ ⲟⲩⲇⲉ ⲗⲁⲁⲩ ⲛ̄ϩⲱⲃ ⲛ̄ⲭⲱϩⲛ̄ ⲏ ⲧⲱⲗⲙ̄ ⲉⲩⲕⲣⲟϥ ⲧⲏⲣⲟⲩ ⲡⲉ.

31. Shenoute, *Canon 1*, YW 78, unpublished (FR-BN 130² f. 1V): ⲙ̄ⲡⲣ̄ⲧⲣⲉ-

ⲡⲉⲕϩⲏⲧ ⲛ̄ⲕⲁϩ ⲛ̄ⲧⲟⲕ ⲡⲁⲉⲓⲱⲧ ⲛ̄ϯⲛⲁⲭⲣⲏ ⲁⲛ ⲉⲣⲟⲕ ⲟⲩⲇⲉ ϭⲉⲗⲁⲁⲩ ϩⲛ̄ ϩⲱⲃ ⲛ̄ⲧⲉⲓ̈ϩⲉ. ⲉⲓⲥ
ϩⲏⲏⲧⲉ ϯⲭⲱ ⲙ̄ⲙⲟⲥ ϫⲉ ⲉⲣϣⲁⲛⲡϫⲟⲉⲓⲥ ϯϭⲉ ⲛⲁⲓ̈ ϯⲧⲱϣ ⲙ̄ⲙⲟⲓ̈ ⲉⲧⲛ̄ⲧⲣⲁⲟⲩⲉⲙ-ⲟⲉⲓⲕ ϩⲛ̄
ⲕⲟⲓⲛⲱⲛⲓⲁ ϣⲁⲛϯⲃⲱⲕ ⲉⲣⲁⲧⲕ̄ ⲙ̄ⲡⲛⲟⲩⲧⲉ.

32. Shenoute, *Canon 1*, YW 78, unpublished (FR-BN 130² f. 1V): ⲕⲛ̄ⲡϣⲁ ⲅⲁⲣ
ⲭⲉ ⲛ̄ⲧⲕ̄-ⲟⲩⲣⲱⲙⲉ ⲛ̄ⲇⲓⲕⲁⲓⲟⲥ. ⲟⲩⲟⲓ̈ ⲇⲉ ⲛⲁⲓ̈ ⲁⲛⲟⲕ ϫⲉ ⲁⲓ̈ⲣ̄-ⲛⲟⲃⲉ· ⲉⲧⲃⲉ ⲡⲁⲓ̈ ⲁⲡⲁϩⲏⲧ
ϣⲱⲡⲉ ⲉϥⲙⲟⲕϩ̄.

33. Shenoute, *Canon 1*, YW 80, unpublished (FR-BN 130² f. 2V): ⲉⲡⲉⲓⲇⲏ
ⲁⲕⲭⲛⲟⲩⲓ̈ ⲇⲉ ϩⲛ̄ ⲟⲩⲙⲓⲛⲉ ⲛ̄ϣⲁⲭⲉ ⲉⲛⲧⲁⲟⲩⲉⲓ̈ⲱⲧ ⲁⲛ ⲧⲉ ⲉϥϣⲁⲭⲉ ⲙⲛ̄ ⲡⲉϥϣⲏⲣⲉ ϩⲛ̄
ⲟⲩⲁⲅⲁⲡⲏ· ⲁⲗⲗⲁ ⲧⲁ-ⲟⲩⲣⲱⲙⲉ ⲧⲉ ⲉϥϣⲁⲭⲉ ⲙⲛ̄ ⲡⲉⲧϩⲓⲧⲟⲩⲱϥ ϩⲛ̄ ⲟⲩⲙⲟⲥⲧⲉ ⲉⲕⲭⲱ
ⲙ̄ⲙⲟⲥ ⲛⲁⲓ̈ ϫⲉ ⲙⲏ ⲛ̄ⲥⲟⲟⲩⲛ ϩⲛ̄ ⲟⲩⲱⲣⲝ̄ ϫⲉ ⲛⲓⲙ ⲡⲉⲛⲧⲁϥⲣ̄-ⲛⲟⲃⲉ.

34. This must be a reference to Genesis 18:27: "Abraham answered, 'Let me take it upon myself to speak to the Lord, I who am but dust and ashes.'" (Shenoute, *Canon 1*, YW 81, unpublished [FR-BN 130² f. 3R]: ⲁⲩⲱ ⲧⲁⲓ̈ ⲧⲉ ⲑⲉ ⲉⲛⲧⲁⲓ̈ⲟⲩⲱϣⲃ̄ ⲛⲁⲕ ϩⲛ̄ ⲟⲩⲛ̄ϣⲟⲧ ⲉϥⲛⲁϣⲧ̄ ⲛ̄ⲑⲉ ⲛ̄ⲁⲙⲛ̄ⲧⲉ ⲉⲓ̈ⲭⲱ ⲙ̄ⲙⲟⲥ ϫⲉ ⲙⲏ ϣⲁⲣⲉⲡⲛⲟⲩⲧⲉ ϣⲁⲭⲉ ⲙⲛ̄ ⲕⲣⲙⲉⲥ· ⲏ ϣⲁϥϭⲱⲗⲡ ϩⲱⲃ ⲉⲃⲟⲗ ⲛ̄ⲕⲁϩ. ⲉϣϫⲉ ⲉⲣⲉⲡⲛⲟⲩⲧⲉ ⲛⲁ-ϣⲁⲭⲉ ⲛⲙ̄ⲙⲁⲓ̈ ⲏ ⲉϥⲛⲁϭⲱⲗⲡ ⲛ̄ⲟⲩϩⲱⲃ ⲛⲁⲓ̈ ⲉⲃⲟⲗ ⲉⲓ̈ⲉ ⲛⲉϥⲛⲁϣⲁⲭⲉ ⲣⲱ ⲛⲙ̄ⲙⲁⲕ ⲡⲉ. ⲁⲩⲱ ⲛⲉϥⲛⲁϭⲱⲗⲡ ⲉⲣⲟⲕ ⲡⲉ ⲛ̄ϩⲱⲃ ⲛⲓⲙ ⲛ̄ⲧⲉⲓ̈ϩⲉ ϫⲉ ⲛ̄ⲧⲕ̄ⲟⲩⲣⲱⲙⲉ ⲉϥⲙ̄ⲡϣⲁ. ⲁⲛⲟⲕ ⲅⲁⲣ ⲡⲉⲧⲟ ⲛ̄ⲥⲟϭ.)

35. Shenoute, *Canon 1*, YW 81–82, unpublished (FR-BN 130² f. 3R/V): ⲁⲛⲟⲕ ⲅⲁⲣ ⲡⲉⲧⲟ ⲛ̄ⲥⲟϭ ϫⲉ ⲙ̄ⲡⲓⲧⲱⲙ ⲉⲣⲱⲓ̈ ⲛ̄ϩⲟⲩⲛ ϩⲛ̄ ⲡⲁⲙⲁ ⲛ̄ϭⲟⲓ̈ⲗⲉ ⲛ̄ⲧⲁϭⲱ ⲉⲓ̈ϣⲉϣ-ⲕⲁϩ ⲉⲭⲱⲓ̈ ⲙⲁⲩⲁⲁⲧ ⲁⲩⲱ ⲉⲓ̈ⲣⲓⲙⲉ ⲉⲓ̈ⲁϣⲁϩⲟⲙ ⲉϩⲣⲁⲓ̈ ⲉⲭⲙ̄ⲡⲙⲁ ⲛ̄ϣⲏⲛ ⲉⲧϯⲟⲩⲱ ⲁⲩⲱ ⲉⲧϯⲕⲁⲣⲡⲟⲥ ϩⲁⲑⲏ ⲛ̄ⲥⲁϥ ⲙ̄ⲛ̄ϣⲟⲙⲧⲉ ⲡⲟⲟⲩ ⲛ̄ϩⲟⲟⲩ. ⲧⲉⲛⲟⲩ ϩⲱⲱϥ ⲁⲟⲩⲕⲱϩⲧ̄ ⲉϥⲟⲟⲩ ⲙⲟⲩϩ ϩⲣⲁⲓ̈ ⲛ̄ϩⲏⲧϥ̄ ⲁⲩⲱ ⲟⲩⲱⲁϩ ⲁϥⲭⲉⲣⲟ ϩⲛ̄ ⲛ̄ⲃⲱ ⲛ̄ⲕⲛ̄ⲧⲉ ⲁⲩⲱ ⲧⲃⲱ ⲛ̄ⲭⲙ̄ⲡⲉϩ ⲙⲛ̄ ⲧⲃⲛ̄ⲛⲉ ⲁⲩⲟⲩⲱϣⲉ ⲁⲩⲱ ⲁⲩⲣⲱⲕϩ̄ ⲁⲩⲱ ⲡⲉϩⲟⲩⲟ ⲛ̄ⲛ̄ϣⲏⲛ ⲧⲏⲣⲟⲩ ⲉⲧϩⲙ̄ⲡⲙⲁ ⲛ̄ϣⲏⲛ ⲁⲩϣⲱⲃϩ̄ ⲉⲃⲟⲗ ⲙ̄ⲡϣⲁϩ ⲉⲧⲭⲉⲣⲟ ⲉⲧⲣⲱⲕϩ̄ ⲛ̄ⲛ̄ϣⲏⲛ ⲉⲛⲧⲁϥⲣ̄-ϫⲟⲓⲥ ⲉⲣⲟⲟⲩ ⲛ̄ϭⲓ ⲡⲕⲱϩⲧ̄.

36. Somewhat facetiously he asks, "What good is it for me to run from a matter of which there is no judgment?" (Shenoute, *Canon 1*, YW 82, unpublished (FR-BN 130² f. 3V): ⲟⲩ ⲉⲣⲟⲓ̈ ⲡⲉ ⲉⲡⲱⲧ ϩⲛ̄ ⲟⲩϩⲱⲃ ⲉⲙⲛ̄ϯⲕⲣⲓⲙⲁ ⲛ̄ϩⲏⲧϥ̄.)

37. See also Emmel's brief description of *Letter Two* in "Shenoute the Monk," 170–71.

38. Shenoute, *Canon 1*, YG 172–74, in Amélineau, *Oeuvres*, 1:445–46.

39. Shenoute quotes the man as demanding Shenoute and/or the monastic father tell him what they think has transpired in his "house," among monks under his charge. (Shenoute, *Canon 1*, XC frg. 1bV, in Amélineau, *Oeuvres*, 1:458.) On this house leader, see also Emmel, "Shenoute the Monk," 161–62. Emmel posits that this person committed the sexual sin(s) that inspired Shenoute to write *Letter One* and is the person Shenoute describes in *Letter One* as trying to convince the monastic leader that nothing untoward has occurred.

40. Shenoute, *Canon 1*, XC 8, unpublished (AT-NB K 9101V): ϥⲥϩⲟⲩⲟⲣⲧ̄ ⲛ̄ϭⲓ ⲡⲉⲧⲛⲁϫⲓⲟⲩⲉ ⲉⲃⲟⲗ ϩⲛ̄ ⲧⲧⲟ ⲙ̄ⲡⲉϥⲥⲟⲛ:— ⲥⲥϩⲟⲩⲟⲣⲧ̄ ⲛ̄ϭⲓ ⲟⲩⲥϩⲓⲙⲉ ⲉⲥⲛⲁϫⲓⲟⲩⲉ ⲉⲃⲟⲗ ϩⲛ̄ ⲧⲧⲟ ⲛ̄ⲧⲉⲧϩⲓⲧⲟⲩⲱⲥ: ϥⲥϩⲟⲩⲟⲣⲧ̄ ⲛ̄ϭⲓ ⲡⲉⲧⲛⲁϫⲓⲟⲩⲉ ⲉⲃⲟⲗ ϩⲛ̄ ⲛⲉϩⲛⲁⲁⲩ ⲙ̄ⲡⲉⲑⲩⲥⲓⲁⲥⲧⲏⲣⲓⲟⲛ· ⲉⲓⲧⲉ ⲟⲩⲟⲉⲓⲕ ⲡⲉ· ⲉⲓⲧⲉ ⲉⲩⲏⲣⲡ̄ ⲡⲉ ⲉⲓⲧⲉ ⲕⲉⲗⲁⲁⲩ ⲛ̄ⲛ̄ⲕⲁ ⲉϩⲉⲛⲉ-ⲃⲟⲗ ⲉⲓⲉ ϩⲛ̄ ⲡⲉⲑⲩⲥⲓⲁⲥⲧⲏⲣⲓⲟⲛ· ⲉⲓⲧⲉ ⲉⲩϩⲓϩⲟⲩⲛ ⲙ̄ⲡⲉⲑⲩⲥⲓⲁⲥⲧⲏⲣⲓⲟⲛ· ⲉⲓⲧⲉ ⲉⲩϩⲓⲃⲟⲗ ⲉⲩⲕⲏ ⲉϩⲣⲁⲓ̈ ⲉⲙⲡⲁⲧⲟⲩϫⲓⲧⲟⲩ ⲉϩⲟⲩⲛ. See also Emmel, "Shenoute the Monk," 165.

41. Shenoute, *Canon 1*, XC 8, unpublished (AT-NB K 9101V): ϥⲥϩⲟⲩⲟⲣⲧ̄ ⲛ̄ϭⲓ ⲡⲉⲧⲛⲁⲧⲁⲙⲓⲉ-ⲟⲩⲉⲓⲇⲟⲥ ⲛ̄ϫⲓⲟⲩⲉ ⲛ̄ϥⲧⲁⲁϥ ⲉⲃⲟⲗ ⲛ̄ϩⲉⲛⲕⲟⲥⲙⲓⲕⲟⲥ ⲡⲁⲣⲁⲧⲉⲅⲛⲱⲙⲏ ⲙ̄ⲡⲉⲛⲉⲓⲱⲧ ⲉⲧϣⲟⲟⲡ ⲛⲁⲛ· ⲉⲓⲧⲉ ϫⲱⲱⲛⲉ. The manuscript fragment ends here. On the translation of ⲕⲟⲥⲙⲓⲕⲟⲥ, see Emmel, "Shenoute the Monk," 161 n. 8.

42. Shenoute, *Canon 1*, XC 17, in Leipoldt, *Opera Omnia*, 3:198.

43. ⲧⲇⲓⲁⲕⲟⲛⲓⲁ is a technical term for the storeroom at Shenoute's monastery. Layton, "Social Structure," 33–34, including n. 39. What Shenoute calls the *ma ntdiakonia* in later texts is likely the same structure as the *diakonia* here in *Canon 1*.

44. Layton, "Social Structure," 33 n. 39; Mahmoud ali Mohammed and Peter Grossmann, "On the Recently Excavated Monastic Buildings in Dayr Anba Shinuda: Archaeological Report," *Bulletin de la Société d'Archéologie Copte* 30 (1991): 53–63; Philip Sellew, paper presented at the Society for Biblical Literature, Toronto, Canada, November 23–26, 2002.

45. *Canon 1*, XC 27–29, in Leipoldt, *Opera Omnia*, 3:205–6. See discussion on pp. 58–59.

46. Shenoute, *Canon 1*, XC 59–60, in Munier, *Manuscrits coptes*, 103–4. On prohibitions against same-sex relations in Egyptian monasticism (including Shenoute), see Terry G. Wilfong, "'Friendship and Physical Desire': The Discourse of Female Homoeroticism in Fifth-Century CE Egypt," in *Among Women: From the Homosocial to the Homoerotic in the Ancient World*, ed. Nancy Sorkin Rabinowitz and Lisa Auanger, (Austin: University of Texas Press, 2002), 304–29; Heike Behlmer, "Koptische Quellen zu (männlicher) 'Homosexualität,'" *Studien zur altägyptischen Kultur* 28 (2000): 27–53; Brooten, *Love between Women*, 348–50.

47. Shenoute, *Canon 1*, XC 7, unpublished (AT-NB K 9101R): ϥⲥϩⲟⲩⲟⲣⲧ̄ ⲛ̄ϭⲓ ⲟⲩⲟⲛ ⲛⲓⲙ ⲉⲧⲛⲁϯⲡⲓ̈ ⲏ ⲉⲧⲛⲁϩⲱⲗϭ̄ ⲉϩⲟⲩⲛ ⲉⲛⲉⲩⲉⲣⲏⲩ ϩⲛ̄ ⲟⲩⲡⲁⲑⲟⲥ ⲛ̄ⲉⲡⲓⲑⲩⲙⲓⲁ ⲉⲓ̈ⲧⲉ ⲕⲟⲩⲓ̈ ⲉⲓ̈ⲧⲉ ⲛⲟϭ ⲉⲓ̈ⲧⲉ ⲉⲓ̈ⲱⲧ ⲉⲓ̈ⲧⲉ ϣⲏⲣⲉ ⲉⲓ̈ⲧⲉ ϩⲟⲟⲩⲧ ⲉⲓ̈ⲧⲉ ⲥϩⲓⲙⲉ.

48. Shenoute, *Canon 1*, XC 7, unpublished (AT-NB K 9101R/V).

49. Emmel has called the rules from this period the "Rule of Pcol." (Emmel, "Shenoute the Monk," 164–65.)

50. Shenoute, *Canon 1*, XC 14–15, in Leipoldt, *Opera Omnia*, 3:196–97.

51. Shenoute, *Canon 1*, XC 16, in Leipoldt, *Opera Omnia*, 3:197. See also Emmel, "Shenoute the Monk," 166–67.

52. Shenoute, *Canon 1*, XC 16, in Leipoldt, *Opera Omnia*, 3:197.

53. Shenoute, *Canon 1*, XC 24, in Leipoldt, *Opera Omnia*, 3:203.

54. Emmel, "Shenoute the Monk," 160–61.

55. Emmel, "Shenoute the Monk," 160–61, esp. n. 26, in which Emmel reasons that the "grave sin" lying behind letter one "entailed *homo*sexuality" due to "the content of many of the rules that Shenoute cites at the beginning of *Canon 1* . . . as well as by repeated echoes of that content later on in the same volume." See also Emmel, *Corpus*, 2:805–6, where he postulates that an incident of "carnal sin" lay behind the dispute between Shenoute and his superior.

56. Shenoute, *Canon 1*, XC 59–60 in Munier, *Manuscrits coptes*, 103–4.

57. On polemics against "gnostic" Christians (whom "orthodox" Christian writers slandered as sexually immoral libertines) and other heretics, see Michael Allen Williams, *Rethinking "Gnosticism": An Argument for Dismantling a Dubious Category* (Princeton, N.J.: Princeton University Press, 1996), 139–88; Virginia Burrus, "The Heretical Woman as Symbol in Alexander, Athanasius, Epiphanius, and Jerome," *HTR* 84 (1991): 229–48.

58. In conceptualizing the multivalent and multireferential nature of speech, I take from Mikhail Bakhtin the notion that every text is written within a context such that at least one already existing system of language and signification stands

behind the text. Someone who speaks about a thing "is not the first person to speak on a topic." Moreover, argues Bakhtin, each text is in fact "constructed while taking into account possible responsive reactions for whose sake, in essence, it is actually created." A speech or a text implicitly invokes the other discourses or systems of meaning that have a history in the community in which the text circulates. ("The Problem of Speech Genres," in *Speech Genres and Other Late Essays*, trans. Vern W. McGee, ed. Caryl Emerson and Michael Holquist [Austin: University of Texas Press, 1986], 93–94; idem, "The Problem of the Text in Linguistics, Philology, and the Human Sciences: An Experiment in Philosophical Analysis," in *Speech Genres*, 105.)

59. Bakhtin, "From Notes Made in 1970–71," in *Speech Genres*, 146.

60. Mary Douglas, *Purity and Danger*, eadem, *Natural Symbols: Explorations in Cosmology*, repr. with a new introduction (London: Routledge, 1996).

61. The classic work on this motif is Phyllis Bird, " 'To Play the Harlot': An Inquiry into an Old Testament Metaphor," in *Gender and Difference in Ancient Israel*, ed. Peggy L. Day (Minneapolis, Minn.: Fortress Press, 1989), 75–94; see also Day, "The Bitch Had It Coming to Her: Rhetoric and Interpretation in Ezekiel 16," *Biblical Interpretation* 8 (2000): 231–54; Judith H. Newman, "Lot in Sodom: The Post-Mortem of a City and the Afterlife of a Biblical Text" in *The Function of Scripture in Early Jewish and Christian Tradition*, ed. Craig A. Evans and James A. Sanders, JSNT Supp. 154, Studies in Scripture and Early Judaism and Christianity 6 (Sheffield: Sheffield Academic Press, 1998), 34–44; T. Drora Setel, "Prophets and Pornography: Female Sexual Imagery in Hosea," in *Feminist Interpretation of the Bible*, ed. Letty M. Russell (Philadelphia: Westminster Press, 1985), 86–95.

62. Shenoute, *Canon 1*, XC 28–29, in Leipoldt, *Opera Omnia*, 3:206.

63. A notable exception is of course Shenoute's account of the rebellion discussed above, pp. 44–45. There "pollution" and "defilement" characterize the community in which theft and disobedience are committed.

64. In Coptic, ϲⲱϣϥ, ⲙ̅ⲛ̅ⲧⲁⲕⲁⲑⲁⲣⲧⲟⲥ, ϫⲱϩⲙ̅. (Shenoute, *Canon 1*, XC 7–8 unpublished [AT-NB K 9101R/V]). The rules against stealing are not characterized as defiled or polluted.

65. Shenoute, *Canon 1*, XC 59–60, in Munier, *Manuscrits coptes*, 103–4.

66. XC 59–60, in Munier, *Manuscrits coptes*, 103–4.

67. Shenoute, *Canon 1*, XC 59, in Munier, *Manuscrits coptes*, 103–4. Cf. Hos. 6:10, "In the house of Israel I have seen a horrible thing; Ephraim's whoredom is there, Israel is defiled."

68. Shenoute, *Canon 1*, YW 87–88, unpublished (FR-BN 130² f. 6R/V): ⲉⲣⲉⲥⲟⲧⲛ̅ ⲛ̅ⲧⲟ ⲉⲛⲓⲙ ⲙⲏ ⲉⲣⲉⲟⲩⲟⲧⲃ̅ ⲛ̅ⲧⲟ ⲉⲧⲁ︦ⲓ ⲉⲛⲧⲁⲡⲭⲟⲉⲓⲥ ⳨ⲧⲛⲉⲥⲁϩⲱⲱⲣⲉ ⲡⲓϣⲱⲗ ⲛ̅ϣ-ⲃⲉⲓⲱ ⲉⲧⲃⲉ ⲛⲉⲥⲛⲟⲃⲉ ⲧⲏⲣⲟⲩ ⲛ̅ⲧⲁⲥⲁⲁⲩ ϩⲛ̅ ⲛⲉⲥⲧⲟϣ ⲧⲏⲣⲟⲩ. ⲏ ⲉⲣⲉϣⲟⲃⲉ ⲛ̅ⲧⲟ ⲉⲧⲁ︦ⲓ ⲉⲛⲧⲁⲡⲭⲟⲉⲓⲥ ⲧⲁⲁⲥ ⲉⲧⲟⲟⲧⲟⲩ ⲛ̅ⲛⲉⲧⲙⲟⲥⲧⲉ ⲙ̅ⲙⲟⲥ ⲉⲁⲩϭⲓ ⲛ̅ⲛⲉⲥϩⲓⲥⲉ ⲙ̅ⲛ̅ ⲛⲉⲥⲙⲟⲕϩ︦ⲥ̅ ⲧⲏⲣⲟⲩ· ⲉⲁⲩⲕⲁⲁⲥ ⲕⲁϩⲏⲩ ⲛ̅ⲛⲉⲥϩⲟⲉⲓⲧⲉ ⲁⲩⲕⲁⲁⲥ ⲉⲥⲁⲥⲭⲏⲙⲟⲛⲉⲓ ⲁⲩⲱ ⲁⲥϣⲱⲡⲉ ⲉⲥϩ-ϭⲟⲗⲏ̅ ⲉⲃⲟⲗ ⲛ̅ϭ[ⲓ] ⲧⲁⲥⲭⲏⲙⲟⲥⲩⲛⲏ ⲛ̅ⲧⲉⲥⲡⲟⲣⲛⲉⲓⲁ ⲛⲁ︦ⲓ ⲧⲏⲣⲟⲩ ⲉⲧⲃⲉ ⲧⲉⲥⲡⲟⲣⲛⲉⲓⲁ ϫⲉ ⲁⲥⲡⲟⲣⲛⲉⲩⲉ ⲁⲥⲟⲩⲁϩϭ︦ ⲛ̅ⲥⲁ ⲛ̅ϩⲉⲑⲛⲟⲥ· ⲁⲩⲱ ⲁⲥϫⲱϩⲙ̅ ϩⲛ̅ ⲛⲉⲥⲟⲩⲱϣ ⲛ̅ϩⲏⲧ· ⲙⲏ ⲉⲛⲉⲥⲱ ⲛ̅ⲧⲟ ⲉⲧⲁ︦ⲓ ⲉⲛⲧⲁⲥⲣ̅-ⲛⲟⲃⲉ ⲙ̅ⲡⲉⲙⲧⲟ ⲉⲃⲟⲗ ⲙ̅ⲡⲛⲟⲩⲧⲉ· ⲉⲁϥⲕⲧⲟϥ ⲁϥϥⲓ ⲛ̅ⲧⲟⲟⲧϭ̅ ⲙ̅ⲡⲉⲥⲟⲩⲟ· ⲙ̅ⲛ̅ ⲡⲉⲥⲛⲉϩ ⲙ̅ⲛ̅ ⲡⲉⲥⲏⲣⲡ ⲙ̅ⲛ̅ ⲛⲉⲥϩⲟⲓⲛⲉⲡ ⲙ̅ⲛ̅ ⲛⲉⲥϩⲃⲱⲱⲥ· ⲉⲁϥⲧⲁϩⲟⲥ ⲉⲣⲁⲧϭ̅ ⲕⲁⲧⲁ ⲛⲉϩⲟⲟⲩ ⲙ̅ⲡⲉⲥⲙⲓⲥⲉ· ⲁⲩⲱ ⲕⲁⲧⲁⲛⲉϩⲟⲟⲩⲉ ⲛ̅ⲧⲁⲥⲉⲓ ⲉϩⲣⲁ︦ⲓ ⲛ̅ϩⲏⲧⲟⲩ ⲉⲃⲟⲗ ϩⲛ̅ⲡⲕⲁϩ ⲛ̅ⲕⲏⲙⲉ· ⲉⲁϥϫ[. .]ⲃⲁ ⲙ̅ⲙⲟⲥ ϩⲛ̅ ⲛⲉϩⲟⲟⲩ ⲛ̅ⲛ̅ⲃⲁϭⲗⲉⲓⲙ ⲛⲁ︦ⲓ ⲉⲛⲧⲁⲥⲧⲁⲗⲉ-ⲑⲩⲥⲓⲁ ⲉϩⲣⲁ︦ⲓ ⲛ̅ϩⲏⲧⲟⲩ. See Jer. 17:3, Eze. 16:39, 23:26, 29; Hos. 2:9, 13, 15 (= LXX 2:11, 15, 17).

69. Shenoute, *Canon 1*, YW 84 , unpublished (FR-BN 130² f. 4V): ⲙ̄ⲡⲉⲉⲓⲙⲉ
ⲣⲱ ϫⲉ ⲡⲥⲁϩⲟⲩ ⲙ̄ⲛ̄ ⲧⲟⲣⲅⲏ ⲙ̄ⲡϭⲱⲛⲧ̄ ⲙ̄ⲛⲟⲩⲧⲉ ⲉϩⲣⲁⲓ̈ ϩⲓϫⲱ ⲉⲧⲃⲉ ⲛ̄ⲟⲩⲃⲟⲧⲉ ⲧⲏⲣⲟⲩ
ⲛ̄ⲑⲉ ⲉⲛⲧⲁⲩϣⲱⲡⲉ ⲉⲝ̄ⲛ̄ⲥⲩⲛⲁⲅⲱⲅⲏ ⲧⲏⲣⲟⲩ ⲉⲛⲧⲁⲩⲣ̄-ⲛⲟⲃⲉ ⲉⲣⲟϥ ϫⲓⲛ ⲛ̄ϣⲟⲣⲡ̄· ⲟⲩⲇⲉ
ⲙ̄ⲡⲉⲉⲓⲙⲉ ϫⲉ ⲁⲡⲛⲟⲩⲧⲉ ⲥⲃ̄ⲧⲱⲧϥ̄ ⲉⲉⲓ ⲉⲃⲟⲗ ϩ̄ⲛ ⲧⲟⲩⲙⲛ̄ⲧⲉ ⲛϥ̄ⲁⲁϥ ⲛ̄ϣ̄ⲙⲙⲟ ⲉⲣⲟ ⲉⲧⲃⲉ
ⲛ̄ⲟⲩⲡⲟⲣⲛⲉⲓⲁ ⲙ̄ⲛ̄ ⲛⲟⲩⲭⲱϩⲙ̄ ⲛ̄ⲑⲉ ⲛ̄ⲧⲁϥⲁⲁϥ ⲛ̄ϣ̄ⲙⲙⲟ ⲉⲛⲥⲩⲛⲁⲅⲱⲅⲏ ⲧⲏⲣⲟⲩ ⲉⲧϣⲟⲟⲡ
ϫⲓⲛ ⲛⲉϩⲟⲟⲩ ⲛ̄ϣⲟⲣⲡ̄· ⲁⲩⲱ ⲧⲁⲓ ⲑⲉ ⲉⲛⲧⲁⲩϣⲱⲡⲉ ⲉⲩⲧⲁⲕⲟ. See also YW 87–88, unpublished (FR-BN 130² f. 6 R/V), where Shenoute quotes Ezek. 16:39, 23:29, and Hos.
2:15.

70. Pachomius, *Epistle 8*; Eng. trans. in Veilleux, *Pachomian Koinonia*, 3:71;
Goehring, "The Fourth Letter of Horsiesius," in *Ascetics*, 225.

71. Martin, *The Corinthian Body*, 199, 220–28, 233; Clark, "Ideology," 166;
Shaw, *Burden of the Flesh*, 64–78, 83–85; and Aline Rousselle, *Porneia: On Desire
and the Body in Antiquity*, trans. Felicia Pheasant (Cambridge, Mass.: Basil Blackwell, 1988), 24–46. On women's impurities, also see Padel, *In and Out of the
Mind*, 102–6.

72. Shenoute, *Canon 1*, YW 81–82, unpublished (FR-BN 130² f. 3R/V): ⲁⲛⲟⲕ
ⲅⲁⲣ ⲡⲉⲧⲟ ⲛ̄ⲥⲟϭ ϫⲉ ⲙ̄ⲡⲓⲧⲱⲙ ⲉⲣⲱⲓ̈ ⲛ̄ϩⲟⲩⲛ ϩⲙ̄ⲡⲁⲙⲁ ⲛ̄ϭⲟⲓⲗⲉ ⲛ̄ⲧⲁϭⲱ ⲉⲓ̈ϣⲉϣ ⲕⲁϩ ⲉϫⲱⲓ̈
ⲙⲁⲩⲁⲁⲧ ⲁⲩⲱ ⲉⲓ̈ⲣⲓⲙⲉ ⲉⲓ̈ⲁϣⲁϩⲟⲙ ⲉϩⲣⲁⲓ̈ ⲉϫⲙ̄ⲡⲙⲁ ⲛ̄ϣⲏⲛⲉⲧϯ ⲟⲩⲱ ⲁⲩⲱ ⲉⲧϯ ⲕⲁⲣⲡⲟⲥ
ϩⲁⲑⲏ ⲛ̄ⲥⲁϥ ⲙ̄ⲛ̄ϣⲙ̄ⲧⲉ ⲡⲟⲟⲩ ⲛ̄ϩⲟⲟⲩ. ⲧⲉⲛⲟⲩ ϩⲱⲱϥ ⲁⲟⲩⲕⲱϩⲧ̄ ⲉϥϩⲟⲟⲩ ⲙⲟⲩϩ ϩⲣⲁⲓ̈
ⲛ̄ϩⲏⲧϥ̄ ⲁⲩⲱ ⲟⲩⲱϩ ⲁϥϫⲉⲣⲟ ϩ̄ⲛ ⲛ̄ⲃⲱ ⲛ̄ⲕⲛ̄ⲧⲉ ⲁⲩⲱ ⲧⲃⲱ ⲛ̄ⲭⲏⲡⲉϩ· ⲙ̄ⲛ̄ ⲧⲃⲛ̄ⲛⲉ ⲁⲩⲟⲩⲱϣⲉ
ⲁⲩⲱ ⲁⲩⲣⲱⲕϩ ⲁⲩⲱ ⲡⲉϩⲟⲩⲟ ⲛ̄ⲛ̄ϣⲏⲛ ⲧⲏⲣⲟⲩ ⲉⲧϩ̄ⲙⲡⲙⲁ ⲛ̄ϣⲏⲛ ⲁⲩϣⲱⲃϩ ⲉⲃⲟⲗ ⲙ̄ⲡϣⲁϩ
ⲉⲧⲭⲉⲣⲟ ⲉⲧⲣⲱⲕϩ̄ ⲛ̄ⲛ̄ϣⲏⲛ ⲉⲛⲧⲁϥ-ϫⲟⲓ̈ⲥ ⲉⲣⲟⲟⲩ ⲛ̄ϭⲓ ⲡⲕⲱϩⲧ̄.

73. Shenoute, *Canon 1*, YG 174–75, in Amélineau, *Oeuvres*, 1:447.

74. E.g., Jer. 4:7; 6:26. There are multiple references to the "destroyer" in
Jeremiah. Shenoute takes this biblical character and remolds it character for his
own use. Also cf. Matt. 3:10.

75. Shenoute, *Canon 1*, YG 174–77, in Amélineau, *Oeuvres*, 1:447–49.

76. The oracles in these passages prove complicated when read together, for
they describe the destruction of both Assyria and Israel. Shenoute, however, adapts
the imagery in them, regardless of their target, for his own use.

77. See also Jer. 5:14 (speaking to Israel: "I am now making my words in
your mouth a fire, and this people wood, and the fire shall devour them"); Mal.
4:1 ("See, the day is coming, burning like an oven, when all the arrogant and all
evildoers will be stubble; the day that comes shall burn them up, says the Lord of
hosts, so that it will leave them neither root nor branch.")

78. Shenoute, *Canon 1*, YG 177–83, in Amélineau, *Oeuvres*, 1:449–53.

79. Shenoute, *Canon 1*, YG 183–84, in Amélineau, *Oeuvres*, 1:453–54.

80. Shenoute, *Canon 1*, YG 128–29, in Elanskaya, *Coptic Manuscripts*, 234–35;
Eng. trans. in ibid., 237, rev.

81. Emmel, *Corpus*, 2:562.

82. Shenoute, *Canon 1*, YG 220, unpublished (FR-BN 130² f. 46R): ⲙⲏ ⲛ̄ⲧⲟ
ⲁⲛ ⲡⲉⲛⲧⲁⲣ̄-ϫⲟⲟⲥ ϫⲉ ⲙⲏ ⲉⲣⲉⲡⲁⲓ̈ ⲟⲩⲱϣ ⲉⲁⲣⲭⲉⲓ ⲉϩⲣⲁⲓ̈ ⲉϫⲱⲛ. ⲉⲧⲃⲉ ⲡⲁⲓ̈ ϯⲧⲁⲙⲟ ⲙ̄ⲙⲟ
ϫⲉ ⲟⲩ ⲙⲟⲛⲟⲛ ϫⲉ ⲉϩ̄ⲛ ⲉⲡⲁⲓ̈ ⲁⲛ ⲉⲛⲉⲧⲉⲣⲉⲛⲉⲉⲩⲉ ⲉⲣⲟⲟⲩ ϩ̄ⲛ ⲡⲟⲩϩⲏⲧ ⲛ̄ⲥⲟϭ ⲉⲧⲭⲱ
ⲛ̄ϩⲉⲛⲙⲛ̄ⲧⲥⲟϭ· ⲁⲗⲗⲁ ⲛ̄ⲁⲅⲅ{ⲉ}ⲗⲟⲥ ⲛ̄ⲗⲉⲓⲧⲟⲩⲣⲅⲟⲥ ⲛ̄ⲧⲉⲡϫⲟⲉⲓⲥ ⲉϩⲛⲁⲩ ⲁⲛ ⲉⲉⲡⲣⲟ-
ⲥⲉⲭⲉ ⲉⲣⲟ ⲉⲧⲃⲉ ⲛ̄ⲭⲱϩⲙ̄ ⲙ̄ⲛ̄ ⲛ̄ⲥⲱⲱϥ ⲙ̄ⲛ̄ ⲛ̄ϫⲓⲟⲩⲉ ⲙ̄ⲛ̄ ⲛ̄ⲕⲉⲡⲉⲑⲟⲟⲩ ⲧⲏⲣⲟⲩ ⲛ̄ⲧⲁⲩⲁⲁⲩ
ϩⲣⲁⲓ̈ ⲛ̄ϩⲏⲧⲉ. Eng. trans. in Emmel, "Shenoute the Monk," 171. See also the very
fragmentary and as yet unplaced XB frg. 2, unpublished (FR-BN Copte 130² f.
93V), as cited and discussed in Emmel, "Shenoute the Monk," 162.

83. Shenoute, *Canon 1*, XB 83, unpublished (FR-BN 130² f. 91R): . . . ⲁⲓ̈ⲛⲁⲩ ⲉϩⲉⲛⲟⲩⲱⲛϩ̅ ⲉⲃⲟⲗ ⲙ̅ⲛ̅ ϩⲉⲛⲋⲱⲁⲛ ⲉⲃⲟⲗ ⲛ̅ⲧⲉⲡⲭⲟⲓⲥ.

84. Philip Rousseau, *Ascetics, Authority, and the Church in the Age of Jerome and Cassian* (Oxford: Oxford University Press, 1978), 21–32. Here, Shenoute breaks slightly with the traditions of his biblical forebears, who did not necessarily seek to lead the community they called to repentance.

85. Shenoute, *Canon 1*, XC 19, in Leipoldt, *Opera Omnia*, 3:199–200.

86. Shenoute, *Canon 1*, XC 23, in Leipoldt, *Opera Omnia*, 3:202.

87. Shenoute, *Canon 1*, XC 23, in Leipoldt, *Opera Omnia*, 3:202–3.

88. Shenoute, *Canon 1*, XC 19, in Leipoldt, *Opera Omnia*, 3:199–200.

89. Shenoute, *Canon 1*, XC 21, in Leipoldt, *Opera Omnia*, 3:201.

90. Shenoute, *Canon 1*, XC 21, in Leipoldt, *Opera Omnia*, 3:201.

91. Shenoute, *Canon 1*, XC 60, in Munier, *Manuscrits coptes*, 104.

92. Shenoute, *Canon 1*, XC 60, in Munier, *Manuscrits coptes*, 104.

93. Shenoute, *Canon 1*, XC 28, in Leipoldt, *Opera Omnia*, 3:206.

94. Shenoute, *Canon 1*, YW 92, unpublished (FR-BN 130² f. 8V): ⲙⲛ̅ⲛ̅ⲥⲁ ⲛⲁⲓ̈ ϯⲉⲡⲓⲕⲁⲗⲉⲓ ⲙ̅ⲡⲛⲟⲩⲧⲉ ⲙ̅ⲙⲛ̅ⲧⲣⲉ ⲉⲭⲛ̅ⲧⲁϯⲯⲩⲭⲏ ϫⲉ ⲛ̅ϯϫⲓ-ⲋⲟⲗ ⲁⲛ.

95. Shenoute, *Canon 1*, XC 148–49, unpublished (FR-BN 130² ff. 94V–95R): ϩⲉⲛⲡⲁⲣⲁⲃⲟⲗⲏ ⲁⲛ ⲛⲉ ϫⲉ ⲛ̅ⲛⲉⲭⲟⲟⲥ ϫⲉ ⲁⲡⲁⲓ̈ ⲟⲩⲱⲛ ⲛ̅ⲣⲱϥ ⲉϩⲣⲁⲓ̈ ⲉⲭⲱⲓ̈ ϩⲛ̅ ϩⲉⲛⲡⲁⲣⲁ-ⲃⲟⲗⲏ ⲙ̅ⲛ̅ ⲟⲩⲋⲓⲛ-ⲱⲁⲭⲉ ⲉⲛϯⲥⲟⲟⲩⲛ ⲙ̅ⲙⲟⲥ ⲁⲛ.

96. Conrad Leyser, *Authority and Asceticism from Augustine to Gregory the Great*, Oxford Historical Monographs (Oxford: Clarendon, 2000), 161.

97. *Vita Prima Pachomii*, 106; Eng. trans. in Veilleux, *Pachomian Koinonia*, 1:370–71.

98. Leyser, *Authority and Asceticism*, 68.

99. Shenoute, *Canon 1*, YW 78, unpublished (FR-BN 130² f. 1V); see n. 32 above.

100. Maud Gleason, "Visiting and News: Gossip and Reputation-Management in the Desert," *JECS* 6 (1998): 502.

101. Ibid., 503.

102. Ibid., 512–16.

Chapter 2

1. Shenoute, *Canon 3*, YA 310, in Leipoldt, *Opera Omnia*, 4:120.

2. Patricia Cox Miller, "Desert Asceticism and 'The Body from Nowhere,'" *JECS* 2 (1994): 137.

3. Shenoute, *Canon 3*, YA 310–11, in Leipoldt, *Opera Omnia*, 4:120–21.

4. Teresa M. Shaw, "*Askesis* and the Appearance of Holiness," *JECS* 6 (1998): 485.

5. Foucault, *Discipline and Punish*, 26–27.

6. Butler, *Gender Trouble*, esp. 128–41. Butler challenges all writers to rethink their conceptions of the body as something existing prior to or apart from discursive signification. Butler revisits the issue of bodily performance in *Bodies That Matter*, where she addresses specifically the ways in which the binary category of "sex" operates as "part of a regulatory practice that produces the bodies it governs" through the process of bodily performance, or "performativity" (1–2).

Moreover, this performance is what in turn constructs a society's notions of sex and gender.

7. Peter Brown, *Body and Society*; Shaw, *Burden of the Flesh*.

8. For the process of "thinking beyond binaries" I am also indebted to Sherry Ortner, who also draws on Bourdieu and other authors of "practice theory" to describe the ways in which societies and cultures "make" individual subjects who are not so constrained by this cultural construction that they lack any agency to change these cultural systems. She theorizes about cultural systems that inform and produce subjects *and* subjects that also possess the capacity to act as agents within these cultural systems. ("Making Gender: Toward a Feminist, Minority, Postcolonial, Subaltern, etc., Theory of Practice," in *Making Gender*, 1–20.)

9. C. Bell, *Ritual Theory*, 81.

10. Ibid., 195.

11. Ibid., 93, 98.

12. Ritual and ritualization are processes in which the "molding of the body within a highly structured environment does not simply express inner states. Rather, it primarily acts to restructure bodies in the very doing of the acts themselves." (Ibid., 100.)

13. Bourdieu, *Outline*, 72. Bourdieu's habitus is "history turned into nature" in that it is a "product of history" which then "produces individual and collective practices . . . in accordance with the schemes engendered by history" that become so endemic to a culture that they are regarded as natural (78, 81–82). A "habitus" is produced and reproduced not only overtly by the enforcement of rules, laws, and the threat of material violence by an identifiable authority or authoritative class but also by objective, "self-regulating" mechanisms and structures—e.g., the modern examples of educational systems, economic systems, etc. The habitus is enforced through "symbolic" violence (e.g., various forms of economic exploitation, reductions in social status or mobility, etc.) as much as, if not more than, through the threat of real, material violence. The habitus of modern life informs practices of every day life unconsciously such that people willingly conform their lives and behaviors to this habitus without the active intention to do so. Likewise, the shifts and changes in practices of daily life inform and continually re-produce the society's habitus.

14. Shenoute regulates his community and its daily practices down to minute detail through a set of specified rules. For Bourdieu, a society's habitus is enforced by self-regulating mechanisms. Explicit rules or laws are hallmarks of a precapitalist society; truly self-regulating mechanisms are only products of postcapitalist societies. In fact, Bourdieu specifically defines habitus as something that operates "without in any way being the product of obedience to rules" and without any "orchestration" by a primary "conductor." (*Outline*, 72.) Shenoute's monastic "rule," however, gestures toward Bourdieu's notion of self-regulating structures. In codifying the rules, Shenoute defers the ultimate authority for the community, its values, and its practices away from himself and onto a somewhat independent mechanism of power for the community: a cultural disposition of constant obedience and submission not to the rules, but to the more abstract institution of the monastic leader in the name of God and tradition.

15. Susan Ashbrook Harvey, "The Stylite's Liturgy: Ritual and Religious Identity in Late Antiquity," *JECS* 6 (1998): 538.

16. Amand Boon, *Pachomiana latina: Règle et épîtres de s. Pachôme, épître de s. Théodore et "Liber" de s. Orsiesius: Texte latin de s. Jérôme*, Bibliothèque de la revue d'histoire ecclésiastique 7 (Louvain: Bureaux de la revue, 1932); Eng. trans. in Veilleux, *Pachomian Koinonia*, 2:139–223. Basil, *Regulae fusius tractatae*, PG 31:889–1052; Eng. trans. in *Basil of Caesarea, Ascetical Works*, ed. and trans. M. Monica Wagner, FC 9 (Washington, D.C.: Catholic University of America Press, 1950). Basil, *Regulae brevius tractatae*, PG 31:1080A–1305B; Eng. trans. in *The Ascetic Works of Saint Basil*, ed. and trans. W. K. Lowther Clarke (London: SPCK, 1925).

17. In contrast to the *Rule of Benedict*; Leyser, *Authority and Asceticism*, 116, 127–28.

18. For this chapter, rules in volumes 3, 5, and 9 of the *Canons* have been consulted. I follow Emmel's codicological reconstruction of the *Canons*. For the reconstruction of manuscript witnesses to *Canon 3* in codices YA, YB, ZC, ZE, ZH, and XL, see Emmel, *Corpus*, 1:145–55, 472, 495–98, 520, 522, 524; 2:570–73, 711–17. I have examined all the witnesses to *Canon 3* (apart from cases of textual parallels) reported by Emmel except for ZC 171–72 (unpublished folio EG-CF 231A) and some unpublished folios of YB and ZE, which have only recently been authenticated as Shenoutean and as copies of *Canon 3*. For the reconstruction of manuscript witnesses to *Canon 5* in codices XS and XL, see Emmel, *Corpus*, 1:164–66, 472, 485–86; 2:575–76, 727–30. I have examined all the witnesses to *Canon 5* (apart from cases of textual parallels) reported by Emmel. For the reconstruction of manuscript witnesses to *Canon 9* in codices DF, FM, XK, YX, YZ, ZA, BV, and XL, see Emmel, *Corpus*, 1:216–33, 392–93, 401–4, 422–23, 471, 473–74, 515, 517, 518; 2:599–605, 778–92. I have examined all the witnesses to *Canon 9* (apart from textual parallels) reported by Emmel except for some unpublished folios and fragments of folios from DF, XK, BV.

19. See also Leipoldt, *Schenute*, 102.

20. William Harmless, *Desert Christians: An Introduction to the Literature of Early Monasticism* (New York: Oxford University Press, 2004), 119, 124.

21. Shenoute, *Canon 3*, YA 421–23, in Leipoldt, *Opera Omnia*, 4:125–26.

22. Shenoute, *Canon 3*, YA 421–28, in Leipoldt, *Opera Omnia*, 4:124–29.

23. See also Emmel, *Corpus*, 1:147–48 and 2:571 on *Canons 1* and *3* and Young, "Five Leaves from a Copy of Shenute's *Third Canon*," *Muséon* 113 (2000): 270. Occasionally, Shenoute alternates "curses" or "woes" with "blessings," suggesting that he may be modeling his literary style on the beatitudes.

24. Shenoute, *Canon 5*, XS 275–76, in Young, *Coptic Manuscripts*, 119–21; Eng. trans. in ibid., 121, rev. The female elder (lit. "old woman") in charge of the women's congregation possesses authority and responsibilities similar to those of the male elder (lit. "old man.") Beneath these primary elders in the monastery's hierarchy are other "elders" and "senior" monks (lit. "old men" and "great men" or "great women"). Cf. the chart in Layton, "Social Structure," 29, which covers "the old man" and "the old woman" (the male and female "eldest" in his translation), "old men" ("elders" in his translation) and "great women" ("senior women" in his translation, "female senior monks" in mine), but not "great men" ("male senior monks" in my translation).

25. E.g., the short rules in Jerome's Latin translation of Pachomius, *Precepts and Institutes*, 18 in Boon, *Pachomiana latina*, 58; Eng. trans. in Veilleux, *Pachom-*

ian Koinonia, 2:172. For longer, descriptive rules see the regulations on the visitors to the monastery and monks' visits to their sick relatives. (Jerome's Latin trans. of Pachomius, *Precepts*, 52–53 in Boon, *Pachomiana latina*, 27–29; Eng. trans. in Veilleux, *Pachomian Koinonia*, 2:154–55.)

26. A notable recent exception is Goehring's article "The Fourth Letter of Horsiesius," in his *Ascetics*, 221–40.

27. Rousseau, *Pachomius*, 48–53. Rousseau reviews the scholarship on the authenticity of the rules attributed to Pachomius and concludes that it is difficult to argue that they existed sixty years prior to their collection and translation by Jerome. Cf. Veilleux, *Pachomian Koinonia*, 2:8.

28. Obvious differences in style and content between the rules attributed to Pachomius and the rules attributed to Horsiesius exist. The analysis in this book of the "Pachomian" rules texts does not deny the differences between the texts, or the diverse theologies and asceticisms that dwelled within the Pachomian communities throughout the fourth century. As Goehring has demonstrated, the monasteries did not have a monolithic view point during this period. On monastic diversity within and nearby the Pachomian establishments, see especially Goehring's essays, "Pachomius's Vision of Heresy," "New Frontiers in Pachomian Studies," "Melitian Monastic Organization: A Challenge to Pachomian Originality," and "Monastic Diversity and Ideological Boundaries," in *Ascetics*, 137–218.

29. Emmel, *Corpus*, 2:571. The fact that Shenoute cites what appear to be preexisting and authoritative regulations for the community in the beginning of *Canon 1*, before he ever assumed leadership of the community, suggests that a rule existed prior to Shenoute's tenure as leader.

30. Krawiec persuasively argues that the women's community received visits and spiritual direction from the leaders of Deir Anba Shenouda *and* the nearby Red Monastery until Shenoute consolidated his authority over the women during his tenure as monastic father. (Krawiec, *Shenoute and the Women*, 53–54.)

31. Goehring, "The Origins of Monasticism," in *Ascetics*, 28; idem, "Pachomius's Vision of Heresy," in *Ascetics*, 138; Hans Quecke, "Ein Pachomiuszitat bei Schenute," in *Probleme der koptischen Literatur*, ed. Peter Nagel (Halle-Wittenberg: Martin Luther Universität, 1968) 155–71. See also Leipoldt, *Schenute*, 11–12, 35–39.

32. Scholarship has narrated this fairly linear evolution of Shenoute's rules from Pachomius's rules. This theory, however, rests upon interpretations of Shenoute's references to a prior "father" or multiple "fathers" as Pachomius and/or Pcol. Leipoldt and others posited a chain of textual transmission from Pachomius to Shenoute. (Revillout, "Les origines du schisme égyptien," 409; Ladeuze, *Étude sur le cénobitisme Pakhômien*, 148, 241, 306–9; Leipoldt, *Schenute*, 99–100.)

33. Shenoute, *Canon 3*, YA 310, in Leipoldt, *Opera Omnia*, 4:120.

34. The identity of the "pages" (*nekhartēs*) or documents to which Shenoute refers is unclear. Cf. Emmel, *Corpus*, 2:571, who translates this phrase instead as "papyrus documents written from of old." It may be a reference to the Bible or to texts from previous monastic leaders or other prominent religious figures.

35. Shenoute, *Canon 3*, YA 423 in Leipoldt, *Opera Omnia*, 4:126.

36. *hennukteris etecinclōpe*: lit., "bats (Gk) which are bats (Cop)."

37. Lit., "places that are dug."

38. Shenoute, *Canon 3*, YA 423–25, in Leipoldt, *Opera Omnia*, 4:126–27. Ps.

118:105 (LXX); John 11:9. Cf. 1 Thess. 5:5. "Deep, dark caves" is literally "dark places that are dug very deep" (*henma nkake eušokh emate*).

39. Shenoute, *Canon 3*, YA 425–28, in Leipoldt, *Opera Omnia*, 4:127–29. See discussion on pp. 118–19. Cf. Matt. 5:44; Luke 6:27; Prov. 25:21.

40. Shenoute, *Canon 5*, XS 360–61, in Leipoldt, *Opera Omnia*, 4:64–65.

41. Leyser, *Authority and Asceticism*, 117.

42. Ibid., 118.

43. Shenoute, *Canon 5*, XS 361–62, in Leipoldt, *Opera Omnia*, 4:65. Cf. 1 Thess. 2:3–7.

44. Shenoute, *Canon 9*, DF 289–90, in Amélineau, *Oeuvres*, 2:519. Cf. John 12:50, 14:31.

45. As Amélineau indicates, Shenoute in this passage quotes not only from the gospel of John but also from the Nicene Creed, which reads, "We believe in one God, the Father almighty, maker of all things visible and invisible. And in one Lord Jesus Christ, the Son of God . . . God from God, light from light, true God from true God, begotten not made. . ." J. N. D. Kelly, *Early Christian Creeds*, 3rd ed. (New York: David McKay, 1972) 215–16; idem, *Early Christian Doctrines*, rev. ed. (San Francisco: HarperCollins, 1978), 231–37.

46. Shenoute, *Canon 9*, FM 113, in Leipoldt, *Opera Omnia*, 4:113. Shenoute refers to the "male elder" many times in the *Canons*, and he seems to function as Shenoute's proxy in the community. In addition to his other responsibilities as the leader of male residence, the "male elder" acts as a courier for Shenoute, who lives in the nearby desert and not in the monastic residence, and as a sort of second in command to Shenoute, a person whose commands must be obeyed as if they were from Shenoute himself. He relays and enforces Shenoute's directives to the men and the women. (Krawiec, *Shenoute and the Women*, 37; cf. Layton, "Social Structure," 28–29.)

47. Shenoute, *Canon 3*, ZC 307, in Leipoldt, *Opera Omnia*, 4:207–8.

48. C. Bell, *Ritual Theory*, 110.

49. Ibid., 110. Bell states that ritualization "sees" this first "evocation of a consensus," etc., but that it "does *not* see the way in which the hegemonic social order is appropriated" (emphasis mine). Bell's understanding of the unseen effects of ritualization is based on the unseen and unspoken results of Bourdieu's objective mechanisms. In Shenoute's monastery, the appropriation of the "hegemonic social order" as redemptive is both "seen" and "unseen."

50. Shenoute, *Canon 5*, XL 107, unpublished (AT-NB 9597R): ϩⲉⲛⲕⲁⲛⲱⲛ ⲉⲃⲟⲗ ϩⲓⲧⲙ̄ⲡⲗⲟⲅⲟⲥ ⲙ̄ⲡϫⲟⲉⲓ̈ⲥ ⲉⲧⲣⲉⲟⲩⲟⲛ ⲛⲓⲙ ⲉⲧⲙⲉ ⲙ̄ⲡⲛⲟⲩⲧⲉ ϩⲛ̄ ⲟⲩⲙⲉ ⲉⲓⲧⲉ ϩⲟⲟⲩⲧ ⲉⲓⲧⲉ ⲥϩⲓⲙⲉ ⲁϩⲉⲣⲁⲧⲟⲩ ϩⲛ̄ ⲟⲩⲱϣ ⲙ̄ⲙⲉ ⲕⲁⲧⲁ ⲛⲉⲅⲣⲁⲫⲏ ϫⲉ ⲁⲓ̈ⲁϩⲉ ⲅⲁⲣ ⲉⲣⲁⲧ ϩⲛ̄ ⲟⲩⲱϣ ⲙ̄ⲙⲉ.

51. See n. 43 above.

52. For Evagrius, the temptations and struggles of the monks fall into eight categories divided into roughly two types: the more physical (such as gluttony and fornication) and the spiritual (such as vainglory and pride). A monk must first conquer the more basic, physical temptations before being able to live the contemplative life of the "gnostikos." See Antoine Guillaumont, introduction to Evagrius Ponticus, *Practicus*, in *Traité pratique ou le moine*, ed. and trans. Antoine and Claire Guillaumont, 2 vols., SC 170–71 (Paris: Les Éditions du Cerf, 1971), 38–84. On the contemplative life, see also Antoine and Claire Guillaumont, introduction

to Evagrius Ponticus, *Gnosticus,* in *Le Gnostique ou à celui qui est devenu digne de la science,* ed. and trans. A. and C. Guillaumont, SC 356 (Paris: Les Éditions du Cerf, 1989), 17–40.

53. Valantasis, "Constructions of Power in Asceticism," 794.

54. Goehring, "The World Engaged: The Social and Economic World of Early Egyptian Monasticism," in *Ascetics,* 39–52, esp. 47–48.

55. Rousseau, *Pachomius,* 88.

56. Ibid., 90, 103.

57. According to Rousseau, life under the rules was a "constant interaction between order and personal liberty." (Ibid., 102.)

58. "About the rule of the assembly, and how to assemble the brothers for the instruction which is useful to their souls, according to what is pleasing to God and in conformity to the advices and rules of the saints. God has given us [that rule] in the light of the scriptures for the liberation of ignorant souls, that they might glorify God in the light of the living, and that they might know how they ought to behave in God's house, without lapse or scandal, not inebriated by what is pleasing to God but standing in the norm of truth, according to the traditions of the apostles and prophets in the manner they teach us how to celebrate in God." (Pachomius, preface to *Precepts and Institutes,* in Boon, *Pachomiana latina,* 53; Eng. trans. in Veilleux, *Pachomian Koinonia,* 2:169.)

59. Pachomius, *Precepts and Institutes* 1–17, in Boon, *Pachomiana latina,* 54–58; Eng. trans. in Veilleux, *Pachomian Koinonia,* 2:169–72.

60. Pachomius, *Precepts and Institutes* 18, in Boon, *Pachomiana latina,* 58–62; Eng. trans. in Veilleux, *Pachomian Koinonia,* 2:172–74.

61. Horsiesius, *Regulations* 42, in L. Th. Lefort, ed., *Oeuvres de s. Pachôme et de ses disciples,* CSCO 159 (Louvain: L. Durbecq, 1956), 93–94; Eng. trans. in Veilleux, *Pachomian Koinonia,* 2:211–12.

62. Horsiesius, *Regulations* 43, in Lefort, *Oeuvres de s. Pachôme,* 94; Eng. trans. in Veilleux, *Pachomian Koinonia,* 2:212.

63. Pachomius, *Precepts* 62, 120, 123, in Boon, *Pachomiana latina,* 32, 45, 46. Eng. trans. in Veilleux, *Pachomian Koinonia,* 2:157, 164.

64. Pachomius, *Precepts* 2, 69, 93, 96, 97 and *Precepts and Judgements* 7, in Boon, *Pachomiana latina,* 13, 33–34, 39, 40, 66; Eng. trans. in Veilleux, *Pachomian Koinonia,* 2:145, 157, 161, 177.

65. Pachomius, *Precepts and Institutes* 18, in Boon, *Pachomiana latina,* 61; Eng. trans. in Veilleux, *Pachomian Koinonia,* 2:174.

66. Pachomius, *Precepts and Judgements* 2, 4, 11, in Boon, *Pachomiana latina,* 64, 65, 67–68; Eng. trans. in Veilleux, *Pachomian Koinonia,* 2:175, 176, 178.

67. Horsiesius, *Regulations* 9, in Lefort, *Oeuvres de s. Pachôme,* 84; Eng. trans. in Veilleux, *Pachomian Koinonia,* 2:199–200.

68. The *Precepts and Institutes* admonish monks not to be overcome by "works of the flesh," and the *Regulations of Horsiesius* warn against the "desires of the flesh" and boasting "according to the flesh." (Pachomius, *Precepts and Institutes* 18, in Boon, *Pachomiana latina,* 58–60; Horsiesius, *Regulations* 4, 36, in Lefort, *Oeuvres de s. Pachôme,* 83, 92; Eng. trans. in Veilleux, *Pachomian Koinonia,* 2:172–73, 198, 209.)

69. Bentley Layton, "Monastic Order in Shenoute's White Monastery Federation," paper presented at the University of Minnesota, Minneapolis, Symposium "Living for Eternity: Monasticism in Egypt," March 8, 2003.

70. Pachomius, *Precepts* 2, in Boon, *Pachomiana latina*, 13; Eng. trans. in Veilleux, *Pachomian Koinonia*, 2:145. Also "No one shall do the laundry with his clothes drawn up higher than is established"; "No one shall . . . bathe or wash [his body] immodestly contrary to the manner established for them"; and "Again when we are seated at the *synaxis*, let us be seated with modesty. Let our garments be gathered about us so as to cover our legs." (Pachomius, *Precepts* 69, 92, in Boon, *Pachomiana latina*, 33–34, 39; Horsiesius, *Regulations* 20, in Lefort, *Oeuvres de s. Pachôme*, 88; Eng. trans. in Veilleux, *Pachomian Koinonia*, 2:157, 161, 204.)

71. Shenoute, *Canon 9*, FM 187–88, in Leipoldt, *Opera Omnia*, 4:162.

72. Shenoute, *Canon 5*, XS 351, in Leipoldt, *Opera Omnia*, 4:59.

73. Shenoute, *Canon 3*, YA 257–58, in Young, "Five Leaves," 271–72; Eng. trans. in Young, "Five Leaves," 272–73, rev.

74. Pachomius, *Precepts* 143, in Boon, *Pachomiana latina*, 51–52; Eng. trans. in Veilleux, *Pachomian Koinonia*, 2:166–67.

75. Shenoute writes of the women's "congregation" as being "in the village," but the precise location is uncertain. (Krawiec, *Shenoute and the Women*, 24, 187 n. 104; cf. Elm, *Virgins of God*, 299–300.)

76. Shenoute, *Canon 5*, XL 136–37, in Munier, *Manuscrits coptes*, 80. Here Shenoute writes about male monks who greet their "mothers," "sisters," or "daughters" with a kiss. Shenoute probably is not referring to the monks' blood relatives (or relatives "according to the flesh"), since in many of his writings about interactions between monks, he stresses that they should not privilege biological ties. Instead, all should be considered brothers, sisters, mothers, and fathers of each other. (Krawiec, *Shenoute and the Women*, 164–71.)

77. Shenoute, *Canon 9*, DF 188–89, in Leipoldt, *Opera Omnia*, 4:107. *Canon 9* contains specific instructions about male and female interactions, including regulations for visiting each other's communities, men who go to the women's community to perform work, men who staff the entrance to the women's community (the "gate house"), and correspondence between Shenoute and the women. For examples, see DF 188–90 in Leipoldt, *Opera Omnia*, 4:107–8 and ZA 223–24, in Young, *Coptic Manuscripts*, 48–59.

78. Horsiesius, *Regulations* 41–42, in Lefort, *Oeuvres de s. Pachôme*, 93–94; Eng. trans. in Veilleux, *Pachomian Koinonia*, 2:210–12. Pachomius, *Precepts* 40–42, 45–46, 71, 74–80, in Boon, *Pachomiana latina*, 23–24, 34, 35–36; Eng. trans. in Veilleux, *Pachomian Koinonia*, 2:151–52, 158–59.

79. See Shenoute, *Canon 5*, XS 319–20, 325–26, in Leipoldt, *Opera Omnia*, 4:53–56. E.g., XS 326: "But if a need exists such that someone seeks a little wine in his (or her) sickness whether it is a man or a woman, whether it is a male junior monk or a female junior monk, and if they ask for a little wine in their sickness, it will be given to them. If they are truly sick, they need it."

80. Shenoute, *Canon 5*, XS 275–76, in Young, *Coptic Manuscripts*, 119–21; Eng. trans. in ibid., 121.

81. Pachomius, *Precepts* 78, 79, 114, in Boon, *Pachomiana latina*, 36, 43; Eng. trans. in Veilleux, *Pachomian Koinonia*, 2:159, 163.

82. Horsiesius, *Regulations* 37, in Lefort, *Oeuvres de s. Pachôme*, 92; Eng. trans. in Veilleux, *Pachomian Koinonia*, 2:210.

83. "For this reason, as for the one who eats his (or her) bread according to

the canons that are established for us, let him (or her) eat it truthfully, so that he (or she) has no sin. . . . Everyone among us, whether male or female, is despised before Jesus when they ask for anything deceitfully, as if they are sick when they are not sick." (Shenoute, *Canon 5*, XS 61–62, in Leipoldt, *Opera Omnia*, 4:78–79.)

84. "No person among us, whether male or female, shall finish eating and go to the infirmary and eat there again, or shall finish eating in the infirmary and go to the refectory and eat there again." Shenoute, *Canon 5*, XS 276, in Young, *Coptic Manuscripts*, 120; Eng. trans. in ibid., 121, rev.

85. Shenoute, *Canon 5*, XS 320, in Leipoldt, *Opera Omnia*, 4:54.

86. Shenoute, *Canon 5*, XS 370, in Leipoldt, *Opera Omnia*, 4:70.

87. Shenoute, *Canon 9*, YX 63–64, in Amélineau, *Monuments*, 4:286–87.

88. Foucault, *Discipline and Punish*, 11.

89. Ibid., 25. As Foucault puts it, "[T]he body is also directly involved in a political field; power relations . . . invest it, mark it, train it, torture it, force it to carry out tasks, to perform ceremonies, to emit signs." See Foucault also on the soul (16–18).

90. Pachomius, *Precepts and Judgements* 4, in Boon, *Pachomiana latina*, 65; Eng. trans. in Veilleux, *Pachomian Koinonia*, 2:176.

91. Krawiec, *Shenoute and the Women*, 28–29, 40–42.

92. A few examples can be found in Pachomius, *Precepts* 9, 10, 32, in Boon, *Pachomiana latina*, 15, 21; Eng. trans. in Veilleux, *Pachomian Koinonia*, 2:146, 150.

93. Pachomius, *Precepts and Judgements* 2, in Boon, *Pachomiana latina*, 64; Eng. trans. in Veilleux, *Pachomian Koinonia*, 2:175–76. Cf. also Pachomius, *Precepts* 136–37, in Boon, *Pachomiana latina*, 49; Eng. trans. in Veilleux, *Pachomian Koinonia*, 2:165.

94. Cf. Rousseau, *Pachomius*, 95–96 on this particular rule.

95. Ibid., 96–97.

96. Ibid., 97.

97. Ibid., 97–98.

98. See Gleason, "Visiting and News," 513–14 for treatment of an anecdote from the *Apophethgmata Patrum* (or *Sayings of the Desert Fathers*) that expresses a similar ambivalence about expulsion.

99. E.g., Shenoute, *Canon 9*, DF 267–68, unpublished (FR-BN 130⁴ f. 96 r/v).

100. E.g., Shenoute, *Canon 9*, DF 262, unpublished (FR-BN 130⁴ f. 95v): ⲛⲉⲧϯ-ⲛ̄ϩⲧⲏⲩ ⲏ ⲉⲧⲉⲓⲣⲉ ⲙ̄ⲡⲙⲉⲉⲩⲉ ϫⲉ ⲉⲓⲥ ⲟⲩⲏⲣ ⲛ̄ⲣⲟⲙⲡⲉ ϫⲓ[ⲛ] ⲛⲧⲁⲛⲛⲟⲩϫⲉ ⲉⲃⲟⲗ ⲛ̄ⲛⲉⲥⲛⲏⲩ ⲉⲧϩⲙ̄ⲡϯⲙⲉ ⲉⲧⲃⲉ ⲙ̄ⲡⲟⲛⲏⲣⲟⲛ. See also *He Who Sits Upon His Throne*, *Canon 6*, in which Shenoute discusses the beating and then expulsion of an elderly monk. (Amélineau, *Oeuvres*, 2:302–8; Emmel, *Corpus*, 1:576–77.)

101. Shenoute, *Canon 5*, XS 320, in Leipoldt, *Opera Omnia*, 4:54; Shenoute, *Canon 9*, BV 114, in Amélineau, *Oeuvres*, 2:349.

102. Shenoute, *Canon 9*, DF 186, in Leipoldt, *Opera Omnia*, 4:105.

103. Monks with family, however, may be entrusted to the "custody of their relatives." (Shenoute, *Is It Not Written*, *Canon 6*, XF 245–46, in Amélineau, *Oeuvres*, 1:66; Eng. trans. in Krawiec, *Shenoute and the Women*, 126–27. Cf. Leipoldt, *Schenute*, 63.)

104. Shenoute, *Canon 9*, DF 178, in Leipoldt, *Opera Omnia*, 4:98.

105. Shenoute, *Canon 9*, DF 180–81, in Leipoldt, *Opera Omnia*, 4:100.

106. Shenoute, *Canon 9*, DF 180–81, in Leipoldt, *Opera Omnia*, 4:100.

107. Shenoute, *Canon 3*, YA 310–11, in Leipoldt, *Opera Omnia*, 4:120–21.

108. Shenoute, *Canon 9*, DF 181, in Leipoldt, *Opera Omnia*, 4:101. See also *Canon 5*, XS 389–90, in Leipoldt, *Opera Omnia*, 4:76–77 in which Shenoute elaborates on a series of scriptural passages in which Israel is destroyed or defiled sinners are dispersed from their homes and regions; and *Canon 9*, XL 387–91, in Leipoldt, *Opera Omnia*, 3:16–18.

109. Shenoute, *Canon 9*, YZ 280-FM 181, in Young, *Coptic Manuscripts*, 55, and Leipoldt, *Opera Omnia*, 4:156; Eng. trans. in Young, *Coptic Manuscripts*, 59, rev.

110. Shenoute, *Canon 3*, YA 311, in Leipoldt, *Opera Omnia*, 4:121. "Your domain" probably refers to the women's community.

111. "God is the one who casts them out." (Shenoute, *Canon 9*, XL 389–90, in Leipoldt, *Opera Omnia*, 3:18.) See also Shenoute, *Canon 5*, XS 320, in Leipoldt, *Opera Omnia*, 4:54.

112. Shenoute, *Canon 9*, DF 185, in Leipoldt, *Opera Omnia*, 4:104–5. See also FM 192 in Leipoldt, *Opera Omnia*, 4:166 for another instruction not to pity expelled monks.

113. See also Weismann's Latin translation ("Iesus enim eos persequitur"). *Sinuthii Archimandritae Vita et Opera Omnia*, CSCO 108, SCopt 12:62.

114. Shenoute, *Canon 3*, YA 426–27, in Leipoldt, *Opera Omnia*, 4:128. Matt. 18:16–22, 10:37; cf. Luke 14:26.

115. Shenoute, *Canon 3*, YA 428, in Leipoldt, *Opera Omnia*, 4:129. Cf. Krawiec, *Shenoute and the Women*, esp. 173–74, regarding Shenoute's further usage of kinship language in the monastic setting.

116. See n. 3 above.

117. In addition, see also Shenoute, *Canon 4*, BZ 345, in Young, *Coptic Manuscripts*, 102 (Eng. trans. in ibid., 112), where Shenoute calls the monastery "a single body" in a letter to the female monks, and Krawiec's treatment of the passage in her *Shenoute and the Women*, 68.

118. Shenoute, *Canon 3*, YA 295, in Leipoldt, *Opera Omnia*, 4:115.

119. Shenoute, *Canon 3*, YA 293–95, in Leipoldt, *Opera Omnia*, 4:114–15.

120. Shenoute, *Canon 3*, YA 295–96, in Leipoldt, *Opera Omnia*, 4:115–16.

121. Shenoute, *Canon 3*, YA 296–97, in Leipoldt, *Opera Omnia*, 4:116.

122. The Coptic for "For this reason, the Lord shall forgive them" reads *etbe pai pjoeis efekō nau ebol*. Just the replacement of one word—*nsōou* instead of *nau*—would cause the passage to read, instead, that the Lord shall "abandon" them.

123. Shenoute, *Canon 3*, YA 299–300 in Leipoldt, *Opera Omnia*, 4:117–18. Jer. 6:19. As Wiesmann's footnotes to the Latin translation indicate, Shenoute also laces this passage with references to 1 Cor. 4:14, Deut. 10:16, 1 Pet. 2:11, and 1 Thess. 4:3, among others. (Wiesmann, *Opera Omnia*, CSCO 108, SCopt 12:70.)

124. Compare this to Origen's and Jerome's ascetic interpretation of Rom. 2:25–29 and 1 Cor. 7:18–20. Circumcision signifies the celibate life, whereas marriage is uncircumcision. Ambrose also interprets circumcision spiritually as celibacy. (Clark, *Reading Renunciation: Asceticism and Scripture in Early Christianity* [Princeton, N.J.: Princeton University Press, 1999], 228–29.)

125. This passage occurs in a fragment of codex FM (pages 113–14), and appears to be part of a narrative section of *Canon 9* that runs from FM 109 through

FM 114 and possibly continues in other witnesses to *Canon 9* through DF 130 and then XK 150. See the manuscript table in Emmel, *Corpus*, 2:778–92.

126. Shenoute, *Canon 9*, FM 113, in Leipoldt, *Opera Omnia*, 4:112–13.

127. "A person who did not ever devastate the hair of his head without me, without asking me first—what then is the matter in which he does not submit to me?" Shenoute, *Canon 9*, FM 113, in Leipoldt, *Opera Omnia*, 4:113.

128. Again, cf. Layton, "Social Structure," 28–29.

129. Shenoute, *Canon 9*, FM 114, in Leipoldt, *Opera Omnia*, 4:113.

130. Shenoute, *Canon 9*, DF 129, in Leipoldt, *Opera Omnia*, 4:94.

131. Shenoute, *Canon 9*, DF 129–30, in Leipoldt, *Opera Omnia*, 4:94.

132. Shenoute's complicated views on sin and disease pervade the *Canons*. He devotes considerable attention to "leprosy" and disease-like pollutions in an extended exegesis of Levitical and other biblical purity codes *Who But God Is the Witness*, in *Canon 8*. An entire copy of *Who But God Is the Witness* is in unpublished codex XO housed at the IFAO in Cairo. A critical edition of the codex is in preparation. On illness and its treatment in early Christian monasteries (including Deir Anba Shenouda), see Andrew T. Crislip, *From Monastery to Hospital: Christian Monasticism and the Transformation of Health Care in Late Antiquity* (Ann Arbor: University of Michigan, 2005).

133. Krawiec, *Shenoute and the Women*, 66–69.

134. Shenoute, *Canon 9*, YZ 221, in Young, "Two Leaves," 294–95; Eng. trans. in ibid., 295–96.

135. Although he refers to the sick person in the third person, it seems likely that he is talking about himself. Shenoute refers to himself in the third person elsewhere in the *Canons*. In *Canon 1*, as in this passage, he refers to himself in the third person when he describes his interactions with other individuals.

136. People will become "ensnared" if they believe that those who say "I love you very much," really love them. He urges "brother or son or husband" and "daughter or wife" not to listen to these professions. (Shenoute, *Canon 9*, YK 181, in Young, *Coptic Manuscripts*, 23–24; Eng. trans. in ibid., 24.)

137. *ouagapē ntapro*, lit. a love that belongs to (or pertains to) the mouth

138. Shenoute, *Canon 9*, YK 181–82, in Young, *Coptic Manuscripts*, 23–24; Eng. trans. in ibid., 25, rev.

139. Shenoute's discussions of illness are sometimes interpreted as references to an actual disease which afflicted Shenoute for several decades (e.g., Emmel, *Corpus*, 2:593–94 on disease references in *Canon 8*).

140. Cf. Crislip, who argues that Egyptian monastic leaders were reluctant to attribute the cause of illness to sin (*From Monastery to Hospital*, 77–78). According to Crislip, the exception to this paradigm was "illness of demonic origin," which he maintains was one condition in which the sick monk is held "responsible for his or her own recovery" (78), as opposed to those suffering from natural disease who required treatment by others for their recovery. Shenoute's discussion of his *own* diseased condition resists these categories, however. He associates the illness with "demonic utterances," imputes the disease to the sin of others, and locates the cure in the actions of himself and others.

141. Shenoute, *Canon 9*, XK 195–96, in Amélineau, *Oeuvres*, 2:512.

142. "Since not a single one came to these congregations because of a house or because of a place or because of a craft; but it was to repent from our sins that

we all came. Or even some came who were (already) sinless, in order that they might struggle not to sin." (Shenoute, *Canon 9*, FM 189, in Leipoldt, *Opera Omnia*, 4:164.)

143. Shenoute, *Canon 9*, FM 189–90, in Leipoldt, *Opera Omnia*, 4:164.

Chapter 3

1. Precise dating of the construction of the church is complicated by the fact that the current site requires further excavation and surveying (see below, nn. 23, 25). Emmel dates the church to about 450 (or sometime in the preceding decade) based on the datable events chronicled in the texts about the building and inscriptions in the extant building at the site. Archaeologist Peter Grossmann dates the church to 455 C.E. based on inscriptions and archaeological research. (W. E. Crum, "Inscriptions from Shenoute's Monastery," *JTS* 5 [1904]: 554–56; Emmel, "The Historical Circumstances of Shenoute's Sermon *God Is Blessed*," in *ΘΕΜΕΛΙΑ: Spätantike und koptologische Studien Peter Grossmann zum 65. Geburtstag* [Wiesbaden: Reichart Verlag, 1998], 93–94; Grossmann, *Christliche Architektur in Ägypten*, Handbook of Oriental Studies, Section One: The Near and Middle East, vol. 62 [Leiden: Brill, 2002], 528–29.)

2. According to the monks at Deir Anba Shenouda, before becoming patriarch, Pope Cyril VI (d. 1971) lived for a time in a cave overlooking Deir Anba Shenouda.

3. See n. 23 below.

4. For Egypt, see Grossmann, *Christliche Architektur*; Darlene Brooks Hedstrom, "'Your Cell Will Teach You All Things': The Relationship between Monastic Practice and the Architectural Design of the Cell in Coptic Monasticism, 400–1000 (Egypt)" (Ph.D. diss., Miami University, 2001); Elizabeth Bolman, "Joining the Community of Saints: Monastic Paintings and Ascetic Practice in Early Christian Egypt," in *Shaping Community: The Art and Archaeology of Monasticism: Papers from a Symposium Held at the Frederick R. Weisman Museum, University of Minnesota, March 10–12*, ed. Sheila McNally, British Archaeological Reports International Series 941 (Oxford: Archaeopress, 2001), 41–56; and eadem, ed., *Monastic Visions: Wall Paintings in the Monastery of St. Antony at the Red Sea* (New Haven, Conn.: Yale University Press and the American Research Center in Egypt, 2002).

5. Dale Martin lays out the multiple ancient philosophical and medical understandings of body, flesh, spirit, and soul as well as Paul's own views on the body. (*Corinthian Body*, 3–37, 128–29). A person's *pneuma*, or vital spirit, was a part of the body that coursed through flesh in the form of blood and sperm. (Rousselle, *Porneia*, 13–15, and on female "sperm," 27–32.)

6. Shaw, *Burden of the Flesh*, 2–3, 29–33.

7. Several examples of Shenoute's discourse of the flesh also occur in his letters to the women monks. In these letters, he chastises the monks for continuing to honor the bonds of the flesh (e.g., family ties, friendship), and he accuses some of the women of showing favoritism to female relatives and friends or of desiring to visit male relatives in the men's community. Shenoute exhorts the women to transform their relationships into bonds of the spirit, in which all monks are equal

in companionship and status to all others (except Shenoute). For an analysis of Shenoute's letters to women and models of kinship in the monastery, see the recent work of Rebecca Krawiec in *Shenoute and the Women of the White Monastery*, 161–74.

8. Since Shenoutean texts continue to be identified among Coptic manuscripts, we may learn more about the context of *Canon 7*.

9. Emmel, *Corpus*, 1:178–204, 2:582–93.

10. Shenoute, *This Great House*, *Canon 7*, XL 273–74, unpublished (FR-BN 130⁴ ff. 139V–140R): ⲡⲉⲓⲏⲟϭ ⲛ̄ⲏ[ⲓ̄], ⲛⲉⲓⲏⲟϭ ⲛ̄ⲏⲓ̄. The other buildings include "other places" and laundries or baths. (XL 274, unpublished [FR-BN 130⁴ f. 140R]: ⲛ̄ⲙⲟⲛ ⲉⲃⲟⲗ ⲧⲱⲛ ϫⲉ ⲉⲛⲛⲁϣϭⲛ̄ϭⲟⲙ ⲉⲕⲉⲧ-ⲡⲉⲓⲏⲟϭ ⲛ̄ⲏⲓ̄ ⲛ̄ⲧⲉⲓ̈ϩⲉ ⲙⲛ̄ ⲛⲉⲓ̈ⲕⲉⲧⲟⲡⲟⲥ ⲛ̄ⲧⲁⲛⲕⲟ-ⲧⲟⲩ ⲛ̄ⲙⲙⲁϥ; cf. Emmel, "Historical Circumstances," 83.)

11. Shenoute, *If Everyone Errs*, XL 282, in Leipoldt, *Opera Omnia*, 3:216.

12. Shenoute, *The Rest of the Words*, *Canon 7*, GO 392, in Leipoldt, *Opera Omnia*, 3:67–68: "The rest of the words in this book, or the others which we spoke and we wrote in the second year after we built this house, at the time when the barbarians were rampaging until they invaded the city called Koeis, at the time when this great multitude dwelled among us as they were fleeing from the Cushites. . . ." Cf. Eng. trans. and discussion in Emmel, *Corpus*, 2:585 and idem, "Historical Circumstances," 85.

13. As there is no complete, published edition of *God Is Holy*, I follow the codicological reconstruction of the extant manuscripts of the text in codices DG, GO, XG, XL, XU, YH, YR, ZS, and ZV in Emmel, *Corpus* 1:178–204, 405–6, 441–43, 464, 472–74, 488–89, 503, 510, 535, 537; 2:745–47. I have examined all the witnesses to *God Is Holy* (apart from cases of textual parallels) reported by Emmel. On the sermon's context, see Emmel, "Historical Circumstances," 82.

14. Shenoute, *God Is Holy*, *Canon 7*, XU 1, in Carl Wessely, ed., *Griechische und koptische Texte theologischen Inhalts*, 5 vols, Studien zur Palaeographie und Papyruskunde 9, 11, 12, 15, 18 (Leipzig: H. Haessel Hachfolger, 1909–17), 1:97; cf. the Eng. trans. in Emmel, *Corpus*, 2:586. This introduction may have been written when *Canon 7* was compiled and serves as a summarizing foreword or prologue. This may still form a portion of the "authentic" Shenoutean corpus, since Shenoute may have compiled the *Canons* himself.

15. As there is no complete, published edition of *A23*, I follow the codicological reconstruction of the extant manuscript fragments in codices GO, XL, and YR as enumerated in Emmel, *Corpus*, 1:441–43, 472–74, 510; 2:748. I have examined all the witnesses to *A23* (apart from cases of textual parallels) reported by Emmel.

16. As there is no complete, published edition of *This Great House*, I follow the codicological reconstruction of the extant manuscripts of the text in codices DG, GN, GO, XG, XL, XU, YH, and YR as enumerated in Emmel, *Corpus*, 1:405–6, 439–40, 441–43, 464, 472–74, 488–89, 503, 510; 2:748–53. I have examined all the witnesses to *This Great House* (apart from cases of textual parallels) reported by Emmel except for unpublished folio fragment GO 186–87 (FR-PL E. 9996).

17. Shenoute, *This Great House*, XL 273–74, unpublished (FR-BN 130⁴ ff. 139V–140R): ⲟⲩ ⲙⲟⲛⲟⲛ ϫⲉ ϥⲧⲟⲟⲩ ⲛ̄ⲉⲃⲟⲧ ⲛⲉⲛⲧⲁⲛⲁⲁⲩ ⲉⲛⲣ̄-ϩⲱⲃ ⲉⲣⲟϥ ⲏ ⲧⲟⲩ ⲧⲏⲣⲟⲩ. ⲁⲗⲗⲁ ϩⲛ̄ ⲛⲉⲓ̈ϩⲁⲁⲩ ⲧⲏⲣⲟⲩ ⲟⲛ ⲛ̄ⲧⲁⲛ̄ⲧⲁⲁⲩ ⲛ̄ⲃⲉⲕⲉ ⲁⲩⲱ ⲛ̄ⲧⲁⲛϫⲟⲟⲩ ⲉⲃⲟⲗ ⲉⲣⲟϥ ϩ2ⲁⲁⲩ ⲛⲓⲙ ⲉⲧϣⲟⲟⲡ ⲛⲁⲛ ⲱⲛⲧⲱⲥ ⲙ̄ⲡⲟⲩϭⲱϫⲃ̄ .... ⲛⲉⲓ̈ⲧⲟⲡⲟⲥ ⲛ̄ⲧⲁⲛⲥⲙⲛ̄ⲧⲟ[ⲩ]

ⲧⲏⲣⲟⲩ ⲉⲧⲣⲉⲛϣ[ⲱ]ⲡⲉ ⲉⲛⲟⲩⲁⲁⲃ ⲛ̄ϩⲏⲧⲟⲩ…. ⲧⲁⲓ ⲧⲉ ⲑⲉ ⲛⲁⲉⲓⲁⲧⲟⲩ ⲛ̄ⲛⲉⲧⲛⲁⲙⲟⲟϣⲉ ⲕⲁⲧⲁ ⲡⲉⲙⲡϣⲁ ⲛ̄ⲛⲉⲩⲁⲅⲅⲉⲗⲓⲟⲛ ⲁⲩⲱ ⲕⲁⲧⲁ ⲡⲉⲙⲡϣⲁ ⲛ̄ⲡⲏⲓ ⲙ̄ⲡⲛⲟⲩⲧⲉ ⲏ ⲛⲉⲛⲓ ⲁⲩⲱ ⲛⲉϥⲧⲟⲡⲟⲥ ⲧⲏⲣⲟⲩ. Cf. Emmel, "Historical Circumstances," 83.

18. As there are no complete, published editions of *I Myself Have Seen* and *If Everyone Errs*, I follow the codicological reconstructions of the extant manuscripts in codices DG, GN, GO, XG, XL, XU, and YR as enumerated in Emmel, *Corpus*, 1:405–6, 439–40, 441–43, 464, 472–74, 488–89, 510; 2:753–57. I have examined all the witnesses to *I Myself Have Seen* and *If Everyone Errs* (apart from cases of textual parallels) reported by Emmel. As Emmel has suggested, *If Everyone Errs* may have been the originally intended ending to *Canon 7*. Its conclusion begins with a summary statement quite similar to the colophon of *God Is Holy*: "For from the beginning of this discourse (*logos*) to its end, all the things that are written in this book find fault with us because of the unnatural things that prevailed upon the majority of people, men and women, and also that we are in the house of God, the Christ, and his places so that we might sanctify ourselves in order that they too (the houses) might become holy." (Shenoute, *If Everyone Errs*, *Canon 7*, XL 281–82, in Leipoldt, *Opera Omnia*, 3:216.) Emmel's hypothesis is further supported by the abrupt shift in topic that occurs in the last three sermons. (Emmel, *Corpus*, 2:584.)

19. As there are no complete, published editions of *The Rest of the Words*, *Continuing to Glorify the Lord*, and *It Is Obvious* I follow the codicological reconstruction of the extant manuscripts in codices DG, GN, GO, XL, XU, YR, and ZS as enumerated in Emmel, *Corpus*, 1:405–6, 439–40, 441–43, 472–74, 488–89, 510, 535; 2:757–61. I have examined all the witnesses to *The Rest of the Words*, *Continuing to Glorify the Lord*, and *It Is Obvious* in *Canon 7* (apart from cases of textual parallels) reported by Emmel. *It Is Obvious* is an excerpt of a longer sermon found in *Discourses 4* (Emmel, *Corpus*, 2:592–93 and idem, "Historical Circumstances," 82).

20. The Coptic Orthodox Church has plans for continued growth at the monastery, having recently built extensive new guest housing, a dining hall and chapel for visitors, and a new church for the monks near their cells. Novices are training to become monks.

21. Mahmoud Ali Mohamed and Peter Grossmann, "On the Recently Excavated Monastic Buildings in Dayr Anba Shinuda: Archaeological Report," *Bulletin de la Société d'archéologie Copte* 30 (1991): 53–63; Grossmann, "Brief Report on a Survey in the Monastery of Apa Shenudi at Suhag (April 2002)," *Bulletin de la Société d'archéologie Copte* 42 (2003): 9–11.

22. W. M. Flinders Petrie, one of the earliest scholars to date the church to Shenoute's lifetime, discussed the site in his research study of the wider area of Atripe: "A much larger settlement and a new church was required by the flourishing monasticism of that age, under Saint Shenudeh. A fresh site was adopted, outside of the existing town, which was partly deserted; the old church was taken down, and the more important parts of it re-used in the great new basilica . . . , and the less useful stone was burnt for lime for the new building. . . . Such seems to have been the growth of the place which became celebrated as the home of the great saint Shenudeh, whose life has been preserved to us." (*Athribis*, British School of Archeology in Egypt 14 [London: London School of Archaeology in Egypt, 1908], 15.) He describes coming upon the remains of a building that he

calls the Coenobium, and he documents this structure along with the walls surrounding the monastery and other brick buildings. (*Athribis*, 13–15.) Other early
studies include G. Lefebvre, "Deir-el-Abiad," in the *Dictionnaire d'archéologie
Chrétienne et de liturgie*, 15 vols. (Paris: Librairie Letouzey et Ané, 1903–53), vol.
4, pt. 1:459–502; Ugo Monneret de Villard, *Les Couvents près de Sohâg (Deyr el-
Abiad et Deyr el-Ahmar)* (Milan: Tipografia Pontificia Arcivescovile S. Giuseppe,
1925–26). Lefebvre provides illustrations dating from 1895 to 1913. Friedrich Deichmann also surveyed the site, focusing primarily on the art and architecture of the
church. ("Zum Altägyptischen in der koptishen Baukunst," *Mitteilungen des Deutschen Archäologischen Instituts—Abteilung Kairo* 8 [1938]: 34–37.)

23. Grossmann, "Dayr Anbā Shinūdah: Architecture" in *The Coptic Encyclopedia*, ed. Aziz S. Atiya, 8 vols. (New York: Macmillan, 1991), 3:769; idem, *Christliche Architektur*, 528; and personal conversations June–July 1999, Cairo. Both the
original structure and the rebuilt, seventh-century church possessed architectural
innovations. (Grossmann, "New Observations in the Church and Sanctuary of
Dayr Anbā Šinūda—the So-Called White Monastery—at Sūhāǧ: Results of Two
Surveys in October, 1981 and January, 1982," *Annales du Service des antiquités de
l'Egypte* 70 [1984]: 71–72; "Dayr Anbā Shinūdah," 768–69; *Christliche Architektur*,
534–36).

24. Hans Georg Severin, "Dayr Anbā Shinūdah: Architectural Sculpture" in
The Coptic Encyclopedia, 3:769.

25. The listing of these two monasteries on the World Monument Fund's
World Monument Watch list was due to the efforts of Elizabeth S. Bolman and
Fawzy Estafanous. Bolman, associate professor of art history at Temple University,
chairs an international and interdisciplinary consortium of scholars pursuing re-
search and conservation at the monasteries. Bolman also directs the Deir Anba
Bishoi wall painting conservation project, which is being administered by the
American Research Center in Egypt, with USAID funding. Grants from ARCE,
the National Endowment for the Humanities, and Dumbarton Oaks fund work at
Deir Anba Shenouda.

26. Grossmann, *Christliche Architektur*, 533–35. On dating, see also n. 1
above.

27. Grossmann, "New Observations"; idem, *Christliche Architektur*, 528–36,
and figs. 150–54. The result of Grossmann's most recent work, including new site
plans, are forthcoming in *Dumbarton Oaks Papers*.

28. Grossmann, *Christliche Architektur*, 534.

29. Ibid., 532; René-Georges Coquin and Maurice Martin, "Dayr Anbā Shinūdah: History" in Atiya, ed., *Coptic Encyclopedia*, 3:761.

30. Severin, "Dayr Anbā Shinūdah: Architectural Sculpture," 769.

31. Among many such descriptions, see Petrie, *Athribis*, 14.

32. Severin, "Dayr Anbā Shinūdah: Architectural Sculpture," 769.

33. Richard Krautheimer, *Early Christian and Byzantine Architecture*, rev.
ed., Pelican History of Art (New York: Penguin Books, 1981), 122–24. Krautheimer
has suggested that the feature of the triconch sanctuary may derive from Italy or
France.

34. Grossmann, *Christliche Architektur*, 530.

35. Ibid., 533–34.

36. Grossmann, "Dayr Anbā Shinūdah: Architecture," 3:769; cf. idem,
Christliche Architektur, 535–36.

37. Severin, "Dayr Anbā Shinūdah: Architectural Sculpture," 769–70; Villard, *Couvents près de Sohâg*, 125; Grossmann, *Christliche Architektur*, 533–34. Some capitals may be original spolia, while others may have been brought to the site during reconstruction.

38. Severin, "Dayr Anbā Shinūdah: Architectural Sculpture," 769–70. The extant architectural sculpture in the sanctuary is the result of a combination of original décor, newer renovations, and even damaged original work "restored" with later material.

39. Deir Anba Shenouda's apse paintings were completed over multiple campaigns; one inscription on the paintings dates to the twelfth century. (Crum, "Inscriptions," 556–57.)

40. Conservation of Deir Anba Bishoi's paintings is underway. See n. 25 above and Bolman, "The Red Monastery Conservation Project, 2004 Campaign: New Contributions to the Corpus of Late Antique Art," forthcoming in a volume on Easter Christian art, edited by Colum Hourihane, published by the Index of Christian Art, Princeton University. Bolman is also working on studying the original appearance of the interior of Deir Anba Shenouda's church with Cédric Meurice and others. On Deir Anba Bishoi's architecture, see Grossmann, *Christliche Architektur*, 536–39; compare plates 150 and 155.

41. Shenoute, *This Great House, Canon 7*, YH frag. 1, in W. Pleyte and P. A. A. Boeser, eds., *Manuscrits coptes du Musée d'Antiquités des Pays-Bas à Leide* (Leiden: Brill, 1897), 318. That this sermon probably celebrated the church's inauguration has been established by Emmel, in "Historical Circumstances," 82–83.

42. Grossmann has observed that it is physically impossible for the number of monks estimated to have resided there to have built the church in four to five months. (Personal conversations, Leiden, August 2000.)

43. A hypothesis proposed by Emmel. (Personal conversations, Leiden, August 2000.)

44. Shenoute, *God Is Holy, Canon 7*, XU 88, in Amélineau, *Oeuvres* 2:145.

45. 1 Cor. 6:15–19; 12:12–26; cf. Rom. 12:4–5. I follow Martin's interpretation of Paul's ideology of the body in *The Corinthian Body*; see esp. chapters 6–7 on the body and pollution.

46. Shenoute, *God Is Holy, Canon 7*, GO 25, unpublished (GB-BL 3581A f. 66R): ⲡⲧⲟⲡⲟⲥ ⲉⲧⲟⲩⲁⲁⲃ ⲙⲡⲛⲟⲩⲧⲉ ⲁⲩⲱ ⲉⲧⲛⲁⲛⲟⲩⲟⲩ ⲉⲩⲟⲩⲉⲱ ϩⲉⲛⲣⲱⲙⲉ ⲟⲛ ⲉⲟⲩⲱϩ ⲛ²ⲏⲧⲟⲩ ⲉⲩⲟⲩⲁⲁⲃ ⲁⲩⲱ ⲉⲛⲁⲛⲟⲩⲟⲩ. ⲡⲉⲣⲡⲉ ⲅⲁⲣ ⲁⲛ ⲙⲡⲛⲟⲩⲧⲉ ⲛϣⲉ ²ⲓ ⲱⲛⲉ ⲙⲛ ⲡⲕⲉⲥⲉⲉⲡⲉ.

47. Shenoute, *God Is Holy, Canon 7*, GO 52, in Amélineau, *Oeuvres*, 2:1. For "despise," Amélineau's text here is *sōōš*, which I read as *sōš*. Amélineau translates it as "souillent," suggesting he reads *sōōš* as *sōōf*, meaning to pollute or defile.

48. Shenoute, *God Is Holy, Canon 7*, GO 88, in Amélineau, *Oeuvres*, 2:145. I have translated *prōme* (lit. "the person" or "the man") as a "humanity" to reflect its usage as a collective singular noun. This should not be confused with the abstract noun *tmnt-rōme* that means the abstract quality "humanity." Cf. the use of *prōme* in *This Great House, Canon 7*, XG fragment 1aV (n. 50 below), where Shenoute clearly refers to all people.

49. I do not identify Shenoute's opponents "Gnostic," although they subscribe to philosophies that have been characterized as "Gnostic." The "Gnostic" label has frequently been applied to theologies involving an inferior creator god or

"demiurge." On the modern creation of "Gnosticism" and a reevaluation of the "Gnostic" label, see Williams, *Rethinking "Gnosticism."*

50. Shenoute, *This Great House, Canon 7*, XG fragment 1aV, in Amélineau, *Oeuvres*, 1:304–5.

51. Shenoute, *This Great House, Canon 7*, XG fragment 1aV–fragment 1bR, in Amélineau, *Oeuvres*, 1:305.

52. Shenoute, *This Great House, Canon 7*, XG fragment 1bR, in Amélineau, *Oeuvres*, 1:305.

53. Shenoute, *This Great House, Canon 7*, XU 304, in Amélineau, *Oeuvres*, 2:4.

54. Shenoute, *This Great House, Canon 7*, DG 331–32, in Amélineau, *Oeuvres*, 2:31.

55. On Shenoute's use of kinship language to construct a new, spiritual monastic family, see Krawiec, *Shenoute and the Women*, 161–74. On familial language that denotes specific ranks in the monastery, also see Layton, "Social Structure," 28–29.

56. Shenoute, *God Is Holy, Canon 7*, GO 52–53, in Amélineau, *Oeuvres*, 2:1–2. "Members of a prostitute" reads literally, "prostitute members" (*mmelos mpornē).*

57. Shenoute, *This Great House, Canon 7*, XU 333, in Amélineau, *Oeuvres*, 2:25.

58. Schroeder, "Prophecy and *Porneia*"; Behlmer, "The City as Metaphor;" see also Chapter 1.

59. See nn. 14, 52, 54, 56, and 57 above and nn. 111 and 122 below; nn. 14, 52, and 54 are examples of these general references to sinfulness.

60. On Rom. 1 see Brooten, *Love Between Women*, esp. 195–302.

61. Clark, "Ideology, History, and the Construction of 'Woman,'" 167–68. Cf. D. S. Wallace-Hadrill, *The Greek Patristic View of Nature* (Manchester: Manchester University Press, 1968) on how early Christian authors positioned the person within the larger system of the created world.

62. After condemning "unnatural" acts, he writes, "Woe to us, because we have defiled ourselves and we have defiled all the earth including even the houses of God and his places. The earth was filled with adultery, fornication, rape, violence, every impiety, like these lands where every defilement that you can enumerate or that you can think of lives." (Shenoute, *This Great House, Canon 7,* YR 290, in Amélineau, *Oeuvres*, 2:483–84.) See also *God Is Holy*, *Canon 7*, DG 154, in Crum, ed., *Catalogue of the Coptic Manuscripts in the British Museum* (London: British Museum, 1905), 80–81: "I said verily and I knew that they are people who commit fornication among themselves or by themselves in every worthless, unnatural act so that they need purity and worthiness." Crum provides the transcription for only a part of this unpublished folio (GB-BL 3581A f. 62). On defilement and "unnatural" behavior in *This Great House*, also see GO fragment 2, unpublished (IT-NB IB17 f. 4R/V).

63. Shenoute, *God Is Holy, Canon 7*, DG 105, unpublished (FR-BN 130^5 f. 16R): ⲛⲟⲉⲓ ⲧⲉⲛⲟⲩ ⲙ̄ⲡⲉⲛϣⲓⲡⲉ ⲉⲓⲙⲉ ⲧⲉⲛⲟⲩ ⲉⲡⲉⲛⲥⲱϣ ϩⲙ̄ ⲡⲧⲣⲉϥⲛⲁⲩ ⲅⲁⲣ ⲉⲡⲣⲱⲙⲉ ⲉⲁϥⲥⲟⲩⲛ ϩⲉⲛⲕⲉⲛⲟⲩⲧⲉ ⲙ̄ⲡⲃⲗ̄ ⲙ̄ⲡϫⲟⲉⲓⲥ ⲡⲛⲟⲩⲧⲉ ⲙⲁⲩⲁⲁϥ ⲙ̄ⲡϥⲥⲱⲧⲙ̄ ⲛ̄ⲥⲁ ⲧⲉϊⲥⲙⲏ ϫⲉ ⲙ̄ⲛⲛⲟⲩⲧⲉ ⲛ̄ⲃⲣ̄ⲣⲉ ⲛⲁϣⲱⲡⲉ ⲛ̄ϩⲏⲧⲕ̄ ⲟⲩⲇⲉ ⲛ̄ⲛⲉⲕⲟⲩⲱϣⲧ̄ ⲛ̄ⲛⲟⲩⲧⲉ ⲛ̄ϣⲙ̄ⲙⲟ· ϩⲙ̄-ⲡⲧⲣⲉϥⲛⲁⲩ ⲉⲡⲣⲱⲙⲉ ⲉⲁϥⲣ̄-ⲁⲥⲉⲃⲏⲥ ϩⲛ̄ ⲙ̄ⲡⲁⲣⲁⲫⲩⲥⲓⲥ ϩⲉⲛϩⲃⲏⲩⲉ ⲛ̄ⲃⲟⲧⲉ.

64. See n. 52 above: "And humanity is the race (*genos*) of God. We use it

badly, in unnatural things without fear. For sin made humanity ignorant that it was from God and that it was a child of God."

65. Shenoute, *God Is Holy*, *Canon 7*, GO 52, in Amélineau, *Oeuvres*, 2:1; see discussion on pp. 142–43.

66. Shenoute, *God Is Holy*, *Canon 7*, XU 1, in Wessely, *Texte*, 1:97.

67. See the entry for *ouop* in Walter E. Crum, *A Coptic Dictionary* (Oxford: Clarendon, 1939), 487–88, esp. the qualitative *ouaab*. This is true in other languages, as well, such as the Greek *hagios*.

68. "In whom will God rest . . . ? I will say also, 'What defiled person will provide an opportunity in him for every uncleanness, Satan, and does not encounter much suffering?'" (Shenoute, *God Is Holy*, *Canon 7*, XU 1, in Wessely, *Texte*, 1:97.)

69. Shenoute, *God Is Holy*, *Canon 7*, XU 1, in Wessely, *Texte*, 1:97.

70. Shenoute, *God Is Holy*, *Canon 7*, XU 78, in Amélineau, *Oeuvres*, 2:144. See also nn. 104–5 below.

71. Shenoute, *God Is Holy*, *Canon 7*, XU 78–79, in Amélineau, *Oeuvres*, 2:144.

72. Shenoute, *God Is Holy*, *Canon 7*, XU 93, in Amélineau, *Oeuvres*, 2:147–48.

73. Shenoute, *God Is Holy*, *Canon 7*, XU 79, in Amélineau, *Oeuvres*, 2:145. Cf. 1 Pet. 2:4.

74. Shenoute, *God Is Holy*, *Canon 7*, DG 132, in Wessely, *Texte*, 1:118. Re "spirit," Wessely reconstructs the text as *mpē e̱t*, which may be a good reading of a damaged manuscript but makes little sense when read in this passage. I suggest instead *mpn̄a̱ e̱t*.

75. Similarly, in *A23*, Shenoute reminds his monks that God watches over the heart and mind of those who keep their bodies holy and pure in the places of God: "The Lord shall watch over the heart and the minds of the people who will keep their body holy in the places of the holy one, the king, God the almighty." (Shenoute, *A23*, *Canon 7*, XL 272, unpublished [FR-BN 130⁴ f. 139R]: ⲡϫⲟⲉⲓⲥ ⲉϥⲉϩⲁⲣⲉϩ ⲉⲡϩⲏⲧ ⲙⲛ̄ ⲙ̄ⲙⲉⲉⲩⲉ ⲛ̄ⲛ̄ⲣⲱⲙⲉ ⲉⲧⲛⲁⲣⲟⲉⲓⲥ ⲉⲡⲉⲩⲥⲱⲙⲁ ⲉϥⲟⲩⲁⲁⲃ ϩⲛ̄ ⲛ̄ⲧⲟⲡⲟⲥ ⲙ̄ⲡⲉⲧⲟⲩⲁⲁⲃ ⲡⲣ̄ⲣⲟ ⲡⲛⲟⲩⲧⲉ ⲡⲡⲁⲛⲧⲟⲕⲣⲁⲧⲱⲣ.)

76. Shenoute, *God Is Holy*, *Canon 7*, XU 88, in Amélineau, *Oeuvres*, 2:145–46.

77. Shenoute, *This Great House*, *Canon 7*, XU 313, in Amélineau, *Oeuvres*, 2:11.

78. Shenoute, *If Everyone Errs*, *Canon 7*, XG 347, in Leipoldt, *Opera Omnia*, 4:19.

79. Shenoute, *I Myself Have Seen*, *Canon 7*, DG 341–42, in Leipoldt, *Opera Omnia*, 3:213.

80. "How will they ever escape from the curse of the anger of the wrath of the Lord? Is God patient with those who commit unclean acts in his places, until they come to his hands and he does to them according to their sins, or even he gives their retribution to them from this place—the one belonging to the person who is pained and who groans over his acts. One appeals to God so that he might give over the soul of the one who defiled his house or his houses to a transformation into their despicable passions and to a dwelling-place of demons, just as Jerusalem was once given over to a transformation and a dwelling-place of dragons—

Jerusalem, on the one hand, so that people might not dwell in it because it did not obey, but the soul that will do unnatural things, on the other hand, so that God will not dwell in it, nor his spirit, because of its ignorance." (Shenoute, *This Great House, Canon 7*, XU 307, in Amélineau, *Oeuvres*, 2:6–7.) Cf. Jer. 9:11, where Jerusalem becomes a den of jackals. Shenoute's rhetoric in *Canon 7* also frequently resembles the temple oracles in Jer. 7 and 8.

81. Shenoute, *I Myself Have Seen, Canon 7*, DG 336, in Leipoldt, *Opera Omnia*, 3:209.

82. "For how or why will Jesus make a house or a place foreign to him if he does not first obliterate the soul or the souls of those who sinned in them before him? Since instead of being filled with the spirit characterized by fear of the Lord, according to what is written, they were filled with the audacious spirit and the unclean spirit." (Shenoute, *This Great House, Canon 7*, XU 310, in Amélineau, *Oeuvres*, 2:8–9.) Cf. Luke 5:26.

83. Shenoute, *I Myself Have Seen, Canon 7*, DG 343, in Leipoldt, *Opera Omnia*, 3:214.

84. Continuing from the previous quote, "But it is a wasteland and a desert, since there was no one good in them. . . . Did a spirit of God come to humanity in the season of its impiety in the beginning, before it knew Jesus? If we do not understand that God did not at first leave people in paradise because of a single transgression, then how will we be received by him if we do all these evil things?" (Shenoute, *I Myself Have Seen, Canon 7*, DG 343–44, in Leipoldt, *Opera Omnia*, 3:214–15.)

85. Shenoute, *God Is Holy, Canon 7*, XU 95–96, in Amélineau, *Oeuvres*, 2:149–50.

86. Shenoute, *God Is Holy, Canon 7*, XU 96–97, in Amélineau, *Oeuvres*, 2:150.

87. Shenoute, *God Is Holy, Canon 7*, XU 100, in Amélineau, *Oeuvres*, 2:153.

88. Shenoute, *God Is Holy, Canon 7*, XG 190, in Wessely, *Texte*, 1:88.

89. "But indeed, as for those who asked for him, he saved them from every evil thing, and he guarded his house and his houses from every disturbance if they prayed and they praised him in them until their consummation." (Shenoute, *God Is Holy, Canon 7*, XG 190, in Wessely, *Texte*, 1:88.)

90. Shenoute, *God Is Holy, Canon 7*, XU 97–99, in Amélineau, *Oeuvres*, 2:150–52.

91. Shenoute, *God Is Holy, Canon 7*, XU 79, in Amélineau, *Oeuvres*, 2:144–45. Cf. "But I will say in this way that the thing on the outside is that of humans so that they might exist in it; the things on the inside, however, are those of Christ who dwells in them, and his father according to the words of truth of the scriptures, the old and the new." (*God Is Holy, Canon 7*, XU 95–96, in Amélineau, *Oeuvres*, 2:149.) In each analogy, humanity is connected to something different, either the inside or the outside. Both analogies, however, represent hierarchies between interior and exterior or divinity and creation in which the "interior" signifies the element that stands closer to God in the hierarchy of creation.

92. Shenoute, *God Is Holy, Canon 7*, XU 79, in Amélineau, *Oeuvres*, 2:145.

93. Shenoute, *God Is Holy, Canon 7*, XU 95, in Amélineau, *Oeuvres*, 2:149.

94. Shenoute, *God Is Holy, Canon 7*, XU 95, in Amélineau, *Oeuvres*, 2:149.

95. Shenoute, *God Is Holy, Canon 7*, XU 94, in Amélineau, *Oeuvres*, 2:148–

49. Cf. Eph. 2:12. Similarly, in *I Myself Have Seen*, Shenoute instructs his monks to worry about spiritual matters, not worldly matters: "For as for those who grieve according to God, God will remove their grief completely, just as also those who mourn will be comforted. As for those who do not grieve according to God, God will give them over completely to grief. . . . For many are those who grieve according to the world because of the things that belong to them, each one according to his sort. Few are those who grieve because of the things of Christ and who do not have anything that pursues them." (Shenoute, *I Myself Have Seen, Canon 7*, DG 342–43, in Leipoldt, *Opera Omnia*, 3:213–14.) Cf. Isa. 61:2–3.

96. Shenoute, *God Is Holy, Canon 7*, XU 104–5, in Amélineau, *Oeuvres*, 2:156.

97. Shenoute, *A23, Canon 7*, XL 272, unpublished (FR-BN 130⁴ f. 139R; see n. 75 above).

98. Shenoute, *This Great House, Canon 7*, XU 305–6, in Amélineau, *Oeuvres*, 2:5–6. Anyone who does not heed the warnings is damned: "This is the way that the curse that is written in scripture and the anger of the wrath of the Lord will come upon every person who will commit these unnatural acts in this house or these houses or these places because they did not obey the voice of their God."

99. Shenoute, *This Great House, Canon 7*, XU 311–12, in Amélineau, *Oeuvres*, 2:10. Shenoute's reasoning here resembles Gen. 18:23–32, where Abraham asks God whether he will destroy the righteous in Sodom along with the wicked. God concedes that he will save Sodom if ten righteous people can be found there.

100. Shenoute, *This Great House, Canon 7*, XU 311–12, in Amélineau, *Oeuvres*, 2:10.

101. Shenoute, *This Great House, Canon 7*, XU 311–12, in Amélineau, *Oeuvres*, 2:10.

102. Shenoute, *This Great House, Canon 7*, XU 313, in Amélineau, *Oeuvres*, 2:11.

103. "For what other hypocrisy is more evil than this: that a congregation wanted some people whose pestilential works they know about to dwell with them more than they wanted Jesus to remain with them." (Shenoute, *This Great House, Canon 7*, XU 313, in Amélineau, *Oeuvres*, 2:11.)

104. Shenoute, *This Great House, Canon 7*, XU 318, in Amélineau, *Oeuvres*, 2:13. The Coptic text reads *pai fkōt noujo ntoou de sejōh mmos*. Coptic has two verbs *jōh*, which mean to "touch" or to "smear." Ezek. 13:10 in the Bohairic reads *thōhs*, which means to "anoint" or to "smear." The Sahidic uses *jōh*. (Crum, *Coptic Dictionary*, 461, 797; Henricus Tattam, ed. and trans., *Prophetae Maiores in dialecto linguae Aegyptiacae Memphitica seu Coptica*, 2 vols. [Hildesheim: Georg Olms Verlag, 1989; orig. pr. 1852], 2:54.)

105. "'I will overturn the wall that you have daubed. I will cast it down upon the earth so that its foundations will be revealed and will collapse. . . . I will fulfill my anger upon this wall so that it will not only collapse very hard on itself, but also upon others that touch it, like a house that fell upon other houses." (Shenoute, *This Great House, Canon 7*, XU 318–19, in Amélineau, *Oeuvres*, 2:13–14.)

106. Shenoute, *This Great House, Canon 7*, XU 319, in Amélineau, *Oeuvres*, 2:14.

107. Matt. 7:1; Luke 6:37; Rom. 14:10

108. Shenoute, *This Great House, Canon 7*, XU 324, in Amélineau, *Oeuvres*, 2:18.

109. Shenoute, *This Great House, Canon 7*, XU 324, in Amélineau, *Oeuvres*, 2:18.

110. Shenoute, *This Great House, Canon 7*, XU 324–25, in Amélineau, *Oeuvres*, 2:18.

111. Shenoute, *This Great House, Canon 7*, XU 327–28, in Amélineau, *Oeuvres*, 2:21. While this gospel passage was popular among Shenoute's ascetic contemporaries for its antifamilial bent, Shenoute uses it not to urge a divorce from biological family but from sinning monastic fathers, mothers, sons, and daughters. Cf. Clark, *Reading Renunciation*, 197–98.

112. Shenoute, *This Great House, Canon 7*, XL 274, unpublished (FR-BN 130⁴ f. 140R): ⲛⲉⲓ̈ⲃⲛⲏⲩⲉ ⲡⲗⲟⲓⲙⲟⲥ. See also the parallel text in YH fragment 1 in Pleyte and Boeser, *Manuscrits*, 318–20. Also see XU 304 in Amélineau, *Oeuvres*, 2:4, where Shenoute asks who is more polluted than people who are "pestilential" or "enslaved to demons."

113. "If we are ignorant because we are people who are not able to know that many are the members of the body in which this disease grows, the one who knows it gives testimony that it moves among them like these snake poisons. As long as it was quiet in these members, it was appearing in these other members." (Shenoute, *If Everyone Errs, Canon 7*, XG 347–48, in Leipoldt, *Opera Omnia*, 4:19–20.)

114. Shenoute, *This Great House, Canon 7*, XU 327–28, in Amélineau, *Oeuvres*, 2:21. Shenoute describes sick and neglected limbs that fall away in *If Everyone Errs, Canon 7*, XG 347, in Leipoldt, *Opera Omnia*, 4:19.

115. Shenoute, *This Great House, Canon 7*, XU 328–29, in Amélineau, *Oeuvres*, 2:21–22.

116. Shenoute, *This Great House, Canon 7*, XU 464, in Amélineau, *Oeuvres*, 2:27.

117. Shenoute, *This Great House, Canon 7*, YR 289–90, in Amélineau, *Oeuvres*, 2:482–84.

118. Shenoute, *This Great House, Canon 7*, XL 279–80, unpublished (FR-BN 130⁴ f. 142R/V): ⲉⲛϣⲁⲛⲭⲟⲟⲥ ⲉⲛϣⲁϫⲉ ⲉⲍⲣⲁⲓ̈ ⲉⲣⲟⲕ ⲡⲛⲟⲩⲧⲉ ⲡⲡⲁⲛⲧⲟⲕⲣⲁⲧⲱⲣ ϫⲉ ⲙ̄ⲡⲣ̄ⲧⲁⲁⲛ ⲉⲧⲟⲟⲧⲟⲩ ⲛ̄ⲛⲉⲓ̈ⲍⲉⲑⲛⲟⲥ ⲉⲧⲡⲉⲍⲧ̄-ⲥⲛⲟϥ ⲉⲃⲟⲗ ⲉⲛⲟ ⲛ̄ⲑⲉ ⲙ̄ⲡⲉⲧⲭⲓ-ⲟⲩⲁ· ⲁⲛⲟⲛ ⲛ̄ⲣⲱⲙⲉ ⲛ̄ⲧⲁⲩⲧⲁⲁⲩ ⲙ̄ⲙⲓⲛ ⲙ̄ⲙⲟⲟⲩ ⲙ̄ⲡⲭⲱⲍⲙ̄ ⲉⲡⲣ̄-ϩⲱⲃ ⲉⲁⲕⲁⲑⲁⲣⲥⲓⲁ ⲛⲓⲙ· ⲁⲛⲙⲉⲍ ⲛ̄ⲧⲟϣ ⲁⲛⲙⲉⲍ ⲙ̄ⲡⲟⲗⲓⲥ ⲁⲩⲱ ⲛ̄ϯⲙⲉ ⲙⲛ̄ ⲛⲉⲍⲓⲟⲟⲩⲉ ⲉⲛⲁϣⲕⲁⲕ ⲉⲃⲟⲗ ⲉⲧⲃⲉ ⲑⲟⲧⲉ ⲛ̄ⲍⲉⲛⲃⲁⲣⲃⲁⲣⲟⲥ ⲉⲛϣϣ ⲉⲃⲟⲗ ϫⲉ ⲟⲩⲟⲓ̈ ⲟⲩⲟⲓ̈· ϩⲟⲉⲓⲛⲉ ϫⲉ ⲉⲧⲃⲉ ⲛⲁϣⲏⲣⲉ· ϩⲉⲛⲕⲟⲟⲩⲉ ϫⲉ ⲉⲧⲃⲉ ⲛⲁⲉⲓⲟⲧⲉ ⲁⲩⲱ ⲛⲁⲥⲛⲏⲩ· ⲉϥⲧⲱⲛ ϭⲉ ϩⲱⲱϥ ⲡⲉⲓⲱⲧ ⲏ ⲉⲥⲧⲱⲛ ⲧⲙⲁⲁⲩ ⲉϥⲧⲱⲛ ⲡⲥⲟⲛ ⲉϥⲧⲱⲛ ⲡⲣⲱⲙⲉ ⲉⲧⲣⲓⲙⲉ ⲁⲩⲱ ⲉⲧⲛⲉⲍⲡⲉ ϫⲉ ⲁⲧⲉϥϣⲉⲉⲣⲉ-ⲡⲟⲣⲛⲉⲩⲉ ⲁⲩⲱ ⲁⲡⲉϥϣⲏⲣⲉ-ⲣ̄-ⲁⲥⲉⲃⲛⲥ ⲁⲩⲱ ⲡⲉϥⲥⲟⲛ.

119. Shenoute, *God Is Holy, Canon 7*, XU 100–101, in Amélineau, *Oeuvres*, 2:153.

120. Those who have succeeded in renouncing their families "are ashamed of the ones who do these things, especially some unclean 'great men' and some pestilential 'great women' who love unnatural things in order to fulfill them more than they love the God who created them. It is not one time that I said, 'Woe to us in the day that Jesus will judge us with them.'" (Shenoute, *God Is Holy, Canon 7*, XU 101, in Amélineau, *Oeuvres*, 2:153.) "Great men" and "great women" are titles of ranks in the monastery. (Layton, "Social Structure," 29.) Layton translates the titles as "senior men" and "senior women."

121. Continuing from the text in the previous note: "Truly, some sons and

daughters—those who have loved God more than their parents and more than their siblings and more than taking a wife and more than taking a husband and who have condemned 'great men' and 'great women' who have grown old in the works of the demons—will raise themselves up on the day of judgment. If there is one who is zealous for souls to present themselves before Christ, then they make known their purity and they will pray for him to strengthen the men who renounced their wives and the women who separated from their husbands so that they might be fulfilled." (Shenoute, *God Is Holy*, *Canon 7*, XU 101–2, in Amélineau, *Oeuvres*, 2:153–54.)

122. Shenoute, *God Is Holy*, *Canon 7*, XU 99–100, in Amélineau, *Oeuvres*, 2:152–53. 2 Tim. 2:20–21; 2 Cor. 4:7.

123. Shenoute, *God Is Holy*, *Canon 7*, XU 100, in Amélineau, *Oeuvres*, 2:153.

124. Shenoute, *If Everyone Errs*, *Canon 7*, XG 349, in Leipoldt, *Opera Omnia*, 4:21.

125. Douglas, *Purity and Danger*, esp. 114–39; eadem, *Natural Symbols*, 54–87; Brown, *Body and Society*, 354–55. Ambrose even calls Mary's womb an *aula pudoris*—a hall of modesty or shame.

126. The clearest description of this comes in Shenoute's *Continuing to Glorify the Lord* in *Canon 7*, published in Leipoldt, *Opera Omnia*, 3:69–74. See also Emmel, "Historical Circumstances," 86–91.

127. For photographs of the festival, see my "'A Suitable Abode for Christ': The Church Building as Symbol of Ascetic Renunciation in Early Monasticism," *Church History* 73 (2004): 475, 510–11. For a similar use of a contemporary event to aid in a mental visualization of an ancient space, see Elizabeth Key Fowden, *Barbarian Plain: Saint Sergius between Rome and Iran*, ClassHer 28 (Berkeley and Los Angeles: University of California Press, 1999), 169–70.

128. Emmel, "Historical Circumstances," 88.

129. I exclude symbolic interpretations of church buildings that do not appear in *ascetic* literature, such as book ten, chapter 4 of Eusebius's *Church History*, which records a dedicatory address celebrating the building of a cathedral at Tyre. The church symbolizes Christianity's triumph over paganism; despite its fantastic appearance, its "marvels pale" in comparison to the beauty of the "spiritual edifice" that is Jesus Christ, who dwells among the Christians and even inside their souls. (10.4.2–72; Eng. trans. in G. A. Williamson, trans., *Eusebius: The History of the Church from Christ to Constantine*, rev. and ed. with a new intro. by Andrew Louth [New York: Penguin Books, 1989], 306–22.)

130. Paulinus's life and literature has received increased scholarly scrutiny in recent years, beginning with Joseph T. Lienhard, *Paulinus of Nola and Early Western Monasticism* (Cologne: P. Hanstein, 1977), and continuing with Catherine Conybeare, *Paulinus Noster: Self and Symbol in the Letters of Paulinus of Nola*, OECS (Oxford: Oxford University Press, 1999), and Dennis E. Trout, *Paulinus of Nola: Life, Letters, and Poems*, ClassHer 27 (Berkeley and Los Angeles: University of California Press, 1999), esp. 23–52 on Paulinus's life.

131. Trout, *Paulinus of Nola*, 53–103.

132. Ibid., 150. On the resources that enabled the construction of the basilica complex at Nola, see also ibid., 153.

133. Paulinus, *Epistle* 32.10–17, *Carmen* 27.360–595, 28.7–59, 180–217 and Eng. trans. in Rudolf Carel Goldschmidt, *Paulinus' Churches at Nola: Texts, Transla-

tions, and Commentary (Amsterdam: N.V. Noord-Hollandsche Uitgevers Maatschappij, 1940), 38–47, 52–65, 72–75, 80–83. The most prized relic at the *Basilica Nova* was a piece of the "true cross" given to Paulinus by Melania the Elder (*Epistle* 32.11 and Eng. trans. in Goldschmidt, *Paulinus' Churches*, 38–41). Conybeare has found Paulinus's descriptions "reticent," particularly when compared to Prudentius's depiction of an imagined Temple of Wisdom. She characterizes Paulinus as exhibiting "relatively little interest in describing material objects as such." (Conybeare, *Paulinus Noster*, 92–93.) When judged against the almost complete lack of particulars regarding the physical space and material appearance of the church in Shenoute's *Canon 7*, however, Paulinus's ekphrasis seems awash with details.

134. "This present of the Lord, this symbol by means of which through Christ's gift the same person comes into being young and dies to his old self, behold it here, in the double church of Felix, now that the buildings have been restored." (Paulinus, *Carmen* 28.196–98 and Eng. trans. in Goldschmidt, *Paulinus' Churches*, 82–83.)

135. "And let us avoid not only committed sin but also the thought of sin, like the morbific smell of a rotting body, a nasty odour, with nostrils pinched together." (Paulinus, *Carmen* 28.241–43 and Eng. trans. in Goldschmidt, *Paulinus' Churches*, 84–85.)

136. Paulinus, *Carmen* 28.223–40 and Eng. trans. in Goldschmidt, *Paulinus' Churches*, 84–85.

137. Paulinus, *Carmen* 28.279–81 and Eng. trans. in Goldschmidt, *Paulinus' Churches*, 86–87.

138. *Carmen* 27 contains two exceptions: a brief hope that the paintings will distract people from food and wine, and a fleeting plea for freedom from "sinful love." (Paulinus, *Carmen* 27.585–95, 623–29 and Eng. trans. in Goldschmidt, *Paulinus' Churches*, 64–67.)

139. Trout, *Paulinus of Nola*, 90–103; see 91, 95–98 for a discussion of Jerome's correspondence with Paulinus in Jerome's epistles 53 and 58.

140. Trout, *Paulinus of Nola*, 153–54.

141. Ibid., 133, 154.

142. For a review of the archaeological evidence at Pbow as it pertains to the literary evidence in the Pachomian chronicles, see Goehring, "New Frontiers," in *Ascetics*, 185–86. This article was originally published in Pearson and Goehring, eds., *The Roots of Egyptian Christianity*, 236–57. The later version should be consulted because it contains additions and emendations that pertain to the archaeological site at Pbow. (See the Addendum in the version in *Ascetics*, 184–86; and "Introduction," in *Ascetics*, 9.)

143. *Paralipomena* 32 in François Halkin, ed., *Sancti Pachomii Vitae Graecae*, SH 19 (Brussels: Société des Bollandistes, 1932), 157–58; Eng. trans. in Veilleux, *Pachomian Koinonia*, 2:55–56. On the use of the term "oratory" to characterize the structure, see Grossmann, "Kirche oder 'Ort des Feierns': Zur Problematik der pachomianischen Bezeichnungen des Kirchengebäudes" *Enchoria* 26 (2000): 41–53.

144. Goehring, "New Frontiers in Pachomian Studies," in *Ascetics*, 185.

145. Again, see Goehring's review of the literature on the site of Pbow in ibid., 184–85.

146. Ibid., 185–86, esp. n. III.

147. Derwas Chitty, *The Desert a City: An Introduction to the Study of Egyptian and Palestinian Monasticism under the Christian Empire* (Oxford: Blackwell, 1966; repr., Crestwood, N.Y.: St. Vladimir's Seminary Press, 1995), 22; also cited in Goehring, "New Frontiers," 185. Chitty, writing decades prior to the archaeological excavations at Pbow, associates the text with the monastery at Tabennese.

148. Arn. van Lantschoot, "Allocution de Timothée d'Alexandrie prononcée à l'occasion de la dédicace de l'église de Pachome a Pboou," *Muséon* 47 (1934) 13–56. Van Lantschoot provides the Arabic version of the text, a French translation, and a commentary. The text is believed to be translated from an earlier Coptic manuscript. Only one known fragment of the Coptic text survives (van Lantschoot, "Allocution," 14).

149. Van Lantschoot admits that the text, presumably due to its style, content, and original language (Coptic), could not have been read by Timothy at the dedication of the church. He finds it likely, however, that it was written before the Arab conquest of Egypt since there is no mention of those events or a similar social disruption. Scholars throughout the twentieth century have objected to attributing the text to Timothy for a variety of sound, historical reasons outlined by van Lantschoot. (Ibid., 14–23).

150. Ibid., 39–42.

151. Ibid., 42–44.

152. Ibid., 44–45.

153. Ibid., 45–46.

154. Ibid., 46–52.

155. Ibid., 52–56.

156. Ibid., 26, 39, 38, 56.

157. Goehring's groundbreaking work on the theological and ideological bent of the Pachomian corpus has demonstrated an increasing concern with the "orthodoxy" the community and its founders as well as the monasteries' relationship with the Alexandrian episcopacy. See esp. "Pachomius's Vision of Heresy in *Ascetics*, 137–61.

158. Van Lantschoot, "Allocution," 50, 52.

159. Conybeare, *Paulinus Noster*, 95.

160. Ibid., 99.

161. Bolman, "Joining the Community of Saints," 43.

162. Ibid., 43.

163. Conybeare, *Paulinus Noster*, 95.

164. Bolman, "Joining the Community of Saints," 46.

Chapter 4

1. David Brakke, "The Egyptian Afterlife of Origenism: Conflicts over Embodiment in Coptic Sermons," *OCP* 66 (2000): 277–93.

2. On the Origenist controversy in Egypt, see Clark, *Origenist Controversy*, 105–21, 151–58.

3. Brakke, "Egyptian Afterlife," 285.

4. Origenist monks were charged with heretically asserting the reverse—that the soul could sin without the body. Ibid., 281.

5. Orlandi, *Shenute Contra Origenistas*. See n. 19 below.

6. Clark, *Origenist Controversy*, 151–57, esp. 157.

7. On Dioscorus's letter to Shenoute, see Herbert Thompson, "Dioscorus and Shenoute," *Bibliothèque de l'École des Hautes Études: Recueil d'Études Égyptologiques* 234 (1922): 367–76; Clark, *Origenist Controversy*, 151–52. On Theophilus's festal letter, see Emmel, *Corpus*, 2:647–48, and Emmel, "Theophilus's Festal Letter."

8. Occasionally, Shenoute also mentions Jews, but there is no evidence that he is referring to Jews living in fourth- or fifth-century Egypt. Rather, Shenoute's "Jews" resemble either the Israelites of the Hebrew Bible or the opponents of Jesus in the New Testament. The very term "Jews" as Shenoute uses it may be a cipher for pagans or heretics. Shenoute's anti-Jewish polemic certainly deserves further study. Michael Foat has begun the conversation on this topic in his dissertation, "I Myself Have Seen."

9. In addition to the texts examined here, see Heike Behlmer, *Schenute von Atripe: De Iudicio (Torino, Museo Egizio, Cat. 63000, Cod. IV)*, Catalogo del Museo Egizio di Torino, 1st ser., Monumenti e Testi, vol. 8 (Turin: Ministero per i Beni Culturali e Ambientali, Sopraintendenza al Museo delle Antichità Egizie, 1996). Additional texts on this topic should receive scholarly attention as more critical editions of Shenoute's works are published. Emmel reports that in *There Is Another Foolishness*, in *Discourses 7*, Shenoute compares the resurrection body to a locust or almond. (*Corpus*, 2:643.) Emmel also suggests that acephalous work number 14 (*A14*) might shed light on the topic. The published fragments of *A14* pertain to the hypocrisy of sinners who pass judgment on others and the use of amulets such as fox paws, snake heads, or crocodile teeth to heal sickness. (See XW 117–20, 126–29, in Young, *Coptic Manuscripts*, 37–45; XY 47–50, in Orlandi, *Shenute Contra Origenistas*, 16, 18; XW 161–62 and XY 55–56, in Orlandi, *Shenute Contra Origenistas*, 18, 20; Eng. trans. in Young, *Coptic Manuscripts*, 45–48, and Foat, "I Myself Have Seen," 110–13, respectively.) The relevant portions must be in the unpublished fragment XY 31–42 (FR-BN 130[2] ff. 32–37) which contains folios of varying legibility.

10. Emmel, *Corpus*, 2:606–8. The *Discourses* consist of the codices in Deir Anba Shenouda's library containing sermons, treatises, and letters Shenoute wrote for a more public audience, an audience that extended beyond the monastery. Emmel suggests that Shenoute probably did not compile the *Discourses* himself, as he likely did with the *Canons*. Rather, they may have been compiled after his death for liturgical or lectionary purposes.

11. I follow Emmel's codicological reconstruction of *The Lord Thundered* and *Discourses 4*. For the reconstruction of the manuscript witnesses in codices DU, GG, YQ, and possibly GM, see Emmel, *Corpus*, 1:243–54, 415–18, 429–31, 437–38, 509, and 2:806–8. I have examined all the witnesses to *The Lord Thundered* (apart from cases of textual parallels) reported by Emmel.

12. Shenoute, *The Lord Thundered*, *Discourses 4*, GG 1–2, in Leipoldt, *Opera Omnia*, 3:84–85.

13. Emmel, *Corpus*, 2:615; Barns, "Shenute as a Historical Source," 153. Shenoute himself writes of destroying at least one other pagan altar in *Not Because a Fox Barks*, translated in Barns, "Shenute as a Historical Source," 156–59.

14. Shenoute, *The Lord Thundered*, *Discourses 4*, GG 1, in Leipoldt, *Opera Omnia*, 3:85; GG 79–80, unpublished (AT-NB 9693R/V): ⲛ̄ⲧⲟⲟⲩ ⲟⲛ ⲛⲉⲧⲟⲩⲭⲱ ⲙ̄ⲙⲟⲥ ⲉⲣⲟⲟⲩ ⲭⲉ ⲡϭⲱⲛⲧ̄ ⲙ̄ⲡⲭⲟⲉⲓⲥ ⲛⲏⲩ ⲉⲭⲛ̄ⲛ̄ϩⲉⲑⲛⲟⲥ ⲧⲏⲣⲟⲩ. . . . ⲱ ⲉⲣⲉⲛⲉⲛⲧⲁⲩⲡⲓⲥ-ⲧⲉⲩⲉ ⲉⲡⲉⲭ̅ⲥ̅ ⲉⲃⲟⲗ ϩⲛ̄ ⲛ̄ⲓⲟⲩⲇⲁⲓ̈ ⲛⲁⲭⲡⲉⲓⲉ-ⲛⲉⲓ̈ⲟⲩⲇⲁⲓ ⲛ̄ⲟⲩⲏⲣ ϩⲛ̄ ⲡⲉϩⲟⲟⲩ ⲉⲧⲙ̄ⲙⲁⲩ· ⲉⲧⲉⲙ̄ⲡⲟⲩ ⲡⲓⲥ[. . . . .] ⲱⲁϩⲟⲩⲛ [. . . . . .] ⲉⲣⲉⲛⲉⲛⲧⲁⲩⲡⲓⲥⲧⲉⲩⲉ ⲇⲉ ⲟⲛ ⲉⲃⲟⲗ ϩⲛ̄ ⲛ̄ϩⲉⲑⲛⲟⲥ ⲛⲁⲭⲡⲓⲉ-ⲛ̄ϩⲉⲑⲛⲟⲥ ⲛ̄ⲟⲩⲏⲣ ⲉⲧⲉⲙ̄ⲡⲟⲩⲡⲓⲥⲧⲉⲩⲉ ⲉⲣⲟϥ.

15. Shenoute, *The Lord Thundered*, *Discourses 4*, DU 18, in Amélineau, *Oeuvres*, 1:368.

16. Shenoute, *The Lord Thundered*, *Discourses 4*, GG 20–21 and DU 48–50, in Amélineau, *Oeuvres*, 2:135–36, 381–82.

17. Shenoute describes the resurrection several times in *The Lord Thundered* and specifically mentions people who do not believe that the body will be raised after death. Shenoute, *The Lord Thundered*, *Discourses 4*, GG 69, in Young, *Coptic Manuscripts*, 146–47; Eng. trans. in ibid., 148–49; GG 31–32 in Young, *Coptic Manuscripts*, 144–45; Eng. trans. in ibid., 145–46; and DU 35–38, in Amélineau, *Oeuvres*, 1:368–72.

18. Shenoute, *The Lord Thundered*, *Discourses 4*, DU 46–47, in Amélineau, *Oeuvres*, 1:379.

19. I follow Emmel's codicological reconstruction of *I Am Amazed*. The text has many codicological difficulties because it appears to have been included in at least two volumes of the *Discourses*—volume seven and somewhere in the badly damaged volumes one, two, and/or three. For the reconstruction of manuscript witnesses DQ, HB, XN, YU, ZN, DS, XE, and DT see Emmel, *Corpus*, 1:407–9, 412–13, 414, 446–47, 459–61, 478, 512, 530; 2:794–99. Tito Orlandi published the text and Italian translation of a portion of *I Am Amazed* in his *Shenute Contra Origenistas*. As Emmel has noted, Orlandi's version does not include fragments that were confirmed as portions of the text only after Orlandi's publication. It also excludes the Coptic translation of Theophilus's festal letter of 401 that was included at the end of the text. Janet Timbie has proposed some revisions to Orlandi's transcriptions in a paper at the annual meeting of the North American Patristics Society in Chicago on May 24, 2001 ("Nestorius in Shenoute's *I Am Amazed*: A Corrected Text Yields New Information"), and in the forthcoming, "Reading and Re-reading Shenoute's *I Am Amazed*: More Information on Nestorius and Others," in *The World of Early Egyptian Christianity: Language, Literature, and Social Context*, ed. James Goehring and Janet Timbie (Washington, D.C.: Catholic University of America Press). I also extend my appreciation to Janet Timbie for sharing with me her copy of the microfilm of DS 190–204 in unpublished British Museum manuscript 8800 ff. 7–13. I have examined all the witnesses to *I Am Amazed* (apart from textual parallels) reported by Emmel.

20. Emmel, "Theophilus," 94, 97 n. 24.

21. Shenoute, *I Am Amazed*, DQ 59, in Orlandi, *Shenute Contra Origenistas*, 50; see also Emmel, *Corpus*, 2:644.

22. Emmel, *Corpus*, 2:648; cf. idem, "Theophilus," 97.

23. Clark, *Origenist Controversy*, 153, 157–58.

24. Ibid., 153.

25. Shenoute, *I Am Amazed*, HB 22 and DQ 77, in Orlandi, *Shenute Contra Origenistas*, 24, 56.

26. Shenoute, *I Am Amazed*, HB 22, in Orlandi, *Shenute Contra Origenistas*, 24.

27. Shenoute, *I Am Amazed*, HB 33, in Orlandi, *Shenute Contra Origenistas*, 32 and DQ 113 in Wessely, *Texte* 1:131.

28. Shenoute, *I Am Amazed*, HB 44, DS 116, in Orlandi, *Shenute Contra Origenistas*, 40, 46.

29. Shenoute, *I Am Amazed*, DQ 59, in Orlandi, *Shenute Contra Origenistas*, 50.

30. I follow Emmel's codicological reconstruction of *Who Speaks Through the Prophet*. This text appears only in codices ZM and DD. For the reconstruction of manuscript witnesses ZM and DD see Emmel, *Corpus*, 1:398–400, 528–29; 2:867. I have examined all the witnesses to *Who Speaks Through the Prophet* reported by Emmel. Regarding the likelihood of this text deriving from the *Discourses*, DD is a lectionary codex; in the lectionary codices, the readings that are documented elsewhere in Shenoute's corpus derive from works in the *Discourses*, not the *Canons* (1:361). ZM is one of a number of codices that contain combinations of texts from either the *Canons* or the *Discourses*, or both (1:308).

31. Shenoute, *Who Speaks Through the Prophet*, ZM 42–43, unpublished (FR-BN 131⁴ ff. 157V-158R): ⲡⲟⲩⲟⲉⲓⲛ ⲛ̄ⲛ̄ϣⲁϫⲉ ⲛ̄ⲛⲉⲅⲣⲁⲫⲏ ⲡⲉ ϣⲁϥϭⲓ ⲛ̄ⲙⲁⲩ ⲛ̄ⲛ̄ϣⲁϫⲉ ⲛ̄ⲕⲁⲕⲉ ⲛ̄ⲛ̄ϩⲉⲗⲗⲏⲛ ⲙⲛ̄ ϩⲁⲓⲣⲉⲧⲓⲕⲟⲥ ⲛⲓⲙ.

32. Shenoute, *Who Speaks Through the Prophet*, ZM 53–54, in Amélineau, *Oeuvres*, 2:189–91.

33. I follow Emmel's codicological reconstruction of *Aʃ*. For the reconstruction of manuscript witnesses YM, TY, and DR to *Aʃ* see Emmel, *Corpus*, 1:410–11, 451–52, 506; 2:873. I have examined all the witnesses to *Aʃ* reported by Emmel. For a description and partial translation, see D. Bell, "Shenoute the Great and the Passion of Christ," *CS* 22 (1987): 291–303.

34. Shenoute, *Who Speaks Through the Prophet*, ZM 42–43, unpublished (FR-BN 131⁴ ff. 157V-158R); see n. 31 above.

35. Frankfurter, *Religion in Roman Egypt*, 79; Wipszycka, "Le Nationalisme." Also, for the Greek term *hellēn*, G. W. H. Lampe provides "pagan" or "gentile" (not "Greek") as definitions. (*A Patristic Greek Lexicon* [Oxford: Clarendon Press, 1961], 451.)

36. Janet Timbie, "State of the Research," 268.

37. Michael Foat has challenged the socioeconomic theory and argues that the term *hellene* is a method by which Shenoute constructs and defines his opponents through the power of language and naming. Foat still places much value in the historical reconstruction of the social group, which Shenoute defines as *hellenes* and remains concerned with determining their identity, even though he admits that they are not an "internally coherent" group. Foat, "I Myself Have Seen," 52.

38. "His sermons juxtapose a peasant audience to 'pagan [*hellēne*]' landlords, whom Shenoute presents as oppressive and corrupt." Frankfurter, *Religion in Roman Egypt*, 77.

39. Ibid., 79.

40. Shenoute, *The Lord Thundered, Discourses 4*, DU 47–49, 55, in Amélineau, *Oeuvres*, 1:379–83; Frankfurter, *Religion in Roman Egypt*, 78.

41. Frankfurter, *Religion in Roman Egypt*, 77. See Shenoute, *Not Because a Fox Barks, Discourses 4*, in Leipoldt, *Opera Omnia*, 3:79–84; Eng. trans. in Barns, "Shenute as a Historical Source," 156–59. On Shenoute's destruction of Gesios's property see also Frankfurter, *Religion in Roman Egypt*, 79; Emmel, "From the

Other Side of the Nile," 107–8. Emmel's reconstruction of Shenoute's conflict with Gesios posits two raids on Gesios's property by Shenoute—one recounted in *Not Because a Fox Barks*, and the other in acephalous work *A4*; the latter is retold in *Vita Sinuthii* 125–26 (Leipoldt, *Opera Omnia*, 1:57; Eng. trans. in D. Bell, *Life of Shenoute*, 77–78).

42. Shenoute, *The Lord Thundered*, *Discourses 4*, DU 45, 50, in Amélineau, *Oeuvres*, 1:378, 382. Frankfurter quotes selections from DU 47 to 50.

43. The passage continues, leading into the quotation from Frankfurter, "The one who bears witness to that which he said, or the one who saw him said that [here Frankfurter picks up the passage] cursed is the one who worships or who pours libations or who makes sacrifices to any other creature." (*The Lord Thundered*, *Discourses 4*, DU 46–47, in Amélineau, *Oeuvres*, 1:379.)

44. Emmel, having arrived at the same hypothesis independently, concurs. ("From the Other Side of the Nile," 109.)

45. On the pagan-Christian debate about Jesus as the Christ, see Goulven Medec, "Le Christ des païens d'après le *De consensu euangelistarum* de saint Augustin," *Recherches Augustiniennes* 26 (1992): 3–67.

46. Besa, *Vita Sinuthii*, 88, in Leipoldt, *Opera Omnia*, 1:43; Eng. trans. in D. Bell, *Life of Shenoute*, 67–68; Heike Behlmer, "Historical Evidence from Shenoute's *De extremo iudicio*," in *Sesto Congresso Internazionale di Egittologia*, ed. G. M. Zaccone and T. R. di Netro, 2 vols. (Turin: International Association of Egyptologists, 1993), 2:14.

47. Emmel, "From the Other Side of the Nile," esp. 108–9. Note that *The Lord Thundered* is not a significant source for his study.

48. "It is about the ones who say that there will be no resurrection that I said these things—these people who are like the pagans, who dream dreams and who say that the body existed from the four elements—water, earth, air, and fire." (Shenoute, *I Am Amazed*, HB 44, in Orlandi, *Shenute Contra Origenistas*, 40; Eng. trans. in Foat, "I Myself Have Seen," 126, rev.)

49. Shenoute, *I Am Amazed*, HB 31, in Orlandi, *Shenute Contra Origenistas*, 30; Eng. trans. in Foat, "I Myself Have Seen," 120, rev.

50. Shenoute, *I Am Amazed*, HB 35, in Orlandi, *Shenute Contra Origenistas*, 34; Eng. trans. in Foat, "I Myself Have Seen," 122, rev. Clark includes this among Shenoute's anti-Origenist passages, although Shenoute does not name Origenists specifically in this section of the treatises. She describes the views Shenoute cites as "probably Gnostic in derivation." (*Origenist Controversy*, 153.) Aloys Grillmeier also characterizes them as Gnostic, with Marcionite or Manichaean leanings. (*Christ in the Christian Tradition*, trans. O. C. Dean [Louisville, Ky.: Westminster John Knox Press, 1996], vol. 2, part 4:194–96.) It seems more likely, however, that if Shenoute caricatures any specific, identifiable heretical group with his slogan about Mary, it would be the Nestorians, since later in *I Am Amazed* he identifies heretics with similar beliefs as followers of Nestorius. See Shenoute, *I Am Amazed*, DQ 59–64, in Orlandi, *Shenute Contra Origenistas*, 50, 52, 54; Eng. trans. in Foat, "I Myself Have Seen," 132–34. In DQ 59–64, Shenoute forcefully argues against Nestorius and presses for Mary's status as *theotokos*, or as he writes in Coptic *tentas-jpe-pnoute*. See pp. 140–41, 143.

51. Shenoute, *I Am Amazed*, DS 115–16, in Orlandi, *Shenute Contra Origenistas*, 46; Eng. trans. in Foat, "I Myself Have Seen," 129, rev.

52. Shenoute also takes issue with those who, in his eyes, deny the full divinity of Jesus Christ as well. He calls such Christians "*hellenes* at heart" because they insist that one should not pray to Christ because Christ himself prayed to God, they claim that God ruled this world with the assistance of an archon, they profess the authority of twelve gospels, and they believe that forty different aeons exist. (Shenoute, *I Am Amazed*, DS 116–17, in Orlandi, *Shenute Contra Origenistas*, 46; Eng. trans. in Foat, "I Myself Have Seen," 129, rev.)

53. On the demonic or Satanic nature of heretics, see *I Am Amazed*, DQ 77–78, in Orlandi, *Shenute Contra Origenistas*, 56; Eng. trans. in Foat, "I Myself Have Seen," 135. Shenoute also claims that all heresies spring from the same root, the devil, in *I Am Amazed*, DS 222, in Emmel, "Theophilus," 95; Eng. trans. in *ibid.*, 96. See also *The Lord Thundered*, *Discourses 4*, GG 18, unpublished (FR–BN 131⁵ f. 65R): ⲡⲥⲁⲧⲁⲛⲁⲥ ⲁⲉ ϩⲱⲱϥ ϣⲁϥⲟⲩⲱϩ ϩⲛ̄ ⲡⲣⲱⲙⲉ ⲉⲧϩⲓϩⲟⲩⲛ ⲛ̄ⲛ̄ϩⲁⲓⲣⲉϯⲕⲟⲥ; and DU 18 and DU 40, in Amélineau, *Oeuvres*, 1:368, 373. On pagans who worship demons, see *The Lord Thundered*, *Discourses 4*, DU 47–49, in Amélineau, *Oeuvres*, 1:379–81. See also Foat's study of Shenoute's *As I Sat on a Mountain*, in which Shenoute calls pagans or barbarians who refuse to become Christians "people of the demons." ("I Myself Have Seen," 31.) On demons, cf. Clark, *Origenist Controversy*, 157.

54. "And every heretic who serves and who worships many gods is unbelieving in him (God)." (Shenoute, *The Lord Thundered*, *Discourses 4*, DU 50, in Amélineau, *Oeuvres*, 1:382.)

55. "The spirit will come into all the dead and they will live. But the Holy Spirit of God, however, has withdrawn from the pagans and the heretics." (Shenoute, *The Lord Thundered*, *Discourses 4*, DU 38, in Amélineau, *Oeuvres*, 1:372.)

56. Shenoute, *The Lord Thundered*, *Discourses 4*, DU 47–48, in Amélineau, *Oeuvres*, 1:380.

57. *oupharmagos.*

58. Shenoute, *The Lord Thundered*, *Discourses 4*, DU 45–46, in Amélineau, *Oeuvres*, 1:378–79.

59. Shenoute, *The Lord Thundered*, *Discourses 4*, GG 9, unpublished (GB-CU 1699K f. 3R): ⲛⲧⲱⲧⲛ̄ ⲁⲉ ⲱ ⲛ̄ϩⲁⲓⲣⲉϯⲕⲟⲥ· ⲛ̄ⲧⲉⲧⲛ̄ ⲟⲩⲥⲡⲉⲣⲙⲁ ⲉⲁⲩⲥⲟⲟⲩϥ ϩⲓⲧⲛ̄ ⲡⲭⲟⲉⲓⲥ ⲡⲛⲟⲩⲧⲉ· ⲛ̄ⲧⲱⲧⲛ̄ ⲛⲉ ⲛ̄ϣⲏⲣⲉ ⲙ̄ⲡⲧⲁⲕⲟ ⲉⲧⲡⲁⲣⲁⲕⲁⲗⲉⲓ ⲛ̄ⲛⲉⲓⲇⲱⲗⲟⲛ ⲛ̄ϣⲉ.

60. "But on account of the lawlessness, however, of the heretics, Satan established them for himself as friends—they and also their philosophers who let their hair grow like women. The Lord Jesus, however, wishes according to that which is written that the ones who believe in him and who love him, who keep his words, are with him in his kingdom, so that they will see him in his glory and they will rest themselves with them forever. But Satan is zealous regarding the one who pleases him, so that he sees all the heretics with him inside the fiery furnace which was prepared for him and his angels as it is written, so that as for the heretics in whom he takes pride and about whom he says, 'They are mine,' his contempt is theirs in hell (*amnte*) forever. Faithfully, according to that which is written, Abraham did not spare his beloved son because of his love for God, but he offered him up as a sacrifice. As for the peoples (*nethnos*), they poured out the blood of their sons and their daughters for demons, as it is written in the Psalms. Some faithless kings and impious people who were among your seed since the beginning, like Gog and Og and the ones who resemble them, and Herod the king, this one

whom the Lord reckoned as a fox, like your own manner also. They are faithful kings, righteous kings who were among the seed of Christians since the beginning until now, such as David and Solomon and Hezekiah and all the ancient kings and righteous kings and rulers who destroyed your temples and who cast down your idols. They are among the Christians." (Shenoute, *The Lord Thundered, Discourses 4*, GG 19–20, in Amélineau, *Oeuvres*, 2:134–35.)

61. Harry O. Maier, "'Manichee!': Leo the Great and the Orthodox Panopticon," *JECS* 4 (1996): 441–60. Maier draws on sociological theories of Lewis A. Coser, *The Functions of Social Conflict* (London: Routledge and Kegan Paul, 1986).

62. Shenoute, *The Lord Thundered, Discourses 4*, GG 20–21, 49–50, 55–56, in Amélineau, *Oeuvres*, 2:135–36, 1:381–85. Some of these passages are used effectively by Frankfurter in *Religion in Roman Egypt*, 77–79.

63. Shenoute, *I Am Amazed*, HB 29, in Orlandi, *Shenute Contra Origenistas*, 28, 30; Eng. trans. in Foat, "I Myself Have Seen," 119; and Hans Quecke in Grillmeier, *Christ in the Christian Tradition*, 2/4:194. My translation follows Quecke, slightly revised.

64. Shenoute, *I Am Amazed*, HB 29–30, in Orlandi, *Shenute Contra Origenistas*, 30; Eng. trans. in Foat, "I Myself Have Seen," 119, rev. Regarding the passage cited here and above in n. 63, cf. Cyril's first and twelfth anathemas of Nestorius: "If anyone does not confess Emmanuel to be God in truth and the holy Virgin on this ground to be Theotokos, since she brought forth after the flesh the Word of God who became flesh, be he anathema. . . . If anyone does not confess that the Word of God suffered in flesh and was crucified in flesh and 'tasted of death' in the flesh and became 'Firstborn from the dead,' inasmuch as he is life and life-giving, as God, be he anathema." (Herbert Bindley, ed. and trans., *The Oecumenical Documents of the Faith*, 4th ed. [London: Methuen, 1950], 113–15; Eng. trans. in ibid., 218–19 rev.)

65. Besa, *Vita Sinuthii*, 128–29, in Leipoldt, *Opera Omnia*, 1:57–58; Eng. trans. in D. Bell, *Life of Shenoute*, 78. Cf. Grillmeier, *Christ in the Christian Tradition*, 2/4:212–13.

66. Griggs, *Early Egyptian Christianity*, 197. A network of roads connected the oasis to the cities along the Nile. (Roger S. Bagnall, *Egypt in Late Antiquity* [Princeton, N.J.: Princeton University Press, 1993], 146.) Shenoute outlived Nestorius and reports of his death in *And It Happened One Day, Discourses 8*, part of which was published in Lefort, "Catéchèse Christologique de Chenoute," *Zeitschrift für Ägyptische Sprache und Altertumskunde* 80 (1955): 40–45.

67. Nestorius's second letter to Cyril; Eng. trans. in Richard A. Norris, *The Christological Controversy* (Philadelphia: Fortress Press, 1980), 135–40, esp. 137–39. See also his first letter to Celestine, where he states that Mary cannot be the mother of "God the Logos" because a parent must be "of the same essence" as the child. (Eng. trans. in Edward Rochie Hardy, ed., in collaboration with Cyril C. Richardson, *Christology of the Later Fathers*, LCC 3 [Philadelphia: Westminster Press, 1954], 348.)

68. Or, as J. N. D. Kelly summarizes the position, that "Mary bore a man, the vehicle of divinity but not God." (*Early Christian Doctrines*, 311.) See esp. Cyril's second letter to Nestorius, where he argues to Nestorius, "It is not the case that first of all an ordinary human being was born of the holy Virgin and that the

Logos descended upon him subsequently." (In Bindley, *Oecumenical Documents*, 96; Eng. trans. in Norris, *Christological Controversy*, 133.)

69. Norman Russell, *Cyril of Alexandria*, Early Church Fathers (London: Routledge, 2000), 34; Susan Wessel, *Cyril of Alexandria and the Nestorian Controversy: The Making of a Saint and of a Heretic*, OECS (Oxford: Oxford University Press, 2004), 229.

70. See Cyril's letter to John of Antioch in Bindley, *Oecumenical Documents*, 142; Eng. trans. also in Norris, *Christological Controversy*, 142–43.

71. Grillmeier, *Christ in the Christian Tradition*, vol. 1, *From the Apostolic Age to Chalcedon (451)*, trans. John Bowden, 2nd rev. ed. (Atlanta: John Knox Press, 1975), 467–78.

72. Grillmeier, *Christ in the Christian Tradition*, 1:473–83; Kelly, *Early Christian Doctrines*, 310–23.

73. Nestorius actually insisted that Jesus Christ's human body was joined with the divinity "so that the nature of the deity associates itself with the things belonging to the body, and the body is acknowledged to be noble and worthy of the wonders related in the Gospels." (Nestorius's Second Letter to Cyril; Eng. trans. in Norris, *Christological Controversy*, 138.)

74. Shenoute, *I Am Amazed*, DQ 59, in Orlandi, *Shenute Contra Origenistas*, 50; Eng. trans. in Foat, "I Myself Have Seen," 132, rev. As Grillmeier notes, Shenoute's representation of Nestorius is not always an accurate depiction of Nestorius's own claims. Shenoute accuses Nestorius of doctrines that he did not advocate, such as an "adoptionist" view of Christ. Nonetheless, this is a critique commonly levied against Nestorius, as in Cyril's second letter to Nestorius: "It is not the case that first of all an ordinary human being was born of the holy Virgin and that the Logos descended upon him subsequently." See n. 68 above.

75. Shenoute, *I Am Amazed*, DQ 60, in Orlandi, *Shenute Contra Origenistas*, 52; Eng. trans. in Foat, "I Myself Have Seen," 132, rev.

76. Shenoute, *I Am Amazed*, DQ 61, in Orlandi, *Shenute Contra Origenistas*, 52, rev.; Eng. trans. in Foat, "I Myself Have Seen," 132, rev. My translation is based on a revision of Orlandi's text after consulting a reproduction of DQ 61 (FR-BN 131⁶ f. 32R) provided by Timbie in "Nestorius in Shenute" and a transcription of sections of DQ 61–62 (FR-BN 131⁶ f. 32R/V) in her "Reading and Rereading." Here is Orlandi's version, with relevant sections underlined and Timbie's new readings of the underlined text in braces { } following: ⲁⲩⲱ ϫⲉ ⲁⲧⲙⲛⲧⲛⲟⲩⲧⲉ ⲃⲱⲕ ⲉⲡⲭⲓⲥⲉ ⲙⲡⲁⲧⲉⲩⲙⲉϩ ⲛ̄ϣⲉ {ⲁⲥⲕⲁⲧⲥⲁⲣⲝ ϩⲓⲡϣⲉ}. ⲁⲩϫⲟⲟⲥ ⲅⲁⲣ ϩⲛ̄ ⲛⲉⲩⲥϩⲁⲓ ϫⲉ ⲡⲁⲓ ⲉⲧⲟϣϣ ⲉⲃⲟⲗ ϫⲉ ⲡⲁⲛⲟⲩⲧⲉ ⲡⲁⲛⲟⲩⲧⲉ ⲉⲧⲃⲉ ⲟⲩ ⲁⲕⲕⲁⲁⲧ ⲛ̄ⲥⲱⲕ ϯⲟⲩⲱϣⲧ ⲛⲁⲩ ϩⲱⲱⲩ ⲙⲛ ⲧⲙⲛⲧⲛⲟⲩⲧⲉ ⲉⲃⲟⲗ ϫⲉ ⲁⲩϩⲱⲧⲣ̄ ⲛ̄ⲙ̄ⲙⲁⲩ {ⲛ̄ⲙ̄ⲙⲁⲥ}. . . . ⲕⲁⲓ ⲅⲁⲣ ⲉⲣⲉⲧⲙⲛ̄ⲧⲛⲟⲩⲧⲉ ⲡⲟⲣⲭ ⲁⲛ ⲉⲡⲥⲱⲙⲁ ⲉⲩϩⲛ̄ ⲡϣⲉ. ϩⲁⲟⲏ {ⲉⲩϩⲓⲡϣⲉ. ⲛ̄ⲑⲉ} ⲙⲡⲁⲓ ϩⲛ̄ ⲟⲩⲡⲁⲣⲁⲇⲉⲓⲅⲙⲁ ⲉⲃⲟⲗ ⲛ̄ϩⲏⲧⲩ̄ ⲛ̄ϩⲛⲧⲩ̄ {ⲛ̄ϩⲛⲧⲛ̄} ⲙⲏ ⲉⲩϣⲁⲛⲙⲟⲩⲟⲩⲧ ⲛ̄ⲟⲩⲣⲱⲙⲉ ⲉϣⲁⲩϫⲟⲟⲥ ϫⲉ ⲁⲩⲙⲉⲩⲧⲟⲩⲣⲱⲙⲉ. ⲙⲏ ⲉϣⲁⲩϫⲟⲟⲥ ⲁⲛ ϫⲉ ⲁⲛⲛⲉⲩⲧⲡⲣⲱⲙⲉ {ⲁⲩⲙⲉⲩⲧⲡⲣⲱⲙⲉ} ⲧⲏⲣⲩ̄ ⲕⲁⲓⲧⲟⲓ ⲛ̄ⲧⲉϯⲯⲩⲭⲏ ⲙⲟⲩ ⲁⲛ.

77. Shenoute, *I Am Amazed*, DQ 62, in Orlandi, *Shenute Contra Origenistas*, 52, 54; Eng. trans. in Foat, 133, rev. Timbie in "Nestorius in Shenute" has suggested the following reading (provided in braces {}) as a revision to Orlandi's text: "even though he was immortal in his whole soul {in his divinity} (ⲉⲩⲟ ⲇⲉ ⲛⲁⲧⲙⲟⲩ ϩⲛ̄ ⲧⲉϯⲯⲩⲭⲏ ⲧ[ⲏⲣⲥ] {ϩⲛ̄ ⲧⲉⲩⲙⲛ̄ⲧⲛⲟⲩⲧⲉ})"; "so he {we} said many times, '[The Word became] flesh {The Word became flesh},' (ⲕⲁⲧⲁ ⲑⲉ ⲛ̄ⲧⲁⲩϫⲟⲟⲥ

{ⲛ̄ⲧⲁⲛⲭⲟⲟⲥ} ⲛ̄ⲟⲁ̄ ⲛ̄ⲥⲟⲡ ⲭⲉ {. . . . .} ⲧⲅⲁⲣ. {ⲁⲡⲗⲟⲅⲟⲥ ⲣ̄-ⲥⲁⲣⲝ})”; “[S]ince the Son is not different from the father, <u>nor is the father (different)</u> {the father is a spirit } . . . (ⲉⲃⲟⲗ ⲭⲉ ⲡ(ϣ)ⲏⲣⲉ ϣⲟⲃⲉ ⲁⲛ ⲉⲡⲉⲓⲱⲧ <u>ⲟⲩⲗⲉ ⲙ̄ⲡⲉⲡⲓⲱⲧ</u> {ⲟⲩⲡ̄ⲛ̄ⲁ̄ ⲡⲉ ⲡⲓⲱⲧ}). . . . ” Cf. Heb. 2:14, John 1:14. The soul/body analogy was “common” in Christology by the year 410, and was used by Cyril. (Wessel, *Cyril*, 80–81, esp. n. 19.)

78. Shenoute, *I Am Amazed*, DQ 63, in Orlandi, *Shenute Contra Origenistas*, 54; Eng. trans. in Foat, “I Myself Have Seen,” 134, rev.

79. Shenoute, *I Am Amazed*, DQ 63–64, in Orlandi, *Shenute Contra Origenistas*, 54; Eng. trans. in Foat, “I Myself Have Seen,” 134, rev.

80. Shenoute, *I Am Amazed*, DQ 64 in Orlandi, *Shenute Contra Origenistas*, 54. Note that Shenoute does not use the Greek term *theotokos* here.

81. Shenoute, *The Lord Thundered, Discourses 4*, DU 18, in Amélineau, *Oeuvres*, 1:368.

82. Shenoute, *I Am Amazed*, DQ 114, in Wessely, *Texte*, 1:132.

83. Clark associates the views of Shenoute's opponents on the eucharist with Evagrian Origenism. (*The Origenist Controversy*, 156–57, where the text cited as “Homily 24” in Amélineau's edition of Shenoute's works has subsequently been identified by Emmel as a fragment of *I Am Amazed*.) This is in part because Shenoute denounces Origenists specifically for denying the presence of Christ in the eucharist in another text. (*And It Happened One Day, Discourses 8*, published in part in Lefort, “Catéchèse Christologique de Chenoute,” 40–45.) For Grillmeier, this passage in *I Am Amazed* is evidence of Gnostic beliefs in Shenoute's community. (*Christ in the Christian Tradition*, 2/4:203–7.) While Shenoute does attack Origenism as a heresy in *I Am Amazed*, he does not identify these particular “heretics” as Origenist. He makes a similar argument about the eucharist in *And It Happened One Day*, however; here he identifies his opponents as followers of Origen. (Lefort, “Catéchèse Christologique,” 45; see also Grillmeier, *Christ in the Christian Tradition*, 2/4:215–16.)

84. Shenoute, *I Am Amazed*, HB 30, in Orlandi, *Shenute Contra Origenistas*, 30; Eng. trans. in Foat, “I Myself Have Seen,” 120, rev.

85. Shenoute, *I Am Amazed*, HB 30, in Orlandi, *Shenute Contra Origenistas*, 30; Eng. trans. in Foat, “I Myself Have Seen,” 120, rev.

86. Shenoute, *I Am Amazed*, HB 31, in Orlandi, *Shenute Contra Origenistas*, 30, 32; Eng. trans. in Foat, “I Myself Have Seen,” 120, rev. Cf. Matt. 26:26–28, Mark 14:22–24, Luke 22:19–20, 1 Cor. 11:24–25.

87. Shenoute, *I Am Amazed*, HB 28, in Orlandi, *Shenute Contra Origenistas*, 28; Eng. trans. in Foat, 119, rev.

88. See also Shenoute, *And It Happened One Day, Discourses 8*, published in part in Lefort, “Catéchèse Christologique de Chenoute,” 40–45 and the discussion of this text in Grillmeier, *Christ in the Christian Tradition*, 2/4:215–16. In this text, also, Shenoute emphasizes the divine corporeality of the son as well as the creation of humanity by the hand of God.

89. See also Clark, *The Origenist Controversy*, 155.

90. Shenoute, *I Am Amazed*, DS 114, in Orlandi, *Shenute Contra Origenistas*, 44; Eng. trans. in Foat, “I Myself Have Seen,” 128–29.

91. Shenoute, *I Am Amazed*, DS 114–15, in Orlandi, *Shenute Contra Origenistas*, 44; Eng. trans. in Foat, “I Myself Have Seen,” 129, rev.

92. Shenoute, *The Lord Thundered*, *Discourses 4*, DU 43 in Amélineau, *Oeuvres*, 1:375–76. See p. 152 for further analysis of this passage.

93. Shenoute, *Who Speaks Through the Prophet*, ZM 43, unpublished (FR-BN 131⁴ f. 158R): ϩⲟⲓⲛⲉ ⲙⲉⲛ ⲅⲁⲣ ⲉⲩⲭⲱ ⲙ̄ⲙⲟⲥ ϫⲉ ⲡⲓⲥⲱⲛⲁ ⲛⲁⲧⲱⲟⲩⲛ ⲁⲛ ⲁⲩⲱ ϫⲉ ⲁⲩⲧ ⲛ̄ⲕⲉⲟⲩⲁ ⲉⲡⲉϥⲙⲁ.

94. "For this reason, not by the power of the one who speaks (Shenoute), but by the grace of the one who says, 'Now I will rise,' says the Lord. 'Now I will be glorified. Now I will be exalted.' Now you will see. Now you will be ashamed. The power of your spirit will be emptied. The flame will eat you. Your words form a fable, which you speak. He will scatter them like dust that the wind blows across the face of the earth." Shenoute, *Who Speaks Through the Prophet*, ZM 43, unpublished (FR-BN 131⁴ f. 158R): ⲉⲧⲃⲉ ⲡⲁⲓ ϩⲣⲁⲓ ϩⲛ̄ ⲧϭⲟⲙ ⲁⲛ ⲙ̄ⲡⲉⲧϣⲁϫⲉ ⲁⲗⲗⲁ ϩⲣⲁⲓ ϩⲛ̄ ⲧⲉⲭⲁⲣⲓⲥ ⲙ̄ⲡⲉⲧⲭⲱ ⲙ̄ⲙⲟⲥ ϫⲉ ⲧⲉⲛⲟⲩ ⲧ̇ⲛⲁⲧⲱⲟⲩⲛ ⲡⲉϫⲉ-ⲡϫⲟⲉⲓⲥ ⲧⲉⲛⲟⲩ ⲧ̇ⲛⲁϫⲓ-ⲉⲟⲟⲩ ⲧⲉⲛⲟⲩ ⲧ̇ⲛⲁϫⲓⲥⲉ ⲧⲉⲛⲟⲩ ⲧⲉⲧⲛⲁⲛⲁⲩ ⲧⲉⲛⲟⲩ ⲧⲉⲧⲛⲁϫⲓ-ϣⲓⲡⲉ ⲧϭⲟⲙ ⲙ̄ⲡⲉⲧⲛ̄ⲡ̄ⲛ̄ⲁ ⲛⲁ-ϣⲱⲡⲉ ⲉⲥⲟⲩⲟⲉⲓⲧ ⲡⲕⲱϩⲧ̄ ⲛⲁⲟⲩⲉⲙ-ⲧⲏⲩⲧⲛ̄ ⲛⲉⲧⲛ̄ϣⲁϫⲉ ⲛ̄ⲧⲟⲃⲧⲛ̄ ϩⲓϣⲃⲱ ⲉⲧⲉⲧⲛ̄ⲭⲱ ⲙ̄ⲙⲟ[ⲥ] ϥⲛⲁϣⲁϣⲟⲩ ⲉⲃⲟⲗ ⲛ̄ⲑⲉ ⲙ̄ⲡϣⲟⲉⲓϣ ⲉϣⲁⲣⲉⲡⲧⲏⲩ ⲑⲟⲗϥ ⲉⲃⲟⲗ ϩⲓⲭⲙ̄ ⲡϩⲟ ⲙ̄ⲡⲕⲁϩ.

95. Shenoute, *I Am Amazed*, HB 41, in Orlandi, *Shenute Contra Origenistas*, 38; Eng. trans. in Foat, "I Myself Have Seen," 125, rev.

96. Shenoute, *I Am Amazed*, HB 42–43, in Orlandi, *Shenute Contra Origenistas*, 38, 40; Eng. trans. in Foat, "I Myself Have Seen," 125–26, rev. Cf. Ps. 96:12–13 (LXX 95:12–13).

97. Shenoute, *The Lord Thundered*, *Discourses 4*, DU 35, in Amélineau, *Oeuvres*, 1:368–69.

98. Shenoute, *The Lord Thundered*, *Discourses 4*, DU 37, in Amélineau, *Oeuvres*, 1:371.

99. Shenoute, *The Lord Thundered*, *Discourses 4*, DU 38, in Amélineau, *Oeuvres*, 1:371.

100. On martyrology in Coptic literature and the importance of the martyrs for Egyptian Christian self-identity in late antiquity and the early Muslim period, see Willy Clarysse, "The Coptic Martyr Cult," in *Martyrium in Multidisciplinary Perspective*, ed. M. Lamberigts and P. van Deun (Leuven: Peeters, 1995), 377–95; L. Th. Lefort, "La chasse aux reliques des martyrs en Égypte au IVᵉ siècle," *La Nouvelle Clio* 6 (1954): 225–30. For more on Shenoute and the martyrs, see Jürgen Horn, *Studien zu den Märtyrern des nördlichen Oberägypten*, vol. 1, *Märtyrerverehrung und Märtyrerlegende im Werk des Schenute: Beiträge zur ältesten ägyptischen Märtyrerüberlieferung*, Göttinger Orientforschungen, 4th ser., vol. 15.1 (Wiesbaden: Harrassowitz, 1986).

101. Shenoute, *Aſ*, TY 63, in Amélineau, *Oeuvres*, 2:120.

102. Shenoute, *Aſ*, DR 118–19, in Leipoldt, *Opera Omnia*, 3:103.

103. Shenoute, *Aſ*, DR 122–23, in Leipoldt, *Opera Omnia*, 3:105.

104. Shenoute, *Aſ*, DR 123–24, in Leipoldt, *Opera Omnia*, 3:106.

105. Shenoute, *Who Speaks Through the Prophet*, ZM 43, unpublished (FR-BN 131⁴ f. 158R): ⲉⲧⲃⲉ ⲡⲁⲓ ϩⲣⲁⲓ ϩⲛ̄ ⲧϭⲟⲙ ⲁⲛ ⲙ̄ⲡⲉⲧϣⲁϫⲉ ⲁⲗⲗⲁ ϩⲣⲁⲓ ϩⲛ̄ ⲧⲉⲭⲁⲣⲓⲥ ⲙ̄ⲡⲉⲧⲭⲱ ⲙ̄ⲙⲟⲥ ϫⲉ ⲧⲉⲛⲟⲩ ⲧ̇ⲛⲁⲧⲱⲟⲩⲛ ⲡⲉϫⲉ-ⲡϫⲟⲉⲓⲥ.

106. Shenoute, *Who Speaks Through the Prophet*, ZM 43, unpublished (FR-BN 131⁴ f. 158R): ϩⲉⲛⲕⲟⲟⲩⲉ ⲇⲉ ϫⲉ ⲉⲣϣⲁⲛⲡⲣⲱⲙⲉⲛⲟⲩ ⲉϣⲁⲣⲉⲧⲉϥⲧⲩⲭⲏ ⲃⲱⲕ ⲉϩⲟⲩⲛ ⲉⲟⲩϩⲁⲣⲡⲁϩ ϩⲉⲛⲕⲟⲟⲩⲉ ⲇⲉ ϫⲉ ⲉϣⲁⲥⲃⲱⲕ ⲉϩⲟⲩⲛ ⲉⲛⲧⲃ̄ⲛⲟⲟⲩⲉ. ϩⲉⲛⲕⲟⲟⲩⲉ ⲇⲉ ϫⲉ

ⲉϣⲁⲥϣⲱⲡⲉ ⲉⲥϩⲏⲁ ϩⲛ̄ ⲡⲁⲏⲣ ϩⲟⲓⲛⲉ ⲇⲉ ⲉⲩⲭⲱ ⲙ̄ⲙⲟⲥ ϫⲉ ⲉϣⲁⲣⲉ-ⲛⲉⲧⲯⲩⲭⲏ ⲛ̄ⲛϩⲉⲗⲗⲏⲛ
ϣⲱⲡⲉ ⲉⲩϣⲁ ⲙⲛ̄ ⲡⲣⲏ ⲙⲛ̄ ⲡⲟⲟϩ ⲙⲛ̄ ⲛ̄ⲥⲓⲟⲩ ϩⲛ̄ ⲙ̄ⲡⲏⲩⲉ.

107. Cf. Clark, *The Origenist Controversy*, 155.

108. Shenoute, *I Am Amazed*, HB 45, in Orlandi, *Shenute Contra Origenistas*, 40; Eng. trans. in Foat, "I Myself Have Seen," 126, rev.

109. Shenoute, *Who Speaks Through the Prophet*, ZM 44, unpublished (FR-BN 131⁴ f. 158V): ⲛ̄ⲙⲁⲛⲓⲭⲁⲓⲟⲥ ⲇⲉ ⲉⲩⲭⲱ ⲙ̄ⲙⲟⲥ ϫⲉ ⲉϣⲱⲡⲉ ⲟⲩⲧⲯⲩⲭⲏ ⲉⲁⲥϩⲱⲧⲃ̄ ⲧⲉ ⲉⲥϣⲁⲛⲙⲟⲩ ϣⲁⲩⲡⲟⲟⲛⲉⲥ ⲉⲩⲥⲱⲙⲁ ⲛ̄ⲕⲉⲗⲉϥⲱⲥ. ⲉⲩⲟⲩⲱϩ ⲇⲉ ⲟⲛ ⲉⲭ̄ⲛ̄ⲧⲉⲩⲙⲛ̄ⲧⲁⲧⲛⲟⲩⲧⲉ ϣⲁⲩϫⲟⲟⲥ ϫⲉ ⲡⲁⲏⲣ ⲧⲉⲧⲯⲩⲭⲏ ⲡⲉ ⲛ̄ⲛ̄ⲍⲱⲟⲛ ⲙⲛ̄ ⲡ̄ⲣⲱⲙⲉ ⲙⲛ̄ ⲛ̄ϩⲁⲗⲁⲧⲉ ⲙⲛ̄ ⲛ̄ⲧⲃⲧ ⲙⲛ̄ ⲛ̄ϫⲁⲧϥⲉ ⲙⲛ̄ ⲛ̄ⲕⲁ ⲛⲓⲙ ⲉⲧϩⲛ̄ ⲡⲕⲟⲥⲙⲟⲥ ⲛ̄ⲑⲉ ⲟⲛ ⲉⲧⲟⲩⲭⲱ ⲙ̄ⲙⲟⲥ ϫⲉ ⲡⲉⲓⲥⲱⲙⲁ ⲡⲁⲡⲛⲟⲩⲧⲉ ⲁⲛ ⲡⲉ ⲁⲗⲗⲁ ⲡⲁⲑⲩⲗⲏ ⲡⲉ. ⲁⲩⲱ ϫⲉ ⲟⲩⲕⲁⲕⲉ ⲡⲉ ⲉϩⲁⲡⲥ̄ ⲟⲛ ⲉⲧⲣⲉϥⲣ̄-ⲕⲁⲕⲉ. ⲧⲡⲉ ⲇⲉ ⲟⲛ ⲙⲛ̄ ⲡⲕⲁϩ ⲉⲩⲭⲱ ⲙ̄ⲙⲟⲥ ϫⲉ ⲛⲁⲡⲛⲟⲩⲧⲉ ⲁⲛ ⲛⲉ.

110. Shenoute, *Who Speaks Through the Prophet*, ZM 44, unpublished (FR-BN 131⁴ f. 158V): ⲡⲁⲅⲅⲉⲗⲟⲥ ⲉⲧⲟⲩⲁⲁⲃ ⲙ̄ⲡϫⲟⲉⲓⲥ ⲁⲑⲁⲛⲁⲥⲓⲟⲥ ⲡⲁⲣⲭⲓⲉⲡⲓⲥⲕⲟⲡⲟⲥ ⲛ̄ⲑⲉ ⲟⲛ ⲛ̄ⲧⲁⲛⲉⲓⲛⲉ ⲉⲧⲉⲡⲗⲁⲛⲏ ⲛ̄ϩⲁϩ ⲛ̄ϩⲁⲓⲣⲉⲧⲓⲕⲟⲥ ⲉⲃⲟⲗ ϩⲓⲧⲛ̄ⲛⲉϥⲉⲡⲓⲥⲧⲟⲗⲏ. Perhaps this reference to Athanasius is an allusion to the *Life of Antony*, in which Athanasius praises Antony for refusing to associate with Manichaeans (as well as Arians, Melitians, and all other "heretics"). (Athanasius, *Vita Antonii* 68, in Bartelink, *Athanase D'Alexandrie*, 314; Eng. trans. in Gregg, *Athanasius*, 81–82.) See also Brown, "The Diffusion of Manichaeism in the Roman Empire," *JRS* 59 (1969); repr. in *Religion and Society in the Age of Saint Augustine* (London: Faber and Faber, 1972), 104 n. 8, 106 n. 6, 109 n. 73, 111.

111. Shenoute, *Who Speaks Through the Prophet*, ZM 59–60, in Amélineau, *Oeuvres*, 2:192.

112. Shenoute, *Who Speaks Through the Prophet*, ZM 60, in Amélineau, *Oeuvres*, 2:192–93; continued in DD 83, unpublished (FR-BN 131⁵ f. 79R): ϩⲣⲁⲓ̈ ϩⲛ̄ ⲡⲁⲓ̈ ⲉⲓⲉ ⲧⲛ̄ⲡⲗⲁⲛⲁ ϫⲉ ⲧⲛ̄[ϣ]ϣ ⲛ̄ⲛⲉⲅⲣⲁⲫⲏ ϫⲉ ⲛⲉⲧⲙⲟⲟⲩⲧ ⲛⲁⲧⲱⲟⲩⲛ ⲉⲛⲛⲉⲛⲱϣ ϫⲉ ⲕⲉⲥⲱⲙⲁ ⲡⲉⲧⲛⲁ[ⲧ]ⲟⲩⲱ ⲉϩⲣⲁⲓ̈ ϩⲛ̄ ⲛ̄ⲥⲱⲙⲁ ⲛ̄ⲛⲉⲧⲙⲟⲟⲩ[ⲧ].

113. Shenoute, *Who Speaks Through the Prophet*, ZM 65 in Wessely, *Texte*, 5:127.

114. Shenoute, *Who Speaks Through the Prophet*, DD 83, unpublished (FR-BN 131⁵ f. 79R): ⲏ̄ ⲛⲉϣⲁⲕ ⲣⲱⲟⲩ ⲛ̄ⲧⲉⲧⲉⲕⲙⲛ̄ⲧⲁⲑⲏⲧ ⲟⲩⲁⲣⲓⲕⲉ ⲉⲛⲉⲡⲣⲟⲫⲏⲧⲏⲥ ⲙⲛ̄ ⲛⲁⲡⲟⲥⲧⲟⲗⲟⲥ ϫⲉ ⲙ̄ⲡⲟⲩϫⲟⲟⲥ ⲛ̄ⲧⲉⲕϩⲉ ϫⲉ ⲕⲉⲥⲱⲙⲁ ⲡⲉⲧⲛⲁⲧ-ⲟⲩⲱ ⲉϩⲣⲁⲓ̈ ϩⲛ̄ ⲡⲥⲱⲙⲁ ⲛ̄ⲛⲉⲧⲙⲟⲟⲩⲧ· ⲏ̄ ϫⲉ ⲙ̄ⲡⲟⲩϫⲟⲟⲥ ϫⲉ ⲧⲁⲓ̈ ⲧⲉ ⲑⲉ ⲛ̄ⲧⲁⲁⲗⲱⲛⲁⲓ ⲡϫⲟⲉⲓⲥ ϫⲟⲟⲥ ϫⲉ ⲁϫⲓⲥⲉ ϩⲟⲩⲛ ϩⲛ̄ ⲛⲉⲓⲕⲉⲉⲥ ⲉⲧϣⲟⲩⲱⲟⲩ ϫⲉ ⲉⲓⲥ ϩⲏⲏⲧⲉ ⲁⲛⲟⲕ ⲧⲛⲁⲉⲓⲛⲉ ⲛ̄ⲕⲉⲥⲱⲙⲁ ⲉϩⲟⲩⲛ ⲉⲣⲱⲧⲛ̄.

115. Shenoute, *Who Speaks Through the Prophet*, DD 83–84, unpublished (FR-BN 131⁵ f. 79R/V).

116. Shenoute, *Who Speaks Through the Prophet*, ZM 63–64, in Munier, *Manuscrits Coptes*, 136–37.

117. Shenoute, *The Lord Thundered*, *Discourses 4*, DU 42–43, in Amélineau, *Oeuvres*, 1:375–76.

118. Shenoute, *The Lord Thundered*, *Discourses 4*, DU 43–44, in Amélineau, *Oeuvres*, 1:376.

119. Shenoute, *The Lord Thundered*, *Discourses 4*, DU 44, in Amélineau, *Oeuvres*, 1:376–77. The resurrection from the death of sin likely refers to baptism. Compare DU 45, in Amélineau, *Oeuvres*, 1:378, where Shenoute likens a pagan who returns to his former ways after baptism to the dog of Prov. 26:11 who returns to his vomit.

120. Shenoute, *The Lord Thundered*, *Discourses 4*, DU 44, in Amélineau, *Oeuvres*, 1:377.

121. Shenoute, *The Lord Thundered*, *Discourses 4*, DU 41–42, in Amélineau, *Oeuvres*, 1:374.

122. Shenoute, *The Lord Thundered*, *Discourses 4*, DU 42, in Amélineau, *Oeuvres*, 1:374–75.

123. Shenoute, *The Lord Thundered*, *Discourses 4*, DU 44, in Amélineau, *Oeuvres*, 1:377.

124. Shenoute, *The Lord Thundered*, *Discourses 4*, GG 69, in Young, *Coptic Manuscripts*, 146–47; Eng. trans. in ibid., 148, rev. Isa. 66:24, Mark 9:48, Rom. 6:12; cf. Hab. 2:5.

125. Shenoute, *The Lord Thundered*, *Discourses 4*, DU 40–41, in Amélineau, *Oeuvres*, 1:373–74.

126. Shenoute, *The Lord Thundered*, *Discourses 4*, DU 40, in Amélineau, *Oeuvres*, 1:373–74.

127. Shenoute, *I Am Amazed*, *Discourses 7*, HB 77, in Amélineau, *Oeuvres*, 1:334.

128. Shenoute, *I Am Amazed*, *Discourses 7*, HB 77–78, in Amélineau, *Oeuvres*, 1:334–35.

129. This section on faith occurs in fragments GG 26–28 and 31–32, in Amélineau, *Oeuvres*, 1:141–43 and Young, *Coptic Manuscripts*, 144–45. (GG 29–30 are no longer extant.) The next extant fragments of *The Lord Thundered*, DU 35–50, in Amélineau, *Oeuvres*, 1:368–83, pick up the theme of the resurrection, and include the passage from Ezek. 37 described above.

130. Shenoute, *The Lord Thundered*, *Discourses 4*, GG 26–28, in Amélineau, *Oeuvres*, 2:141–42.

131. Shenoute, *The Lord Thundered*, *Discourses 4*, GG 27, in Amélineau, *Oeuvres*, 2:141–42.

132. Shenoute, *The Lord Thundered*, *Discourses 4*, GG 27, in Amélineau, *Oeuvres*, 2:142.

133. Shenoute, *The Lord Thundered*, *Discourses 4*, GG 27–28, in Amélineau, *Oeuvres*, 2:142–43.

134. Shenoute, *I Am Amazed*, *Discourses 7*, HB 45, in Orlandi, *Shenute Contra Origenistas*, 40; Eng. trans. in Foat, "I Myself Have Seen," 126, rev.

135. Shenoute, *I Am Amazed*, *Discourses 7*, HB 45, in Orlandi, *Shenute Contra Origenistas*, 42; Eng. trans. in Foat, "I Myself Have Seen," 126, rev.

136. Shenoute, *I Am Amazed*, *Discourses 7*, HB 45–46, DS 110–11, in Orlandi, *Shenute Contra Origenistas*, 42; Eng. trans. in Foat, "I Myself Have Seen," 127, rev. According to Shenoute, the same group of heretics refuses to pray to Christ (since "he himself prayed"), reads from twelve gospels, and believes in forty aeons. (HB 49–50, DS 115–17, in Orlandi, *Shenute Contra Origenistas*, 44, 46; Eng. trans. in Foat, "I Myself Have Seen," 129.) These accusations are similar to his earlier charges against the Melitians regarding reading apocryphal books, professing multiple universes or *kosmoi*, and claiming that Jesus was a "creature." Cf. Shenoute, *I Am Amazed*, HB 19–22, in Orlandi, *Shenute Contra Origenistas*, 22, 24. Grillmeier believes Shenoute refers to Gnostic beliefs (*Christ in the Christian Tradition*, 2/4:193.)

137. Shenoute, *I Am Amazed*, *Discourses 7*, DS 111, in Orlandi, *Shenute Contra Origenistas*, 42; Eng. trans. in Foat, "I Myself Have Seen," 127, rev.

Conclusion

1. Miller, "Body from Nowhere," 141.

2. Shenoute, *A26* in Behlmer, *De Iudicio*, 32–33; Eng. trans. in David Brakke, *Demons and the Making of the Monk: Spiritual Combat in Early Christianity* (Cambridge, Mass.: Harvard University Press, 2006), 101. On Jesus as judge who sends the wicked to hell, also see *Canon 9*, DF 15–16, unpublished (AT-NB 9345). For more on the volitional aspect of sin, see *As We Began to Preach, Discourses 4* in Emile Chassinat, *Le quatrième livres des entretiens et épitres de Shenouti*, MIFAO 23 (Cairo: Imprimerie de l'Institut français d'archéologie orientale, 1911), 62–84.

Abbreviations

AT-NB	Österreichische Nationalbibliothek Papyrussamlung, Vienna; call numbers begin with a "K" (Koptisch)
ClassHer	Transformation of the Classical Heritage Series
CoptSt	Coptic Studies
CS	*Cistercian Studies*
CSCO	Corpus Scriptorum Christianorum Orientalium
CSEL	Corpus Scriptorum Ecclesiasticorum Latinorum
CSS	Cistercian Studies Series
EG-C	Coptic Museum in Cairo; call numbers begin with "Copte"
EG-CF	Institut français d'archéologie orientale, Cairo
FC	Fathers of the Church
FR-BN	Bibliothèque nationale, Paris; call numbers begin with "Copte"
FR-PL	Musée du Louvre, Paris; call numbers begin with "E"
FR-SU	Bibliothèque nationale et universitaire, Strasbourg
GB-BL	British Library, London; call numbers begin with "Or."
GB-CU	Cambridge University Library, Cambridge; call numbers begin with "Or."
GB-OB	Bodleian Library, Oxford
HTR	*Harvard Theological Review*
IT-NB	Biblioteca Nazionale "Vittorio Emanuele III," Naples
JAAR	*Journal of the American Academy of Religion*
JECS	*Journal of Early Christian Studies*
JJP	*Journal of Juristic Papyrology*

JNES	*Journal of Near Eastern Studies*
JRS	*Journal of Roman Studies*
JSNT Supp.	Journal for the Study of the New Testament, Supplement Series
JTS	*Journal of Theological Studies*
LCC	Library of Christian Classics
OCP	*Orientalia Christiana Periodica*
OECS	Oxford Early Christian Studies Series
Or	*Orientalia*
PG	*Patrologia Graeca*, ed. J. P. Migne
PL	*Patrologia Latina*, ed. J. P. Migne
SAC	Studies in Antiquity and Christianity
SC	Sources Chrétiennes
SCopt	Scriptores Coptici
SH	Subsidia Hagiographica
TU	Texte und Untersuchungen zur Geschichte der altchristlichen Literatur
VT	*Vetus Testamentum*

Bibliography

Primary Sources: Publications

Amélineau, Émile. *Monuments pour servir à l'histoire de l'Égypte chrétienne aux IVᵉ, Vᵉ, VIᵉ, et VIIᵉ siècles.* Mission archéologique française au Caire, Mémoires 4. Paris: Ernest Leroux, 1888–95.

———. *Oeuvres de Schenoudi: Texte copte et traduction française.* 2 vols. Paris: Ernest Leroux, 1907–14.

Apophthegmata Patrum. PG 65: 72–440; PL 73: 739–1062. French translation in *Les Sentences des Pères du désert: Les apophtegmes des Pères,* translated by J. Dion and G. Oury. Solesmes: Abbaye Saint-Pierre de Solesmes, 1966. And *Les Sentences des Pères du désert: Collection alphabétique,* translated by Lucien Regnault. Solesmes: Abbaye Saint-Pierre de Solesmes, 1981. And *Les Sentences des Pères du désert. Troisième recueil et tables,* translated by Lucien Regnault. Solesmes: Abbaye Saint-Pierre de Solesmes, 1976. English translation in *The Sayings of the Desert Fathers: The Alphabetical Collection,* translated by Benedicta Ward. London: Mowbrays, 1975.

Athanasius. *Vita Antonii.* In *Athanase D'Alexandrie: Vie d'Antoine,* edited by G. J. M. Bartelink. SC 400. Paris: Éditions du Cerf, 1994. English translation in *Athanasius: The Life of Antony and Letter to Marcellinus,* translated by Robert C. Gregg. Classics of Western Spirituality. New York: Paulist Press, 1980.

Barns, John W. B. "Shenute as a Historical Source." In *Actes du Xᵉ congrès international de papyrologues: Varsovie-Cracovie 3–9 septembre 1961,* edited by Józef Wolski, 151–59. Wroclaw: Zaklad Narodowy Imienia Ossolinskich Wydawnictwo Polskiej Akademii Nauk, 1964.

Basil. *Regulae brevius tractatae.* PG 31:1080A–1305B. English translation in *The Ascetic Works of Saint Basil,* translated and edited by W. K. Lowther Clarke. London: SPCK, 1925.

———. *Regulae fusius tractatae.* PG 31:889–1052. English translation in *Basil of Caesarea, Ascetical Works,* edited and translated by M. Monica Wagner. FC 9. Washington, D.C.: Catholic University of America Press, 1950.

Bell, David N., trans. *Besa: The Life of Shenoute.* With an introduction by Armand Veilleux. CSS 73. Kalamazoo, Mich.: Cistercian Publishers, 1983.

———. "Shenoute the Great and the Passion of Christ." *CS* 22 (1987): 291–303.

———. "Shenoute the Great: The Struggle with Satan." *CS* 21 (1986): 177–85.

Bindley, Herbert, ed. and trans. *The Oecumenical Documents of the Faith.* 4th edition. London: Methuen, 1950.

Boon, Amand, ed. *Pachomiana latina: Règle et épîtres de s. Pachôme, épître de s. Théodore et "liber" de s. Orsiesius: Texte latin de s. Jerome.* Bibliothèque de la revue d'histoire ecclésiastique 7. Louvain: Bureaux de la revue, 1932.

Brakke, David. "Shenute: On Cleaving to Profitable Things." *Orientalia Lovaniensia Periodica* 20 (1989): 115–41.

Chassinat, Emile. *Le quatrième livres des entretiens et épitres de Shenouti.* MIFAO 23. Cairo: Imprimerie de l'Institut français d'archéologie orientale, 1911.

Crum, Walter E. *Catalogue of the Coptic Manuscripts in the British Museum.* London: British Museum, 1905.

————. *Coptic Monuments.* Cairo: Imprimerie de l'Institut français d'archéologie orientale, 1902.

————. "Inscriptions from Shenoute's Monastery." *JTS* 5 (1904): 552–69.

Elanskaya, Alla I. *The Literary Coptic Manuscripts in the A. S. Pushkin State Fine Arts Museum in Moscow.* Supplements to Vigiliae Christianae 18. Leiden: Brill, 1994.

Evagrius Ponticus. *Gnosticus.* Edited and translated by Antoine and Claire Guillaumont. *Le Gnostique ou à celui qui est devenu digne de la science.* SC 356. Paris: Les Éditions du Cerf, 1989.

————. *Practicus.* Edited and translated by Antoine and Claire Guillaumont. *Traité pratique ou le moine.* 2 volumes. SC 170–71. Paris: Les Éditions du Cerf, 1971.

Gregory Nazianzen. *Oration 42.* In *Grégoire de Nazianze discours 42–43: Introduction, texte critique, traduction et notes.* Edited and translated by Jean Bernardi. SC 384. Paris: Éditions du Cerf, 1992. English Translation in *S. Cyril of Jerusalem, S. Gregory Nazianzen.* Vol. 7 of *Nicene and Post-Nicene Fathers of the Christian Church, Second Series.* Edited and translated by Philip Schaff and Henry Wace. New York: Christian Literature Company, 1894. Repr., Grand Rapids, Mich.: W. B. Eerdmans, 1952.

Halkin, François, ed. *Sancti Pachomii Vitae Graecae.* SH 19. Brussels: Société des Bollandistes, 1932.

Hardy, Edward Rochie, ed., in collaboration with Cyril C. Richardson. *Christology of the Later Fathers.* LCC 3. Philadelphia: Westminster Press, 1954.

Harmless, William. *Desert Christians: An Introduction to the Literature of Early Monasticism.* New York: Oxford University Press, 2004.

Koschorke, Klaus, Stefan Timm, and Frederik Wisse. "Schenute: De Certamine Contra Diabolum." *OC* 59 (1975): 60–77.

Kuhn, Karl. *Letters and Sermons of Besa.* 2 vols. CSCO 157–58. SCopt 21–22. Louvain: Imprimerie orientaliste, 1956.

Lefort, L. Th. "Catéchèse Christologique de Chenoute." *Zeitschrift für Ägyptische Sprache und Altertumskunde* 80 (1955): 40–45.

————, ed. *Oeuvres de s. Pachôme et de ses disciples.* 2 vols. CSCO 159–60. SCopt 23–24. Louvain: L. Durbecq, 1956.

————, ed. *S. Pachomii vita bohairice scripta.* CSCO 89. SCopt 7. Paris: E typographeo reipublicae, 1925; reprint, Louvain: Sécretariat du CSCO, 1953.

Leipoldt, Johannes, ed., with the assistance of W. E. Crum. *Sinuthii Archimandritae Vita et Opera Omnia.* 3 vols. (numbered 1, 3, and 4). CSCO 41, 42, 73. SCopt 1, 2, 5. Paris: Imprimerie nationale, 1906–13. Latin trans. in Hermann Wiesmann, trans., *Sinuthii Archimandritae Vita et Opera Omnia.* 3 vols. (numbered 1, 3, and 4). CSCO 96, 108, 129. SCopt 8, 12, 16. Paris: Imprimerie nationale, 1931–36.

Munier, Henri. *Manuscrits coptes: CGC Nos. 9201–9304.* Cairo: Imprimerie de l'Institut français d'archéologie orientale, 1916.

Norris, Richard A., ed. *The Christological Controversy*. Philadelphia: Fortress Press, 1980.

Orlandi, Tito, ed. and trans. *Shenute Contra Origenistas: Testo con introduzione e traduzione*. Rome: C.I.M., 1985.

Penn, Michael. "Introduction and Translation: Apa Shenoute's 'On the Piety of Women.'" *Coptic Church Review* 16 (1995): 26–29.

Pleyte, W., and P. A. A. Boeser, eds. *Manuscrits coptes du Musée d'Antiquités des Pays-Bas à Leide*. Leiden: Brill, 1897.

Rufinus. *Commentary on the Apostles' Creed*. In *Rufin et Fortunat, 2 commentaires du Credo des apôtres*, edited and translated by Françoise Bilbille Gaven and Jean-Claude Gaven. Collection Les Pères dans la foi 68. Paris: Migne, 1997. English translation in *Commentary on the Apostles' Creed*, translated by J. N. D. Kelly. ACW 20. Westminster, Md.: Newman Press, 1955.

Tattam, Henricus, ed. and trans. *Prophetae Maiores in dialecto linguae Aegyptiacae Memphitica seu Coptica*. 2 vols. 1852. Reprint, Hildesheim: Georg Olms, 1989.

Van Lantschoot, Arn. "Allocution de Timothée d'Alexandrie prononcée à l'occasion de la dédicace de l'église de Pachome a Pboou." *Muséon* 47 (1934): 13–56.

Veilleux, Armand, trans. *Pachomian Koinonia I: The Life of Saint Pachomius and His Disciples*. CSS 45. Kalamazoo, Mich.: Cistercian Publications, 1980.

———, trans. *Pachomian Koinonia II: Pachomian Chronicles and Rules*. CSS 46. Kalamazoo, Mich.: Cistercian Publications, 1981.

———, trans. *Pachomian Koinonia III: Instructions, Letters, and Other Writings of Saint Pachomius and His Disciples*. CSS 47. Kalamazoo, Mich.: Cistercian Publications, 1982.

Wessely, Carl, ed. *Griechische und koptische Texte theologischen Inhalts*. 5 vols. Studien zur Palaeographie und Papyruskunde 9, 11, 12, 15, 18. Leipzig: H. Haessel Hachfolger, 1909–17.

Williamson, A., trans. *Eusebius: The History of the Church from Christ to Constantine*. Revised and edited with a new introduction by Andrew Louth. New York: Penguin Books, 1989.

Wisse, Frederik. "The Naples Fragments of Shenoute's 'De certamine contra diabolum.'" *OC* 75 (1991): 123–40.

Young, Dwight W. "Additional Fragments of Shenoute's *Eighth Canon*." *Archiv für Papyrusforschung und verwandte Gebiete* 44 (1998): 47–68.

———. *Coptic Manuscripts from the White Monastery: Works of Shenute*. 2 vols. Mitteilungen aus der Papyrussammlung der Österreichischen Nationalbibliothek (Papyrus Erzherzog Rainer), Neue Series 22. Vienna: Österreichische Nationalbibliothek in Kommission bei Verlag Brüder Hollinek, 1993.

———. "Five Leaves from a Copy of Shenoute's *Third Canon*." *Muséon* 113 (2000): 263–94.

———. "Pages From a Copy of Shenoute's *Eighth Canon*." *Or* 67 (1998): 64–84.

———. "Two Leaves from a Copy of Shenoute's Ninth Canon." In *Weiner Zeitschrift für die Kunde des Morgenlandes*, edited by Arne A. Ambros, Hermann Hunger, and Markus Köhbach, 281–301. Vienna: Instituts für Orientalistik, 1998.

Zoega, Georg. *Catalogus Codicum Copticorum Manu Scriptorum Qui in Museo Borgiano Velitris Adservantur*. Rome: Sacra Congregatio de Propaganda Fide, 1810. Reprint, Hildesheim: Georg Olms, 1973.

PRIMARY SOURCES: UNPUBLISHED MANUSCRIPTS

Biblioteca Nazionale "Vittorio Emanuele III," Naples (IT-NB)
   IB 4
   IB 17
Bibliothèque nationale, Paris (FR-BN)
   Copte 78
   Copte 129^{12}
   Copte 129^{13}
   Copte 130^{1}
   Copte 130^{2}
   Copte 130^{3}
   Copte 130^{4}
   Copte 130^{5}
   Copte 130^{8}
   Copte 131^{4}
   Copte 131^{5}
   Copte 131^{6}
   Copte 131^{7}
   Copte 131^{8}
   Copte 132^{2}
   Copte 132^{3}
   Copte 132^{4}
   Copte 140^{5}
Bodleian Library, Oxford (GB-OB)
   Clarendon Press b.4
British Library, London (GB-BL)
   Or. 3581A
   Or. 8800
Cambridge University Library, Cambridge (GB-CU)
   Or. 1699E
Coptic Museum in Cairo (EG-C)
   C.G. 8007a, b, c
   inv. 2631/99; Hyvernat photos 13/14
   inv. 2631/101; Hyvernat photos 7/8
   inv. 2631/110; Hyvernat photos 25/26
   inv. 2634/149; Hyvernat photos 97/98
Institut français d'archéologie orientale, Cairo (EG-CF)
   Copte 2
Musée du Louvre, Paris (FR-PL)
   E. 9991
   E. 9996
Österreichische Nationalbibliothek Papyrussamlung, Vienna (AT-NB)
   K 911
   K 912
   K 915
   K 918
   K 919

K 920
K 932
K 934
K 975
K 1712
K 9006
K 9101
K 9313
K 9341
K 9343
K 9345
K 9346
K 9596
K 9597
K 9693
K 9750
K 9751
K 9757
K 9762
K 9798

SECONDARY SOURCES

Althusser, Louis. "Ideology and Ideological State Apparatuses (Notes towards an Investigation)." In *Lenin and Philosophy and Other Essays*, translated by Ben Brewster, 170–90. New York: Monthly Review Press, 1971.
Atiya, Aziz S., ed. *The Coptic Encyclopedia*. 8 vols. New York: Macmillan, 1991.
Bagnall, Roger. *Egypt in Late Antiquity*. Princeton, N.J.: Princeton University Press, 1993.
Bakhtin, M. M. "From Notes Made in 1970–71." In *Speech Genres*, 132–58.
———. "The Problem of Speech Genres." In *Speech Genres*, 60–102.
———. "The Problem of the Text in Linguistics, Philology, and the Human Sciences: An Experiment in Philosophical Analysis." In *Speech Genres*, 103–31.
———. *Speech Genres and Other Late Essays*. Translated by Vern W. McGee. Edited by Caryl Emerson and Michael Holquist. Austin: University of Texas Press, 1986.
Barrett, Michèle. *The Politics of Truth: From Marx to Foucault*. Stanford, Calif.: Stanford University Press, 1991.
Behlmer, Heike. "The City as Metaphor in the Works of Two Panopolitans: Shenoute and Besa." In *Perspectives on Panopolis*, edited by Egberts et al., 13–29.
———. "Historical Evidence from Shenoute's *De extremo iudicio*." In *Sesto Congresso internazionale di Egittologia*, edited by G. M. Zaccone and T. R. di Netro, 2 vols., 2:11–19. Turin: International Association of Egyptologists, 1993.
———. "Koptische Quellen zu (männlicher) 'Homosexualität.'" *Studien zur altägyptischen Kultur* 28 (2000): 27–53
———. *Schenute von Atripe: De Iudicio (Torino, Museo Egizio, Cat. 63000, Cod.*

IV). Catalogo del Museo Egizio di Torino, 1st ser. Monumenti e Testi, vol. 8. Turin: Ministero per i Beni Culturali e Ambientali, Sopraintendenza al Museo delle Antichità Egizie, 1996.

Bell, Catherine. *Ritual Theory, Ritual Practice*. New York: Oxford University Press, 1992.

Bird, Phyllis. "To Play the Harlot: An Inquiry into an Old Testament Metaphor." In *Gender and Difference in Ancient Israel*, edited by Peggy L. Day, 75–94. Minneapolis, Minn.: Fortress Press, 1989.

Bolman, Elizabeth. "Joining the Community of Saints: Monastic Paintings and Ascetic Practice in Early Christian Egypt." In *Shaping Community: The Art and Archaeology of Monasticism: Papers from a Symposium Held at the Frederick R. Weisman Museum, University of Minnesota, March 10–12*, British Archaeological Reports International Series 941, edited by Sheila McNally, 41–56. Oxford: Archaeopress, 2001.

———, ed. *Monastic Visions: Wall Paintings in the Monastery of St. Antony at the Red Sea*. New Haven, Conn.: Yale University Press and the American Research Center in Egypt, 2002.

Bourdieu, Pierre. *Outline of a Theory of Practice*. Translated by Richard Nice. Cambridge: Cambridge University Press, 1977.

Bowman, Alan K. *Egypt after the Pharaohs, 332 BC–AD 642: From Alexander to the Arab Conquest*. Berkeley and Los Angeles: University of California Press, 1986.

Boyarin, Daniel. *Carnal Israel: Reading Sex in Talmudic Culture*. Berkeley and Los Angeles: University of California Press, 1993.

Brakke, David. *Athanasius and the Politics of Asceticism*. OECS. Oxford: Clarendon, 1995. Reprint, *Athanasius and Asceticism*, Baltimore: Johns Hopkins University Press, 1998.

———. "The Body in Early Christian Sources." *Bulletin of the American Society of Papyrologists* 37 (2000): 119–34.

———. *Demons and the Making of the Monk: Spiritual Combat in Early Christianity*. Cambridge, Mass.: Harvard University Press, 2006.

———. "The Egyptian Afterlife of Origenism: Conflicts over Embodiment in Coptic Sermons." *OCP* 66 (2000): 277–93.

———. "Ethiopian Demons: Male Sexuality, the Black-Skinned Other, and the Monastic Self." *Journal of the History of Sexuality* 10 (2001): 501–35.

Brooks Hedstrom, Darlene. " 'Your Cell Will Teach You All Things': The Relationship between Monastic Practice and the Architectural Design of the Cell in Coptic Monasticism, 400–1000 (Egypt)." Ph.D. diss., Miami University, 2001.

Brooten, Bernadette J. *Love Between Women: Early Christian Responses to Female Homoeroticism*. Chicago: University of Chicago Press, 1996.

Brown, Peter. *Authority and the Sacred: Aspects of the Christianisation of the Roman World*. Cambridge: Cambridge University Press, 1995.

———. *The Body and Society: Men, Women, and Sexual Renunciation in Early Christianity*. New York: Columbia University Press, 1988.

———. "The Diffusion of Manichaeism in the Roman Empire." *JRS* 59 (1969): 92–103; reprinted in *Religion and Society in the Age of Saint Augustine*, 94–118. London: Faber and Faber, 1972.

————. *Power and Persuasion in Late Antiquity: Towards a Christian Empire.* Madison: University of Wisconsin Press, 1992.

Burrus, Virginia. "The Heretical Woman as Symbol in Alexander, Athanasius, Epiphanius, and Jerome." *HTR* 84 (1991): 229–48.

Burton-Christie, Douglas. *Word in the Desert: Scripture and the Quest for Holiness in Early Christian Monasticism.* New York: Oxford University Press, 1993.

Butler, Judith. *Bodies That Matter: On the Discursive Limits of "Sex."* New York: Routledge, 1993

————. *Gender Trouble: Feminism and the Subversion of Identity.* New York: Routledge, 1990.

Butler, Judith, and Joan Scott, eds. *Feminists Theorize the Political.* New York: Routledge, 1992.

Castelli, Elizabeth. "Virginity and Its Meaning for Women's Sexuality in Early Christianity." *Journal of Feminist Studies in Religion* 2 (1986): 61–88.

Certeau, Michel de. *The Writing of History.* Translated by Tom Conley. New York: Columbia University Press, 1988.

Chitty, Derwas. *The Desert a City: An Introduction to the Study of Egyptian and Palestinian Monasticism under the Christian Empire.* Oxford: Blackwell, 1966. Reprint, Crestwood, N.Y.: St. Vladimir's Seminary Press, 1995.

Clark, Elizabeth A. *Ascetic Piety and Women's Faith: Essays on Late Ancient Christianity.* Lewiston, N.Y.: Edwin Mellen Press, 1986.

————. "Foucault, the Fathers, and Sex." *JAAR* 56 (1988): 619–41.

————. "Ideology, History, and the Construction of 'Woman' in Late Ancient Christianity." *JECS* 2 (1994): 155–84.

————. *Jerome, Chrysostom and Friends: Essays and Translations.* New York: Edwin Mellen Press, 1979.

————. "The Lady Vanishes: Dilemmas of a Feminist Historian after the 'Linguistic Turn.'" *Church History* 67 (1998): 1–31.

————. *The Origenist Controversy: The Cultural Construction of an Early Christian Debate.* Princeton, N.J.: Princeton University Press, 1992.

————. *Reading Renunciation: Asceticism and Scripture in Early Christianity.* Princeton, N.J.: Princeton University Press, 1999.

Clarysse, Willy. "The Coptic Martyr Cult." In *Martyrium in Multidisciplinary Perspective,* edited by M. Lamberigts and P. van Deun, 377–95. Leuven: Peeters, 1995.

Conybeare, Catherine. *Paulinus Noster: Self and Symbols in the Letters of Paulinus of Nola.* OECS. Oxford: Oxford University Press, 2000.

Coquin, René-Georges, and Maurice Martin. "Dayr Anbā Shinūdah: History." In *The Coptic Encyclopedia,* edited by Atiya, 3:761–65.

Crislip, Andrew Todd. *From Monastery to Hospital: Christian Monasticism and the Transformation of Health Care in Late Antiquity.* Ann Arbor: University of Michigan, 2005.

Crum, Walter E. *A Coptic Dictionary.* Compiled with the help of many scholars. Oxford: Clarendon, 1939.

Day, Peggy L. "Adulterous Jerusalem's Imagined Demise: Death of a Metaphor in Ezekiel XVI." *VT* 50 (2000): 285–309.

————. "The Bitch Had It Coming to Her: Rhetoric and Interpretation in Ezekiel 16." *Biblical Interpretation* 8 (2000): 231–54.

Deichmann, F. W. "Zum Altägyptischen in der koptishen Baukunst." *Mittei-lungen des Deutschen Archäologischen Instituts—Abteilung Kairo* 8 (1938): 34–37.

Depuydt, Leo. "In Sinuthium Graecum." *Or* 59 (1990): 67–71.

Derrida, Jacques. "What Is a 'Relevant' Translation?" *Critical Inquiry* 27 (2001): 174–200.

Douglas, Mary. *Natural Symbols: Explorations in Cosmology.* Reprint, with a new introduction. London: Routledge, 1996.

———. *Purity and Danger: An Analysis of Concepts of Pollution and Taboo.* London: Routledge & K. Paul, 1966.

Dreyfus, Hubert L., and Paul Rabinow. *Michel Foucault: Beyond Structuralism and Hermeneutics.* 2nd ed. With an Afterword by and an interview with Michel Foucault. Chicago: University of Chicago Press, 1982.

Eagleton, Terry. *Ideology: An Introduction.* New York: Verso, 1991.

Egberts, A., B. P. Muhs, and J. van der Vliet, eds. *Perspectives on Panopolis: An Egyptian Town from Alexander the Great to the Arab Conquest. Acts from an International Symposium Held in Leiden on 16, 17 and 18 December 1998.* Papyrologica Lugduno-Batava 31. Leiden: Brill, 2002.

Elm, Susanna. "A Programmatic Life: Gregory of Nazianzus' *Orations* 42 and 43 and the Constantinopolitan Elites." *Arethusa* 33 (2000): 411–27.

———. *"Virgins of God": The Making of Asceticism in Late Antiquity.* Oxford Classical Monographs. Oxford: Oxford University Press, 1994.

Emmel, Stephen. "The Christian Book in Egypt: Innovation and the Coptic Tradition." In *The Bible as Book: The Manuscript Tradition,* edited by John L. Sharpe III and Kimberly Van Kampen, 35–43. London: British Library; New Castle, Del.: Oak Knoll Press, in association with The Scriptorium, Center for Christian Antiquities, 1998.

———. "From the Other Side of the Nile: Shenute and Panopolis." In *Perspectives on Panopolis,* edited by Egberts et al., 95–113.

———. "The Historical Circumstances of Shenute's Sermon *God Is Blessed.*" In ΘΕΜΕΛΙΑ: *Spätantike und koptologische Studien Peter Grossmann zum 65. Geburtstag,* edited by Martin Krause and Sofia Schaten, 81–96. Wiesbaden: Reichert Verlag, 1998.

———. "Shenoute the Monk: The Early Monastic Career of Shenoute the Archimandrite." In *Il Monachesimo tra eredità e aperture: Atti del simposio "Testi e temi nella tradizione del monachesimo cristiano" per il 50° anniversario dell'Istituto monastico di Sant'Anselmo, Roma, 28 maggio–1° giugno 2002.* Edited by Maciej Bielawski and Daniël Hombergen, 151–74. Studia Anselmiana 140. Rome: Pontificio Ateneo di S. Anselmo, 2004.

———. *Shenoute's Literary Corpus.* 2 vols. CSCO 599–600. Subsidia 111–12. Louvain: Peeters, 2004.

———. "Theophilus's Festal Letter of 401 as Quoted by Shenute." In *Divitiae Aegypti: Koptologische und verwandte Studien zu Ehren von Martin Krause,* edited by Cäcilia Fluck et al., 93–98. Wiesbaden: Dr. Ludwig Reichert Verlag, 1995.

Foat, Michael. "I Myself Have Seen: The Representation of Humanity in the Writings of Apa Shenoute of Atripe." Ph.D. diss. Brown University. 1996.

Foucault, Michel. "Afterword." In *Michel Foucault,* by Dreyfus and Rabinow, 208–26.

———. *The Care of the Self.* Vol. 3 of *The History of Sexuality.* Translated by Robert Hurley. New York: Vintage Books, 1988.

———. *Discipline and Punish: The Birth of the Prison.* Translated by Alan Sheridan. 2nd ed. New York: Vintage Books, 1995.

———. *The History of Sexuality: An Introduction.* Vol. 1 of *The History of Sexuality.* Translated by Robert Hurley. New York: Vintage Books, 1978.

———. *Power/Knowledge: Selected Interviews and Other Writings, 1972–1977.* Edited by Colin Gordon. Translated by Colin Gordon et al. New York: Pantheon Books, 1980.

———. *The Use of Pleasure.* Vol. 2 of *The History of Sexuality.* Translated by Robert Hurley. New York: Vintage Books, 1990.

———. "Writing the Self." Translated by Ann Hobart. In *Foucault and His Interlocutors,* edited and introduced by Arnold I. Davidson, 234–47. Chicago: University of Chicago Press, 1997.

Fowden, Elizabeth Key. *Barbarian Plain: Saint Sergius between Rome and Iran.* ClassHer 28. Berkeley and Los Angeles: University of California Press, 1999.

Frankfurter, David. *Elijah in Upper Egypt: The Apocalypse of Elijah and Early Egyptian Christianity.* SAC. Minneapolis, Minn.: Fortress Press, 1993.

———. *Religion in Roman Egypt: Assimilation and Resistance.* Princeton, N.J.: Princeton University Press, 1998.

———. "Syncretism and the Holy Man in Late Antique Egypt." *JECS* 11 (2003): 339–85.

Fraser, Nancy, and Linda J. Nicholson. "Social Criticism without Philosophy: An Encounter between Feminism and Postmodernism." In *Feminism/Postmodernism,* edited by Nicholson, 19–38.

Frend, W. H. C. *The Early Church.* Knowing Christianity. Philadelphia: J. B. Lippincott, 1966.

———. *The Rise of the Monophysite Movement: Chapters in the History of the Church in the Fifth and Sixth Centuries.* Cambridge: Cambridge University Press, 1972.

Gabra, Gawdat. *Coptic Monasteries: Egypt's Monastic Art and Architecture.* Cairo: The American University in Cairo Press, 2002.

Gaddis, Michael. *There Is No Crime for Those Who Have Christ: Religious Violence in the Christian Roman Empire.* ClassHer 39. Berkeley and Los Angeles: University of California Press, 2005.

Gleason, Maud. "Visiting and News: Gossip and Reputation-Management in the Desert." *JECS* 6 (1998): 501–21.

Goehring, James E. *Ascetics, Society, and the Desert: Studies in Early Egyptian Monasticism.* SAC. Harrisburg, Pa.: Trinity Press, 1999.

———. "Chalcedonian Power Politics and the Demise of Pachomian Monasticism." In *Ascetics,* 241–61. Claremont, Calif.: Institute for Antiquity and Christianity, 1989.

———. "The Dark Side of the Landscape: Ideology and Power in the Christian Myth of the Desert." In *The Cultural Turn in Late Ancient Studies: Gender, Asceticism, and Historiography,* edited by Dale B. Martin and Patricia Cox Miller, 136–49. Durham, N.C.: Duke University Press, 2005.

———. "The Encroaching Desert: Literary Production and Ascetic Space in Early Christian Egypt." *JECS* 1 (1993): 281–96. Reprint in *Ascetics,* 73–88.

―――. "The Fourth Letter of Horsiesius and the Situation in the Pachomian Community following the Death of Theodore." In *Ascetics*, 221–40.

―――. "Melitian Monastic Organization: A Challenge to Pachomian Originality." In *Studia Patristica: Papers Presented at the Eleventh International Conference on Patristic Studies Held in Oxford 1991: Biblica et Apocrypha, Orientalia, Ascetica*, edited by Elizabeth A. Livingstone, vol. 25, 388–95. Leuven: Peeters, 1993. Reprint in *Ascetics*, 187–95.

―――. "Monastic Diversity and Ideological Boundaries in Fourth-Century Christian Egypt." *JECS* 5 (1997): 61–84. Rev. edition in *Ascetics*, 196–218.

―――. "New Frontiers in Pachomian Studies." In *The Roots of Egyptian Christianity*, edited by Pearson and Goehring, 236–57. Reprint in *Ascetics*, 162–86.

―――. "Pachomius's Vision of Heresy: The Development of a Pachomian Tradition." *Muséon* 95 (1982): 241–62. Reprint in *Ascetics*, 137–61.

―――. "The World Engaged: The Social and Economic World of Early Egyptian Monasticism." In *Gnosticism and the Early Christian World: In Honor of James M. Robinson*, edited by Goehring et al., 134–44. Forum Fascicles 2. Sonoma, Calif.: Polebridge Press, 1990. Reprint in *Ascetics*, 39–52.

Goldschmidt, Rudolf Carel. *Paulinus' Churches at Nola: Texts, Translations, and Commentary*. Amsterdam: N.V. Noord-Hollandsche Uitgevers Maatschappij, 1940.

Gould, Graham. *The Desert Fathers on Monastic Community*. OECS. Oxford: Clarendon Press, 1993.

Griggs, C. Wilfred. *Early Egyptian Christianity from Its Origins to 451 CE*. CoptSt 2. Leiden: Brill, 1990.

Grillmeier, Aloys. *Christ in Christian Tradition*. Volume 1, *From the Apostolic Age to Chalcedon (451)*. Vol. 1 of *Christ in Christian Tradition*. Translated by John Bowden. 2nd rev. ed. Atlanta: John Knox Press, 1975.

―――. *Christ in Christian Tradition*. Vol. 2, *From the Council of Chalcedon (451) to Gregory the Great (590–604), Part 1: Reception and Contradiction*. Translated by Pauline Allen and John Cawte. Atlanta: John Knox Press, 1987.

―――. *Christ in Christian Tradition*. Volume 2, *From the Council of Chalcedon (451) to Gregory the Great (590–604), Part 2: The Church of Alexandria with Nubia and Ethiopia after 451*. Translated by O. C. Dean. Louisville, Ky.: Westminster John Knox Press, 1996.

Grossmann, Peter. "Brief Report on a Survey in the Monastery of Apa Shenudi at Suhag (April 2002)." *Bulletin de la Société d'archéologie Copte* 42 (2003): 9–11.

―――. *Christliche Architektur in Ägypten*. Handbook of Oriental Studies, Section One: The Near and Middle East 62. Leiden: Brill, 2002.

―――. "Dayr Anbā Shinūdah: Architecture." In *The Coptic Encyclopedia*, edited by Atiya, 3:766–69.

―――. "Kirche oder 'Ort des Feierns': Zur Problematik der pachomianischen Bezeichnungen des Kirchengebäudes." *Enchoria* 26 (2000): 41–53.

―――. "New Observations in the Church and Sanctuary of Dayr Anbā Šinūda—the So-Called White Monastery—at Suhāğ: Results of Two Surveys in October, 1981 and January, 1982." *Annales du Service des antiquités de l'Egypte* 70 (1984): 69–73.

Guérin, H. "Sermons inédits de Senouti: Thèse soutenue a l'École du Louvre." *Revue égyptologique* 10 (1902): 148–64; 11 (1904): 15–34.

Harpham, Geoffrey Galt. *The Ascetic Imperative in Culture and Criticism*. Chicago: University of Chicago Press, 1987.

Harvey, Susan Ashbrook. "The Stylite's Liturgy: Ritual and Religious Identity in Late Antiquity." *JECS* 6 (1998): 523–39.

Horn, Jürgen. *Studien zu den Märtyrern des nördlichen Oberägypten*. Vol. 1, *Märtyrerverehrung und Märtyrerlegende im Werk des Schenute: Beiträge zur ältesten ägyptischen Märtyrerüberlieferung*. Göttinger Orientforschungen, 4th ser., vol. 15.1. Wiesbaden: Otto Harrassowitz, 1986.

Kelly, J. N. D. *Early Christian Creeds*. 3rd ed. New York: David McKay, 1972.

———. *Early Christian Doctrines*. Rev. ed. San Francisco: HarperCollins, 1978.

Krautheimer, Richard. *Early Christian and Byzantine Architecture*. Rev. ed. Pelican History of Art. New York: Penguin Books, 1981.

Krawiec, Rebecca. *Shenoute and the Women of the White Monastery: Egyptian Monasticism in Late Antiquity*. New York: Oxford University Press, 2002.

Krueger, Derek. *Writing and Holiness: The Practice of Authorship in the Early Christian East*. Divinations. Philadelphia: University of Pennsylvania Press, 2004.

Kuhn, Karl. "A Fifth-Century Abbot." *JTS*, 2nd series, 5 (1954): 36–48, 174–87; 6 (1955): 35–48.

Ladeuze, Paulin. *Étude sur le cénobitisme Pakhômien pendant le IVᵉ siècle et la première moitié du Vᵉ*. 1898. Reprint, Frankfurt: Minerva, 1961.

Lampe, G. W. H. *A Patristic Greek Lexicon*. Oxford: Clarendon Press, 1961–68.

Layton, Bentley. *A Coptic Grammar with Chrestomathy and Glossary: Sahidic Dialect*. Porta Linguarum Orientalium Neue Serie 20. Wiesbaden: Harrassowitz, 2000.

———. "Monastic Order in Shenoute's White Monastery Federation." Paper presented at the University of Minnesota, Minneapolis, Symposium "Living for Eternity: Monasticism in Egypt." March 8, 2003.

———. "Social Structure and Food Consumption in an Early Christian Monastery: The Evidence of Shenoute's Canons and the White Monastery Federation AD 385–465." *Muséon* (2002): 25–55.

Lefebvre, G. "Deir-el-Abiad." In the *Dictionnaire d'archéologie Chrétienne et de liturgie*. 15 vols. Paris: Librairie Letouzey et Ané, 1903–53. Vol. 4, pt. 1, pp. 459–502.

Lefort, L. Th. "Athanase, Ambroise, et Chenoute 'Sur la virginité.'" *Muséon* 48 (1935): 55–73.

———. "La chasse aux reliques des martyrs en Égypte au IVᵉ siècle." *La Nouvelle Clio* 6 (1954): 225–30.

Leipoldt, Johannes. *Schenute von Atripe und die Entstehung des national ägyptischen Christentums*. TU 25.1. Leipzig: J. C. Hinrichs, 1903.

Leyser, Conrad. *Authority and Asceticism from Augustine to Gregory the Great*. Oxford Historical Monographs. Oxford: Clarendon, 2000.

Lienhard, Joseph T. *Paulinus of Nola and Early Western Monasticism*. Cologne: P. Hanstein, 1977.

Maier, Harry O. "'Manichee!': Leo the Great and the Orthodox Panopticon." *JECS* 4 (1996): 441–60.

Martin, Dale B. *The Corinthian Body*. New Haven, Conn.: Yale University Press, 1995.

McLynn, Neil. "Gregory of Nazianzus." In *Late Antiquity: A Guide to the Post-classical World*, edited by G. W. Bowersock, Peter Brown, and Oleg Grabar, 476–77. Cambridge, Mass.: Harvard University Press, 1996.

Medec, Goulven. "Le Christ des païens d'après le *De consensu euangelistarum* de saint Augustin." *Recherches Augustiniennes* 26 (1992): 3–67.

Miller, Patricia Cox. "Desert Asceticism and 'The Body from Nowhere.'" *JECS* 2 (1994): 137–53.

Mohamed, Mahmoud Ali, and Peter Grossmann. "On the Recently Excavated Monastic Buildings in Dayr Anba Shinuda: Archaeological Report." *Bulletin de la Société d'Archéologie Copte* 30 (1991): 53–63.

Monneret de Villard, Ugo. *Les Couvents près de Sohâg (Deyr el-Abiad et Deyr el-Ahmar)*. Milan: Tipografia Pontificia Arcivescovile S. Giuseppe, 1925–26.

Montserrat, Dominic. *Sex and Society in Græco-Roman Egypt*. New York: Kegan Paul International, 1996.

Newman, Judith H. "Lot in Sodom: The Post-Mortem of a City and the Afterlife of a Biblical Text." In *The Function of Scripture in Early Jewish and Christian Tradition*, edited by Craig A. Evans and James A. Sanders, 34–44. JSNT Supp. 154. Studies in Scripture and Early Judaism and Christianity 6. Sheffield: Sheffield Academic Press, 1998.

Nicholson, Linda J., ed. *Feminism/Postmodernism*. New York: Routledge, 1990.

Orlandi, Tito. "A Catechesis against Apocryphal Texts by Shenute and the Gnostic Texts of Nag Hammadi." *HTR* 75 (1982): 85–95.

———. "Coptic Literature." In *The Roots of Egyptian Christianity*, edited by Pearson and Goehring, 51–81.

———. "The Future of Studies in Coptic Biblical and Ecclesiastical Literature." In *Future of Coptic Studies*, edited by Wilson, 143–63.

———. "The Library of the Monastery of Saint Shenute at Atripe." In *Perspectives on Panopolis*, edited by Egberts et al., 211–31.

Ortner, Sherry B. *Making Gender: The Politics and Erotics of Culture*. Boston: Beacon Press, 1996.

———. "Making Gender: Toward a Feminist, Minority, Postcolonial, Subaltern, etc., Theory of Practice." In *Making Gender*, 1–20.

Padel, Ruth. *In and Out of the Mind: Greek Images of the Tragic Self*. Princeton, N.J.: Princeton University Press, 1992.

Pearson, Birger A., and James E. Goehring, eds. *The Roots of Egyptian Christianity*. SAC. Philadelphia: Fortress Press, 1986.

Petrie, W. M. Flinders. *Athribis*. British School of Archeology in Egypt 14. London: London School of Archaeology in Egypt, 1908.

Quecke, Hans. "Ein Pachomiuszitat bei Schenute." In *Probleme der koptischen Literatur*, edited by Peter Nagel, 155–71. Halle-Wittenberg: Martin Luther Universität, 1968.

Revillout, E. "Les origines du schisme égyptien. Premier récit: Le précurseur et inspirateur, Sénuti le prophète." *Revue de l'histoire des religions* 8 (1883): 401–67, 545–81.

Riley, Denise. "Does Sex Have a History?" In *Feminism and History*, edited by Scott, 17–33.

Rousseau, Philip. *Ascetics, Authority, and the Church in the Age of Jerome and Cassian*. Oxford Historical Monographs. Oxford: Oxford University Press, 1978.

———. *Basil of Caesarea.* ClassHer 20. Berkeley and Los Angeles: University of California Press, 1994.

———. *Pachomius: The Making of a Community in Fourth-Century Egypt.* Class-Her 6. Rev. edition. Berkeley and Los Angeles: University of California Press, 1999.

Rousselle, Aline. *Porneia: On Desire and the Body in Antiquity.* Translated by Felicia Pheasant. Cambridge, Mass.: Basil Blackwell, 1988.

Rubenson, Samuel. *The Letters of St. Anthony: Monasticism and the Making of a Saint.* SAC. Minneapolis, Minn.: Fortress Press, 1995.

Russell, Norman. *Cyril of Alexandria.* Early Church Fathers. London: Routledge, 2000.

Schroeder, Caroline T. "Prophecy and *Porneia* in Shenoute's Letters: The Rhetoric of Sexuality in a Late Antique Egyptian Monastery." *JNES* 65 (2006): 81–97.

Scott, Joan Wallach, ed. *Feminism and History.* Oxford: Oxford University Press, 1996.

———. *Gender and the Politics of History.* New York: Columbia University Press, 1988.

———. "Gender: A Useful Category of Analysis." In *Feminism and History,* 152–80.

———. *Only Paradoxes to Offer: French Feminists and the Rights of Man.* Cambridge, Mass.: Harvard University Press, 1996.

Setel, T. Drora. "Prophets and Pornography: Female Sexual Imagery in Hosea." In *Feminist Interpretation of the Bible,* edited by Letty M. Russell, 86–95. Philadelphia: Westminster Press, 1985.

Severin, Hans Georg. "Dayr Anbā Shinūdah: Architectural Sculpture." In *The Coptic Encyclopedia,* edited by Atiya, 3:769–70.

Shaw, Teresa M. "*Askesis* and the Appearance of Holiness." *JECS* 6 (1998): 485–99.

———. *The Burden of the Flesh: Fasting and Sexuality in Early Christianity.* Minneapolis, Minn.: Fortress Press, 1998.

Shisha-Halevy, Ariel. *Coptic Grammatical Categories: Structural Studies in the Syntax of Shenoutean Sahidic.* Analecta Orientalia 53. Rome: Pontificium Institutum Biblicum, 1986.

Thompson, Herbert. "Dioscorus and Shenoute." *Bibliothèque de l'École des Hautes Études: Recueil d'Études Égyptologiques* 234 (1922): 367–76.

Thompson, John B. *Ideology and Modern Culture: Critical Social Theory in the Era of Mass Communication.* Stanford, Calif.: Stanford University Press, 1990.

Timbie, Janet. "Dualism and the Concept of Orthodoxy in the Thought of the Monks of Upper Egypt." Ph.D. diss., University of Pennsylvania, 1979.

———. "Nestorius in Shenoute's *I Am Amazed*: A Corrected Text Yields New Information." Paper presented at the North American Patristics Society Annual Meeting. May 24, 2001.

———. "Reading and Re-reading Shenoute's *I Am Amazed*: More Information on Nestorius and Others." In *The World of Early Egyptian Christianity: Language, Literature, and Social Context,* edited by James Goehring and Janet Timbie. Washington, D.C.: Catholic University of America Press, forthcoming.

———. "The State of Research on the Career of Shenoute of Atripe." In *The Roots of Egyptian Christianity,* edited by Pearson and Goehring, 258–70.

Trout, Dennis E. *Paulinus of Nola: Life, Letters, and Poems.* ClassHer 27. Berkeley and Los Angeles: University of California Press, 1999.

Valantasis, Richard. "Constructions of Power in Asceticism." *JAAR* 63 (1995): 775–821.

Veilleux, Armand. "Chénouté ou les écueils du monachisme." *Collectanea Cisterciensia* 45 (1983): 124–31.

Wallace-Hadrill, D. S. *The Greek Patristic View of Nature.* Manchester: Manchester University Press, 1968.

Wessel, Susan. *Cyril of Alexandria and the Nestorian Controversy: The Making of a Saint and of a Heretic.* OECS. Oxford: Oxford University Press, 2004.

Wilfong, Terry G. "'Friendship and Physical Desire': The Discourse of Female Homoeroticism in Fifth-Century CE Egypt." In *Among Women: From the Homosocial to the Homoerotic in the Ancient World*, edited by Nancy Sorkin Rabinowitz and Lisa Auanger, 304–29. Austin: University of Texas Press, 2002.

———. "Reading the Disjointed Body in Coptic: From Physical Modification to Textual Fragmentation." In *Changing Bodies, Changing Meanings: Studies on the Human Body in Antiquity*, edited by Dominic Montserrat, 116–36. New York: Routledge, 1998.

———. *Women of Jeme: Lives in a Coptic Town in Late Antique Egypt.* New Texts from Ancient Cultures. Ann Arbor: University of Michigan Press, 2002.

Williams, Michael Allen. *Rethinking "Gnosticism": An Argument for Dismantling a Dubious Category.* Princeton, N.J.: Princeton University Press, 1996.

Wilson, R. McL., ed. *The Future of Coptic Studies.* CoptSt 1. Leiden: Brill, 1978.

Wilson, Robert R. *Prophecy and Society in Ancient Israel.* Philadelphia: Fortress Press, 1980.

Wipszycka, Ewa. "Le nationalisme a-t-il existé dans L'Egypte byzantine?" *JJP* 22 (1992): 83–128.

Index

Abraham, 136, 155, 173 n.34, 195 n.99, 204 n.60

Adam, 107, 128

adornment, 95, 97–100, 110–12, 118–21

adultery, 43, 38, 70. *See also* fornication

altar, 29, 35, 36

Ambrose (bishop of Milan), 116, 185 n.124, 197 n.125

anchorites. *See* monasticism, anchoritic and semianchoritic

Antinoopolis, 129

Antony, 16, 17, 90, 168 n.51, 209 n.110

Apollinarianism, 141

Apophthegmata Patrum, 17, 52, 90

architecture, 22, 91; Shenoute on, 109, 110. *See also* adornment; church building

Arianism, 128, 141, 209 n.110

asceticism, 3, 5, 14, 24, 168 n.51; as model for laity, 156. *See also* discipline, ascetic

Athanasius (bishop of Alexandria), 130, 149, 209 n.110

Atripe, 1, 163 n.1

Augustine, 1, 166 n.25

Bakhtin, Mikhail, 39, 174–75 n.58

barbarian invasions, 93, 117, 188 n.12

Basil, rules of, 59

basilica. *See* church building

Bell, Catherine, 56–58, 66

Benedict, rule of, 59

Besa, 6, 163 nn. 2, 4

Bible. *See* scripture

bishops of Alexandria, 6, 10, 23, 123. *See also names of individual bishops*

blasphemy, 50

body, the, 161; of Christ, 22, 92; as dwelling place for God, 105–7, 115–16, 194 nn. 82, 91; harmony of social body, 55, 75–76, 78; human body, 12, 22, 40, 80, 83, 126–27, 152–57, 159, 187 n.5; of the individual, 3, 47; monastery as, 3, 13, 21–22, 53, 79–88, 100–105, 125; people as members of Christ's, 101–2, 105–6, 109, 117–18; and production

of knowledge, 54, 56–57, 160, 184 n.89; relationship between individual social bodies, 3, 40, 54–58, 67, 79–89, 92, 111–14; and ritual, 58, 67; as sacred, 22, 126, 128, 156–57; Shenoute's, 85–86; as social construction, 11–12, 57, 177–78 n.6. *See also* discipline, of the body; discourse, of the body; eucharist; ideology, and the body; pollution, bodily or physical; purity, bodily; resurrection; sin, and the body

Bolman, Elizabeth, 123

boundaries, 13–14, 116, 168 n.49

Bourdieu, Pierre, 56–58

Brakke, David, 16–17, 126

Brown, Peter, 5, 57, 116

Butler, Judith, 11–12, 56, 57

Canons, as division of Shenoute's literary corpus, 19–21, 59–60, 68, 70, 72, 126–29, 188 n.14, 202 n.30

castration, 77

celibacy, 4, 9, 11, 44, 69, 74, 115, 126

Chitty, Derwas, 121

Christology, 22, 133, 137, 139–45, 157, 204 n.52. *See also* theology

church building: at Deir Anba Shenouda, construction and reconstruction of, 2, 21–22, 90, 93–98, 100, 116, 188 n.12, 191 n.42; at Deir Anba Shenouda, decorative sculpture, 94, 97–99; at Deir Anba Shenouda, excavations of, 2, 90, 94, 96, 187 n.1, 189–90 nn. 22, 25; at Deir Anba Shenouda, wall paintings in, 95, 97–99, 191 n.40; as distraction from asceticism, 110; as exemplar for asceticism, 100, 105–10, 118–19, 121–25, 156, 158; as house of God, 89, 91–92, 93, 101, 105–8, 125, 193–94 nn. 80, 82; as monastic body, 92, 101, 105–9, 115; purity of, 105–11, 156, 193 nn. 75, 80; and salvation, 97, 107, 109, 110, 116, 123; theological and ideological meanings of, 91–92, 97, 111, 118–25. *See also* altar; Pachomian monasteries, basilica at Pbow; Pachomian mon-

Acknowledgments

I HAVE ACCRUED a great many debts over the long course of this project. I wish first and foremost to thank my mentor at Duke University, Elizabeth A. Clark. Her high scholarly standards and innovative research have been a model for me as they have been for countless other young scholars. Her support and insightful criticism on my work pushed me never to lose sight of Shenoute's importance for the study of late antiquity, and not just for Coptic studies. I am also grateful to other faculty at Duke and the University of North Carolina for their suggestions and guidance on the entire manuscript: Orval S. Wintermute, Lucas Van Rompay, Bart Ehrman, Dale Martin, Jean O'Barr, and Melvin K. H. Peters.

Many other friends and colleagues kindly read portions of the manuscript over the years in its various stages and recommended much-needed improvements: Betsy Bolman, David Brakke, Catherine Chin, Stephanie Cobb, Kirsti Copeland, George Demacopoulos, Bonnie Effros, Georgia Frank, the late John P. Frank, Michael Gaddis, Kim Haines-Eitzen, Andrew S. Jacobs, Scott McDonough, Ann Meredith, Patricia Cox Miller, Gil Renberg, Tina Shepardson, Christopher Whitsett, and the members of the Cornell Society for the Humanities in the academic years 2002–4. Annabel Wharton and James E. Goehring directed me to important sources about architecture and Egyptian monasticism, respectively. Stephen Emmel offered crucial advice regarding the scope of my overall project early in its formulation as well as additional support over subsequent years. I thank Rebecca Krawiec most of all, for her formal comments and our invaluable conversations over the years. The guidance and assistance of the editorial board and staff of the Divinations series and the University of Pennsylvania Press have unquestionably made this a stronger book. I thank Derek Krueger and Jerome Singerman, in particular. The comments of the anonymous readers of my manuscript also provided vital corrections and suggestions, for which I am extremely grateful.

My research on Shenoute's unpublished manuscripts and the archaeological site of Shenoute's monastery (Deir Anba Shenouda) could never have been completed without the generous assistance of many people and institutions. Dwight Young and Anne Boud'hors graciously granted me permission to use unpublished manuscripts to which they possess the publication rights and which are housed at the Österreichische Nationalbibliothek and the Institut français d'archéologie orientale (IFAO) in Cairo. At the IFAO, I would like to thank former Director Nicholas Grimal, Librarian Nadine Cherpion, Archivist Anne Minault-Gout, and the rest of the IFAO staff for facilitating my research there. Monika Hasitzka and Cornelia Römer of the Österreichische Nationalbibliothek graciously provided me with reproductions of many of their unpublished Shenoutean folios. For my research on manuscripts at the Coptic Museum in Cairo, I am indebted to former Director Alfy Henary, the Coptic Museum Board of Directors, and the Egyptian Supreme Council of Antiquities for permission to conduct my research and to Dr. Samiha Abd El-Shaheed, the former director of the manuscript collection there. The staff of the American Research Center in Egypt also provided assistance during my first trip to Egypt; I thank Amira Khattab, Amir Khattab, and former Director Mark Easton especially. I appreciate the assistance of the Coptic Orthodox Church and Bishop Ioannes in facilitating my visits to Deir Anba Shenouda in July 1999 and February 2002. I am grateful for the hospitality shown to me by the monks of Deir Anba Shenouda (especially Abouna Shenouda and Abouna Pachomius) and for the aid and friendship of Bassem Botros and Mina Awad Karam while at the monastery. Without generous counsel and assistance from Betsy Bolman, Stephen Davis, and Peter Grossmann while I was in Cairo, my work would have come to a screeching halt in June of 1999. Peter Grossmann kindly permitted me to reproduce his site plans of Deir Anba Shenouda as well. I also spent time conducting research in the Semitics Library at the Catholic University of America. I owe thanks to the library and to its director, Monica Blanchard, for access to copies of unpublished Shenoutean manuscripts. Janet Timbie lent me personal copies of manuscripts as well as her own essays prior to publication, and she and David Johnson graciously responded to my inquiries.

Several friends and colleagues have provided additional inspiration along the way. I thank Flora Keshgegian and Susan Ashbrook Harvey, who first introduced me to the seductions of studying Christianity in late antiquity. I owe a special debt to my parents, Mary and Milton Schroeder, as well as to my sister, Katherine Schroeder. I thank Bradley Johnson Schroeder for his patience. Eric Johnson supported and encouraged my research, even when it entailed personal and professional sacrifices on his part.

My scholarship has benefited greatly from the contributions of the remarkable individuals I have had the privilege to meet over the course of this project. Any errors or oversights in this book are, of course, solely my own.

My research in Egypt in 1999 was supported by grants from a Duke University Travel Award Fund. Funds from an Anne Firor Scott Research Award (sponsored by the History Department and Women's Studies Program at Duke) and an Aleane Webb Research Fellowship (sponsored by Duke) supported the purchase of microfilms and photographs of unpublished manuscripts in European libraries and museums. A Charlotte W. Newcombe Fellowship administered by the Woodrow Wilson National Fellowship Foundation funded an invaluable year of full-time writing. Most of the additions and revisions to this book were completed during a fellowship in the humanities at Cornell University and Ithaca College from 2002 to 2004; I thank those institutions and the Woodrow Wilson National Fellowship Foundation for providing me with that honor and opportunity. I am grateful for the time to complete final revisions during a fellowship with the Introduction to the Humanities Program at Stanford University in 2005 and 2006.

Earlier versions of my research were first published in "Purity and Pollution in the Asceticism of Shenute of Atripe," in vol. 35 of *Studia Patristica*, ed. M. F. Wiles and E. J. Yarnold (Leuven: Peeters, 2001), 142–47; "'A Suitable Abode for Christ': The Church Building as Symbol of Ascetic Renunciation in Early Monasticism," *Church History* 73 (2004): 472–521; and "Shenoute of Atripe on the Resurrection," *ARC* 33 (2005): 123–37. Some material in Chapter 1 first appeared in "Prophecy and *Porneia* in Shenoute's Letters: The Rhetoric of Sexuality in a Late Antique Egyptian Monastery," *JNES* 65 (2006): 81–97, published by the University of Chicago Press.

This book is dedicated to three exceptional women to whom I attribute my choice of career in the academic study of religion. Each of these women passed away while I was working on this project. This book is for Pearl Meeske, who helped raise me, and Edna Taylor, my paternal grandmother—two women whose deep compassion and yet strikingly divergent religious convictions revealed to me the abiding role of religion in people's lives. This book is also for Theresa Murphy, my maternal grandmother, whose life and work demonstrated for me what it means to be a true intellectual.